ENGLISH PROSE FICTION

1558–1700

A Critical History

PAUL SALZMAN

D0769107

CLARENDON PRESS · OXFORD
1985

Oxford University Press, Walton Street, Oxford OX2 6DP

London New York Toronto
Delhi Bombay Calcutta Madras Karachi
Kuala Lumpur Singapore Hong Kong Tokyo
Nairobi Dar es Salaam Cape Town
Melbourne Auckland
and associated companies in
Beirut Berlin Ibadan Mexico City Nicosia

Oxford is a trade mark of Oxford University Press

Published in the United States
by Oxford University Press, New York

British Library Cataloguing in Publication Data

Salzman, Paul
English prose fiction 1558–1700.
1. English fiction—Early modern, 1500–1700
—History and criticism
I. Title
823'.3'09   PR836
ISBN 0-19-812805-3

Library of Congress Cataloging in Publication Data
Salzman, Paul.
English prose fiction, 1558–1700.
Bibliography: p.
Includes index.
1. English fiction—Early modern, 1500–1700—History
and criticism. 2. Fiction—15th and 16th centuries—
History and criticism. 3. Fiction—17th century—
History and criticism.   I. Title.
PR836.S24   1985   823'.3'09   84-12184
ISBN 0-19-812805-3

Set by Macmillan India Ltd, Bangalore
Printed in Great Britain
at the University Press, Oxford
by David Stanford
Printer to the University

Preface

In recent years the novel has replaced poetry as the major area of literature to attract critics and theorists alike. Despite increasing interest in forms of prose fiction which do not conform to the stereotype of the Victorian novel, little attention has been paid to the development of fiction in England before the work of Defoe, Richardson, and Fielding. Some aspects of Elizabethan fiction have been studied, and Sidney's *Arcadia* has attracted a good deal of interest in recent years, but no satisfactory overview of the fiction has appeared. Margaret Schlauch's *Antecedents of the English Novel* searches anachronistically for realism in Elizabethan fiction; Walter Davis's more ambitious *Idea and Act in Elizabethan Fiction* tries to force many disparate works into a thematic pattern.[1] The seventeenth century is still uncharted, and anyone interested in the development of prose fiction after the death of Elizabeth is forced to turn to unreliable or outdated works such as J. J. Jusserand's *The English Novel in the Time of Shakespeare* (1890), Charlotte Morgan's *The Rise of the Novel of Manners* (1911), or a section of E. A. Baker's *History of the English Novel*.[2] The important bibliographical research of Charles Mish has made an analysis of seventeenth-century fiction a much easier task, and I have made extensive use of his checklist, complementing it with my own bibliography.[3] This book is intended to provide a clear outline of the development of prose fiction from the accession of Elizabeth to the end of the seventeenth century; it surveys every mode of fiction, from the popular chivalric romance to the sophisticated heroic romance.

The book is in two parts, not primarily in order to emphasize any distinction between Elizabethan and seventeenth-century

---

[1] Margaret Schlauch, *Antecedents of the English Novel 1400–1600* (London, 1963); Walter R. Davis, *Idea and Act in Elizabethan Fiction* (Princeton, 1969).

[2] E. A. Baker, *The History of the English Novel* (1929, rpt. New York, 1957), Vol. 3, pp. 11–106.

[3] Charles C. Mish, *English Prose Fiction 1600 to 1700: A Chronological Checklist* (Charlottesville, 1967); and see also his valuable survey of short fiction, 'English Short Fiction in the Seventeenth Century', *Studies in Short Fiction*, 6 (1968–9), 233–330.

fiction, although there are some major differences, but because the two areas have been treated differently. I have been able to sum up critical positions and engage in detailed critical analysis in the case of major Elizabethan writers like Sidney, Nashe, and Deloney, who have already attracted a body of criticism; while seventeenth-century fiction is an unknown area, requiring a much more extensive presentation of basic information. Elizabethan writers also produced a number of idiosyncratic works best treated singly, while the great increase in the production of fiction during the seventeenth century makes it comparatively easy to generalize about various distinct modes. However, I have avoided a monotonous compilation of bibliographical lists, or endless summaries of little-known works, and instead, concentrated on one or two examples of each mode of fiction.

Early fiction should be approached on its own ground, not viewed as a series of failed attempts at creating the novel form. The fiction discussed in this book influenced major writers throughout the period, from Shakespeare to Dryden, and it demands serious consideration. I have written not just for the specialist, but for anyone with an interest in Elizabethan and seventeenth-century literature, or with a general interest in prose fiction.

My work on early fiction began at Monash University under the kind supervision of Dr Geoffrey Hiller. My Ph.D. thesis, a study of seventeenth-century fiction, was written at Pembroke College, Cambridge, supervised by Dr J. C. A. Rathmell. The greater part of this book was written during my two years as a Research Associate at the University of Adelaide. I would like to acknowledge the encouragement and support of many friends and colleagues in Australia and England: Dr Harold Love, Professor David Bradley, Professor Ian Jack, Dr Richard McCabe, Ms Katherine Duncan-Jones, Dr Howard Erskine-Hill, Ms Marion Campbell, and Professor Ken Ruthven. I owe a special debt to Dr Kerryn Goldsworthy, who painstakingly improved my style. I would also like to thank the following libraries: The British Library; the Cambridge University Library; the Pepys Library, Magdalene College, Cambridge; the Bodleian Library; and the libraries of King's College, Trinity

College, St. John's College, and Peterhouse College, Cambridge. I owe my greatest debt to the close friends who supported me during this lengthy period.

Reliable, modern editions of texts have been used when available. In all quotations from early texts the use of u and v and the use of the long s have been normalized, unusual printer's contractions expanded, and roman substituted for black-letter gothic type. Original spelling and punctuation have been retained except for the silent correction of some obvious errors.

Contents

Abbreviations

BHS	Bulletin of Hispanic Studies
ELH	English Literary History
ELN	English Language Notes
ELR	English Literary Renaissance
HLQ	Huntington Library Quarterly
JEGP	Journal of English and Germanic Philology
MLN	Modern Language Notes
MLQ	Modern Language Quarterly
MLR	Modern Language Review
MP	Modern Philology
N&Q	Notes and Queries
PBSA	Papers of the Bibliographical Society of America
PMLA	Publications of the Modern Language Association of America
PQ	Philological Quarterly
RES	Review of English Studies
SEL	Studies in English Literature 1500–1900
SP	Studies in Philology
YES	Yearbook of English Studies

Chapter 1

Introduction: Elizabethan Fiction

Over the last twenty years scholars have corrected the impression that 'Elizabethan fiction was an obscure, slight and unsatisfactory affair.'[1] Books by Margaret Schlauch and Walter Davis on Elizabethan fiction in general, and numerous studies of Sidney, Nashe, Gascoigne, and Deloney in particular, have restored the fiction to something like the high regard in which it was held when it was written.[2] Despite this attention some obvious questions about Elizabethan fiction must still be asked. 'How new was it, and what are its particular characteristics?' are questions which also imply an enquiry about its origins. The quest for the first English 'novel' is, one hopes, an outdated game today; the purpose of this book is not to make an anachronistic search for the beginning of a modern genre.[3] But while viewing early fiction as a genre with its own unique characteristics, one still wishes to know what these characteristics are in relation to earlier modes—is Sidney writing a new kind of fiction in comparison with Malory?

Before the sixteenth century, English narrative took the form of verse, rather than prose. Malory may have signalled the end of medieval romance, but his narrative also points forward to the Elizabethan interest in prose as a medium for telling a story.[4] The account of Elizabethan fiction in the following pages will be both generic and roughly chronological. Classification into various types of narrative—courtly, Sidneian, popular, and so on—only serves to emphasize the great variety of approaches to prose

---

[1] E. A. Baker, *The History of the English Novel*, (1929, rpt. New York, 1957), Vol. 2, p. 15.

[2] Margaret Schlauch, *Antecedents of the English Novel* (London, 1963); Walter R. Davis, *Idea and Act in Elizabethan Fiction* (Princeton, 1969).

[3] In this sense it is regrettable that William Ringler's interesting article '*Beware the Cat* and the Beginnings of English Fiction', *Novel*, 12 (1979), 113–26, is so keen to establish a new 'first novel'.

[4] See Ronald S. Crane, *The Vogue of Medieval Chivalric Romance During the English Renaissance* (Menasha, Wisconsin, 1919), p. 7.

narrative which were taken by the Elizabethans. This eclecticism must be borne in mind during any discussion of what was new in the fiction. While each mode of fiction had its own tradition, there was considerable interaction between them.

Prose fiction was nurtured by the conditions which led to the outpouring of vernacular literature at the end of the sixteenth century. A new interest in the possibilities of prose style can be seen in the work of Lyly, Sidney, and Nashe; vernacular prose was developed and explored with an increasing sense of its possibilities.[5] With the exception of Sidney's *Defence of Poetry*, virtually all the statements made about prose fiction in the sixteenth century are to be found in the prefaces to individual works, and these statements are predominantly concerned with questions of prose style. Many popular writers claim that they utilize a plain, simple, or 'low' style. Richard Johnson, for example, in the preface to the second part of *The Seven Champions Of Christendome* (1597), writes 'I have no eloquent phrase to invite thy willingnes to read, onely a little barren invention' (A).

One cannot, however, always take these professions at face value. Deloney, in the preface to the second part of *The Gentle Craft*, writes 'expect not herein to find any matter of light value, curiously pen'd with pickt words, or choise phrases, but a quaint and plaine discourse'.[6] Deloney here distinguishes himself from deliberate stylists like Lyly, yet he makes quite extensive use of euphuism in his fiction.

An individual style is seen as part of the attraction of fiction, and intentional complexity, even obscurity, may be paraded as a virtue. For example, in the preface to *Menaphon*, Robert Greene writes:

if Gentlemen you find my style either magis humile in some place, or more sublime in another, if you find dark Aenigmas or strange conceipts as if Sphinx on the one side, and Roscius on the other were playing the wagges; thinke the metaphors are well ment, and that I did it for your pleasures, whereunto I ever aymed my thoughts: and desire you to take a little paines to prie into my imagination.[7]

[5] See George Philip Krapp, *The Rise of English Literary Prose* (1915, rpt. New York, 1965), *passim*.
[6] *The Novels of Thomas Deloney*, ed. Merritt Lawlis (Bloomington, 1961), p. 174.
[7] Robert Greene, *Works*, ed. A. B. Grosart (1881–6, rpt. New York, 1964), Vol. 6, pp. 7–8.

This attractive obscurity is related to the allegorical reading of poetry, although at a fairly crude level, as can be seen in Brian Melbancke's comment in the preface of *Philotimus* (1583): 'Poetrye, wee saye, is nothinge else, but an heape of forged fictions, beaten out of the braynes of fantasticall fellowes when their heades were intoxicate, and indeede it is true, the moste bee fables, yet parrable-wyse, conteynynge great misteryes' (Di). Melbancke refers to 'my obscuritie, wherewith I haue endarkened my style' (π 4).

The idiosyncratic and spectacular styles of Lyly and Sidney fuelled the interest in stylistic display. Thomas Lodge does make some statements (belied by his own work) which seem to anticipate Bacon's criticism of the time when 'men began to hunt more after wordes than matter'.[8] In the preface to *William Longbeard*, Lodge writes that 'In olde time menne studied to illustrate matter with words, now we strive for words beside matter.'[9] This attitude to style, however, had little effect on fiction before the seventeenth century.

The 'high' mode of Elizabethan fiction was romance, exemplified in Sidney's *Arcadia*. The characteristic Elizabethan treatment of romance, as opposed to medieval romance, can be illustrated by a comparison between Thomas Lodge's *Rosalynde* (1590), the principal source for *As You Like It*, and its own source, the fourteenth-century verse romance *Gamelyn*. We may begin with the obvious but none the less important point that Lodge uses prose as the medium for the romance, a prose refined by the previous labours of both Lyly and Sidney. *Gamelyn* provides Lodge with the circumstances which drive Rosader (Gamelyn; Shakespeare's Orlando) to Arden. *Gamelyn* is a rough but vigorous narrative, and its hero is an altogether fiercer character than Rosader, who is influenced by Renaissance notions of courtly behaviour. Not content with his display of strength in the wrestling scene common to all versions of the story, Gamelyn also throws his brother's porter down a well when he refuses to open the gate (ll. 303–6). Gamelyn and Adam flee to the woods (chased by the sheriff) and join a group of outlaws, who make

---

[8] 'Advancement of Learning', *Critical Essays of the Seventeenth Century*, ed. J. E. Spingarn (Oxford, 1957), Vol. 1, p. 2.

[9] *The Complete Works of Thomas Lodge*, ed. Edmund Gosse (1883, rpt. New York, 1963), Vol. 2, p. 4.

Gamelyn their king. Not a single woman appears in *Gamelyn*, and we are merely told 'sithen wedded Gamelyn a wif both good and fair' (l. 898). Lodge responds to the pastoral romance, totally altering Rosader's time in the forest, creating Arden—that intensified pastoral realm where characters explore love and their own personalities—and creating Rosalynde, who provided Shakespeare with the basic material for the witty heroine of *As You Like It*.[10]

The nature of Elizabethan romance can also be seen in comparison with Malory. In his brilliant analysis of the structure of medieval romance, Eugene Vinaver suggests that the method of interlace (*entrelacement*) was used by Sidney in the revised version of the *Arcadia*.[11] Perhaps the medieval romance structure provided some impetus, but the revival of interest in Greek romance, particularly Heliodorus' *Aethiopica* which Sidney praises in the *Defence of Poetry*, was a more immediate influence on the structure of the *New Arcadia*. Sidney uses the *in medias res* opening, with its retrospective narrative method, derived from the structure of the epic. Medieval interlace may open up to an eternity, a seamless web of adventure, but it has a definite narrative beginning, and a different approach to time from that of the Renaissance romance.[12] Interlace produces proliferating characters whose adventures all occur in the present and are interwoven by the narrator. The structure chosen by Sidney juxtaposes the past with the present, in particular the previous adventures of Pyrocles and Musidorus retold by them during their sojourn in Arcadia.

The Elizabethan romance as practised by Sidney, Lodge, and Greene favours a pastoral setting, especially a classical one. The medieval fascination with Arthur is of course still present in Spenser, and Ben Jonson told Drummond that 'for a heroic poem . . . there was no such ground as King Arthur's fiction and that S[ir] P. Sidney had an intention to have transformed all his *Arcadia* to the stories of King Arthur'.[13] Whatever Sidney's

[10] Peter V. Marinelli, *Pastoral* (London, 1971), pp. 46–9; Harold E. Toliver, *Pastoral Forms and Attitudes* (Berkeley, 1971), Chaps. 2 and 3.

[11] Eugene Vinaver, *The Rise of Romance* (Oxford, 1971), p. 93; see also Rosemond Tuve, *Allegorical Imagery* (Princeton, 1966), p. 367, n. 22.

[12] Vinaver, p. 76; for the development of a new sense of time in general during the Renaissance, see Ricardo J. Quinones, *The Renaissance Discovery of Time* (Cambridge, Mass., 1972), *passim*.

[13] Ben Jonson, *Complete Poems*, ed. George Parfitt (Harmondsworth, 1975), p. 464.

intention may have been, however, his revision of the *Arcadia* did
not alter its classical Greek setting and characters.

In a debased form, the medieval romance tradition found its
way into Elizabethan fiction through the popular appeal of the
Spanish and Portuguese chivalric romances, the *Amadis* and
Palmerin cycles.[14] The translations and imitations of these
chivalric romances represent an important area of fiction written
for what Louis Wright, somewhat anachronistically, has called
the Elizabethan middle-class reader.[15] Sidney may have borrowed from *Amadis*, and even admired it to some extent, but he
saw it as outmoded and a work 'which God knoweth wanteth
much of a perfect poesy'.[16]

The sophisticated Elizabethan romance, as already mentioned, received an impetus from the Greek romances, which
were readily available in the mid-sixteenth century.[17] Heliodorus
in particular provided an example of a highly wrought structure.
Samuel Wolff points out that 'the Greek romances give to *plot*—
the mere happening of things—a place much more important
than they give to character.'[18] Longus' *Daphnis and Chloe* is part of
the pastoral influence reinforced by continental examples such as
Sannazaro's *Arcadia*. The Greek romances stressed a 'world of
chance',[19] but the tempering influence of the continental
pastoral of Sannazaro and Montemayor provided the balance
which enabled Sidney, Lodge, and Greene to write romances of
harmony rather than chaos.

The sudden proliferation of modes of fiction at this time reflects
the increase in literacy during the last quarter of the sixteenth
century. E. H. Miller estimates 50 per cent literacy by 1600, and
H. S. Bennett provides interesting figures which link this with a
sudden increase in the production of fiction in the second half of
the sixteenth century: the period 1558 to 1603 produced three

[14] See H. Thomas, *Spanish and Portuguese Romances of Chivalry* (Cambridge, 1920); John
J. O'Connor, *Amadis de Gaule and Its Influence on Elizabethan Fiction* (New Brunswick, N.J.,
1970); Mary Patchell, *The Palmerin Romances in Elizabethan Prose Fiction* (London, 1947).

[15] Louis B. Wright, *Middle Class Culture in Elizabethan England* (Chapel Hill,
Nth. Carolina, 1935), *passim*.

[16] *Miscellaneous Prose of Sir Philip Sidney*, ed. K. Duncan-Jones and J. Van Dorsten
(Oxford, 1973), p. 92.

[17] See Samuel Lee Wolff, *The Greek Romances in Elizabethan Prose Fiction* (1912, rpt. New
York, 1961), pp. 8–10.

[18] Ibid., p. 137.

[19] Davis, p. 160.

times the amount of fiction found from 1475 to 1558.[20] The
principal characteristic of Elizabethan fiction (and to a lesser
extent the fiction of the seventeenth century) is its diversity,
which reflects both the increased reading public and the writers'
interest in experiment. Women played an important part in this
new reading public, and were addressed by Lyly in *Euphues*,
Sidney in the *Old Arcadia*, and frequently by Greene, who was
called 'the Homer of women' by Nashe.[21] Later chapters will
outline the various modes of fiction read at the time and explore
this varied reading public in more detail.

[20] E. H. Miller, *The Professional Writer in Elizabethan England* (Cambridge, Mass.,
1959), p. 39; H. S. Bennett, *English Books and Readers 1558–1603* (Cambridge, 1965), p. 248.
[21] Wright, p. 110.

Chapter 2

The Novella

'The short story in prose . . . had never really been acclimatized in England during the middle ages.'[1] Yet during the early years of Elizabeth's reign, the novella achieved an extremely high level of popularity. Boccaccio found favour in England, through extensive translation, two hundred years after he wrote *The Decameron*. The 1560s and 70s saw a sudden interest in the work of continental writers of novellas—Boccaccio, Bandello (via French translations by Belleforest and Boaistuau), Marguerite de Navarre—together with a reworking of classical stories in the manner of the novella. This early period was almost entirely devoted to translation and adaptation. Later writers still relied heavily upon their predecessors; Painter in particular supplied subsequent writers of both prose and drama with a large amount of source material.

The fashion for translations of novellas began in 1566, with the first part of William Painter's *The Palace of Pleasure*, containing sixty novellas; this was augmented by a second part in 1567, with further additions in 1575. Painter's immediate popularity is attested to by the four editions of his collection which appeared in the space of a decade, and by the imitations which followed. He is, perhaps, the most obvious provoker of Ascham's outburst in *The Scholemaster* (1570) against 'fonde bookes, of late translated out of *Italian* into English, sold in every shop in London, commended by honest titles the soner to corrupt honest maners'.[2] Ascham saw these 'bawdie bookes' as a threat to English morality: 'ten *Morte Arthures* do not the tenth part so much harm as one of these bookes made in *Italie* and translated in England.'[3]

Ascham's condemnation did little to prevent the increasing

---

[1] Mary A. Scott, *Elizabethan Translations from the Italian* (Cambridge, Mass., 1916), p. xl.

[2] *Elizabethan Critical Essays*, ed. G. G. Smith (1904, rpt. Oxford, 1959), Vol. 1, p. 2.

[3] Ibid., pp. 3 and 4.

vogue for Italianate stories, but Painter's collection was not taken
entirely from Italian sources. The first twenty-nine stories in the
Palace of Pleasure are classical ones, translations of Livy,
Herodotus, Aelian, Plutarch, Quintus Curtius, and Aulus
Gellius. These are followed by ten novellas taken from Boccaccio,
six from Bandello, two from Giovanni Fiorentino, one from
Straparola, and sixteen from Marguerite de Navarre, ending (in
the augmented edition) with a tale from Massanio. In 1567
Geoffrey Fenton's *Tragical Discourses* followed close on the heels of
Painter, containing thirteen stories from Bandello, four of them
the same as Painter's; both Fenton and Painter chose to follow the
French versions of Bandello by Belleforest and Boaistuau.[4]
    The third major collection of novellas was George Pettie's
Petite Pallace of Pettie his Pleasure (1576), containing eleven
classical tales and one medieval saint's life, but very much under
the influence of the continental novella, with numerous references to stories translated by Painter and Fenton. Pettie's
popularity took over from Painter, and his little collection went
through six editions between 1576 and 1613.

I. Painter and Fenton

Painter's main assets as a story-teller are negative rather than
positive. He does not distract from his plot with excessive
rhetoric; his style is, to quote C. S. Lewis, 'tolerably plain'; he has
a good sense of drama, of the vivid scene, which helped endear
him to dramatists who based plays on his stories. Yvonne Rodax
makes a similar point, while emphasizing Painter's important
ability to lend an English quality to his stories whether their
sources are classical or continental:

Painter has actually left little personal imprint upon his work, yet he has
imparted to it an indefinably English stamp. He has accomplished this
through his choices—selecting for the most part stories of action,
bloodshed and adventure—and by his use of local terms and realistic
detail.[5]

This comment perhaps flattens out Painter's collection too much,

    [4] See René Pruvost, *Mateo Bandello and Elizabethan Fiction* (Paris, 1937), Chaps. 2–4.
    [5] Yvonne Rodax, *The Real and the Ideal in the Novella* (Chapel Hill, Nth. Carolina, 1968), p. 96.

for he skilfully combines his 'bloodshed' with much lighter, humorous stories, which show some influence from the jestbook. Story 21, a brief anecdote, is '*A merie geste, vttered by Hannibal to King Antiochus*' (I. 88), and the two stories taken from Fiorentino (Nos. 47 and 48) are comic in the fabliau tradition.[6]

Painter himself emphasizes the variety of his collection in his dedication to the Earl of Warwick:

In these Histories be depainted in liuelye colours, the vglie shapes of insolencye and pride, the deformed figures of incontinencie and rape, the cruell aspects of spoyle, breach of order, treason, ill lucke and ouerthrow of States and other persons. Wherein also be intermixed, pleasaunte discourses, merie talke, sportinge practises deceitfull devices, and nipping tauntes, to exhilarate your honor's minde. (I. 5)

He sees the attraction of his 'histories' as stemming in part from their vividness, their ability to present a scene before the eyes of the reader: 'like a liuely image [they] representeth before our eies the beginning, end and circumstance of eche attempt' (II. 150). On the other hand, he stresses too the moral purpose of his translations, which are (in the traditional formula) intended to 'render good examples, the best to be followed, and the worst to be auoyded' (I. 5). In the preface to the second part, he even itemizes the morals to be drawn from each story (II. 154–7)

A good example of one of Painter's classical stories is his account of Candaules and Gyges, taken from Herodotus (I. 8–12). Painter prefaces the events of the story with an introductory paragraph of his own, containing a series of generalizations which tell the reader, in advance, the moral import of the story that follows. The theme is encapsulated in the opening sentence: 'Of all Follies wherewith vayne men be affected, the follie of immoderate loue is moste to bee detested' (I. 46).

While Painter goes on to give a very exact translation of Herodotus, he is at times concerned to add some slight sense of motivation to Herodotus' bold statements: 'Now Candaules conceived a passion for his own wife, and thought she was the most beautiful woman on earth', becomes 'Candaules king of Lydia, had a marueilous beautifull gentlewoman to his Queene

---

[6] References are to William Painter, *The Palace of Pleasure*, ed. Joseph Jacobs (London, 1890), 3 vols.

and wife, whome hee loued very dearlye, and for that great loue whiche he bare her, thought her the fayrest creature of the world' (I. 46–7).

Already Painter is interpreting, casting Herodotus' cold statement of fact to fit his introductory moral perspective, but also to allow the reader some insight into why a man might behave as irrationally as Candaules later does. Herodotus' words are then translated almost exactly, but Painter ends his story with another generalized, moral statement: 'A goodly example to declare, that the secrets of Marriage, ought not to be disclosed: but with reverence to be covered, lest God do plague such offences with death or other shame, to manifest to the world, howe dearely hee esteemeth that honourable state' (I. 48).

Painter tackles Boccaccio a little differently; he is able to mimic the compressed, spare quality of the stories in the *Decameron*. His thirtieth novella is an extremely accurate translation of Boccaccio's tale of Melchisedech and the three rings (*Decameron*, I. 3). In this case, Painter gives the reader no moralizing introduction or conclusion. Similar accuracy is evident in the following novella (Painter 31, *Decameron*, I. 8).

Twenty-five of Painter's stories (almost exactly a quarter) are taken from Bandello. René Pruvost's important study of Bandello's influence on Elizabethan fiction indicates widespread translation, adaptation, and allusion.[7] The major task of translation was undertaken by Painter, and by Geoffrey Fenton, who published *Certaine Tragicall Discourses* in 1567, a volume containing thirteen tales from Bandello.

Both Painter and Fenton rely on the French translations of Bandello by Belleforest and Boaistuau, although Painter knew the original, and used it in one case.[8] The two French translators tried to tame the fierce qualities of Bandello, producing 'a series of Bandéllian plots overlaid with moral harangues, discourses, anticlerical outbursts (almost Protestant in tone) and the complicated machinery of courtly love . . . '.[9] Painter's own moralizing impulse was drawn to this treatment, and he also rejected Bandello's harsh style in favour of smoother French

---

[7] Pruvost, *passim*.

[8] Ibid., p. 24; and see Frank S. Hook, ed., *The French Bandello: A Selection* (Columbia, 1948), University of Missouri Studies, Vol. 22, No. 1, pp. 9–38.

[9] Rodax, p. 95.

rhetoric: 'choosing rather to follow Launay and Belleforest the French Translatours, than the barren soile of his own vain, who being a Lombard, doth frankly confesse himselfe to be no fine Florentine, or trimme Thoscane, as eloquent and gentle Boccaccio was' (I. 11).

Once again, Painter introduces English references, an increase of concrete detail, and a firmer moral stance.[10] The work of Geoffrey Fenton, however, reveals the extent to which Painter still concentrates on the action of the story, for Fenton carries the process of rhetorical expansion much further, providing soliloquies for his characters.[11] The two translators share four stories (Painter II. 24/ Fenton 7; P. II. 27/F. 11; P. II. 29/F. 13; P. II. 30/F. 1), and a comparison of their treatments of one story will make the differences between them clear.

The violent story of the Countess of Celant (Bandello I. 4) gave both Painter and Fenton an opportunity to relate a sensational tale while at the same time drawing a moral conclusion. Bianca Maria, the title character, is married at 16 to Viscount Hermes, who recognizes her 'wanton spirit' and keeps her, accordingly, in check. After his death she marries the Count of Celant, who promises her liberty within the marriage; she soon leaves him to live a promiscuous life in Pavia. She is courted by Valperga, Count Massino, soon tires of being his mistress, and turns to his friend Roberto Sanseverino, Count Gaiazzo. When Valperga, after this ill-treatment, makes her character known, she tries to persuade Sanseverino to challenge him. His refusal to attack his friend leads to his rejection by the Countess of Celant, who returns her favours to Valperga, and tries to persuade him to murder Sanseverino. The two friends put their heads together and realize the wickedness of the Countess, whose true character they then proceed to reveal at every opportunity, driving her out of Pavia to Milan. There she captures the heart of Pietro de Cardone, an inexperienced young Sicilian, who is easily persuaded to take revenge on the Countess's two former lovers for their 'slander'. He kills Valperga, and reveals the Countess's part in the murder after he is imprisoned, saving his own life, and condemning her. The Countess confesses her faults on the scaffold before being beheaded.

[10] See Pruvost's analysis, pp. 163–80.   [11] Ibid., pp. 180–95.

Painter and Fenton both rely on Belleforest's version of this
story, which softens Bandello's unrepentant Countess,[12] and has
a moral tone which appealed to the English writers. The story of
the wicked but repentant Countess was obviously an attractive
one: not only was it translated by Painter and Fenton, but George
Whetstone produced a poetic version in *The Rock of Regard* (1576)
based on their prose versions.[13]

Both translators emphasize, from first to last, the moral to be
drawn from the Countess's dissolute behaviour: 'Women need to
be watched' is a motto adumbrated at length in the opening
paragraph of both versions. Painter cannot resist some
localization:

If England doe not by experience see Maydens of Noble Houses
Infamed through to mutch vnbrideled and frank maner of Lyfe, and
their parents desolate for such villanyes, and the name of their houses
become Fabulous and Ridiculous to the people: surely that manner of
Espiall and watch ouer Children may be noted in Nations not very farre
conuening from vs . . . (III. 44)

Painter, here as elsewhere, tells his story plainly and simply.
Fenton is far from being uninterested in the narrative, but he is a
much more elaborately rhetorical writer than Painter. Elements
later to become greatly expanded in the full euphuistic style of
Lyly are already apparent in Fenton. The episode in which the
Count of Celant rebukes his wife is followed, in Fenton's version,
by a series of reflections couched in euphuistic *exempla*:

For the fierce elephant standes not in awe of his Keaper by force of any
stripes, but is made tractable to bende his lardge bodie whilest he
mounte upon his backe, by certeine familiar voices and stroakinges of
his keper, wherewith he overcometh the naturall rudenes and crueltie of
the beaste. The tygre will take foode at the handes of the wildman
norished in the caves and desert habitacions amongst theim, where no
stripes, nor other awe of man, can move any moderacion to his wodnes
or cruell nature: so, likewise, some women, albeyt they are founde to
reteine some sparkes of civil humanitie, beinge more easelye broughte
to a reformacion by gentle order, then reclaimed by the smart of any
torture or crueltie. (II. 18–19)[14]

[12] See ibid., pp. 129–31.
[13] Ibid., p. 72.
[14] References are to Geoffrey Fenton, *Certain Tragicall Discourses*, ed. Robert L. Douglas
(London, 1898), 2 vols.

Fenton's rhetorical interest is not necessarily a distraction from the story; and at times his interest in detail leads to a greater vividness, a more arresting description, than can be found in Painter.[15] In the story of the Countess of Celant, the Countess, on the death of her first husband, repairs to Casal, where her primping is described by Painter: 'bendinge her only study to gay and trimme Apparell, and imployed the mornings with the vermilion rud to colour hir cheekes by greater curiosity than the most shameless Curtisan of Rome' (III. 48). This is faithful to Belleforest: 'aussi tout son estude n'estoit qu'a se parer, & altiffer, à employer tous les matins à se vermillonner les joües, avec plus de curiosité que la plus eshontée courtisanne de Rome.'[16] Fenton's sharper eye tells us that 'her chiefe and common exercise ther was to force a frizilacion of her haire with the bodkind, converting the naturall cooloor into a glistening glee, suborned by arte to abuse God and nature; by alteringe the complexion of her face by a dye of fadinge cooloors devised by pollecye, and that with more curosytie then the moste shameles Curtisan in Rome' (II. 8).

Fenton tends to expand the speeches given to his characters; for example, the soliloquy of the Count after his wife deserts him is 118 words long in Painter, and 257 words long in Fenton (and 116 in Belleforest; see Painter II. 56, Fenton II. 22). This does impart a greater psychological interest to the characters; Fenton and Painter begin a long continuing division between writers interested in rhetoric and characters' thoughts, and writers interested in action.

Fenton's moral stance is also harsher, more uncompromising, than Painter's. Painter hastens to apologize to his readers: 'Beare with me good Ladyes (for of you alone I craue this pardon) for introducing the Whoorish lyfe of the Countesse, and hir bloody enterprise . . .' (III. 78), while Fenton avoids an interpolation which might reduce the moral driven home by Belleforest. Fenton is fascinated by 'Tragicall' stories; his collection is much less varied than Painter's, although it achieves a certain intensity through this concentration. Fenton tells us:

I greve that the worlde (at this presente) swarmeth with so greate a

---

[15] On this point, see Rodax, pp. 100–1.
[16] Hook, *The French Bandello*, op. cit., pp. 131–2.

number of insensed men readye to dye for a pleasure of so small moment
as the contentmente of the bodie, so I wishe that as in writynge thies
tragicall affaires I have founde the faulte of mine owne life, that also the
reste of the younglings of our countrey in reding my indevor, may
breake the slepe of their large follye . . . (II. 313)

While Painter is also keen to teach 'Good lessons', he emphasizes
pleasure as much as profit: 'I haue mollified and sweetened with
the course of pleasaunt matters' (III. 431–2). Both approaches to
the novella proved influential.

II. Pettie

A Petite Palace of Pettie his Pleasure appeared in 1576, when the
novella was at the height of its popularity. George Pettie's
collection of eleven classical tales and one saint's life has been
seen by Douglas Bush as deriving from Painter and Fenton, in
particular from the attitude of Belleforest to the novella.[17] Pettie
shows considerable familiarity with Painter and Fenton, and
often allows his characters, in an obvious disregard of historical
verisimilitude, to 'recall' the plight of characters in their novellas.
Camma, for example, says 'Did *Juliette* die upon the corps of her
Romeo, and shall my body remayne on earth *Synnatus* beyng
buried?' (p. 34).[18]

Despite these allusions, Pettie's collection is very different from
those of his admired predecessors. All his stories except that of
Alexius are based, albeit loosely, on tales taken from Ovid, Livy,
Tacitus, and Hyginus.[19] Although he refers to, or has his
characters refer to, novellas found in Painter, he avoids translat-
ing any of them himself. His collection is different both in content
and style, just as his stance, in telling his stories, is original.

The style of these stories is a step closer to the elaborate rhetoric
of euphuism than Fenton's, although it is by no means the same as
Lyly's.[20] Pettie continues the process seen in Fenton of using the
events of the story as a source of soliloquies and rhetorical display.
While he is not as extreme in this as Lyly was to be two years later

[17] Douglas Bush, '*The Petite Pallace of Pettie His Pleasure*', *JEGP* 27 (1928), 166–9.
[18] References are to *A Petite Palace of Pettie His Pleasure*, ed. Herbert Hartman (New
York, 1938).
[19] See Bush, p. 163.
[20] See J. Swart, 'Lyly and Pettie', *English Studies*, 23 (1941), 9–18, *passim*.

in *Euphues*, he is always intent on displaying his wit, his sophistication. He is not a modest translator, like Painter, but an interpreter—a very peacock of an interpreter, parading his superior knowledge and style.

The stories' inherent attractions have gone largely unnoticed by scholars intent on seeking out the sources of euphuism in them. Only Yvonne Rodax has noted that 'Pettie exhibits an ironic lightness and gaiety'.[21] He takes the fashionable moral stance, wielded so heavily by Fenton and even Painter, and plays with it a little. In true Renaissance spirit, we are told in the preface by one R.B. that Pettie did not intend his work for publication, and the printer tells the reader that it has been published 'to pleasure you, the friendly Readers' (p. 8). R.B. addresses 'the gentle Gentlewomen Readers', and the ruse is undermined by Pettie's constant asides, in the course of his stories, addressed to 'Gentlewomen', as Fenton addresses his 'deare ladies' and Painter his 'good ladies'. R.B. indicates Pettie's change in emphasis from the heavier morality of Fenton and Painter: 'I dare not compare this woorke with the former Pallaces of Pleasure, because comparisons are odious, and because they containe Histories, translated out of grave authors & learned writers: and this containeth discourses, devised by a greene youthfull capacitie, and reported in a manner *ex tempore* . . .' (p. 4). Pettie's 'letter' to R.B. is again written in a tone of gentlemanly *sprezzatura*, modestly referring to the stories as 'trifles' for R.B.'s 'owne private pleasure' (p. 5). A *frisson* is added by the information that 'divers discourses touch neerely divers of my nere freindes: but the best is, they are so darkely figured forth, that only they whom they touch, can understand whom they touch . . .' (p. 5).

Proud to be a fashionable writer, Pettie excuses the anachronisms I have mentioned above by saying, 'If this mislike you in my discourses, that I make *Camma*, use the example of the countesse of *Salisbury*, the Dutches of *Savoy*, and sutch who were of far later yeeres, then the auncient *Camma* is, with the like in divers other of the stories: you must consider that my *Camma* is of fresher memory then any of them, and I thinke in your judgment of fresher hew then the fayrest of them' (pp. 5–6). Similarly, Pettie

[21] Rodax, p. 103.

points to his use of 'new fashions in phrases and wordes' (p. 6).

The stories in *The Palace of Pleasure* are chiefly love stories, always handled lightly, and at times mockingly. Soliloquies, letters, and moralizing apostrophes from the narrator are threaded through each tale; all three provide Pettie with the opportunity to display his stylistic gifts. He does not treat his mythological material naïvely, but views it at a distance. An example of this, and of his rapidly shifting tone, is his version of the story of Minos and Pasiphae. Pasiphae's light behaviour, her trifling with Verecundus, has led to her husband's intense jealousy, and Pettie sees this, for a moment, as part of a moral scheme:

But you shall understand (Gentlewomen) this was not all her punishment, nay this was but a trifle in respect of that which after followed, a matter in haynousnesse so horrible, in desire so detestable, and in lust so lothsome, that it is no lesse strange to bee tolde, then hard to bee beleeved . . . (p. 224)

What is referred to is, of course, Pasiphae's attraction to the bull: 'I dare not say shee fell in love with the bull, least I should drive you rather to laughinge at my story then listninge to it, but surely so it was' (p. 224).

Pettie then shifts ground:

But Gentlewomen, because you shal not enter into colorick conceites against me, for publishing in this presence, a hystorie whiche seemeth so mutch to sounde to the shame of your sexe, I meane not to justifie the truth of it, but rather will prove it false by the opinion of one *Servius*, who writeth, that *Pasiphae* in deede played false with one *Taurus* (which signifieth a Bul) secretary to her husband in the house of *Dedalus*, and after being delyvered, had two sonnes, the one lyke *Minos*, the other lyke *Taurus*, and thereupon the Poets faigned the fable aforsaide: but whether beeing a woman shee used the carnall company of a beast, or whether lyke a lewde wife shee gave her husbande the badge of a beast, her offence was sutch, that I cannot (though gladly I woulde) excuse it. (p. 225)

Of course, if Pasiphae did not actually desire a real bull, she was scarcely visited by a 'lust so lothsome'. And Pettie's apparently forthright moral judgement is immediately qualified: 'Yet must I needes say that in my fancy her husbande deserved some blame: for no doubt his suspicion without cause, caused her in sutche sorte to transgresse marriage lawes' (pp. 225–6). Didacticism is a fashionable pose taken up by Pettie; it provides the chance for impressive speeches: '(Gentlewomen) I am setled in this opinion, that no suspicion of jelousie ought to cause a woman to transgresse the boundes of honesty' (p. 226). The reader is teased by Pettie's mixture of condemnation and justification.

The soliloquies spoken by Pettie's characters revolve around moral choices (although they are primarily rhetorical display, and only secondarily explorations of motivation). Scilla muses on her love for King Minos, her father's enemy:

And shall I then preferre mine owne pleasure before my father's profit? why every one ought to be nerest to them selves, and their wisdome is nothing worth which are not wise for them selves. Nay rather shall I preferre the commodytie of King *Minos* before the commodytie of King *Nysus*? why *Nysus* is my Father: why *Minos* will be my Phere: why *Nysus* gave me lyfe: why *Minos* wyll yeelde mee love: why *Nysus* made mee a maide: why *Minos* will make mee a mother: why *Nysus* cherished mee being young: why *Minos* wyll make mutch of mee beeinge olde: why nature bindeth mee to love my father: why God commaundeth mee to love my husband . . . (p. 163)

She is overcome by her love, cuts off her father's golden hair which maintains him on his throne, is scorned by Minos, and drowns herself.

Here again Pettie toys with his moral, advising his gentle-women readers 'that you pull not of your fathers haire that is, yᵗ you pul not their hearts out of their bodies, by unadvisedly castinge your selves away in matching in marriage with those who are not meet for you' (p. 164), at the same time saying 'But (Soveraigne) now your father is gone, I will give you more sound advice: I will admonishe you all not to pull of your owne haire, that is not to binde your selves to the froward fansi of your politique parents, but to make your choice in marriage according to your owne mindes . . .' (pp. 164–5). This is a piece of key-hole sermonizing, a tongue-in-cheek whisper to the reader: 'But mum, *lupus in fabula*, I must (I say) admonish you yᵗ as your parents gave you your bodies, so they may dispose of them' (p. 126). The *Petite Palace* has, in effect, two audiences: the gentlewomen created by the narrator, cajoled by him, and spun around by his ambiguous moralizing until they are dizzy; and an invisible audience of fellow young wits, enjoying Pettie's dexterity, his sleight of hand.

The narrative skills displayed by Pettie are most apparent in his version of the Tereus and Procne story. He begins with a serious reflection on the theme of man's miserable condition throughout his life, from childhood when 'our weake mindes are troubled with many toyes' (p. 41) to old age when 'wee covetously carke for coin, wee toyle for trash, wee thinke wee never have inough . . .' (ibid.). But of course Pettie has promised his readers delight, not dole: 'And surely the consideration of this our miserable estate doth so resolve mee with sorrow, that if your Presence did not sprinkle mee with some deawe of delight, I should hardly frame my wittes to procure you pleasure by any pleasant history . . .' (p. 42).

Tereus woos Progne [sic] with a fair speech, and they are soon married. Tereus' attack on Philomela is unmotivated: 'For being in ship together, hee began filthily to fixe his fancy upon her . . .' (p. 48). The revelation of his deed in Philomela's embroidery is seen as divine justice: 'See the just judgement of god, who will suffer no evill done secretly, but it shal bee manifested openly' (p. 51).

Until now, Pettie has given little thought to his characters, but to drive home the horror of Progne's revenge, he suddenly brings Tereus' son Itys alive, through some excellent dialogue:

in came *Itys* the pretty elfe beeing two or three yeeres of age, and seeing his mother sit sadly sayd unto her, Mam how doost, why doest weepe, and tooke her about the necke and kist her, saying I will goe and call my dad to come and play with thee: but shee like a tirannous Tiger flong him from her saying: Away impe of impiety, how like thy father thou art, not onely in favour, but in flattery also: I will make thy Dad sport shortly: the imp rose againe, and came running dugling to her saying, why do you beate me mam, I have learned my Criscrosse today so I have, and my father sayth he wil buie mee a golden coate, and then you shannot kisse mee so you shannot . . . (p. 54)

Pettie can, if he desires, create that most difficult of all characters, a small child, to enhance the *frisson* for his reader. He is only occasionally interested in achieving this type of verisimilitude; it is part of his general versatility as a writer. The reader is soon held back from the story again: 'It were hard here gentlewomen for you to give sentence, who more offended of the husband or the wife . . .' (p. 55).

The reader is left off-balance, wondering what response is

required of him (or, perhaps I should say, of her). Pettie's cynicism is hidden by his wit, although we can detect it; his stories are treated as grounds for rhetorical brilliance, sly humour, and didacticism. He knows full well that he is an entertainer, not a preacher: 'You Gentlewomen', he says at the end of the story of Alexius,

may also learne hereby, not to repose any permanent pleasure in practising with your husbands, but only to use their companie as a solace, to sweeten ye sowernesse of this life withal, and to thinke that sutch supersticious love towards your husbands, doth withdraw you from the true love which you ought to beare towards god. But I could preache better to you in a more pleasant matter, I will leave this text to maister parson, who while he is unmaried I warrant you will disswade you so earnestly from sutch idolatrous doting on your husbands, that hee will not stick to tell you beesides Scripture that you ought to have no respect of persons, but to love an other man or him selfe so well as your husbandes. (pp. 270–1)

III. The Development of the Novella

Painter and Fenton begin two distinct traditions in the Elizabethan novella: the story which concentrates primarily on plot, on action, and the story which concentrates on rhetoric, on reflection by characters and narrator. The interest in rhetoric became dominant, as Pettie's work makes clear, and it was continued by Greene in framed tales such as *Planetomachia* (1585) and *Penelope's Web* (1587). The popularity of *Euphues* increased this interest in such rhetoric as might be applied to a story.

By the time Pettie's collection appeared the prose 'history' was considered to be a most fashionable field for literary endeavour. Henry Wotton, in the preface to his collection, *A Courtlie Controversie of Cupids Cautels* (1578), writes:

considering howe greatly tragicall histories haue bin commended and esteemed of late dayes, euen in such sorte as it seemeth a shame vnto all Gentlemen and Gentlewomen, nurtured in the schole of curtesie, but principally vnto Courtiers, to be ignoraunt thereof . . . (A4)

Painter's plainer style and interest in narrative is still evident in Barnaby Rich's collection, *Rich His Farewell to Military Profession* (1581). Critics have praised this collection, perhaps excessively,

for its humour and attention to narrative detail.[22] It proved
extremely popular, and provided source material for a large
number of plays, including *Twelfth Night*, *The Merry Wives of
Windsor*, and perhaps *Othello*.[23] The collection is very varied,
beginning with 'Sappho Duke of Mantona', a shortened romance derived in part from Heliodorus, and continuing with some
stories in the continental novella style, and some closer to the
fabliau.

Rich is certainly interested in telling his stories without any
excessive elaboration, and in this sense he resembles Painter. At
one stage of his second story, 'Appolonius and Silla', he cuts short
any soliloquies with the aside: 'Gentlewomen accordyng to my
promise, I will heare for breuities sake, omit to make repetition of
the long and dolorous discourse recorded by *Silla*, for this sodaine
departure of her Apolanius, knowyng you to bee as tenderly
harted as *Silla* her self . . .'.[24] Rich is not adding very much to
the techniques of Painter or Pettie, but rather showing great skill
in handling a diverse range of stories. He relies upon an enormous
range of sources for his plots, incidents, characters, and even
language, drawing on Painter, Pettie, Gascoigne, Lyly, Udall,
Golding, Underdowne, Cinthio, Belleforest, and Straparola.[25]

Also to prove fruitful was the combination of sensational Italian
novella and a moralizing narrator. It can be seen (with
moralizing predominating) in Thomas Beard's *The Theatre of
God's Judgements* (1597), and (with sensational plots predominating) in John Reynolds' *The Triumphs of God's Revenges* (1621).
The didactic stance was inextricably associated with the novella,
although a writer like Pettie might toy with it in a sophisticated
fashion. Nearly all Elizabethan fiction claims to be written to
teach as well as delight, to borrow Sidney's characterization of
the purpose of poetry. Whetstone states that his miscellany *The
Rock of Regard* (1576), containing the prose tale of Rinaldo and

---

[22] See *Rich's Farewell to Military Profession*, ed. Thomas Malory Cranfill (Austin, 1959),
pp. lviii–lix; Margaret Schlauch gives the false impression that Rich is original in his
references to his gentlewomen readers, see 'English Short Fiction in the 15th and 16th
Centuries', *Studies in Short Fiction*, 3 (1966), 426.

[23] Cranfill, pp. xlvii–liii.

[24] Ibid., p. 69.

[25] Ibid., p. xvii.

Giletta as well as poetry, 'imparteth necessarie matter of direction, for vnstaid youth' (π 2). This didacticism, however, seldom prevents the major writers and translators of novellas from entertaining.

Chapter 3

Courtly Fiction: I. Gascoigne

George Gascoigne's *Adventures of Master F.J.* is seen today as an 'ingeniously contrived' narrative—although its high reputation was established only quite recently, following C. T. Prouty's edition of *A Hundreth Sundrie Flowres* and biography of Gascoigne, both published in 1942.[1] As is so often the case with early fiction, certain bibliographical complexities need to be taken into account. In 1573 *A Hundreth Sundrie Flowres* appeared anonymously, containing a quantity of poetry, two plays (*Supposes* and *Jocasta*) and 'A Discourse of the Adventures passed by Master F.J.'.[2] Gascoigne indirectly acknowledged authorship by bringing out a revised collection in 1573, entitled *The Posies of George Gascoigne*. In a dedication addressed to 'the reverende Divines' (p. 3), Gascoigne apologizes for the offences contained in the earlier volume: 'sundrie wanton speeches and lascivious phrases, but further I heare that the same have beene doubtfully construed, and (therefore) scandalous' (p. 3).[3] The contents have been rearranged into 'Flowers', 'Hearbes', and 'Weedes'. Among the weeds is a revised version of *Master F.J.*

The first version tells the story of F.J.'s affair with Mistress Elinor, 'in the north partes of this Realme' (p. 51).[4] In the preface to *The Posies*, Gascoigne explains that:

I understande that sundrie well disposed mindes have taken offence at certain wanton wordes and sentences passed in the fable of *Ferdinando Jeronimi*, and the Ladie *Elinora de Valasco*, the which in the first edition was termed the adventures of master F.I. And that also therwith some busie conjectures have presumed to thinke that the same was indeed

---

[1] M. R. Rohr Philmus, 'Gascoigne's Fable of the Artist as a Young Man', *JEGP* 73 (1974), 29; C. T. Prouty, *George Gascoigne* (New York, 1942); C. T. Prouty, ed., *George Gascoigne's A Hundreth Sundrie Flowres* (Columbia, Missouri, 1942).

[2] See the introduction to Prouty's edition for full bibliographical details, op. cit., pp. 9–13, 17–19.

[3] References are to *The Posies*, ed. John W. Cunliffe (Cambridge, 1907).

[4] References are to Prouty's edition of *A Hundreth Sundrie Flowres*.

written to the scandalizing of some worthie personages, whom they woulde seeme thereby to know. Surely (right reverend) I smile to see the simplicitie of such, who being indeed starke staring blind, would yet seeme to see farre into a milstone. And the rather I scorne their rash judgements, for that in talking with xx of them one after another, there have not two agreed in one conjecture. Alas, alas, if I had bene so foolishe as to have passed in recitall a thing so done in deede, yet all the world might thinke me verie simple if I woulde call John, John, or Mary, Mary. But for the better satisfying of all men universally, I doe here protest unto you (reverend) even by the hope of my salvation, that there is no living creature touched or to be noted therby. And for the rest you shall find it now in this second imprinting so turquened and turned, so clensed from all unclenly wordes, and so purged from the humor of inhumanitie, as percase you woulde not judge that it was the same tale. (p. 7)

Instead of the English tale related, with accompanying poems, by G.T. in the first version, Gascoigne turned his story into a purported translation 'out of the Italian riding tales of *Bartello*' (p. 383). The detailed differences between the two versions will be discussed below.

Gascoigne was unsuccessful in his attempt to quell biographical speculation about his story. Such speculation may have been responsible for the seizure of 'half a hundred of Gascoignes poesies' in 1576, and seems to indicate that the revision was inadequate.[5] Modern scholars have also entered the fray. The most convincing case for reading *Master F.J.* as partly autobiographical was stated by C. T. Prouty, who was, at the same time, compelled to refute some wild speculation about the identity of F.J. by B. M. Word.[6] Prouty's assertions have, in turn, been countered by Robert Adams.[7] We have too little evidence for any certain conclusion to be reached. A commonsense view might well note Gascoigne's protestations, in the preface to *The Posies*, that *Master F.J.* was not intended to be a *roman à clef*. If it was related to actual events, and so caused scandal, surely the solution would be to omit it from *The Posies*, rather than revise it in a manner which removes some erotic details (though not all), but leaves the events of the story untouched.

[5] C. T. Prouty, *George Gascoigne*, p. 194.

[6] Ibid., p. 193; and see Prouty's introduction to *A Hundreth Sundrie Flowres*, pp. 19–28.

[7] Robert P. Adams, 'Gascoigne's "Master F.J." as Original Fiction', *PMLA* 73 (1958), 315–26, *passim*.

Master F.J., particularly in its first form, is presented as part of an anthology. This format was a popular one, and some consideration of similar works to Gascoigne's *Hundreth Sundrie Flowres*, ignored by critics of *Master F.J.*, should throw further light on the story's nature. Collections of prose and verse were very fashionable in the 1560s and 70s, and along with them flourished an interest in courtly love and *questioni d'amore*,[8] both part of an interest in correct courtly behaviour which found its most important expression in Castiglione's *Cortegiano*, translated by Sir Thomas Hoby in 1561.

While *Master F.J.* embodies some of the ideals of courtly love,[9] it also undercuts through irony the more conventional exposition of courtly love found in the anthologies and fiction published in the late 1560s and early 1570s. Edmund Tilney's *Flower of Friendshippe* (1568) is perhaps more discourse than prose fiction, but it contains many conventions found in courtly fiction, particularly the *questioni d'amore*. A number of works which appeared after *Master F.J.* also indicate how its attack on conventional attitudes to love is quite unique. Gascoigne's friend George Whetstone published two works in imitation of him: *The Rocke of Regard* (1576) and *An Heptameron of Ciuill Discourses* (1582).

The Rocke of Regard contains 'the discourse of Rinaldo and Giletta', a much more conventional story than *Master F.J.* It is difficult to accept Prouty's characterization of it as a 'slavish imitation';[10] Rinaldo begins, like F.J., as a conventional courtly lover—but he remains one. *Rinaldo and Giletta* is a much more predictable story than *Master F.J.*; essentially an account of crossed love, it relates how Rinaldo eventually overcame his wicked rival Fitzaldo, and married Giletta. John Grange's *Golden Aphroditis* (1577), although its use of initials for its characters may owe something to Gascoigne, is also a conventional story; its protagonist N.O. holds firm to his courtly ideals, and succeeds in marrying A.O. in the end.

Gascoigne turns these conventional stories on their heads, particularly in the first version of *Master F.J.* Gascoigne himself

---

[8] See Violet M. Jefferey, *John Lyly and the Italian Renaissance* (Paris, 1928), pp. 3–49.
[9] See Frank B. Fieler, 'Gascoigne's Use of Courtly Love Conventions in "The Adventures Passed by Master F.J." ', *Studies in Short Fiction*, 1 (1963), 26–32, *passim*.
[10] *George Gascoigne*, p. 221, n. 102.

stands in an ambiguous relationship to court fashions: his fortunes rose and fell, and with them his ability to live the courtier's life.[11] His satire cuts through the courtly pose; *The Steele Glas*, as Prouty notes, 'ranges over the whole of contemporary life'.[12] *Master F.J.* is more than just a satire, but it certainly takes a satirical view of F.J.'s courtly pretensions.

Next to Sidney's *Arcadia*, Gascoigne's short work is perhaps the most impressively constructed in Elizabethan fiction; the *presentation* of the story is at the centre of the reader's attention from the very beginning. Three 'characters' stand, initially, between us and the protagonist F.J. They are the printer, A.B.; one H.W., who tells the reader how he delivered to the printer the 'divers discourses & verses' we read in *A Hundreth Sundrie Flowres* (p. 49); and H.W.'s 'familiar friend Master G.T.' (p. 49), who has compiled the collection! *Master F.J.* is very much part of a supposed anthology. The careful attempt to persuade the reader that the author(s) had no desire for publication is merely a very complex example of typical Elizabethan mock-modesty (discussed in the previous chapter in relation to Pettie). Gascoigne owns the anthology in *The Posies*; perhaps the attempt to present it as a compilation was simply a method of building an effective disguise for his anonymity. (One can, of course, see this as evidence of the autobiographical nature of *Master F.J.*, but I would still stress the ubiquitous convention of anonymity as reason enough.)

G.T. is a 'presenter', a careful compiler; perhaps an editor:

I have thought good (I say) to present you with this written booke, wherein you shall find a number of *Sonets*, layes, letters, Ballades, Rondlets, verlayes and verses, the workes of your friend and myne *Master F.J.* and divers others, the which when I had with long travayle confusedly gathered together, I thought it then *Opere precium*, to reduce them into some good order. (pp. 50–1)

When his elaborate introduction to the anthology is completed, with the reader perhaps slightly confused by the shuffling of material between G.T., H.W., and A.B., G.T. plunges into the midst of the 'history' he is presenting:

[11] Ibid., pp. 3–100.
[12] Ibid., p. 249; for a full treatment, see Ronald C. Johnson, *George Gascoigne* (New York, 1972), Chap. 6.

The said F.J. chaunced once in the north partes of this Realme to fall in company of a very fayre gentlewoman whose name was Mistresse *Elinor*, unto whom bearinge a hotte affection, he first adventured to write this letter following. (p. 51)

The reader has three kinds of source material before him which supply him with information about F.J.'s affair with Elinor: F.J.'s own poems and letters and Elinor's replies; reported events and dialogue, of the kind vouched for by G.T. with the claim 'My friend F.J. hath tolde me divers times . . .' (p. 53); and G.T.'s commentary, his distanced reaction to (and perhaps ordering of) these events. The reader's response to F.J.'s story shifts as these three sources of information alternate. This shifting response is emotional rather than moral; only the second version of the story takes an overt moral stance, and even there it is muted. We are not in the moralistic world of the novella: we sympathize with F.J. as much as we judge him, and we do so because we have his own words before us, as well as the worldly commentary of G.T.[13] F.J.'s first love affair is exposed to the banter of G.T. (which is not without its own sympathy) in the re-telling, and also to the advice of Dame Fraunces, F.J.'s unselfish admirer. Her patient tolerance of F.J.'s foibles balances G.T.'s harsher view.[14]

F.J. begins his love affair in copy-book style, in the manner of a fashion-conscious courtier under the influence of the attitudes found in Castiglione. His first letter to Elinor alludes to the icy-fire oxymoron so favoured by Petrarchans: '*I must say that I have found fire in frost*' (p. 51); 'I feele a *continuall frost, in my most fervent fire*' (p. 52). Elinor is correctly modest and retiring in her response:

She toke occasion one daye, at his request to daunce with him, the which doinge, she bashfully began to declare unto him, that she had read over the writinge, which he delivered unto hir, with like protestation, that (as at deliverie thereof, she understode not for what cause he thrust the same into hir bosome) so now she coulde not

---

[13] Here I differ from the moralizing interpretations found in Charles W. Smith, 'Structural and Thematic Unity in Gascoigne's *The Adventures of Master F.J.*', *Papers on Language and Literature*, 2 (1966), 99–108; and the much more impressive article by Lynette McGrath, 'George Gascoigne's Moral Satire: the Didactic Use of Convention in *The Adventures Passed by Master F.J.*', *JEGP* 70 (1971), 432–50.

[14] This is stressed in Paul A. Parrish, 'The Multiple Perspectives of Gascoigne's "The Adventures of Master F.J."', *Studies in Short Fiction*, 10 (1973), pp. 82–4.

perceyue thereby any part of his meaning, neverthelesse at last semed to take uppon hir the matter, and though she disabled hir selfe, yet gave him thankes as &c. (p. 52)

However, the use of indirect speech, reported through G.T., slightly deflates Elinor's response, with its dismissive '&c.' We are then presented with a poem by F.J.: 'the first verses that ever he wrote uppon like occasion' (p. 52), a very conventional poem in Elinor's praise, judged quite indulgently by G.T. in his role as critic ('may in my judgement be well allowed', ibid.), and perhaps containing a clue to the physical desire which F.J. is concealing in conventional courtly-love language and behaviour: '*You can conject by chaùnge of hew, what humors feede my blood*' (ibid.).

Elinor's first letter to F.J. initiates his realization that he is not paying court to an innocent woman: he suspects that she did not write the letter herself. G.T. indicates Elinor's true nature more directly: 'For as by the stile this letter of hirs bewrayeth that it was not penned by a womans capacitie, so the sequell of hir doings may discipher, that she had mo ready clearkes then trustie servants in store' (p. 53). From this point on, the narrative explores the tension between F.J.'s determination to keep up appearances (that is, to play the role of courtly lover), and the cruder reality of his affair with Elinor.

G.T. shifts the reader's involvement in events, giving us a glimpse of the characters at close hand, then distancing them. We have access directly to the more public encounters of Elinor and F.J., but private assignations, or at least the exact details of them, are reported second-hand. So in a repetition of the rehearsal of courtly convention seen in their first encounter, Elinor spurns F.J., but is persuaded to accept his devotion:

I perceive now (quod she) how mishap doth follow me, that having chosen this walk for a simple solace, I am here disquieted by the man that meaneth my distruction: & therwithal, as half angry, began to turne hir back, when as my friend F.J., now awaked, gan thus salute hir.

Mystres (quod he) and I perceive now, y^t good hap haunts me, for being by lack of oportunitie constreined to commit my welfare unto these blabbing leaves of bewraying paper (shewing y^t in his hand) I am here recomforted w^t the happy view of my desired joye, & therewithall reverently kissing his hand, did softly distreine hir slender arme & so stayed hir departure. The first blow thus profered & defended, they

walked & talked traversing divers wayes, wherein I doubt not but y^t my
friend F.J. could quit himself reasonably well. And though it stood not
with the duty of a friend that I should therein require to know his
secrets, yet of him selfe he declared thus much, that after long talk shee
was contented to accept his proferd service . . . (pp. 54–5)

Gascoigne has a fine sense of dialogue, and a very visual
approach to this scene. Movement is as important as speech—
perhaps more so. Elinor turns away from F.J.; the sexuality
beneath the encounter is encapsulated in his soft yet firm hold on
her 'slender arme'. G.T.'s response to the situation is mildly
humorous, and his detachment is stressed by his inability to
report what was said by Elinor and F.J. on their walk, thereby
ensuring that the reader is conscious of the fact that he is reading
a 'discourse' of F.J.'s adventures, not a first-hand, direct account.

From this point on, the affair proceeds through a series of
economical, partly symbolic scenes. Elinor retreats to her bed
with a rather suspicious 'bleeding at the nose', made ambiguous
by G.T.'s aside: 'whether it were by sodain chaunge, or of wonted
custome' (p. 56). F.J. pretends that he does not know who Elinor
is (thus keeping up appearances), and offers to cure her. This
gives him the opportunity for an intimate conversation in full
view of the assembled company. F.J.'s success in staunching the
blood intimates that he will be successful in other areas; it
certainly sets the seal on Elinor's admiration. Her next letter to
F.J. is her own, not the work of her secretary, and Elinor
continues the courtly nature of the affair by agreeing to be F.J.'s
'she' (p. 58). Immediately following this epistolatory declaration of faith, G.T. alerts us to Elinor's true nature by reminding
us of her previous relationship: 'Shee had in the same house a
friend, a servaunt, a Secretary: what should I name him? such
one as shee esteemed in time past more than was cause in tyme
present' (p. 58). The sexuality behind F.J.'s courtly pose is also
emphasized again: 'he thought good now to smyte while the yron
was hotte, and to lend his Mistresse suche a penne in hir
Secretaries absence, as he should never be able at his returne to
amende the well writing thereof' (p. 58). In public, in a series of
questioni d'amore led by Elinor, the pose of humble courtly lover
('my hand is on my harte', p. 58) is maintained.

The elegant banter that night over supper provides a brief
vignette, a glimpse of the polished society which forms the

background to the affair: 'This gentleman hath a passion', says one of the ladies,

the which once in a daye at the least doth kill his appetite. Are you so well acquainted with the disposition of his body qd. the Lord of the house? by his owne saying, qd. she, and not otherwise. Fayre Ladie qd. F.J. you either mistoke me or overheard me then, for I told of a comfortable humor which so fed me with continual remembrance of joye, as y^t my stomack being ful thereof doth desire in maner none other vittayles. (p. 60)

F.J. is able to parry the snide remarks, which indicate how careful he and Elinor will have to be. Of course a distanced, courtly love affair would be quite acceptable, but F.J. wants more than that. The taunter is Frances, in love with F.J., and obviously jealous at this time, but later to be his friend and confidante. Frances almost succeeds in thwarting the affair before it has really begun: Gascoigne uses a dance scene to explore the tensions between F.J., Frances, and Elinor, a device favoured much later by dramatists.

The centre of the story shifts, for a moment, from Elinor (who retreats in a huff that night) to Frances, who reveals her true affection the following morning, taking the name Hope from F.J., and calling him her Trust. A more honourable, certainly a more hopeful, alternative is briefly before F.J., but he rejects it. At this quiet moment, G.T.'s intrusions cease. Frances tells F.J. what, we realize, he already knows: 'shee seemed to accuse Dame *Elynor*, for the most unconstant woman lyving' (p. 66). F.J. may try to maintain a courtly-love pose in public, but he cannot deceive himself. G.T. extols Frances's virtues, but makes it quite plain that F.J. is now pursuing Elinor because he will be able to achieve an easier sexual victory: 'F.J. had cast his affection on the other (being a married woman)' (p. 67). Here the ideal of courtly love, the elevated affair with the married woman, is reduced to the crudest level:

Now if any man will curiously aske the question why F.J. should chuse the one and leave the other, over and besides the common proverbe? (*So many men, so many minds*) thus may be answered: we see by common experience, y^t the highest flying faucon, doth more commonly pray upon the corn fed crow, & the simple shiftles dove, then on the mounting kyte: & why? because the one is overcome with lesse difficultie then that other. (p. 67)

One may wonder how much the cynical G.T. is projecting this motive onto F.J., who is, after all, involved in his first love affair. However, F.J.'s actions leave the reader in little doubt.

The first sexual encounter between Elinor and F.J. provides another opportunity for an appropriate use of symbolism. F.J. prepares for his assignation: 'taking his night gowne, did under the same convey his naked sword' (p. 69). The scene is a brilliant piece of comedy, as F.J.'s obvious sexual intent, thinly veiled quite literally now, is met with mock-modesty which soon turns to alacrity:

The Moone was now at the full, the skies cleare, and the weather temperate, by reason whereof he might the more playnely and with the greater contentation behold his long desired joyes, and spreding his armes abrode to embrace his loving Mistresse, he sayd: oh my deare Lady when shall I be able with any desert to countervayle the least parte of this your bountiful goodnesse? The dame (whether it were of feare in deede, or that the wylynes of womanhode had taught hir to cover hir conceites with some fyne dissimulation) stert backe from the knight, and shriching (but softly) sayd unto him. Alas servaunt what have I deserved, that you come against me with naked sword as against an open enimie. (p. 69)

It takes little time for the woman who shrichs softly to succumb:

But why hold I so long discourse in discribing the joyes which (for lacke of like experience) I cannot set out to ye full? Were it not that I knowe to whom I write, I would the more beware what I write. F.J. was a man, and neither of us are sencelesse, and therfore I shold slaunder him (over and besides a greater obloquie to the whole genealogie of *Enaeas*) if I should imagine that of tender hart he would forbeare to expresse hir more tender limbes against the hard floore. (p. 69)

G.T. here nudges the reader, and his rather prurient comment at this stage reflects back on himself, rather than on F.J. F.J.'s attempt to conceal this assignation is foiled by the ever-observant Frances:

the Ladie *Fraunces* being no lesse desirous to see an issue of these enterprises, then F.J. was willing to cover them in secresy, did watch & even at the entring of his chamber doore, percyved the poynt of his naked sworde glistring under the skyrt of his night gowne: whereat she smyled & said to hir selfe, this geare goeth well about. (pp. 69–70)

Frances slips into F.J.'s chamber and steals the sword which has figured so prominently in the night's events.

F.J. is determined to maintain the literary decorum with which he began his interest in Elinor, and immediately writes a ballad to her. This receives ambiguous judgement from G.T. ('some will accompt it but a dyddeldome', p. 72), who indirectly acknowledges its attempt to romanticize a sexual encounter. The ballad's mythological references are a very thin veil indeed, and its concluding lines make plain what has occurred:

> *Yet honored still the Moone with true intent:*
> *Who taught us skill,*
> *To worke our will,*
> *And gave us place, till all the night was spent.*   (p. 72)

Elinor, as we might expect, is more inclined to broadcast what has occurred:

onely in hir night gowne gyrt to hir, with a coyfe trymmed *Alla Piedmonteze*, on the which she ware a little cap crossed over the crowne with two bends of yellowe Sarcenet or Cipresse, in the middest whereof she had placed (of hir owne hand writing) in paper this word, *Contented*. (p. 72)

F.J.'s poems illustrate his obsession with Elinor; while G.T.'s over-literal comments on them ('By this challenge I gesse, that either hee was in an extasie or els sure I am nowe in a lunacie, for it is a proud challenge made to *Beautie* hir selfe . . .', p. 76) reduce our faith in his critical acumen. Both G.T. and Elinor reveal a literary naïvety parallel to F.J.'s emotional naïvety when they cavil at a poem in praise of 'my Hellen' (p. 75)—G.T. going to great lengths in his explanation of F.J.'s relationship with a woman called Helen.[15]

F.J.'s confidence grows, and becomes a rather unpalatable cockiness when he strikes up a friendship with Elinor's husband, and makes obvious play with the fact that the husband has to borrow F.J.'s hunting horn: 'the horne was to hard for him to wynde, whereat F.J. tooke pleasure, and sayde to him selfe, blowe tyll thou breake that: I made thee one with in these fewe dayes, that thou wilt never cracke whiles thou livest' (p. 78). F.J. even writes a mocking poem on the theme, and his callousness (which seems to have gone unnoticed by critics) hints at his later decline. He retires to his bed melodramatically when Elinor's secretary returns, and sullenly refuses to respond to her cajoling.

---

[15] See Parrish, p. 81.

G.T. holds up the story at this delicate moment in order to recount a tale from Ariosto, to illustrate the pangs caused by jealousy and suspicion. F.J.'s passion has weakened him physically, he is languishing through a fit of pique, all of which seems to reflect his weakened character. A second interpolated story is provided by Dame Pergo, this time realistic—a story of unrequited love related in some ways to Frances's affection for F.J.

When Elinor visits F.J. in his room at night, her expression of love is too much for him. He swoons, but is revived by an act of intense sensuality which instantly conveys Elinor's powerful sexuality: 'returning to life, the first thing which he felt, was that his good mistres lay pressing his brest w^t the whole weight of hir body, and biting his lips with hir friendly teeth' (p. 91). But as she prepares to join him in bed, his jealousy returns, resulting in him plainly expressing 'with whom, of whom, by whom, and too whom shee bent hir better liking' (p. 92). A quarrel ensues, and Elinor repels F.J.'s advances:

But the Dame denied flatly, alleadging that shee found no cause at all to use such curtesie unto such a recreant, adding further many wordes of greate reproche: the which did so enrage F.J. as that having now forgotten all former curtesies, he drewe uppon his new professed enimie, and bare hir up with such a violence against the bolster, that before shee could prepare the warde, he thrust hir through both hands, &c. wher by the Dame swoning for feare, was constreyned (for a time) to abandon hir body to the enemies curtesie. (p. 92)

Here we see the harshness brought out in F.J. by his affair, the coarsening of his character—no longer concerned, in the privacy of his room at night, to maintain a courtly pose. The *double entendre* of the sword picks up the earlier symbolic use, and fully indicates the degeneration of the whole affair. This is not to suggest that F.J. is solely responsible; the wily G.T. does not take the attack on Elinor quite so seriously: 'having now recovered her chamber (bicause shee founde hir hurt to be nothing daungerous) I doubt not, but shee slept quietly the rest of the night' (p. 92). (Or is this simply a chauvinist remark by G.T.?)

G.T.'s crude view of things seems ultimately justified, as Elinor returns to her secretary: 'his quils & pennes not worn so near as they were wont to be, did now prick such faire large notes, y^t his Mistres liked better to sing faburden under him, than to descant any longer uppon F.J.['s] playne song' (p. 93). Frances discovers them, and Gascoigne reminds us of F.J.'s decline by a pointed parallel in the change of season: 'Dame *Pergo* heard a Cuckoe chaunt, who (because the pride of the spring was now past) cried Cuck cuck Cuckoe in hir stamering voyce' (ibid.). The bird's cry too is wryly appropriate. The selfless Frances continues to help F.J. She tells the third interpolated story—a tale of a selfless husband who copes with his wife's adultery. It evidently reflects on Pergo, but demands that F.J. sympathize with the husband; which he does, although he marvels at 'a rare tractabilitie in the lover' (p. 100). Frances makes another effort to heal the breach between Elinor and F.J. The affair becomes literary, rather than actual, with F.J. trading poems for rebuffs, and finally facing humiliating laughter from Elinor, the secretary, and Pergo. F.J.'s poem of rejection is his public renunciation—it soon circulates throughout the household.

F.J. takes some convincing of Elinor's nature—his stubborn refusal to let go is an indication that he has not really matured through his experience. Elinor has to be blatant: 'And if I did so (quod she) what then?' is her reply to F.J.'s accusation that she is granting her favours to the secretary (p. 104). F.J.'s cynical last poem ends the first version of the history: one can agree, in a sense, with G.T.'s description of it as a 'thriftlesse Historie' (p. 105); little has been gained by any character.

In his revision, as I have already mentioned, Gascoigne turned his story into a pseudo-translation from the Italian. We lose the services of G.T. as a narrator, and this certainly reduces the irony, in the interaction of various points of view, present in the first version. The morals implicit in the first version are made more explicit: F.J., now called Ferdinando Jéronimi, has been invited to visit the Lord of Valasco for the specific purpose of arranging to marry Francischina (Frances). The revision omits some erotic detail, and the poem mocking Elinor's husband ('*As some men say there is a kind of seed*', p. 78). The impact of the affair is softened somewhat through these omissions, although in general the story remains the same.

The most important alteration is a new conclusion for the story, telling us that after Ferdinando left Valasco's castle he 'departed to his house in *Venice*: spending there yᵉ rest of his dayes in a dissolute kind of lyfe: & abandoning the worthy Lady

Fraunc[ischin]a, who (dayly being gauled with the griefe of his great ingratitude) dyd shortlye bring hir selfe into a myserable consumption: whereof (after three yeares languishing) she dyed . . .' (p. 453). On the other hand, 'Notwithstanding al which occur[rente]s the Lady *Elinor* lived long in yᵉ continuance of hir accustomed change: & thus we see that where wicked lust doeth beare the name of love, it doth not onelye infecte the lyght minded, but it maye also become confusion to others which are vowed to constancie' (ibid.).

The cruder moralizing is not as attractive as G.T.'s ambiguous comments, but this does seem an appropriate fate for F.J., who is far too fixed in his conception of himself, and of the role he desires to play (or at least be seen to play). The first version of the story moves the reader beyond simple moral judgement (and security). It is many things: a satire directed against attempts to play out courtly codes when they conflict with the reality of a situation; a kaleidoscopic account of a love affair, viewed from the perspective of a naïve young man, a cynical older man, and a trusting, wise friend; a comedy revealing the disjunction between literary and moral interpretations of events; a cautionary tale of blind passion and missed opportunities.

Chapter 4

Courtly Fiction: II. Lyly

Master F.J. is an example of courtly fiction which went virtually unnoticed, while five years later Lyly established a fashion with *Euphues*, which was an unparalleled success: 'All our ladies were then his scholars, and that beauty in court which could not parley Euphuism was as little regarded as she which now [1632] there speaks not French.'[1] *Euphues* ran to nineteen editions by 1636 (the last five including the sequel *Euphues and his England*). *Master F.J.* and *Euphues* share the influence of the *questioni d'amore*, and both are comic explorations of courtly behaviour, but unlike Gascoigne, Lyly created a flamboyant style to assist in his exploration, a style which attracted the attention of his contemporaries (whether they approved or disapproved) and which has remained at the centre of modern critical consideration of his fiction. The questions about the nature and derivation of euphuism have, I believe, been satisfactorily answered; while any discussion of Lyly's fiction will involve a consideration of euphuism, I do not intend to elaborate its sources and character.[2]

Lyly's indebtedness to Pettie has been considered from a stylistic point of view,[3] but a more interesting connection is both writers' use of irony combined with didacticism. Lyly's fiction has a solid, didactic surface: advice is constantly offered to Euphues while he is a young wanton, and offered by him after he has reformed; paradigms of correct behaviour are outlined by the older generation for the improvement of the younger (by Eubulus in *The Anatomy of Wit*, and by Fidus in *Euphues and his England*); in numerous soliloquies characters offer themselves

---

[1] G. K. Hunter, *John Lyly: The Humanist as Courtier* (London, 1962), p. 72.

[2] The nature of euphuism is conveniently summarized by Hunter, pp. 261–79, drawing on the work of M. W. Croll, and superseding it. Reference should also be made to Jonas A. Barish, 'The Prose Style of John Lyly', *ELH* 23 (1956), 14–35. Origins are also considered by Hunter, pp. 270–2; and see William Ringler, 'The Immediate Source of Euphuism', *PMLA* 53 (1938), 678–86.

[3] See J. Swart, 'Lyly and Pettie', *English Studies*, 23 (1941), 9–18.

advice, constantly balancing alternative courses of conduct.
However, the didacticism, particularly that emanating from
Euphues, is frequently treated humorously. The reader must
beware of being lulled by Lyly's style into ignoring the context of
each speech.

The balance of narrative action and rhetorical elaboration is
also relevant here. There is very little narrative action in *Euphues*;
the actual story can be very briefly summarized. But so, for that
matter, can the story of Richardson's *Pamela*. It is necessary to
focus on *how* Lyly tells his story.

Euphues The Anatomy of Wit divides into two almost equal
halves: the story of Euphues' friendship with Philautus, his
attraction to Philautus' love Lucilla, and Lucilla's betrayal of
Euphues which leads to a reconciliation between the two friends;
and in the second half, the presentation of Euphues as a didactic
figure, writing advice to all and sundry. The story is related to the
theme of the prodigal son, the didactic side to what G. K. Hunter
has called the Humanist interest in 'the relation of wit to
wisdom'.[4] At first, Euphues appears as a brash but inexperienced
young man (not unlike F.J. in this): 'This younge gallant, of more
wit then wealth, and yet of more wealth then wisdome, seeing
himselfe inferiour to none in pleasant conceipts, thought himselfe
superiour to al in honest conditions . . .' (I. 184).[5]

This boldness is to be deflated by misadventure in love,
changing Euphues from the callous betrayer of his friend to a
moral exemplar. This change is interconnected with Lyly's style,
for euphuism is intimately concerned with antithesis, as Albert
Feuillerat pointed out long ago: *Euphues* 'n'est en somme qu'une
antithèse longuement prolongée'.[6] This idea was expanded by
Jonas Barish, in an excellent article which stresses the tendency of
euphuism to view man and nature in conjunction as essentially
paradoxical: euphuism, he says, encapsulates 'the precarious
closeness of extremes . . .'.[7] Structural balance and antithesis,
and illustrative paradox, are at the heart of euphuism: 'The fine

---

[4] Hunter, p. 51; and see John Dover Wilson, 'Euphues and The Prodigal Son', *The Library*, 10 (1909), 337–61.

[5] All references are to *The Complete Works of John Lyly*, ed. R. Warwick Bond (Oxford, 1902).

[6] Albert Feuillerat, *John Lyly* (Cambridge, 1910), p. 412.

[7] Barish, p. 21.

christall is sooner crazed then the harde marble, the greenest
Beeche burneth faster then the dryest Oke, the fairest silke is
soonest soyled, and the sweetest wine tourneth to the sharpest
vinegar . . .' (I. 189). The insistence of this style, its constant
setting up of oppositions, makes Euphues' change appropriate.
Influenced by a single affair, he changes from wanton to wise,
from prodigal to paragon. The structure of *Euphues The Anatomy
of Wit* is similar to the structure of a euphuistic sentence: an
antithesis is set up between the unreformed and reformed
Euphues.

Two recent articles have drawn attention to the ambiguity of
Lyly's work. Madelon Gohlke sees a kind of deceit at the heart of
the story: 'people do not say what they mean.'[8] Unfortunately,
this insight leads to an anachronistic view of the characters as
psychological cases, and to absurdities such as the notion that the
resumption of friendship between Euphues and Philautus after
the rejection of Lucilla indicates 'the power of the homosexual
bond over the heterosexual one . . .'.[9] But Gohlke is right to note
that language is often used as a screen in *Euphues*. Theodore
Steinberg also discusses this aspect, focusing on what he sees as
Euphues' hypocrisy.[10] His view of *Euphues* reduces ambiguity to
simple opposition. *Euphues* satirizes extremes; courtesy is a
desirable trait if it is not excessive.

The ambiguity of language in *Euphues* stems from its rhetorical
function. It is used as a weapon of persuasion and as resistance
to persuasion. The work opens with what is virtually a debate
between Euphues and Eubulus, in which Eubulus warns
Euphues that he is open to temptation, particularly through his
pride: 'Alas *Euphues* by how much the more I loue the highe
climbinge of thy capacitie, by so muche the more I feare thy fall'
(I. 189). Euphues' reply is shot through with persuasive but
illogical imagery. The argument revolves around the nature/
nurture controversy: Eubulus has claimed that Euphues will be
prey to bad influences; Euphues replies with a series of examples
showing that 'education can haue no shew, where the excellencie
of nature doth beare sway' (I. 191). By quickly moving on to
personal abuse, however, Euphues soon shows that he is wanting

[8] Madelon Gohlke, 'Reading "Euphues" ', *Criticism*, 19 (1977), 105.
[9] Ibid., p. 113.
[10] Theodore Steinberg, 'The Anatomy of *Euphues*', *SEL* 17 (1977), 27–38.

in courtesy, either by nature or nurture: 'The similytude you
rehearse of the waxe, argueth your waxinge and melting
brayne . . .' (ibid.). Pride carries Euphues on in a wave of self-
admiration:

As touchinge my residence and abidinge heere in *Naples*, my youthly
and lusty affections, my sportes and pleasures, my pastimes, my
common dalyaunce, my delyghtes, my resorte and company, and
companions, which dayly vse to visite mee, althoughe to you they
breede more sorrowe and care, then solace and comforte, bicause of
your crabbed age: yet to mee they bring more comforte and ioy, then
care & griefe, more blisse then bale, more happines then heauines:
bicause of my youthfule gentlenes. (I. 192)

If Lyly has a serious purpose, it is to demonstrate how 'wit', in
the sense of an intelligence in full flight, a projection of character
through language, can be abused: 'Heere ye may beholde
gentlemen, how lewdly wit standeth in his owne lyght . . .'
(I. 195). The condemnation is aimed at the misdirection of wit:

I go not about (gentlemen) to inueigh against wit, for then I wer
witlesse, but frankely to confesse mine owne lyttle wit, I have euer
thought so supersticiously of wit, that I feare I haue committed Idolatry
agaynst wisedome, and if Nature had dealte so beneficially with mee to
haue given me any wit, I should haue bene readyer in the defence of it
to haue made an Apologie, then any way to tourne to Apostacie . . .
(I. 196)

Every action which occurs in *Euphues* leads to reflection, every
character, through dialogue and soliloquy, explores his or her
reaction to a situation, and throughout this process, fuelled by the
tendency of Lyly's style towards antithesis, alternative responses
are posited. So Lucilla, when she feels a mounting affection for
Euphues, 'entred into these termes and contrarieties' (I. 205).
She weighs up her choices, balances the 'contrarieties', and
Euphues does likewise. In the very act of choosing a course of
behaviour, these characters make their deception quite plain by
actually articulating the judgement passed on them by the
reader:

Shall I not then hazarde my lyfe to obtaine my loue? and deceiue
Philautus to receiue *Lucilla*? Yes *Euphues*, where loue beareth sway,
friendshippe can haue no shew: As *Philautus* brought me for his shadowe
the last supper, so will I vse him for my shadow til I haue gayned his

Saint. And canst thou wretch be false to him that is faithfull to thee? Shall hys curtesie be cause of thy crueltie? Wilt thou violate the league of fayth, to enherite the land of folly? Shal affection be of more force then friendshippe, loue then law, lust then loyaltie? Knowest thou not that he that looseth his honestie hath nothing els to loose? (I. 209–10)

These highly wrought soliloquies are a development from the novella; we have already seen their use by Pettie, who influenced Lyly considerably. Like Pettie, Lyly addresses his audience directly—they are 'gentlemen' in *Euphues the Anatomy of Wit*, 'gentlemen' and 'gentlewomen' in *Euphues and his England*. The authorial asides are didactic rather than ironic: 'Heere you may see gentlemen the falshood in felowship, the fraude in friendship . . .' (I. 215).

The formal nature of euphuism may blind the modern reader to the skilful use of the soliloquy to convey nuances of emotional reaction. An excellent example is contained in a soliloquy spoken by Lucilla after she meets Euphues. Lucilla tries to convince herself that she should follow her desires:

Time hath weaned me from my mothers teat, and age ridde me from my fathers correction, when children are in their swathe cloutes, then are they subiect to the whip, and ought to be carefull of the rigour of their parents. As for me seeing I am not fedde with their pap, I am not to be ledde by their perswasions. Let my father vse what speaches he lyst, I will follow mine owne lust. Lust *Lucilla*, what sayst thou? No, no, mine owne loue I should haue sayd, for I am as farre from lust, as I am from reason, and as neere to loue as I am to folly. Then sticke to thy determination, & shew thy selfe, what loue can doe, what loue dares doe, what loue hath done. (I. 207)

In this soliloquy, Lyly has Lucilla make what the modern reader might call a Freudian slip—the substitution of 'lust' for 'loue', which reveals what is really on her mind, and so reflects her true character. Euphuism is a persuasive rhetorical style, and in this example, Lucilla is using it to persuade herself to undertake a particular course of action. The rhythmic repetition and alliteration in the last sentence quoted is coloured by Lucilla's admission that love is really lust and what it actually 'does' is lead to deception, when Lucilla decides to have both Euphues and Philautus for the time being: 'and I hope so to behaue my selfe as *Euphues* shall thinke me his owne, and *Philautus* perswade himselfe I am none but his' (I. 207).

Euphuism may thus be used to bolster a false argument, and the reader has to concentrate in order to discover how the truth is being twisted. The care with which Lyly has constructed the arguments he gives to his characters has been indicated by Walter King.[11] But euphuism argues through analogy rather than logic, through the proliferation of supporting examples. In this sense, although *Euphues The Anatomy of Wit* is divided equally into narrative and didactic material provided by the reformed Euphues, both parts are essentially concerned with persuasion. Euphues' 'Cooling Carde' to all lovers, his letter to the matrons and maidens of Italy, his oration on nurture and upbringing ('Euphues and his Ephoebus'), his debate with Atheos on God, are all pedagogic, and use euphuism for the same purpose as the narrative section of the work. It is misleading to detach the didactic section, and concentrate on the narrative: both sections were obviously given equal importance by Lyly.

As regards Lyly's approach to narrative, it is notable that he has an intellectual, rather than a visual, apprehension of his characters. We learn almost nothing about their physical characteristics, or about the appearance of their environment, for Lyly animates ideas, not objects. We do learn about the characters in *Euphues* from what they say, from how they argue, from the illustrations they use: language is the key to character. For example, Philautus reveals that he, like Euphues, is a young man who scorns the wisdom of the aged:

Touchinge our accesse bee thou secure, I will flappe *Ferardo* in the mouth with some conceyte, and fill his olde heade so full of newe fables that thou shalt rather bee earnestly entreated to repaire to his house, then euyll entreated to leaue it. As olde men are very suspitious to mistrust euerye thinge, so are they verye credulous to beleeue any thinge, the blinde man doth eate many a Fly . . . (I. 214)

After his reformation, Euphues immediately assumes a very superior tone, a preacher's pose, to lend weight to his admonitions:

Musing with my selfe beeing idle howe I myght be well imployed (friend *Philautus*) I could finde nothing either more fitte to continue our friendshippe, or of greater force to dissolue our follye, then to write a remedy for that which many iudge past cure, for loue (*Philautus*) with y^e

11 Walter N. King, 'John Lyly and Elizabethan Rhetoric', *SP* 52 (1955), 149–61.

which I haue bene so tormented, that I haue lost my time, thou so troubled that thou hast forgot reason . . . (I. 246)

This new Euphues is able to write stoic (and very comfortless) advice to Eubulus on the death of his daughter; advice which still seems to reveal a very callow contempt for old age: 'take ye death of thy daughter patiently, and looke for thine own speedely, so shalt thou perfourme both the office of an honeste man, and the honour of an aged father . . .' (I. 311). He also takes a very superior tone in his letter to Philautus on Lucilla's death, and the reader sympathizes with Philautus' 'sigh', rather than Euphues' triumphant moralizing.

The sequel which followed *Euphues The Anatomy of Wit* has not been accorded much attention by critics interested in euphuism as a style, and it is surprisingly absent from Theodore Steinberg's account of Lyly as a comic satirist. It is, in many ways, a more ambitious work, and allows Lyly to give his comic perspective much more freedom, with an increased emphasis on narrative action. Following the success of his first work, Lyly, like Pettie, turns to a female audience (although he continues to address his 'gentlemen' readers). In the preface addressed to the ladies, he presents his book as a trifle to be toyed with rather than taken seriously:

It resteth Ladies, that you take the paines to read it, but at such times, as you spend in playing with your little Dogges, and yet will I not pinch you of that pastime, for I am content that your Dogges lye in your laps, so *Euphues* may be in your hands, that when you shall be wearie in reading of the one, you may be ready to sport with the other; or handle him as you doe your Iunckets, that when you can eate no more, you tye some in your napkin for children, for if you be filled with the first part, put the second in your pocket for your wayting Maydes: *Euphues* had rather lye shut in a Ladyes casket, then open in a Schollers studie. (II. 8–9)

Lyly's new approach involves a considerable use of irony, reinforced by the interesting technique of stories within stories. Our view of Euphues himself is now balanced between satire and a certain amount of respect. Euphues is now a fully-fledged analyst of other people's affairs, a completely self-assured dispenser of advice on all occasions. The minute he sets sail for

England with Philautus, he launches into a long, didactic speech: 'we cannot better bestowe our time on the Sea, then in aduise how to behaue our selues when we come to ye shore' (II. 13). He tells Philautus a story in illustration of a basic theme found in Lyly's fiction: the repentant prodigal. It is an attempt by Euphues to warn the hapless Philautus about his 'light' behaviour, and as such seems to be excessive, judging by our knowledge of Philautus' character. Unfortunately, Philautus' reaction to the story is less than ideal. To begin with, he becomes seasick: 'You must imagine (bicause it were too long to tell all his iourney) that he was Sea sicke (as thou beginnest to be *Philautus*)' (II. 29). Then he becomes sleepy: '*Philautus* not accustomed to these narrow Seas, was more redy to tell what wood the ship was made of, then to aunswer to *Euphues* discourse: yet between waking and winking, as, one halfe sicke and some-what sleepy, it came in his braynes, aunswered thus . . .' (II. 32–3).

Lyly's satirical view of Euphues becomes even more overt when Euphues gives Philautus a thumb-nail sketch of England. Drawing on information sadly out of date, he explains that the English use brass and iron rings instead of coins, and that 'All the *Brittaines* doe die them-selues with woad, which setteth a blewish colour vpon them, and it maketh them more terrible to beholde in battaile' (II. 32). As Euphues relies on Caesar for his knowledge of England, our respect for his 'learning' decreases markedly. This misinformation also serves to highlight Euphues' later favourable view of England. Lyly is writing a chauvinist account of England, and Euphues becomes one of England's most fervent supporters. *Euphues and his England* concludes with '*Euphues Glasse for Europe*', which draws on William Harrison's *Description of Britaine* (the opening of Holinshed's Chronicle of 1577) and provides an expansive, adulatory description of England. It also includes extensive praise of Elizabeth.

Lyly introduces Euphues and Philautus to English courtly society, and Philautus becomes the centre of interest, as he falls in love with Camilla, but eventually concedes to her match with Surius and marries Frauncis instead. Euphues is still fixed in his role, and despite his admiration for English society, and English women, he leaves England, and we leave him as a hermit at the 'Mount of *Silixsedra*' (II. 228).

Philautus' happy sojourn in English society is paralleled by a

cautionary tale told by Fidus to Euphues and Philautus when
they first arrive in England. Fidus recalls his début, at the age of
20, as a courtier: 'Who so conuersant with the Ladyes as I? Who
so pleasaunt? Who more prodigall?' (II. 49). Then a gentleman
had warned him against women, much as Eubulus warned
Euphues, or as Fidus himself now warns Philautus. (And here
Lyly seems to indicate that such advice is only ever useful with
hindsight; that it is, in a sense, detached from experience and so
fruitless.) Disregarding the gentleman's warning, Fidus falls in
love with a lady called Iffida, and courts her—and at this point of
the story Euphues, as little interested in the details of love as
Philautus was in moral maxims, begins to drowse ('And nowe
Philautus, for I see *Euphues* begynne to nodde', II. 56). Un-
deterred by this silent criticism, Fidus continues his tale: Iffida
tells him a typical *questioni d'amore* story, but he provides the
wrong answer. Having thus alienated her, he is thereafter
consistently met with rebuffs; and when he tries his own *questioni
d'amore* story he receives an unexpected reply. Iffida refuses to
play the game: asked if she would choose a handsome, a witty, or
a wealthy lover, she first states that she would not settle for less
than a man who combined all three qualities. Then, when
pressed, she claims that she would choose wealth: 'for beautie
without riches, goeth a begging, and wit with-out wealth,
cheapeneth all things in the Faire, but buyeth nothing' (II. 72).

This infuriates Fidus, who does, however, receive a more
sympathetic visit from Iffida when he falls ill through his
unrequited love for her. She explains that she is remaining true to
Thirsus, who is presently overseas. When news later reaches
Iffida that Thirsus is dead, her grief banishes all thought of Fidus;
but when, after five years, she has begun to regard him with some
favour, fate intervenes and she dies of a fever. At this, Fidus
recalls, he left the court and has lived a solitary life ever since.

This story is repeated, with significant variations, when
Philautus enters the courtly world and falls in love with Camilla.
Unlike Fidus, he is able, eventually, to transfer his affections, and
avoid the solitary life. Philautus is integrated with the sophisticated society depicted in *Euphues and his England*, while Euphues,
like Fidus, is only a transient participant: he withdraws from the
courtly world even before he leaves England. In order to reach
his position of content, Philautus has to endure a similar affair to

Fidus': the beautiful Camilla is not for him, and he must give up his vain pursuit.

When Philautus first succumbs to Camilla's charms, he reveals, in an interesting soliloquy, that he has internalized Euphues, who now stands as a kind of overarching conscience whose advice can easily be anticipated:

O my *Euphues*, would I had thy wit, or thou my wil. Shal I vtter this to thee, but thou art more likely to correct my follyes with counsaile, then to comfort me with any pretie conceit. Thou wilt say that she is a Lady of great credit, & I heere of no countenaunce. I but *Euphues*, low trees haue their tops, smal sparkes their heat, the Flye his splene, ye Ant hir gall, *Philautus* his affection . . . (II. 90)

Notice that the pejorative sense of 'wit' found at the beginning of *Euphues* ('This younge gallant of more wit than wealth') has now been replaced by what Theodore Steinberg sees as an ambiguous assessment of wit's worth.[12] Rather this is an acknowledgment that wit must be seen in context: it may be used or misused. In this particular case, Euphues' wit, as Philautus well knows, is an intellectual apprehension of the dangers inherent in Philautus' new passion.

When Euphues himself breezes in, immediately after Philautus' soliloquy, full of praise for English women ('it is as rare to see a beautifull woman in *England* w^{t}out vertue, as to see a faire woman in *Italy* w^{t}out pride', II. 91), Philautus turns to the attack. He criticizes Euphues for renouncing his 'cooling card'. We are treated to the spectacle of Euphues apparently commending Philautus' action, but only in the abstract; the love-sick Philautus condemning Euphues for renouncing his asceticism; and Euphues himself highly offended at being lectured to by his friend. Euphues announces that 'I was neuer wise inough to giue thee counsaile, yet euer willing to wish thee well' (II. 102)—at which the reader raises an eyebrow—and he leaves in a huff. Philautus returns to his fruitless courtship of Camilla, and his decision to seek help from a countryman called Psellus, supposedly skilled in magic, gives Lyly a further occasion for satire. Psellus is seen by Philautus as a figure possessing the power of a John Dee (or perhaps, as love potions are in question, one should say a Simon Forman). Psellus comes out with a large amount of

[12] Steinberg, p. 30.

mumbo-jumbo, and nine love potions, containing ever more
grisly ingredients—but he punctures the spell by telling
Philautus that all this is nonsense: 'Love dwelleth in the minde, in
the will and in the heart, which neyther Coniurer canne alter nor
Phisicke' (II. 118). With this sensible rationalism, Lyly mocks
the popular appeal to magic, and also Philautus' attempt to
evade the reality of the situation. Philautus is never without a
guide to conduct, but Psellus has a much lighter touch than
Euphues.

Philautus' advances to Camilla are made against the background of sophisticated courtly games, seen also in *Master F.J.*;
these have been discussed by Violet Jefferey.[13] As Philautus is
spurned, he turns back to his friend Euphues. Their letters
provide an interesting example of euphuism utilized for persuasive purposes. As the letters pass to and fro, Euphues initially
resisting Philautus' overtures, the illustrations from natural
history increase to become a veritable torrent of supporting
examples (for both sides). Philautus must yield to Euphues'
influence, must once again accept him as a guide. The imagery
subtly conveys the power, and perhaps even cruelty, involved in
this submission:

A *Phoenix* is no foode for *Philautus*, that dayntie toothe of thine must bee
pulled out, els wilt thou surfette with desire, and that Eagles eye pecked
out, els wilt bee daseled with delyght. My counsaile must rule thy
conceipte, least thou confound vs both. (II. 153–4)

Euphues tries to persuade Philautus that love should not strive for
possession: 'I haue read of many, and some I know, betweene
whom there was as feruent affection as might be, that neuer
desired any thing, but sweete talke, and continuall company at
bankets . . .' (II. 159). This even calls forth a response from the
author: 'I must needes conclude with *Philautus*, though I shoulde
cauill with *Euphues*, that the ende of love is the full fruition of the
partie beloved, at all times and in all places' (II. 160).

The permutations of love are finally explored in a long scene
depicting a dinner held by Flavia, a noblewoman who has
befriended Euphues and Philautus. She organizes three dispu-
tations: one between Camilla and her lover Surius, one between
Philautus and Frauncis, and one between Martius and herself.

[13] Violet M. Jefferey, *John Lyly and the Italian Renaissance* (Paris, 1928).

Camilla is asked by Surius how she would respond to a declaration of love from 'one wounded with your beautie (for vnder that name I comprehende all other vertues) . . .' (II. 163). This question becomes concerned with the Neoplatonic notion of beauty, which is repudiated by Camilla, who sees a man in love with her beauty as someone 'enflamed wᵗ lust rather then loue' (II. 164), but defended by Surius, who reminds Camilla that 'a Lady endewed with bewtie, pulleth on curtesie, curtesie mercy, and one vertue linkes it selfe to another, vntill there be a rare perfection' (II. 165). The discussion which follows prepares the ground for Surius' declaration of his intentions to Camilla.

Martius and Flavia, the older members of the company, debate the dangers of men having access to women, 'Knowing yt there is nothing more pernicious to either, then loue, and that loue breedeth by nothing sooner then lookes' (II. 170). Martius dodges this extreme solution to the problem of love by arguing that anyone in love would go mad if prevented from seeing the person loved. After Surius has entered the debate in protest, it is reduced to some pretty patter about loving and fishing. These debates should indicate to Philautus that his approach to Camilla has extended beyond due bounds. He is teased by Frauncis, and asks her if a lover should be constant or secret. This evasive attempt at self-justification is quickly dealt with by Frauncis, who points out that 'It is no question *Philautus* to aske which is best, when being not ioyned there is neuer a good' (II. 177). Frauncis tries to argue Philautus out of his increasingly foolish infatuation.

Euphues is invited to pass judgement on these debates, and for once produces a very sensible notion of compromise, a kind of *via media* of love. Philautus then turns to Frauncis, and Euphues leaves England, with a final, liberal dispensation of advice. His glass for Europe is yet another moral lesson, set before the women of Italy as an example. In the final letter of the work, Euphues the bachelor advises Philautus on marriage. We are left with a largely satirical view of Euphues, with a most alluring style, with a narrative of some verve and, of course, considerable wit.

Like all extreme styles, euphuism passed from being in vogue to being ridiculed, but Lyly's fiction continued to be popular after his style became outmoded, and its success led to numerous imitations. Even works which do not imitate Lyly may conjure up his fiction in a sub-title: for example, John Dickenson's *Arisbas: Euphues Amidst His Slumbers* (1594). Any critic of Lyly's style will come to appreciate it after a brief perusal of the lamer imitations which appeared. Austen Saker's *Narbonus* (1580), for example, has no sense of parison—of the rhythm of balanced clauses which provides the vigour behind Lyly's style—and produces a lumpy string of euphuistic similes:

The Riuer Nilus ingendreth the foule Crocadile, and castes vp the precious perles: the filthy Toade hath a faire stone in hir heade: the Serpents skin is very medicinable for sundry things, where contrary, the Bee hath Hony in her mouth and a sting in her tayle: the swetest rose hath some pricke, the clearest Well, some dyrte in the bottom . . . (sig. Bi^v)

Robert Greene's first imitation of Lyly, *Mamillia* (1583), is more successful, if somewhat tedious. Greene is more interested in narrative action than Lyly, a concern apparent in his later fiction. Both Greene, and Thomas Lodge in *Rosalynde* (1592), were able to draw on euphuism as they constructed their own approaches to fiction.[14] Less fruitful were a number of eccentric, ornate styles which followed in euphuism's wake. Brian Melbancke's *Philotimus* (1583), for instance, makes use of rhyming prose, produced through extensive borrowing from various miscellanies.[15]

As euphuism fell from favour, attacks on it increased; by the time Shakespeare poked fun at it in *Henry IV* it was thoroughly out of season. In the course of a decade, Greene turned from imitation to refutation of euphuism. In *Menaphon* (1589), his most impressive romance, Greene has assimilated Sidney's example, and engages in a searching examination of how characters use language to project an image to the world.[16] Euphuism is portrayed as both outmoded and affected. Melicertus and

---

[14] See Nancy R. Lindheim, 'Lyly's Golden Legacy: *Rosalynde* and *Pandosto*', *SEL* 15 (1975), 3–20.
[15] See Hyder E. Rollins, 'Notes on Brian Melbanck's "Philotimus"', *SP* 1 (1929), 40–57; 'Notes on the Sources of Melbanck's "Philotimus"', *Harvard Studies and Notes in Philology and Literature*, 18 (1935), 177–98.
[16] See Walter R. Davis, *Idea and Act in Elizabethan Fiction* (Princeton, 1969), p. 174.

Samela, their true identities unknown to each other, exchange euphuistic speeches, and Greene comments on the exchange:

Samela made this replie, because she heard him so superfine, as if Ephaebus had learnd him to refine his mother tongue, wherefore thought he had done it of an inkhorne desire to be eloquent; and Melicertus thinking that Samela had learned with Lucilla in Athens to anatomize wit, and speake none but Similes . . .[17]

Melicertus' true noble rank is revealed to Samela when he recites a poem free from the conventions of euphuism. Despite this rejection, some elements of Lyly's style are still present in Greene's work, but they have been amalgamated into Greene's own style.

A more amusing view of euphuism may be found in Barnaby Rich's *The Adventures of Don Simonides* (1581), described not altogether appropriately by Walter Davis as a 'sixteenth century *Sentimental Journey*'.[18] I would also question Davis's contention that 'Simonides is a Euphues who never learns', for Rich makes it plain at the end of *The Second Tome* (1584) that Simonides recognizes his folly and does indeed repent.[19] While he does not write a 'cooling card', he pronounces what could be called a 'cooling speech' (sigs. Tiii^v, and Vi). Rich's narrative pays much greater attention to events than Lyly's, but his exploration of stylistic variation is important. Already apparent in the first part of *Don Simonides*, where Rich alters his style to suit the changes in the narrative (see, for example, Lamia's racy speech, sigs. Hiii^v–Mii), changing styles are at the centre of *The Second Tome*, which begins with a debate between Sebastian the Friar, Sandalian the lawyer, and de Feragosa the soldier, each character speaking in a distinct, appropriate style.

Don Simonides himself, after numerous adventures, actually meets Euphues. The euphuism spoken by Simonides is parodic, and Euphues' moralizing has little effect on his actions. Simonides reforms after he has visited England, in imitation of Euphues, and returned to Seville. Rich is no longer writing courtly fiction, and the figure of Euphues is no longer treated with the sophisticated irony we find in *Euphues and his England*.

---

[17] Robert Greene, *Works*, ed. A. B. Grosart (1881–6, rpt. New York, 1964), Vol. 6, p. 82.
[18] Davis, p. 127.   [19] Ibid.

Chapter 5

Sir Philip Sidney and the *Arcadia*

'Will you needes haue a written Pallace of Pleasure, or rather a printed Court of Honour? Read the Countesse of Pembrookes Arcadia, a gallant Legendary, full of pleasurable accidents and proffitable discourses . . .'.[1] Gabriel Harvey's praise of the *Arcadia* in *Pierces Supererogation* (1593) may stand as representative of numerous adulatory comments by Sidney's contemporaries. Sidney's romance maintained this popularity through the following century, and its influence on seventeenth-century fiction is the subject of a later chapter (Chapter 10, below). As tastes changed, interest in the *Arcadia* did eventually wane, and did not revive until the appearance of Albert Feuillerat's edition of 1912. It is only in the last few decades that critics have accorded it the enthusiastic and detailed interest that greeted its first appearance.

Sidney may have begun the *Arcadia* as early as 1577, if we rely on the statement of Edmund Molyneux in a note contributed to Stowe's continuation of Holinshed (1587).[2] The bulk of the first version was probably written at Wilton and Ivy Church between March and August 1580.[3] The *Old Arcadia* then underwent at least four stages of revision (which may be examined in detail in Jean Robertson's excellent edition) before Sidney began the *New Arcadia*. The only surviving manuscript of the *New Arcadia*, held by the Cambridge University Library, is dated 1584, although some controversy has arisen over this date, with William Ringler arguing for it as the date of composition, Jean Robertson as merely the date of the transcription.[4] Sidney probably began the

[1] G. Gregory Smith, ed., *Elizabethan Critical Essays* (Oxford, 1904), Vol. 2, p. 282.

[2] Jean Robertson, ed., *The Countess of Pembroke's Arcadia (The Old Arcadia)* (Oxford, 1973), p. xv; references are to this edition; references to the *New Arcadia (NA)* are to Albert Feuillerat, ed., *The Prose Works of Sir Philip Sidney* (Cambridge, 1912), Vol. 1.

[3] Ibid., p. xvi.

[4] William Ringler, ed., *The Poems of Sir Philip Sidney* (Oxford, 1962), pp. 529–31; Robertson, pp. lvi-vii; and see Mary Mahl, 'Sir Philip Sidney's Scribe: *The New Arcadia* and the *Apology for Poetry*', *ELN* 10 (1972), 90–1; Dorothy Connell, *Sir Philip Sidney: The Maker's Mind* (Oxford, 1977), p. 115.

New Arcadia after 1582, and must have stopped writing before he left England for his fatal journey to the Netherlands in 1585.

Although manuscripts of the *Old Arcadia* were in circulation after Sidney's death—Abraham Fraunce used one as a source for illustrations in his *Arcadian Rhetoric* (1588)—it was the *New Arcadia* which was published by William Ponsonby, under the supervision of Sidney's close friend Fulke Greville, in 1590. The printed text adds chapter divisions and arranges the eclogues, but concludes in mid-sentence during Book Three. In response to this 'disfigured' *Arcadia*, in 1593 Sidney's sister Mary published a text which joined the last three books of the *Old Arcadia* onto the incomplete revision; this text rearranges the eclogues and makes some alterations in the text to smooth the new conjunction.[5] The full text of the *Old Arcadia* only emerged in 1907 with the discovery by Bertram Dobell of long-forgotten manuscripts. We thus have three versions of the *Arcadia* to consider: the original *Old Arcadia*, the revised but incomplete *New Arcadia*, and the 1593 composite *Arcadia*. C. S. Lewis's plea that we should concentrate on the 1593 *Arcadia* as 'the text which really affected the English mind' has been largely ignored by scholars and critics who have explored the distinct characteristics of the two other texts.[6]

The adulation which greeted the appearance of the *Arcadia* has engendered a view that it appeared *ex nihilo* as far as any English tradition of prose fiction is concerned. The most recent assessment of the *Arcadia*'s relation to its sources, by A. C. Hamilton, exaggerates the paucity of a native tradition of fiction.[7] Yet the first version of the *Arcadia* is not entirely unrelated to the fiction that we have discussed in preceding chapters. It is in the manner of Pettie and Lyly that the *Old Arcadia*'s witty narrator directly

---

[5] Scholars once ascribed some alterations to Mary's bowdlerization, but it is now agreed that major changes are in accordance with Sidney's intentions; on this whole matter see K. T. Rowe, 'The Countess of Pembroke's Editorship of the *Arcadia*', *PMLA* 54 (1939), 122–38, and 'Elizabethan Morality and the Folio Revisions of Sidney's *Arcadia*', *MP* 37 (1939), 151–72; and William Lee Godshalk, 'Sidney's revisions of the *Arcadia* Books III–V', *PQ* 43 (1964), 171–84.

[6] C. S. Lewis, *English Literature in the Sixteenth Century* (Oxford, 1954), p. 333; R. W. Zandvoort's detailed study, *Sidney's 'Arcadia': A Comparison Between the Two Versions* (Amsterdam, 1929) has *not* been superseded by Robert E. Levine, *A Comparison of Sidney's Old and New Arcadia* (Salzburg, 1974).

[7] A. C. Hamilton, 'Sidney's *Arcadia* as Prose Fiction: Its Relation to Its Sources', *ELR* 2 (1972), 32–3; and also his *Sir Philip Sidney: A Study of his Life and Work* (Cambridge, 1977), p. 9.

addresses his audience of 'fair ladies'. The disengaged narrator (which we have also noted in *Master F.J.*) may be related to the courtier's *sprezzatura* which led Sidney to refer to the *Arcadia* as 'this idle work of mine' in the dedicatory letter to his sister (p. 3).[8] In the late 1570s, the art of prose narrative was practised in a manner which made it an attractive possibility. What we can see occurring in Sidney's romance is an expansion of the shorter and more limited form of courtly fiction into a mode which could encompass the aims of poetry which Sidney outlined in his *Defence* (in all probability written when Sidney was bringing the *Old Arcadia* to a conclusion).[9]

Sidney combined the newly fashionable pastoral with the much less fashionable chivalric romance (drawing for the former on Sannazaro's *Arcadia* and Montemayor's *Diana*, for the latter on *Amadis de Gaule*),[10] creating a new, if hybrid, form of fiction. The *Arcadia* could also be seen as a response to the recently popular *Euphues*. Comparisons between Sidney and Lyly usually focus on questions of style, and indicate the differences between euphuism and the Arcadian style.[11] As G. K. Hunter points out, quoting from Drayton's epistle to Henry Reynolds, it was Sidney who 'did first reduce/Our tongue from Lyly's writing then in use'.[12] We can deduce that Sidney was quite conscious of this potential rivalry from his comment in *A Defence of Poetry*:

So is that honey-flowing matron Eloquence apparelled, or rather disguised, in a courtesan-like painted affectation: one time, with so far-fet words that may seem monsters but must seem strangers to any poor Englishman; an other time, with coursing of a letter, as if they were bound to follow the method of a dictionary; another time, with figures and flowers, extremely winter-starved. But I would this fault were only peculiar to versifiers, and had not as large possession among prose-printers . . .[13]

---

[8] This narrative address is also found in Ariosto, as Robertson points out, p. xxii; for a detailed discussion of the *Old Arcadia*'s narrator see Richard Lanham, *The Old Arcadia* (New Haven, 1965), Chap. 4, *passim*.

[9] *Miscellaneous Prose of Sir Philip Sidney*, ed. K. Duncan-Jones and J. Van Dorsten (Oxford, 1973), pp. 62–3.

[10] See Hamilton, 'Sidney's *Arcadia* as Prose Fiction', p. 30; Robertson, pp. xx–xxiii.

[11] For example, see P. Albert Duhamel, 'Sidney's *Arcadia* and Elizabethan Rhetoric', *SP* 45 (1948), 134–50; for a computer analysis of Sidney's style in comparison to Lyly, Nashe, and Lodge, see Robert Cluett, 'Arcadia Wired', *Language and Style*, 7 (1974), 119–35.

[12] G. K. Hunter, *John Lyly: The Humanist as Courtier* (London, 1962), p. 286.

[13] *Miscellaneous Prose*, p. 117.

The vogue for euphuism was eclipsed by the *Arcadia*'s appearance, and Sidney dramatically altered the course of prose fiction in England. Despite this stylistic contrast, Sidney's didactic purpose (as espoused in the *Defence*) is not unlike the education of the courtier which is exemplified in Euphues' and then Philautus' growth in knowledge through experience. Sidney's didactic intentions are still the subject of critical controversy; argument revolves around the treatment of Pyrocles and Musidorus either as exemplary heroes, or as imperfect agents who contribute to the near downfall of Arcadia—a question complicated by the different treatment of the princes in the *Old Arcadia* and the *New Arcadia*. The princes in the revised romance are closer to 'right' prince Cyrus in Xenophon.[14] They are less at fault in their dealings with the princesses, and have, in A. C. Hamilton's words, a 'greater moral awareness'.[15] Even in the *New Arcadia* the princes are involved in a learning experience, undertaking what Josephine Roberts calls a 'heroic journey' towards architectonic knowledge.[16]

In a recent book, Stephen Greenblatt has explored the conscious sense of what he calls 'self-fashioning' in the work of several Renaissance figures.[17] In his chapter on *The Faerie Queene*, Greenblatt places Spenser's poem in the context of the role-playing which formed an essential part of the courtier's life, especially under Elizabeth.[18] Guyon's destruction of the Bower of Bliss is seen as a reaction against its threat, through its undeniable allure, to the heroic quest: 'The Bower of Bliss must be destroyed not because its gratifications are unreal but because they threaten 'civility'—civilization—which for Spenser is achieved only through renunciation and the constant exercise of power.'[19]

Spenser probably did not become acquainted with Sidney until 1579, and any direct influence between the two writers was minimal.[20] However, Spenser pointed to Sidney as the man

> Who first my Muse did lift out of the floore,
> To sing his sweet delights in lowlie laies . . .

[14] Ibid., p. 79.   [15] *Sir Philip Sidney*, p. 145.
[16] Josephine A. Roberts, *Architectonic Knowledge in the New Arcadia* (Salzburg, 1978).
[17] Stephen Greenblatt, *Renaissance Self-Fashioning From More to Shakespeare* (Chicago and London, 1980).
[18] Ibid., pp. 161–9, and Chap. 4 *passim*.   [19] Ibid., p. 173.
[20] See Ringler, pp. xxxi–iv.

Admittedly, this couplet does occur in a dedication to Sidney's sister.[21] The *Arcadia* may be seen to parallel, in some important ways, the *Faerie Queene*'s didactic purpose, which was to 'fashion a gentleman or noble person in vertuous and gentle discipline'.[22] When the princes enter Arcadia, passion impels them towards a renunciation of their former heroic status.[23] In Fulke Greville's words, Sidney depicts the 'dark webs of effeminate Princes', woven in an Arcadia which degenerated with Basilius' retirement—as all states do 'when Soveraign Princes, to play with their own visions, will put off publique action'.[24] The princes in the *Old Arcadia* are reduced through their disguises to actors (role-players) rather than heroes. This has led to critical divergence ranging from Richard Lanham's reading of the romance as almost totally comic, to Franco Marenco's notion of it as 'a gloomy, almost desperate book', a Calvinist expression of moral condemnation.[25] The same divergence was present amongst Sidney's contemporaries; against Greville's harsh attitude towards the princes we can set Gabriel Harvey's opinion: 'What should I speake of those two braue Knightes, Musidorus and Pyrocles, combined in one excellent knight, Sir Philip Sidney . . .'.[26]

In the *New Arcadia* the events of the Captivity Episode bring the need for the princes' heroic prowess into Arcadia itself—although this also occurs with the appearance of the lion and bear in Book One, a scene which may symbolize the unleashing of destructive passion in Arcadia, or be viewed simply as an opportunity for the princes to display their heroism.[27] As the episode develops, Pamela and Philoclea become the pattern by

[21] Ibid., p. xxxiii.

[22] Edmund Spenser, *Works*, ed. Edwin Greenlaw *et al.* (1932, rpt. Baltimore, 1966), Vol. 1, p. 167.

[23] See Mark Rose, *Heroic Love* (Cambridge, Mass., 1968), Chap. 2.

[24] Fulke Greville, *Life of Sir Philip Sidney*, ed. Nowell Smith, (Oxford, 1907), p. 13 and p. 11.

[25] Lanham, *passim*; Franco Marenco, 'Double Plot in Sidney's Old "Arcadia"', *MLR* 64 (1969), 250, and see his *Arcadia Puritana* (Bari, 1968); Marenco's view is echoed by Clifford Davidson, 'Nature and Judgement in the *Old Arcadia*', *Papers on Language and Literature*, 6 (1970), 348–65; Robert Levine takes an extreme view which sees the princes, even in the *New Arcadia*, as being completely undercut and viewed satirically by Sidney, op. cit., *passim*.

[26] *Pierce's Supererogation* (1593), in Smith, Vol. 2, p. 263.

[27] Marenco sees the scene as degrading, 'Double Plot', pp. 253–5; Jon S. Lawry as heroic, in *Sidney's Two Arcadias: Pattern and Proceeding* (Ithaca, N. Y., 1972), p. 61.

which one might fashion a heroic gentlewoman, replacing the princes as exemplars. The ability of poetry to hold out examples is stressed in the *Defence*, and Fulke Greville is at pains to suggest that the *Arcadia* fleshed out ideas: 'his intent, and scope was, to turn the barren Philosophy precepts into pregnant Images of life . . .'.[28] Sidney, like Spenser, was engaged in a process of fashioning—Pamela, Philoclea, Pyrocles, and Musidorus are tested and tempered by their experiences; at the same time the reader is engaged in a process of discovery: 'his end in them', Greville writes, 'was not vanishing pleasure alone, but morall Images, and Examples, (as directing threds) to guide every man through the confused *Labyrinth* of his own desires, and life . . .'.[29]

This account of Sidney's didactic purpose may be of some use in analysing two important areas of modern critical argument: the generic classification of the two *Arcadias*, and the purpose of the concluding trial scene. Scholars initially considered the *Old Arcadia* to be an inferior attempt by Sidney which was superseded by his revision, and thus concentrated on a classification of the *New Arcadia*. Kenneth Myrick first elaborated the notion of the *New Arcadia* as a heroic poem, taking the idea from Sidney's own definition of the 'heroical poem' in his *Defence of Poetry*.[30] E. M. W. Tillyard's consideration of the revised version as an epic is a development of this view, and the notion that Sidney's revision increased the *Arcadia*'s heroic and epic qualities is now widely accepted, despite Walter Davis's insistence that it is simply an expanded pastoral romance.[31]

Recently the genre of the *Old Arcadia* has come under consideration. Richard Lanham's stimulating if controversial discussion, which undertakes a rhetorical analysis and emphasizes Sidney's comedy, concludes that the *Old Arcadia* is a comic

---

[28] Greville, p. 15.   [29] Ibid., p. 223.

[30] *Miscellaneous Prose*, p. 81; Kenneth Myrick, *Sir Philip Sidney as a Literary Craftsman* (Lincoln, Nebraska, 2nd edn., 1965), Chap. 6; Myrick's classification is echoed by A. C. Hamilton, *Sir Philip Sidney*, p. 123; Alan Isler sees both *Arcadias* as heroic poems, but gives the term a different definition, drawing on Elizabethan notions of epic and romance, in 'Heroic Poetry and Sidney's Two *Arcadias*', *PMLA* 83 (1968), 368–79; Jon Lawry also considers both *Arcadias* to be heroic poems, op. cit., pp. 1–13.

[31] E. M. W. Tillyard, *The English Epic and Its Background* (London, 1954), pp. 294–319, and for a fuller consideration of the *New Arcadia* as an epic see Rodney Delasanta, *The Epic Voice* (The Hague, 1967), Chap. 3. Walter R. Davis, *A Map of Arcadia* (New Haven, 1965), Chap. 7; like much of Davis's otherwise stimulating consideration of Sidney, this idea is marred by his choice of the 1593 composite text, a fault also of his discussion in *Idea and Act in Elizabethan Fiction* (Princeton, 1969), Chap. 3.

novel—an unwise and jarring anachronism.[32] A more useful
approach shared by a number of scholars stresses the dramatic
structure, the careful division into five acts, and views it as a
Terentian comedy.[33] The move from dramatic structure in the
Old Arcadia to epic in the *New* reflects Sidney's strengthening of
the *Arcadia*'s didactic purpose: 'that feigning notable images of
virtues, vices, or what else, with that delightful teaching'.[34]

Sidney's incomplete revision of the *Arcadia* has enticed readers
with a textual puzzle of the *Edwin Drood* variety. Critics have
pondered over the probable ending of the *New Arcadia*, and over
explanations for its unfinished state.[35] The trial scene which
concludes the *Old Arcadia* and the composite 1593 text (whether
or not Sidney intended to conclude the revised version in this
way) has also been the focus for critical argument over Sidney's
didactic purpose. The trial scene was probably prompted by the
conclusion of Heliodorus' *Aethiopica*, where Hydaspes has to sit in
judgement on his daughter Chariclea (unlike Euarchus, he
spares her when he discovers who she is).[36] Such a scene also
allows Sidney to display his rhetorical skill by recreating in a
work of fiction a setting for the forensic oratory which was one of
the classical inspirations for the systems of rhetoric so influential
in the Renaissance. However, some questions are raised by the
trial of the princes and Gynecia: does Euarchus exercise
necessary judgement or excessive severity? Are the princes rightly
condemned? Does the 'trick ending' leave the dilemma unsolved
and the reader uneasy?[37]

[32] Lanham, p. 382.

[33] Marenco, 'Double Plot', p. 250; Robert W. Parker, 'Terentian Structure and
Sidney's Original *Arcadia*', *ELR* 2 (1972), 61–78; Clark L. Chalifour, 'Sir Philip Sidney's
Old Arcadia as Terentian Comedy', *SEL* 16 (1976), 51–63; Robertson, p. xxxvii; Josephine
Roberts suggests that Sidney borrowed a number of characters' names from Terence's
plays, op. cit., pp. 183–5.

[34] *Miscellaneous Prose*, p. 81.

[35] A sensible explanation for the conclusion of the *New Arcadia* in mid-sentence is
offered by Godshalk, op. cit., p. 117; see also Elizabeth Dipple, 'The Captivity Episode
and the *New Arcadia*', *JEGP* 70 (1971), 418–31; Nancy R. Lindheim, 'Vision, Revision
and the 1593 text of the *Arcadia*', *ELR* 2 (1972), 136–40; Robert Kimbrough, *Sir Philip
Sidney* (New York, 1971), p. 142; Lawry, p. 166; Arthur K. Amos, *Time, Space and Value:
The Narrative Structure of the 'New Arcadia'* (Lewisburg, 1977), pp. 186–7.

[36] Hamilton, 'Sidney's *Arcadia* as Prose Fiction', pp. 42–7.

[37] See Kenneth T. Rowe, *Romantic Love and Parental Authority in Sidney's Arcadia*
(Michigan, 1947); Elizabeth Dipple, '"Unjust Justice" in the *Old Arcadia*', *SEL* 10
(1970), 83–101; Richard McCoy relates the trial to a personal dilemma in Sidney,
stemming from a tension between authority and individuality under Elizabeth's reign, see
Sir Philip Sidney: Rebellion in Arcadia (New Brunswick, 1979), pp. 124–37.

While Euarchus' justice is necessary to balance the chaos initially caused by Basilius' weakness, the reader also sympathizes with the princes (whose guilt is significantly lessened in Sidney's revision). Margaret Dana rightly states that 'Sidney's intent in the trial sequence is to create a situation as astonishing and ironic as possible.'[38] The tragi-comic ending neatly satisfies the reader's potentially conflicting desires for, on the one hand, right judgement (Euarchus' reason) and, on the other, the lovers' triumph (passion)—this initial conflict but ultimate reconciliation of reason and passion is enacted in the poetic dialogue at the beginning of the second eclogues (*OA*, pp. 135–6; *NA*, pp. 339–40).[39]

In recent years critical attention has shifted back to the *New Arcadia*. Sidney's revision entailed an imitation of the structure of Greek romance, with an *in medias res* opening and the use of retrospective narration. This considerably increased the complexity of what John Hoskins, in his *Directions for Speech and Style* (*c.* 1600), called 'the web . . . of his story', but Sidney also took great pains to interweave the stories, and connect (usually through familial ties) the large cast of characters.[40] Following William Ringler's account of thematic progression in the four sets of eclogues which divide the five books of the *Old Arcadia*, Walter Davis has related the themes of the eclogues to the action of the romance.[41]

Much more elaborate structural features have been posited for both the *Old* and *New Arcadias* by Jon Lawry, who analyses a series of 'triads' in both, and for the *New Arcadia* by Arthur Amos, who finds the first book dominated by 'space', the second by 'time', and the third by 'value'.[42] These patterns tend to be anachronistic impositions which detract from the structural

---

[38] Margaret E. Dana, 'The Providential Plot of the *Old Arcadia*', *SEL* 17 (1977), p. 52.

[39] For an important consideration of Sidney's mixing of genres, which unfortunately does not distinguish between the *Old* and *New Arcadias*, see Stephen J. Greenblatt, 'Sidney's *Arcadia* and the Mixed Mode', *SP* 70 (1973), 269–78.

[40] John Hoskins, *Directions For Speech and Style*, ed. H. H. Hudson (Princeton, 1935), p. 41; A. C. Hamilton has constructed family trees for the major characters, see *Sir Philip Sidney*, p. 175.

[41] Ringler, pp. xxxviii–ix; Davis, *Idea and Act*, p. 113, and for an elaborate consideration of structure and narrative method see his 'Narrative Methods in Sidney's *Old Arcadia*', *SEL* 18 (1978), 13–33.

[42] Lawry, *passim*; Amos, *passim*.

features reflecting Sidney's thematic concerns. A more fruitful approach has come from scholars who have looked carefully at the effect of retrospective narrative, and the resulting web of interconnecting stories. Nancy Lindheim has differentiated the kinds of stories told by the two princes, noting that they 'present alternative views concerning the nature and exercise of moral virtue'.[43] This approach has been expanded by Josephine Roberts in her consideration of Sidney's elaborate didactic purpose.[44] As the attention devoted to Sidney's narrative method has intensified, the *New Arcadia* has yielded an increased richness of meaning.[45]

Sidney began work on the *Arcadia* during a period of enforced retirement from the court, and this is reflected in the theme of inaction which is present in both versions.[46] Sidney complained bitterly, in a letter to Edmund Denny, written in 1580, that 'the vnnoble constitution of our tyme, doth keep vs from fitte imployments. . . .'[47] Just as Basilius' retirement sets in motion the events which disrupt Arcadia, so the princes, through their disguises, are trapped into roles which separate them from their previous heroic existence; as Pyrocles complains:

Alas, incomparable *Philoclea*, thou ever seest me, but dost never see me as I am: thou hearest willingly all that I dare say, and I dare not say that which were most fit for thee to heare. Alas who ever but I was imprisoned in libertie, and banished being still present? To whom but me have lovers bene jailours, and honour a captivitie? (*NA*, p. 252)

Sidney ultimately abandoned his literary activities for a plunge into action which was still a form of self-fashioning—right down to the exemplary death and succeeding legend. In the *New*

---

[43] Nancy R. Lindheim, 'Sidney's *Arcadia* Book II: Retrospective Narrative', *SP* 64 (1967), 162.

[44] Roberts, op. cit., *passim*; and see also Elizabeth Dipple, 'Metamorphosis in Sidney's *Arcadias*', *PQ* 50 (1971), 47–62.

[45] See, for example, the important consideration of Sidney's imagery by Myron Turner, 'The Disfigured Face of Nature: Image and Metaphor in the revised *Arcadia*', *ELR* 2 (1972), 116–35.

[46] See Neil Rudenstine, *Sidney's Poetic Development* (Cambridge, Mass., 1967), p. 16; Hamilton, *Sir Philip Sidney*, p. 34.

[47] James M. Osborn, *Young Philip Sidney 1572–1577* (New Haven, 1972), p. 537; Richard McCoy sees an ambivalence in all of Sidney's work stemming from his personal dilemma, op. cit., *passim*.

Arcadia, despite the increased emphasis on heroic achievement, Pyrocles and Musidorus are forced into a series of acutely self-conscious games, as they bring their active past lives into conjunction with their present situation through their need to relate their own stories. Pamela and Philoclea achieve a type of heroism in the Captivity Episode, but it is a passive, stoical heroism, a resistance to Cecropia.

The tension between speech and action which Sidney explores is apparent throughout Elizabethan fiction: in Lyly's rhetorical display which subsumes narrative action; in Gascoigne's ironic juxtaposition of F.J.'s courtly pose—what he *says* about his affair—and his tawdry behaviour; in Nashe's explosive use of a variety of styles and modes to relate Jack Wilton's adventures. Sidney's desire that he might 'awake some other spirit to exercise his pen in that wherewith mine is already dulled' (*OA*, p. 417) was more than answered by the powerful influence of the *Arcadia* on the fiction of the following century. The *Arcadia* stands alone as the greatest achievement in fiction during the period considered in this book, but it is related to the themes as well as the methods of the fiction that surrounded it.

Chapter 6

The Development of Romance

I. Robert Greene

During the 1580s prose fiction was dominated by the work of Robert Greene, who published fifteen works of fiction between 1580 and 1590. Greene has already been discussed above in relation to the novella and euphuistic fiction. His output encompassed every fashion: euphuism, the novella, the pastoral romance, the cony-catching pamphlet, the repentance pamphlet. By René Pruvost, Greene is seen as passing through eleven periods of composition, which Walter Davis sensibly reduces to four: 'experiments in the Euphuistic mode (1580–84); collections of short tales or novella (1585–88); pastoral romances strongly influenced by Greek romance (1588–89); and pamphlets of repentance and roguery, in the main non-fictional (1590–92)'.[1] It is not surprising that Greene helped to sustain this facility by plagiarizing, a practice not at all confined to him, and not especially disreputable.[2] Greene began by imitating Lyly, and never entirely abandoned euphuism despite the fact that he satirizes it in *Menaphon* (1589)—although his later works make sporadic, rather than consistent, use of it.

During the 1580s and 90s the fashionable romance (as distinct from the popular chivalric romance influenced by *Amadis* and its imitators) drew on three main sources of inspiration: Greek romance, pastoral, and Sidney's *Arcadia*. Imitation of Sidney is almost entirely limited to lip-service until the early years of the seventeenth century (see Chapter 10). The Greek romance has already been mentioned as an important influence on Sidney, particularly Heliodorus' *Aethiopica*. In 1587, a new edition

---

[1] René Pruvost, *Robert Greene et ses romans*, Publications de la Faculté des lettres D'Alger, II. 9 (Paris, 1938), Chaps. 3–13; Walter R. Davis, *Idea and Act*, p. 139.
[2] See R. G. Goree, 'Concerning Repetitions in Greene's Romances', *PQ* 3 (1924), 69–75; R. W. Dent, 'Greene's *Gwydonius: The Carde of Fancie*: A Study of Elizabethan Plagiarism', *HLQ* 24 (1961), 151–62.

appeared of Heliodorous in the translation by Underdowne. *Clitophon and Leucippe*, by Achilles Tatius, was available in Latin (1554), Italian (1560), and French (1568), although an English translation did not appear until 1597. Angel Day's translation of Longus' *Daphnis and Chloe* also appeared in 1587, reinforcing the influence of pastoral forms on the fiction of the 1580s and 90s.[3]

The pastoral romances of this period retreat from Sidney's ambitious mingling of the pastoral and the chivalric, and from his interest in large, epic structure. They are much shorter, much less experimental, but the best examples are very polished performances indeed. From the time of Virgil's *Eclogues* onwards, the pastoral tradition was an enduring one,

But Arcadia was forever being rediscovered. This was possible because the stock of pastoral motifs was bound to no genre and to no poetic form. It found its way into the Greek romance (Longus) and from thence into the Renaissance. From the romance, pastoral poetry could return to the eclogue or pass to the drama (Tasso's *Aminta*; Guarini's *Pastor Fido*). The pastoral world is as extensive as the knightly world.[4]

The fashionable output of Greene and other writers of pastoral romances had an important influence on Elizabethan drama, most notably on Shakespeare, who based *The Winter's Tale* on Greene's *Pandosto* (which was reprinted, after its appearance in 1588, in 1592, 1595, and 1607—*The Winter's Tale* was seen by Simon Forman in 1611, though its first performance may have been earlier), and *As You Like It* on Lodge's *Rosalynde* (which was reprinted, after its appearance in 1590, in 1592, 1596, and 1598—*As You Like It* is generally dated 1599).

Walter Davis, following Samuel Wolff, has placed great emphasis on the influence of Greek romance on Greene.[5] In the Greek romance, the intricate plot was elevated to the centre of interest in fiction, and fortune was used as a device to forward the plot, and to provide astounding incidents. This alters the

---

[3] The most useful studies of the Greek romance form are Ben E. Perry, *The Ancient Romances* (Berkeley, 1907) and Arthur Heiserman's stimulating *The Novel Before the Novel* (Chicago, 1977).

[4] E. R. Curtius, *European Literature and the Latin Middle Ages*, trans. Willard Trask (1953, rpt. London, 1979), p. 187; and see W. W. Greg, *Pastoral Poetry and Pastoral Drama* (London, 1906); Helen Cooper, *Pastoral* (Ipswich, 1977); and Thomas Rosenmeyer, *The Green Cabinet* (Berkeley and Los Angeles, 1969).

[5] Samuel Lee Wolff, *The Greek Romances in Elizabethan Prose Fiction* (1912, rpt. New York, 1961), pp. 367–458; Davis, pp. 156–78.

emphasis of euphuistic fiction, with its interest in speeches, rhetoric, and character at the expense of action. But Davis ignores the combination of the Greek romance interest in plot with the reflective concerns of the pastoral. In fact, Greene's romances contain a number of potentially conflicting interests: in incident, in the pastoral landscape, and in the set speech or euphuistic description. This may be attributed to Greene's adept use of the prevailing fashions which would ensure the popularity of his fiction. He could appeal to a variety of interests simultaneously.

While Greene dutifully imitated Lyly in *Mamillia* (Part One 1580, Part Two 1583), he quickly assimilated euphuism as a useful style, and soon produced works which are written in a more original manner. In *Gwydonius The Carde of Fancie* (1584), while the style is still predominantly euphuistic, the plot is a product of Greene's interest in startling action; it is intended to evoke wonder and amazement in the reader. The plot depends upon sudden alterations in character: Gwydonius quickly changes from a wastrel ('He was so endued with vanitie, so imbrued with vice, so nursed up in wantonnesse, and so nusled up in wilfulnesse . . .', p. 13)[6] to a paragon, and in the romance's dramatic conclusion he fights against his father. Helmut Bonheim has pointed to Greene's elaborate use of 'binary structures', to his pairing of characters and of speeches.[7] This has the virtue of allowing a range of characters to be interconnected: Gwydonius woos Duke Orlanio's daughter Castania, while Castania's brother Thersandro pursues Gwydonius' sister Lewcippa. Sidney uses this device to explore differences in character and situation when he follows the fortunes of Pyrocles and Musidorus in their pursuit of Philoclea and Pamela, but Greene uses it simply to expand his plot, for he is not really interested in character analysis.

Arbasto, The Anatomie of Fortune (1584) shows only the dark side of fortune: 'to stay upon fortunes lotte, is to treade on brittle Glasse' (title-page). This romance does face up to the implications of Fortune as a force which rules a wholly contingent

    [6] References are to Alexander B. Grosart, ed., *The Life and Complete Works in Prose and Verse of Robert Greene* (London, 1881–6), Vol. 4.
    [7] Helmut Bonheim, 'Robert Greene's *Gwydonius: The Carde of Fancy*', Anglia, 96 (1978), 50.

world. As Walter Davis notes, 'The only possible response to life
so conceived is to withdraw from it, and that is what Arbasto does
after his series of tragic denouements.'[8] The romance is a much
less inspired performance than *Gwydonius*, and it clings even more
closely to Greene's euphuistic style, which relies on strings of
'natural history' similes, and lacks the rhythmic control of Lyly.

After *Arbasto*, Greene concentrated on collections of novellas:
Planetomachia (1585),[9] *Penelopes Web* (1587), *Euphues his Censure to
Philautus* (1587), *Alcida Greenes Metamorphosis* (1588), and *Greenes
Orpharion* (1588?). These collections are quite eclectic, and draw
on a variety of sources.[10] *Philomela, The Lady Fitzwaters Nightingale*
(1587? pub. 1590) is an Italianate tale in the euphuistic mode,
one of Greene's less inspiring efforts.

Perimedes The Blacke-Smith (1588) is a more interesting work.
Perimedes and his wife tell three tales to each other. The first,
told by Perimedes, is like a miniature Greek romance. It uses all
the traditional narrative methods which promote the abrupt
changes brought about by fortune in Greek romance: the capture
of children by pirates, separation of husband and wife, the long
passage of time which allows the children to grow up and then
take part in adventures which will reunite them with their
parents. In many Greek romances, fortune the separator and
time the restorer wage a battle: 'Time, *Mariana*, is the nourse of
hope, and oft thwarteth fortune in hir decrees . . .'.[11]

In the same year that he produced *Perimedes*, Greene published
his most famous romance, *Pandosto. The Triumph of Time. Pandosto*
is almost invariably viewed through the distorting lenses of *The
Winter's Tale*; indeed it is almost impossible to read it without
reference to Shakespeare's transformation of it.[12] *Pandosto* is a
quite masterly combination of pastoral and Greek romance
motifs. The story caught Shakespeare's imagination with its
abrupt changes of fortune and extreme situations. The most
dramatic alteration by Shakespeare is the statue-scene, the

---

[8] Davis, p. 145.

[9] For the tale in *Planetomachia* missing in Grosart's edition, see D. Bratchell, ed., *Robert
Greene's Planetomachia* (Trowbridge, 1979).

[10] See Pruvost, *Robert Greene*, pp. 200–29, 234–49, 263–72, 309–31.

[11] *Perimedes The Blacke-Smith*, Grosart, Vol.. 7, p. 26.

[12] See John Lawlor, '*Pandosto* and the Nature of Dramatic Romance', *PQ* 41 (1962),
96–113; Geoffrey Bullough, *Narrative and Dramatic Sources of Shakespeare*, Vol. 8 (London,
1975), pp. 119–21, 136–55.

reappearance of Hermione: in *Pandosto* Bellaria (Hermione's source) does in fact die, and Shakespeare decided to introduce even more cause for awe and wonder than Greene's romance provided.

Greene begins with a didactic paragraph setting out the main theme of the romance: 'Among al the passions wherewith humane mindes are perplexed, there is none that so galleth with restlesse despight, as the infectious soare of Jealousie . . .' (p. 156).[13] He takes pains to explain Pandosto's jealousy of Bellaria's association with his friend Egistus (Shakespeare's Polixenes).[14] Bellaria is particularly attentive to her husband's friend, 'oftentimes comming her selfe into his bed chamber' (p. 158). The plot of *Pandosto* is initiated by an understandable jealousy; only its increasing intensity and irrationality is questionable. Behind the dramatic alterations of the plot stands uncaring fortune: 'Fortune envious of such happy successe, willing to shewe some signe of her inconstancie, turned her wheele . . .' (p. 157). Walter Davis notes that the romance is almost nihilistic in its implications: 'beneath the split between people and the events of their lives in *Pandosto* lies the almost cynical or Calvinistic assumption of the inconsequentiality of human purposes . . .'.[15] It is perhaps more accurate to say that Greene's interest in creating surprising plots leads him to take an arbitrary attitude to his characters. There is a degree of moral justice in *Pandosto*: in Greene's world, it would not be appropriate for Bellaria to return from death. Only the innocent generation, Dorastus and Fawnia, can be granted happiness at the end of the romance; Pandosto, having come close to committing incest with Fawnia, kills himself 'in a melancholie fit' (p. 199). '*Temporis filia veritas*', truth is the daughter of time, proclaims the title-page— but time is undeniably a harsh mother. The revelation of truth does not bring happiness to everyone.

After the horrors of Pandosto's court, transformed by his consuming jealousy into an image of hell, devoid of all justice and humanity ('he determined that both Bellaria and the yong infant should be burnt with fire', p. 166), Fawnia is entrusted to the cruel sea, but she reaches the pastoral haven of 'Sycilia' (p. 173). Greene, like Sidney, does not completely idealize the shepherd's

---

[13] References are to Bullough, op. cit.
[14] See Lawlor, pp. 96–7.   [15] Davis, p. 170.

life. His equivalent of Sidney's 'low' shepherds is Porrus and his wife, who are rather endearing. Despite their foibles, the simple shepherds contrast most favourably with Pandosto's callous nature.

Fawnia is able to grow up in this pastoral refuge without fear, until Egistus' son Dorastus sees her, and so allows the world of the Court to reassert itself. Like an angry sea, fortune threatens the pastoral island at the centre of *Pandosto*. Fawnia cannot escape her origins, and Greene emphasizes that nature is more powerful than nurture, giving Fawnia an unconsciously ironic speech: 'I am born to toile for the Court, not in the Court, my nature unfit for their nurture: better live then in meane degree, than in high disdaine' (p. 182). Egistus' objection to his son's desire for Fawnia is a milder echo of Pandosto's anger.

Dorastus of course loves the princess beneath the shepherdess, and Greene creates another delicate moment of irony when he has Fawnia make a speech in praise of pastoral life which impresses Dorastus to the extent that he sees in her wit the revelation of a courtly mind:

Sir, what richer state then content, or what sweeter life then quiet? We shepheards are not borne to honor, nor beholding unto beautie, the less care we have to feare fame or fortune: we count our attire brave inough if warme inough, and our foode dainty, if to suffice nature: our greatest enemie is the wolfe; our onely care in safe keeping our flock: in stead of courtly ditties we spend the daies with cuntry songs: our amorous conceites are homely thoughtes; delighting as much to talke of Pan and his cuntrey prankes, as Ladies to tell of Venus and her wanton toyes. Our toyle is in shifting of the fouldes, and looking to the Lambes, easie labours: oft singing and telling tales, homely pleasures; our greatest welth not to covet, our honor not to climbe, our quiet not to care. Envie looketh not so lowe as shepheards: Shepheards gaze not so high as ambition: we are rich in that we are poore with content, and proud onely in this, that we have no cause to be proud.

This wittie aunswer of Fawnia so inflamed Dorastus fancy, as he commended him selfe for making so good a choyce, thinking, if her birth were aunswerable to her wit and beauty, that she were a fitte mate for the most famous Prince in the worlde. (pp. 181–2)

This impressive description of idealized pastoral life encapsulates a central paradox of the mode: this kind of appreciation of the shepherd's life is enunciated by a transient individual, not truly part of that life. Fawnia is merely a fellow-traveller, not a true shepherd.

In Greene's harsh romance world, the pastoral interlude only benefits those who are already free from evil. It does not bring about miraculous conversions of hate to love, as does Lodge's Arden, but merely provides a haven for those threatened by their enemies. Pandosto is offered no miraculous respite; although he becomes repentant, the loss of his wife is permanent, melancholy remorse pursues him, and he commits suicide. Fortune and time may reveal truth, but they offer no salves for the wounds which they have opened.

Between his two most accomplished works of fiction, *Pandosto* and *Menaphon*, Greene published *Ciceronis Amor* (1589), a work which has attracted some attention as an early example of fictionalised biography—although Greene's interest in Cicero is not at all one that involves historical accuracy.[16] The wooing of Terentia by Lentulus and Fabius, and her eventual marriage to Cicero, is a fairly straightforward narrative, devoid of surprising incidents or the machinations of fortune.[17] Walter Davis has drawn attention to the pastoral interlude which occurs when the characters enter the 'vale of Love';[18] the shepherd's tale of Phillis and Corydon leads to Terentia's encounter with Fabius, who throws off his identity as a simpleton and becomes ennobled through his love for her.[19] Charles Larson sees the pastoral tale as a prefiguring of 'the happy conclusion of the affair between Terentia and Cicero and . . . the entire interlude influences Terentia to the extent that after it is over she frankly avows her love for Cicero . . .'.[20] Because the world of *Ciceronis Amor* is relatively benign, in comparison with *Pandosto*, the pastoral interlude has much less impact.

Walter Davis has called *Menaphon* (1589) 'Greene's masterpiece', which may mislead those unacquainted with Greene's work to hold unduly high expectations of this romance.[21] *Menaphon* is an accomplished romance, written at a time when Greene was the most experienced author of prose fiction in

---

[16] See Charles Larson, 'Robert Greene's *Ciceronis Amor*: Fictional Biography in the Romance Genre', *Studies in the Novel*, 6 (1974), 256–67.
[17] Ibid., p. 264.   [18] *Ciceronis Amor*, Grosart, Vol. 7, p. 177.
[19] See Davis, pp. 77–8.   [20] Larson, p. 265.
[21] Davis, p. 171.

England, and in it he skilfully utilizes the wide range of romance motifs with which he was familiar. Samuel Wolff has pointed to a number of parallels between *Menaphon* and Sidney's *Arcadia*.[22] They seem to me to be minor allusions, and may indicate that Greene saw a manuscript of the *Old Arcadia* (it is unthinkable that he saw the manuscript of the *New Arcadia*, which is why he did not imitate its structure—not because of an inability to master it, as Wolff maintains).[23]

Thomas Nashe, in the precocious preface which he wrote for *Menaphon*, rightly notes the restrained nature of Greene's 'eloquence'; the romance is written in the middle-style: 'I come (sweet friend) to thy *Arcadian Menaphon*; whose attire though not so statelie, yet comelie, dooth entitle thee above all other, to that *temperatum dicendi genus*, which *Tullie* in his *Orator* tearmeth true eloquence' (p. 5).[24] Greene's style has become flexible in accordance with his interest in plot, in filling the romance form with incidents.

The opening of *Menaphon* is similar to that of the *Old Arcadia*: Democles, King of Arcadia, has consulted the oracle and received an obscure but suitably threatening reply. In Greene's Arcadia there is, initially, a complete separation of the court from the country, and Democles does not retreat into the pastoral world. Greene turns his attention to the King's shepherd Menaphon, who surveys an Arcadia which is traditionally harmonious:

> *Menaphon* looking over the champion of *Arcadie* to see if the Continent were as full of smiles, as the seas were of favours, sawe the shrubbes as in a dreame with delightfull harmonie, and the birdes that chaunted on their braunches not disturbed with the least breath of a favourable *Zephirus*. (p. 24)

Menaphon is an extremely ironic romance. Menaphon meditates on the evils of love, and even sings a song directed against it:

> Some say Loue
> Foolish Loue
> > Doth rule and gouerne all the Gods,
> I say Loue,
> Inconstant Loue.
> > Sets mens senses farre at ods. (p. 27)

---

[22] Wolff, p. 443.   [23] Ibid., p. 444.
[24] References are to G. B. Harrison, ed., *Greene's Menaphon and Lodge's A Margarite of America* (Oxford, 1927).

But then he catches sight of Sephestia and becomes an immediate convert: 'now he swore no benigne Planet but *Venus*, no God but *Cupide*, no exquisite deitie but Loue' (p. 33). In the course of the romance, Sephestia, who is disguised as Samela, is courted by Maximius, her husband, who believes that his wife is dead, and who is himself disguised as the shepherd Melicertus. And Greene increases the level of irony and complication by having Sephestia's son Pleusidippus spirited away by pirates so that he can return (aged about 15) and court his own mother (ignorant of course of her identity).

Walter Davis has noted the importance of style in *Menaphon*: characters are very conscious of the way they speak, of the type of song they sing.[25] This is most evident when Melicertus and Samela begin by exchanging euphuistic compliments until Melicertus recites a sophisticated poem which makes Samela realize that he is much nobler than he appears to be (pp. 59–60). Their courtship is paralleled by that of Doron and Carmela, who provide low comedy by their use of imagery taken from the humblest side of rural life:

> *Carmela deare, even as the golden ball*
> *That* Venus *got, such are thy goodly eyes,*
> *When cherries iuce is iumbled there with all,*
> *Thy breath is like the steeme of apple pies.*
>
> *Thy lippes resemble two Cowcumbers Fair,*
> *Thy teeth like to the tuskes of fattest swine,*
> *Thy speach is like the thunder in the aire:*
> *Would God thy toes, thy lips and all were mine.* (p. 102)

Melicertus easily beats Menaphon in a contest (to see who will lead a force to rescue Samela) which requires the competitors to describe their love in an eclogue (pp. 89–94).

Greene manages to outdo Sidney in the possible complications of an amorous triangle when Democles also pursues Samela, without realizing that she is his daughter. But Greene's romance is much simpler than Sidney's, and one appreciates the greatness of the *Arcadia* in comparison to *Menaphon*, which is simply a very competent piece of work by a skilled professional. One of the most attractive aspects of *Menaphon*, apart from the poetry, is Greene's humour. It comes through clearly in a sparkling exchange between Menaphon, Pesana, Melicertus, and Samela:

[25] Davis, p. 173.

Were I a sheepe [says Samela], I should bee garded from the foldes with iollie Swaines, such as was *Lunas* Loue on the hills of *Latmos*; their pipes sounding like the melodie of *Mercurie*, when he lulld asleepe *Argus*: but more, when the Damzells tracing along the Plaines, should with their eyes like Sunne bright beames, drawe on lookes to gaze on such sparkling Planets: then wearie with foode, shoulde I lye and looke on their beauties, as on the spotted wealthe of the richest Firmament; I should listen to their sweete layes, more sweete than the Sea-born *Syrens*: thus feeding on the delicacie of their features, I should like the *Tyrian* heyfer fall in love with *Agenors* darling. I but quoth *Melicertus*, those faire facde Damzells oft draw foorth the kindest sheepe to the shambles. And what of that sir aunswered Samela, would not a sheepe so long fed with beautie, die for loue. If he die (quoth *Pesana*) it is more kindness in beastes, than constancie in men: for they die for loue, when larkes die with leekes. If they be so wise quoth *Menaphon*, they shew but their mother witts; for what sparkes they have of inconstancie, they drawe from their female fosterers, as the sea dooth ebbes and tides from the Moone. So be it sir answered *Pesana*, then no doubt your mother was made of a Weathercocke, that brought foorth such a wavering companion: for you master *Menaphon* measure your looks by minutes and your loues are like lightning, which no sooner flash on the eie, but they vanish. (p. 54)

This type of dialogue owes much to the *questioni d'amore* as transmitted by Lyly, but in Greene's hands it is less precious, less drawn-out, more convincing as true conversation. He skilfully distinguishes each character's pattern of speech. *Menaphon* is not as dark a romance as *Pandosto*: pastoral regeneration is in the ascendency, and Democles is allowed to live and preside over the marriages at the close.

After the publication of *Menaphon* Greene began his long series of repentance pamphlets which involved a renunciation of the 'follies' of fiction: 'Follies I tearme them, because their subjects haue bene superficiall, and their intents amorous, yet mixed with such morrall. principles, that the precepts of vertue seemed to crave pardon for all those vaine opinions love set downe in hir periods.'[26] *Greene's Mourning Garment* (1590?) is a curious work, which returns to some of the elements of euphuism in its style and theme, but which also includes a pastoral section, the frame for which is a prodigal son story (Rabbi Bilessi and his son Philador). Greene's didactic interest gives the narrative a very static quality,

---

[26] *Greenes Farewell to Follie* (1592), Grosart, Vol. 9, p. 227.

and the over-all structure is much less convincing than the earlier romances. Greene uses classical verse forms in this work, an attempt to include the fashionable experimentation of Sidney in a very traditional work of fiction.

Greene's Mourning Garment sets up the usual contrast between the corruption of the town (Saragunta), and the simple purity of pastoral life. An enormous variety of motifs both old and new are squeezed into this curious rag-bag work. Its eclectic disorder perhaps indicates that Greene's farewell to fiction was prompted by loss of inspiration. However, with *Pandosto* and *Menaphon* he made a substantial contribution to the development of romance.

II. William Warner's *Syrinx*

Greene drew much inspiration from the work of William Warner, both from his poem *Albion's England* (1586–1606) and from his prose work *Pan his Syrinx* (1584).[27] *Syrinx* is a powerful romance, drawing on Lyly for its style, but on Greek romance (particularly Heliodorus) for its structure.[28] Warner's control over an intricate structure is most impressive. While *Syrinx* is by no means as complex as the *New Arcadia*, Warner is much more adept at weaving a plot together in a smaller compass than Greene, and it is perhaps unfortunate that Greene did not follow his example. Warner makes his structure explicit by setting out an elaborate table of contents, which divides the work into seven sections (each referred to as a calamus, a reed of Pan's pipe). The sections are also named after the individual whose story is the centre of attention: Arbaces, Thetis, Belopares, Pheone, Deipyrus, Aphrodite, and Opheltes.[29] The story of Arbaces enfolds the other six stories. He is a Median nobleman separated from his wife Dircilla and son Sorares by the war with Assyria. Sorares, who has been raised at the Assyrian court, 'replaces' his father on the island where he has been shipwrecked without their relationship being revealed; while Sorares' sons Atys and Abynados search for him, the six inset-tales are related, before a series of reconciliations resolve the frame-tale.

---

[27] See Wolff, pp. 442–3, and Wallace A. Bacon, ed., *William Warner's Syrinx* (Evanston, Illinois, 1950), pp. lxxii–lxxviii.
[28] Bacon, pp. lvii–lxi.
[29] Warner took his names from Cooper's *Chronicle*, see Bacon, pp. xliii—xliv.

Warner relies heavily on the vagaries of fortune to advance his narrative, and in this he is most faithful to the ethos of the Greek romance. The effects of fortune create a wayward and threatening world (as well as a series of surprises for the reader):

Fortune is only constant in [inconstancy]; and as touching bliss, it may be that your opinion is heretical, for that true bliss indeed performeth a perpetuity, whereas the flattering pleasures of this world cannot promise one hour's certainty, and therefore it may not be aptly termed bliss whereof a change is to be doubted. (p. 99)[30]

However, there is a curious tension in *Syrinx* between the contingent action brought about by fortune, and the static, euphuistic moralizing which constantly interrupts the action. An unsettling disjunction exists between the often horrifying events in the romance, and the carefully balanced disquisitions on women (pp. 119–27) or pride (pp. 148–53).

Warner certainly has a didactic purpose, which is much more effective when integrated with the narrative than when separated into euphuistic speeches. At the beginning of the romance, Arbaces explains to Sorares how the Medians began to fight each other on the island when they unloaded their treasure. Greed for wealth fires a vicious contest, and after their ship is burnt, the survivors find a grisly but symbolically apt punishment for Chebron, who initiated the conflict: 'we pressed him to death under an huge heap of gold, whose bones under the pile are yet extant' (p. 29). The Assyrians fall victim to exactly the same greed, and repeat all the actions of the Medes, allowing Arbaces to sail away on their ship. Ironically, the gold is of no use whatsoever on the island, a point which is economically made when Arbaces says 'having gold we vainly persuaded ourselves not to want anything' (p. 28), but the false logic of this statement is vividly underlined by the sight that greets the visiting Assyrians: 'the piles of gold, being in a manner overgrown with moss and rust' (p. 30).

Walter Davis believes that the brutal world depicted by Warner is completely nihilistic, and encourages the withdrawal of Arbaces and his family.[31] Certainly there is a good deal of baroque brutality depicted in *Syrinx*. We hear of Thetis, punished for her adultery by being forced to eat her dead lover (p. 35);

---

[30] References are to Bacon.   [31] Davis, pp. 161–2.

cannibalism practised by a group of marooned sailors (p. 70); the beheading of Tymetes (p. 133). The story of Aphrodite is particularly cruel, ending as it does with the death of almost every participant. Warner does, however, introduce a balancing story or two: that of Deipyrus, and the story of Opheltes with its '*comical*' conclusion (p. 159). The frame-tale of Arbaces does not simply end with the reunion of a divided family, it also involves an important story of regeneration. When Dircilla was on the island, she discovered that its inhabitants were savages, who fed upon 'raw flesh' (p. 180). Dircilla's previous worldly vanity now seems quite ludicrous: 'all seemed then vain which before time I had in most value' (p. 183). This parallels Arbaces' experience with the gold that became worthless on the island. Humbled in this way, Dircilla is able to reform the savages, who at close range lose their apparent brutality and take on a much more idyllic aspect. Significantly, Dircilla sees her sojourn as an escape from Fortune: 'By assistance, I say, of these—that is, patience, time, place, people, and this sweet and [unthreatened] liberty (the only remembrance of thee, *Arbaces*, and of *Sorares*, my son, excepted) I made not only resistance for the time, but at length a final conquest of Fortune' (p. 185). Warner is not just describing a nihilistic, contingent world; he suggests that it can be altered.

III. Thomas Lodge

Thomas Lodge is a fascinating minor Elizabethan figure, who combined a varied literary output with an eventful personal life (including voyages with Clarke and Cavendish), ending his days as a highly regarded physician.[32] He produced two plays (*The Wounds of Civil War* and *A Looking Glass for London and England*, the latter in collaboration with Robert Greene); a considerable amount of poetry, including the important early examples of Roman satire in *A Fig For Momus*; translations of Josephus and Seneca; and six works of prose fiction.

Lodge appended his first romance, *Forbonius and Prisceria*, to his pamphlet *An Alarm Against Usurers* (1584). Frederick Beaty has argued that Lodge is imitating the *Old Arcadia*, but the parallels

---

[32] See the biographical studies: N. Burton Paradise, *Thomas Lodge: The History of an Elizabethan* (New Haven, 1931); C. J. Sisson, *Thomas Lodge and Other Elizabethans* (Cambridge, Mass., 1933); Edward A. Tenney, *Thomas Lodge* (Ithaca, New York, 1935).

which he points out are not particularly convincing.[33] Lodge did
dedicate the pamphlet to Sidney, but without mentioning the
Arcadia. *Forbonius and Prisceria* is an extremely slight work, a five-
finger exercise in the pastoral mode, and offers no hint of the
impressive romance which was to appear six years later.

Rosalynde (1590) is, next to the *Arcadia*, the most accomplished
pastoral romance written in this period. While Shakespeare
made a number of major additions to the romance when he wrote
As You Like It (most notably the creation of Jacques and
Touchstone), much of the charm of Shakespeare's Rosalind and
her adventures in Arden is present in Lodge's work. There is
obviously no point in criticizing *Rosalynde* for lacking the
balancing satire of *As You Like It*; we must explore Lodge's
romance on its own terms.[34] Lodge's skill is such that *Rosalynde*
appears to be deceptively simple. His carefully woven plot is
particularly effective, and his flexible style, which utilizes
euphuism in a number of set speeches and soliloquies but
elsewhere is relatively plain, gives the romance an appealing
lapidary quality; it has an alluring inevitability which holds the
reader's attention.

Rosalynde begins with a euphuistic and didactic speech made
by Sir John of Bourdeaux to his sons, a speech full of platitudes
many of which have no relevance at all to subsequent events.
Despite his warning to 'beware of Love, for it is far more perilous
than pleasant' (p. 162), love is not really a threatening experience for Saladyne and Rosader.[35] This severe set-piece,
complete with a poetic 'scedule' containing further wise saws,
belies the very light touch in the rest of the romance. When
Saladyne comes into conflict with his younger brother Rosader,
Lodge's style changes, and the pace of the romance quickens:

in came *Saladyne* with his men, and seeing his brother in a browne
studie, and to forget his wonted reverence, thought to shake him out of
his dumps thus. Sirha (quoth hee) what, is your heart on your halfe

[33] Frederick L. Beaty, 'Lodge's Forbonius and Prisceria and Sidney's Arcadia', *English
Studies*, 49 (1968), 38–45.
[34] *Pace* Robert B. Pierce, 'The Moral Languages of *Rosalynde* and *As You Like It*', *SP* 68
(1971), 167–76; and see Charles Whitworth Jr., '*Rosalynde* As You Like It and As Lodge
Wrote It', *English Studies*, 58 (1977), 114–17.
[35] References are to Geoffrey Bullough, *Narrative and Dramatic Sources of Shakespeare*,
Vol. 2 (London, 1958).

penie, or are you saying a Dirge for your fathers soule? what, is my dinner readie? (pp. 166–7)

Lodge is able to intertwine the strands of his plot in a much more subtle manner than his friend Robert Greene. Rosader and Rosalynd are drawn to each other when Rosader takes part in a wrestling match at court, encouraged by his brother, who has bribed the Norman wrestler to kill Rosader.

The drama in the first part of the romance is not chivalric, or even courtly, but domestic, as Rosader rebels against Saladyne's oppression. This part of the romance draws on the fourteenth-century *Tale of Gamelyn*, once thought to be by Chaucer. Rosader's rebellion is not quite as violent as Gamelyn's until he finally attacks his brother and his friends when he has been completely humiliated. Before this, Lodge turns to Rosalynd and Alinda, who are ordered to leave the court by Alinda's father, the usurper King Torismond. Rosalynd has fallen in love with Rosader, and expresses her passion in one of the many impressive poems which contribute to the romance's charm:

> *Love in my bosome like a Bee*
> *   doth sucke his sweete:*
> *Now with his wings he playes with me,*
> *   now with his feete.*
> *Within mine eies he makes his neast,*
> *His bed amidst my tender breast,*
> *My kisses are his daily feast;*
> *And yet he robs me, of my rest.*
> *Ah wanton, will ye?*   (p. 175)

Rosalynd disguises herself as a man, and the two friends flee to the forest of Arden. Lodge's Arden already harbours the exiled King Gerismond, who lives there like Robin Hood 'with a lustie crue of Outlawes' (p. 196). Arden also displays many traditional pastoral features. The first sign of life encountered by Rosalynd (now calling herself Ganimede) and Aliena (Alinda's new name) in Arden is a poem carved on a pine tree by the lovesick shepherd Montanus (it is worth noting that Shakespeare transfers this activity to Orlando). Aliena immediately recognizes the conventions behind this sight: 'No doubt (quoth *Aliena*) this poesie is the passion of some perplexed shepheard . . .' (p. 181). As well as poetic shepherds, Arden has the serene landscape of pastoral (although its flora differs from that of Arcadia):

The ground where they sat was diapred with *Floras* riches, as if she ment to wrap *Tellus* in the glorie of her vestments: round about in the forme of an Ampitheater were most curiouslie planted Pine trees, interseamed with Limons and Citrons, which with the thicknesse of their boughes so shadowed the place, that *Phoebus* could not prie into the secret of that Arbour; so united were the tops with so thicke a closure, that *Venus* might there in her jollitie have dallied unseen with her deerest paramour. (p. 183)

Arden is protective: a landscape which shelters love, and which will offer Rosalynd, along with her disguise, the freedom to woo Rosader. Walter Davis has emphasized the element of role-playing which occurs there. The characters are granted a beneficial freedom: 'each character enters Arden under a conscious mask, finds his true self, and thus achieves meaningful discipline.'[36] Charles Larson has corrected Davis's view, pointing out that not all the characters play roles, but I cannot accept Larson's notion that Arden is less than ideal, even threatening.[37] In comparison with Sidney's Arcadia, Arden is a true haven. Lodge's lion is not at all as menacing as the lion and bear which pursue Philoclea and Pamela. Lodge's Coridon reveals much less about the realities of country life than Shakespeare's Corin, while Montanus is accorded much more sophisticated expressions than Sylvius. Arden's protection nurtures Gerismond, reconciles Rosader and Saladyne, and eventually awards Montanus his love, Phoebe.

There is no real threat to Arden, and it is not seen as a threat to the martial prowess of the members of the court who have retreated into it. Saladyne and Rosader (after their marriages) ably support Gerismond against Torismond. Montanus is made 'Lord over all the Forrest of *Arden*' (p. 256), an acknowledgement of the elevated position to which the expression of his love has brought him. Lodge is at pains to point out that in *Rosalynde* the pastoral world is triumphant; unlike some of Greene's romances, where the power of Fortune holds sway:

Heere Gentlemen may you see in *Euphues Golden Legacie*, that such as neglect their fathers precepts, incurre much prejudice; that division in

---

[36] Walter R. Davis, 'Masking in Arden: The Histrionics of Lodge's *Rosalynde*', *SEL* 5 (1965), 163.

[37] Charles Larson, 'Lodge's *Rosalynde*: Decorum in Arden', *Studies in Short Fiction*, 14 (1977), 117–27, *passim*.

Nature as it is a blemish in nurture, so tis a breach of good fortunes; that vertue is not measured by birth but by action; that yonger brethren though inferiour in yeares, yet may be superiour to honours; that concord is the sweetest conclusion, and amitie betwixt brothers more forceable than Fortune. (p. 256)

It is significant that Rosader becomes a forester in Arden, not a shepherd. He is in many ways a stronger character than Shakespeare's Orlando; love does not remove his dignity quite so completely. It is left to Montanus to express the pastoral view of love and the transformation which it creates, in an eclogue with Coridon which echoes Musidorus' poem in the *Arcadia*:

> *My sheepe are turnd to thoughts, whom froward will*
> *Guides in the restlesse Laborynth of love,*
> *Feare lends them pasture wheresoere they move,*
> *And by their death their life renueth still,*
>
> *My sheephooke is my pen, mine oaten reede*
> *My paper, where my manie woes are written;*
> *Thus, silly swaine (with love and fancie bitten)*
> *I trace the plaines of paine in wofull weede.* (p. 186)

Lodge uses paired and contrasted characters very effectively: the opposed but then reconciled brothers, Rosader and Saladyne; the good King Gerismond and the usurper Torismond; the extroverted Rosalynd and her more traditional friend Alinda; Corin the 'low' shepherd and Montanus, the shepherd elevated by love. The one character who stands out from these pairs is, of course, Rosalynd, who is endowed with the wit and intelligence to utilize the freedom granted to her by Arden and by her disguise. While Walter Davis is correct in his view of Rosalynd as a character who achieves freedom through taking on a mask, a role, she is also able to escape from the constricting role forced upon women by the conventions of courtship:

You may see (quoth *Ganimede*) what mad cattell you women be, whose hearts sometimes are made of Adamant that will touch with no impression; and sometime of waxe that is fit for everie forme: they delight to be courted, and then they glorie to seeme coy; and when they are most desired then they freese with disdaine: and this fault is so common to the sex, that you see it painted out in the shepheards

passions, who found his Mistris as froward as he was enamoured.
(p. 181)

As Ganimede playing at being Rosalynd, she is able to avoid this
game of hypocrisy. The resultant witty comedy adds a new
dimension to the convention of disguise in romance. Arden, as
already noted, is a more welcoming landscape than Arcadia: the
disguise of gender which lands Pyrocles in such hot water enables
Rosalynd to woo Rosader and to make Phoebe susceptible to the
pangs of love and, ultimately, the suit of Montanus.

Lodge implicitly contrasts Aliena's response to Saladyne's
courtship with Rosalynd's energetic control over her own
destiny: 'At this word marriage *Aliena* stood in a maze what to
answere: fearing that if she were too coye to drive him away with
her disdaine; and if she were too courteous to discover the heat of
her desires' (p. 237). Rosalynd can be delightfully direct:

Nay Forrester . . . if thy busines be not the greater, seeing thou saist
thou art so deeply in love, let me see how thou canst wooe: I will
represent *Rosalynde*, and thou shalt bee as thou art, *Rosader*; see in some
amorous Eglogue, how if *Rosalynde* were present, how thou couldst court
her . . . (p. 211)

If Sidney gave the romance an intellectual vigour, Lodge gave it,
through Rosalynd, an exhilarating freshness in the delineation of
character.

Lodge turned away from the pastoral romance in his next work
of fiction, *Robert Second Duke of Normandy (Robin the Devil)* (1591).
Walter Davis has noted a number of works which strive for a type
of historical accuracy written in the 1590s;[38] and Lodge, in his
preface, pictures himself as a historian:

Gentlemen, I haue vppon the earnest request of some my good friends,
drawne out of the old and ancient antiquaries, the true life of *Robert*
second Duke of *Normandie* . . . wherein I stand not so much on the
termes, as the trueth, publishing as much as I haue read, and not so
much as they have written. (p. 4)[39]

The result is a mish-mash of legend, romance, novella, and
allegory, rather than anything very recognizable as a historical

---

[38] Davis, *Idea and Act*, p. 195.
[39] References are to Edmund Gosse, ed., *The Works of Thomas Lodge* (1883, rpt. New York, 1963), Vol. 2.

work. Lodge's 'realism' has been defended by Claudette Pollack, but her analysis simply reveals a vivid attention to detail (particularly violent detail).[40] Pollack notes Lodge's use of novella conventions, and also the influence of the *Faerie Queene* (Book II) on the scene in which Robert is converted.[41] This underlines Lodge's eclecticism, and *Robert Second Duke of Normandy* is an extremely uneven work, which despite some vivid moments is an unsatisfactory whole.

Lodge continued in this 'historical' vein with *The Life and Death of William Longbeard* (1593). Like its predecessor, this is essentially a popular work, drawing on the jest-book, outlining the life of a legendary figure.[42] Both works indicate Lodge's search for a popular form, rather than any particular development in his fiction. Between them he produced *Euphues Shadow, The Battle of the Senses* (1592), a much more conventional romance than *Rosalynde*. *Euphues Shadow*, as its title implies, is much more euphuistic in style than *Rosalynde*. At the beginning of the work, Philamis is lectured by Anthenor as Euphues was by Eubulus. Anthenor, like Sir John of Bourdeaux, writes a didactic poem, in Anthenor's case addressed 'to all young gentlemen' (p. 16).[43] The *questioni d'amore* which follow also draw on Lyly (pp. 23–8).

Lodge then includes an inset chivalric story full of exotic incident such as the sight (in '*Libia*') of 'an angrie *Rinocerotes* pursuing a tender and yoong infant' (p. 39). This old-fashioned story sits uncomfortably next to the sophisticated *questioni d'amore*. Finally Lodge includes a pastoral section. The dialogue at the end of the romance once again recalls Lyly. *Euphues Shadow* is surprisingly clumsy in comparison with *Rosalynde*.

Fortunately, Lodge's final work of fiction does fulfil some of the promise of *Rosalynde*. Lodge claimed that *A Margarite of America* (1596) was a translation from a Spanish book which he found in the Jesuit College at Santos, on his voyage with the hapless Sir Thomas Cavendish.[44] It seems doubtful that the work is a translation, although it has an element of bloody violence

---

[40] Claudette Pollack, 'Romance and Realism in Lodge's "Robin the Devil"', *Studies in Short Fiction*, 13 (1976), 491–7, *passim*.

[41] Ibid., pp. 494–5.   [42] See Davis, pp. 197–8.

[43] References are to Gosse, Vol. 2.

[44] For accounts of the voyage, see Tenney, pp. 116–17; Paradise, pp. 38–42; Sisson, pp. 105–7.

reminiscent of the continental novella.[45] Whatever Lodge's inspiration, the world depicted in *A Margarite of America* seems to question quite consciously the harmony depicted in *Rosalynde*, and to show that romance conventions and courtly ideals could be manipulated for a malevolent purpose.

Lodge experiments with a dramatic *in medias res* opening, describing a potential battle between the emperors of Mosco and Cusco which is averted by a wise old man. To resolve the conflict, a match is proposed between Arsadachus, the emperor of Mosco's son, and Margarita, the emperor of Cusco's daughter. The bulk of the romance follows the violent career of Arsadachus, a character whose calculating malice holds the reader's horrified attention as firmly as Iago's does. Claudette Pollack has described Lodge's portrayal of Arsadachus as dependent upon a combination of Machiavelli and Castiglione.[46] Lodge contrasts the extremely naïve character of Margarita, who refuses to believe that her love Arsadachus is a villain until the very end of the romance (when he kills her), with the cynicism of Arsadachus.

The setting of the romance has given rise to some confusion. While it contains some pastoral features, its atmosphere is certainly not 'entirely pastoral', but a blend of pastoral, chivalric, and novella elements.[47] Josephine Roberts has argued that Lodge wrote a dystopia set in the New World, a picture of its violence and evil.[48] But the setting of *A Margarite of America* is not as consistent as this implies. Cusco is of course the South American city, but Mosco, with its 'dukedome of *Volgradia*' (p. 119),[49] stems from a fantastic Russia invented by Lodge. The characters show no signs of being inhabitants of the New World.

Arsadachus is able to prey upon people who too readily accept the conventions of courtly behaviour, of the romance lover. Appearance counts for a good deal in the world of the romance, and perhaps Lodge realized the dangers of such an attitude when carried over into the real world. Arsadachus seems to be the

---

[45] Claudette Pollack convincingly argues against its being a translation, 'Lodge's *A Margarite of America*: An Elizabethan Medley', *Renaissance and Reformation*, 12 (1976), 1.

[46] Ibid., pp. 2–6.   [47] Ibid., p. 8.

[48] Josephine A. Roberts, 'Lodge's *A Margarite of America*: A Dystopian Vision of The New World', *Studies in Short Fiction*, 17 (1980), 407–14, *passim*.

[49] References are to G. B. Harrison, ed., *Greene's Menaphon and Lodge's A Margarite of America* (Oxford, 1927).

perfect romance hero: he writes poetry, he is able to take a witty part in *questioni d'amore*, he knows how to take part in a delicate lovers' dialogue:

Princesse said he, by what means might loue be discovered if speech were not? By the eies (my lord said she) which are the keys of desire, which both open the way for loue to enter, and locke him vp when he is let in. How hap then (said he) that *Cupid* among the poets is fained blinde? In that (my lord quoth she) he was maskt to poets memorie . . . (pp. 167–8)

Margarita indicates that she gives excessive credence to the eye, to appearance, in love. Lodge establishes a constant level of irony in his treatment of Arsadachus' ability to project the right appearance. One of his poems, if read carefully, clearly warns that he is not what he seems, that he harbours destructive intentions:

> *Iudge not my thoughts, ne measure my desires,*
> *By outward conduct of my searching eies,*
> *For starres resemble flames, yet are no fires:*
> *If vnder gold a secret poison lies,*
> *If vnder softest flowers lie Serpents fell . . .* (p. 181)

In the *questioni d'amore* conducted by Asaphus, the role of the five senses in love is again discussed, and Margarita defends sight a second time, maintaining with unconscious irony that:

It must be the eie then which can discern the rude colt from the trained steed, the true diamond from the counterfet glasse, the right colour from the rude, and the perfect beautie from the imperfect behauiour: had not the eie the prerogative, loue should bee a monster, no myracle. . . (p. 179)

But Arsadachus, the accomplished lover, *is* a monster, who tries to seduce Margarita's friend Philenia, murders her and her husband Minecius, and wreaks havoc on his return to Cusco.

Arsadachus' cruelty is extreme, but he inhabits an extremely harsh and violent world. Arsadachus' father is incensed when his son marries Diana, and orders Argias, Diana's father, to be torn to pieces by four horses: 'then casting his mangled members into a litter, hee sent them to *Diana* in a present' (p. 197). The cold violence of this society is reinforced by numerous descriptions of glittering, splendid displays, pageants, and a joust, which involve a lavish use of precious stones, alluring to the eye but hard and cold:

These armes were of beaten golde far more curious then those that *Thetis* gave hir *Achilles* before *Troy*, or *Meriores* bestowed on *Vlysses* when he assaulted *Rhesus*, being full of flames and half moones of saphires, chrisolites, and diamonds. In his helme he bare his mistresse fauour, which was a sleeue of salamanders skinne richly perfumed, and set with rubies. (p. 166)

The violence unleashed by Arsadachus along with his Machiavellian accomplices, Thebion and Argias, cannot be controlled. The wise Arsinous, who has retreated to a cell and studied magic, cannot convince Margarita that she must learn not to trust so much in appearance. When he conjures up an image of Arsadachus, Margarita tries to embrace it: 'was it euer seene (quoth he smilingly) a ladie to bee so besotted on a shadow? Ah pardon me (said *Margarita*) I held it for the substance' (p. 213). The box prepared by Arsinous which Margarita gives to Arsadachus when he leaves Mosco contains a potion which brings on Arsadachus' final madness (because he has been unfaithful to Margarita), during which he kills Diana, and dashes out the brains of his little son.

A Margarite of America has a brilliant, polished surface, beneath which seethes calculating malevolence. The romance certainly teeters close to sheer nihilism, but it is an exaggeration to maintain that Arsadachus 'will not reform', that he dies with no moral consciousness at all.[50] He does recognize his evil nature before he commits suicide:

I see with mine inward eies the ghosts of these poore slaughtered soules calling for iustice at my hands; stay me not therefore from death, but assist me to die, for by this means you shall ridde your countrey of a plague, the world of a monster. (p. 224)

Lodge is able to utilize the violence of the novella and romance conventions to create a fascinating exploration of the Machiavellian manipulation of appearance when characters rely on outward, rather than inward, eyes.

---

[50] Davis, p. 199; see also Roberts, p. 413.

IV. The Romance in the 1590s

After its publication in 1590 and 1593, Sidney's *Arcadia* did not exert a strong influence on fiction until the early years of the seventeenth century (see below, Chapter 10). John Dickenson did express a debt to Sidney in the preface to *Arisbas* (1594):

I hope that it shall not minister iust occasion of offence to any, that my blushing Muse reuerencing the steps wherein he traced, and houering aloofe with awefull dread, doth yet at last warily approach and carefully obserue the directions of so worthie a guide, & in part, glance at the vnmatchable height of his heroique humour. (A4)

However, Dickenson subtitled his romance *Euphues amidst his slumbers*, although *Arisbas* is not euphuistic. Lyly's influence lingered, at least as a selling-point, for quite some time. (Perhaps the change is truly signalled when *Menaphon* is retitled *Greenes Arcadia* in 1610.)

Arisbas is set in Arcadia, where Arisbas has come to seek his lost love Timoclea (whose name clearly recalls Philoclea's). He is a prince of Cyprus in disguise; the separation occurs during a ship-wreck—these romance motifs are deftly utilized by Dickenson. However, his initially firm plot soon becomes much more diffuse, as Arisbas is told about life in Arcadia by the shepherd Damon. Dickenson's Arcadia has a strong mythological content, and a delicate atmosphere. Through it move figures like Zephyrus and Pomona, and Dickenson's poetry is also concerned with mytho-logical themes. His Arcadia is not threatened by political disruption as is Sidney's. However, it is a fallen world, for it has been deserted by the Gods who once frequented it: 'when our Country was haunted with the almost-daily presence of heauens high inhabitantes, though now bereaued of so great a good through our owne ingratitude' (E2).

Arisbas associates himself with Pyrocles in a poem entitled 'Cupids Palace':

> Pyrocles such fancie knew,
> Fancie giving Loue his due,
> Which did on Philoclea looke,
> Bathing in a Christall brooke.
> He disguisde a virgin seemd,
> And his name was Zelmane deemd.

O how sweetly did he praise,
In those lines those louely laies,
All perfections in her planted?   (G)

But Arisbas' reunion with Timoclea has the inevitability of
Daphnis' union with Chloe.[51] The romance is almost entirely
static, and the small amount of action is contained in retrospective narration (such as Timoclea's account of her adventures,
after Arisbas finds her; H2—H4ᵛ). In spite of its self-conscious
associations with the *Arcadia, Arisbas* is much closer to *Rosalynde* in
its pastoral concerns. It deserves to be better known.

Emanuel Forde's *Ornatus and Artesia* (1598?) may serve as an
example of the popularization of the sophisticated romance in
the 1580s and 90s. With Forde, what was once fresh and original
has become truly formulaic. *Ornatus and Artesia* might be
described as a slick piece of work by a writer who was well aware
of public taste. It is an adroit but undemanding performance,
making good use of Greek romance techniques to separate the
two lovers, Ornatus and Artesia, and to keep the plot under
control. Ornatus' disguise as a woman leads to the expected
complications when Artesia's uncle is attracted to him. A few
chivalric incidents eke out the action which moves to its
inevitable conclusion. Clichés about the monotonies of the
romance form, about its two-dimensionality, which bear no
relation to Sidney or the best work of Lodge and Greene, are born
out by derivative romances like *Ornatus and Artesia.*[52]

Despite the existence of derivative works, the romance form
developed by Sidney, Greene, and Lodge provided some of the
most impressive works of Elizabethan fiction. It is worth noting
that contemporary readers appreciated their quality. The
Arcadia was, of course, one of the most popular books of the
seventeenth century. *Rosalynde* went through eleven editions up
to 1642; *Menaphon* six up to 1632; and *Pandosto* ten up to 1632;
while minor works tended to disappear, usually with
justification.

[51] Davis associates their union with the changing seasons, p. 76.
[52] Another good example of the derivative romance is *Loves Load-Starre* (1600), by
Robert Kittowe, expanded from a story in *The Cobler of Canterburie* (1590) derived from
Boccaccio (v. 6); see John D. Hurrell, '*Loves Load-Starre*: A Study in Elizabethan Literary
Craftsmanship', *Boston University Studies in English*, 1 (1955), 197–209.

Chapter 7

Rhetoric and 'Realism': Nashe and Others

If we turn from the work of the romance-writers to the work of Thomas Nashe, we must resist the temptation to draw a simple opposition, to see Nashe as 'realistic' in contrast to Sidney. The modern reader, whose understanding of 'realism' as a literary term may be misleading in this context, should be alerted to Nashe's rhetorical art and particularly to his idiosyncratic use of narrative voice, rather than given an anachronistic characterization of *The Unfortunate Traveller* as a 'novel'. With Nashe's work, and some of the writings of Greene, Chettle, and Breton, fiction is constantly shading into other genres: into the jest-book, the cony-catching pamphlet, the polemical treatise.

During the 1590s Nashe took up the mantle of Robert Greene. Nashe was a precocious polemicist, proud of his quick wit and his learning which, like Greene, he wore lightly. It is misleading to see Nashe as an Elizabethan 'journalist', although such a description does perhaps help to evoke his eclecticism and range of interests.[1] He was too idiosyncratic to achieve the truly popular appeal of Greene. His most important work of prose fiction, *The Unfortunate Traveller*, remained out of print from its first appearance in 1594 until Grosart's edition of 1883. Nashe's eventual rejection of patronage with the mock-dedication of *Lenten Stuff* (1598) may also indicate his inability to find anyone truly appreciative of his originality.

Nashe's first work, *The Anatomy of Absurdity* (1589), written while he was still at Cambridge, aligns itself with the most up-to-date thoughts about fiction. Lyly's style is condemned (although Nashe has not avoided the influence of euphuism):[2] 'Minerals, stones, and herbes, should not haue such cogged natures and

---

[1] See Donald J. McGinn, *Thomas Nashe* (New York, 1981), *passim*.
[2] See G. R. Hibbard, *Thomas Nashe: A Critical Introduction* (London, 1962), pp. 17–18.

names ascribed to them without cause . . .' (i. 10).[3] The old
chivalric romances are scorned:

What els I pray you doe these bable bookemungers endeuour, but to
repaire the ruinous wals of *Venus* Court, to restore to the worlde that
forgotten Legendary licence of lying, to imitate a fresh the fantasticall
dreames of those exiled Abbie-lubbers, from whose idle pens proceeded
those worne out impressions of the feyned no where acts, of Arthur of the
rounde table, Arthur of litle Brittaine, sir Tristram, Hewon of Burdeux,
the Squire of low degree, the foure sons of Amon, with infinite others.
(p. 11)

In his preface to Greene's *Menaphon* (1589), Nashe also associated
himself with the fashionable pastoral romance, but only by way
of commendation, for his own literary talent lay in a quite
different direction.

The Anatomy of Absurdity is written in a derivative style, but
Nashe was soon caught up in the Marprelate controversy, which
had an important influence on the exciting and individual style
which he perfected in *Pierce Penilesse, The Unfortunate Traveller*,
and *Lenten Stuff*. In 1588 'Martin Marprelate' made his first
appearance with a pamphlet entitled *Oh read ouer D. John Bridges*,
the opening shot in a lively war waged against the established
church by the Puritans. 'Martin', long thought to be John Penry,
has recently been identified as Job Throkmorton, and with the
appearance of this engaging *persona*, religious controversy was
raised (or lowered, depending on one's point of view) to the level
of literary display.[4] Raymond Anselment aptly describes
'Martin's' style as 'dramatic satire', and emphasizes the rhetorical basis of its protean character.[5] Ponderous attempts to deal
with 'Martin' only supplied further fuel for his satire, and in
desperation the authorities turned to the 'professional' writers for
aid. It is now generally acknowledged that Nashe's contribution
was *An Almond For A Parrot* (1590).[6] To hold the reader's interest,
Nashe had to assume a *persona* and a dramatic style. The

---

[3] All references are to *The Works of Thomas Nashe*, ed. R. B. McKerrow, rev. F. P.
Wilson (Oxford, 1958), 4 vols.

[4] Donald J. McGinn, *John Penry and the Marprelate Controversy* (New Brunswick, N. J.,
1966); Leland H. Carlson, *Martin Marprelate Gentleman: Job Throkmorton Laid Open in His
Colours* (San Marino, 1981).

[5] Raymond Anselment, 'Rhetoric and the Dramatic Satire of Martin Marprelate',
SEL 10 (1970), 103–19, *passim*.

[6] McGinn, *Thomas Nashe*, p. 44.

pamphlet purports to be written by 'Cuthbert Curry-Knaue', a name which is taken up in *The Defence of Cony-Catching* (1592), purportedly written by Cuthbert Cony-Catcher. The flippant dedication to William Kempe ('*Monsieur du kempe, Iestmonger and* Vice-regent generall to the Ghost of Dicke Tarlton', iii. 341) sets the tone for the pamphlet, which casually buttonholes Martin and the reader: 'Welcome, Mayster *Martin*, from the dead, and much good ioy may you haue of your stage-like resurrection' (iii. 344). Consciously or unconsciously, Nashe gradually developed an idiosyncratic colourful *persona*, expressed in a flexible style. The need to meet Martin on his own ground provoked Nashe's exploration of the style which achieved full literary distinction in his next work, *Pierce Penilesse* (1592).[7]

I. *Pierce Penilesse*

In this, his most popular work, Nashe takes up the cause of the writer who must live by his wits, who is always vulnerable. Pierce is not exactly Nashe himself; he is a larger-than-life controlled expansion of Nashe's own situation, but close enough to reality for his satire to sting. *Pierce Penilesse* may be seen as part of a general interest in satire in the 1590s, although in this work it has a more conservative appearance than the poetic satire of Hall or Marston. Pierce introduces himself as a figure brought to a state of desperation by poverty and lack of literary success; he has the satirical stance of the Outsider: 'Wherevpon (in a malecontent humor) I accused my fortune, raild on my patrones, bit my pen, rent my papers, and ragde in all points like a mad man' (i. 157). He sees a universal neglect of talent in his society:

This is the lamentable condition of our Times, that men of Arte must seeke almes of Cormorantes, and those that deserue best, be kept vnder by Dunces, who count it a policie to keepe them bare, because they should follow their bookes the better: thinking belike, that, as preferment hath made themselues idle, that were earst painefull in meaner places, so it would likewise slacken the endeuours of those Students that as yet striue to excell in hope of aduauncement. (p. 160)

Deciding to seek aid from the devil, Pierce sets off in search of 'this

---

[7] See Travis L. Summersgill, 'The Influence of the Marprelate Controversy on the Style of Thomas Nashe', *SP* 48 (1951), 145–60, and Hibbard, Chap. 2.

olde Asse'. His quest enables Nashe to direct some satire at the
lawyers, and at this stage the general points-scoring suddenly
produces a vivid vignette, a description of

an old, stradling Vsurer, clad in a damaske cassocke, edged with Fox
fur, a paire of trunke slops, sagging down like a Shoomakers wallet, and
a short thrid-bare gown on his backe, fac't with moatheaten budge;
vpon his head he wore a filthy, course biggin, and next it a garnish of
night-caps, which a sage butten-cap, of the forme of a cow-sheard, ouer
spread very orderly: a fat chuffe it was, I remember, with a gray beard
cut short to the stumps, as though it were grimde, and a huge, woorme-
eaten nose, like a cluster of grapes hanging downe-wards. (pp. 162–3)

This technique of creating an arresting caricature by exag-
gerated physical details plays an important part in Nashe's work.
Perhaps the most impressive example is the satirical portrait of
Gabriel Harvey in *Have With You to Saffron-Walden* (1596).

Pierce's supplication is, as G. R. Hibbard points out, 'essentially a series of variations on the old formula of the Seven Deadly
Sins'.[8] Nashe always has his eye on the contemporary scene, and
the pamphlet is also undoubtedly spiced with some political
satire, although scholars are not in complete agreement about the
identities of its targets.[9] But the range of Nashe's satirical survey is
very wide, enabling him, among other things, to enter into the
debate over the theatre by mounting a stringent defence of plays
(pp. 211–15). The most attractive aspect of *Pierce Penilesse* is the
way Nashe brings his caricatures to life in a manner which, as
Hibbard suggests, may well have influenced Ben Jonson in his
creation of characters based on humours.[10] The pamphlet is
much too diverse in its aims to be considered as a true work of
prose fiction, but many individual elements add to the fiction-
writer's technique.

II. Henry Chettle and Nicholas Breton

The popularity of Nashe's pamphlet is reflected in the prompt
appearance of other works which acknowledge its influence.

[8] Hibbard, p. 69.
[9] Donald J. McGinn, 'The Allegory of the "Beare" and the "Foxe" in Nashe's *Pierce
Penilesse*', *PMLA* 61 (1946), 431–53; Anthony G. Petti, 'Political Satire in *Pierce Penilesse*'
Neophilologus, 45 (1961), 139–50.
[10] Hibbard, p. 74.

Henry Chettle, an acquaintance of Nashe and Greene, produced a sprightly little pamphlet entitled *Kind-Harts Dreame* in the same year as *Pierce*. Its sub-title implies that it is akin to a sequel: '*Deliuered by seuerall Ghosts vnto him to be publisht, after* Piers Penilesse *Post had refused the carriage*' (p. 3).[11] The pamphlet describes how Kind-hart sees in a dream five individuals who present him with petitions which have been refused by the knight of the post who offered to carry Pierce's supplication to the devil. The five are Anthony Now Now, a ballad singer; Doctor Burcot, a physician; Robert Greene; Richard Tarleton; and William Cuckoe, a cony-catcher. Chettle skilfully provides each character with a suitable style for his oration.[12]

Kind-Harts Dreame lacks the satirical power of *Pierce Penilesse*. It is a whimsical work, particularly in its depiction of notorious individuals like Greene and Tarleton. Chettle shows Nashe's influence in his colloquial style as well as in his frequent direct references to *Pierce Penilesse*. His second and more substantial work of fiction was much more original.

In 1595 Chettle published *Piers Plainnes Seaven Yeres Prentiship*. This work joins together the world of romance and the world of Nashe. Walter Davis has pointed out that Chettle uses two quite distinct styles, 'an exalted formal style, rhetorical and Euphuistic' for the story of the romance figures Celydon, Celinus, Hylenus, Aemilius, Rhodope, and Aeliana, and 'a relaxed extemporal style heavily influenced by the Marprelate tracts and Nashe' for Piers's adventures.[13]

Chettle juxtaposes three worlds: the pastoral, to which Piers has retreated after his tumultuous adventures; the tough, picaresque world of his apprenticeship period; and the elevated but dangerous world of the court.[14] A less complex work, which also draws on Nashe's exploitation of first-person narrative, was published by Nicholas Breton in 1597. In *The Miseries of Mavillia* the narrative is divided into five 'miseries' related by Mavillia herself. Breton's plain style owes little to Nashe, although his use of colloquial conversation is impressive, particularly in the early

---

[11] References are to Henry Chettle, *Kind-Harts Dreame*, ed. G. B. Harrison (London, 1923).
[12] See Walter R. Davis, *Idea and Act*, p. 203.
[13] Ibid., pp. 203–4.
[14] For further consideration of this aspect of *Piers Plainnes* see below, Chap. 15, Sec. III.

part of the narrative, which effectively portrays a child's point of view. A good example is the description of Mavillia's treatment at the hands of a laundress:

when I would crie A little drinke, some bread and butter, I would go to bed: Peace, you little whore, would she say, learne to lie in the strawe, you are like: tarrie and be hanged, is meate so good cheape? I will make you grate on a crust, ha, you monkie, you shall have butter with a birchen rod: then if I cried, take me up, clap, clap, clap, clap, set me downe again, crie till thy heart burst, I thinke it longs to be knocked on the head . . . (pp. 114–15)[15]

Breton's rather naïve narrative is an interesting curiosity. Chettle's subtler use of Piers's first-person narrative, the carefully created speaking voice which is conscious of its audience ('I saw Menalcas smile even now, when I cald Brocage a mysterie . . .', p. 143) derives from Nashe's seminal work of fiction, *The Unfortunate Traveller*.

III. *The Unfortunate Traveller*

The Unfortunate Traveller has appealed to twentieth-century readers more than any other work of early fiction. Often this attraction has stemmed from over-emphasis of certain features which bear some resemblance to the concerns of modern novelists—its 'nihilism', its 'picaresque' nature, its violence. Elizabethan readers were not so impressed, judging by the fact that it did not reappear after the two editions of 1594. (*Pierce Penilesse*, Nashe's most popular work, went through five editions between 1592 and 1595.) Any analysis of *The Unfortunate Traveller* must begin with a consideration of the debates which have been waged over its nature. It is a work which is shaped by Nashe's individual style and personality, and it does not fit into any easily identifiable category.

Some scholars, notably Fredson Bowers, have seen *The Unfortunate Traveller* as a picaresque novel.[16] The Spanish

---

[15] References to *The Works of Nicholas Breton*, ed. Ursula Kentish-Wright (London, 1929), Vol. 2.

[16] Fredson T. Bowers, 'Thomas Nashe and the Picaresque Novel', *Humanistic Studies in Honour of John Calvin Metcalf* (Charlottesville, 1941), pp. 12–27; Arnold Kettle, *An Introduction to the English Novel* (London, 1951), Vol. 1, p. 23; Madelon S. Gohlke, 'Wits Wantonness: *The Unfortunate Traveller* as Picaresque', *SP* 73 (1976), 397–413.

picaresque tradition did not have a strong influence on English
fiction until the seventeenth century (see below, Chapter 13).
Nashe may have been familiar with *Lazarillo de Tormes* (1553),
which was translated into English in 1576 by David Rowland,
with a second edition in 1586. But Jack Wilton, the narrator of
The Unfortunate Traveller, is not a victim of poverty like Lazarillo;
and he plays his tricks in the early part of his narrative for sheer
enjoyment—he is not a rogue out of dire necessity, as is
Lazarillo.[17] Nashe revels in his linguistic skill in *The Unfortunate
Traveller*, changing his style to suit the rapid alterations of tone,
incident, and theme.[18]

Neil Rhodes has recently placed Nashe in the context of the
grotesque in sixteenth-century literature.[19] He points out that
Elizabethan journalistic satire is 'the product of an uneasy
relationship between sermon and festive comedy, priest and
clown', and that the resulting tension between 'laughter and
revulsion' reveals the presence of the literary grotesque.[20] The
grotesque is also associated with 'a fascinated sense of the body',
as exemplified by Rabelais,[21] and with the 'absence of a
satisfactory authorial role' for popular prose writers.[22] However,
in *The Unfortunate Traveller* the question of Jack Wilton's status as
an independent character is more problematic than this formula
implies. Nashe carefully establishes Jack's identity as a page in
'*The Induction to the dapper Mounsier Pages of the Court*' (ii. 207). The
dramatic address to the pages has the immediacy of the opening
of *An Almond For A Parrat*: 'Gallant Squires, haue amongst you: at
Mumchaunce I meane not, for so I might chaunce come to short
commons, but at *nouus, noua, nouum*, which is in English, newes of
the maker' (p. 207).[23] The pages are enlisted in support of the
book, which is written in their praise. Nashe emphasizes the first-

[17] For a closer analysis of *Lazarillo*, see below, Chap. 13, Sec. III.
[18] The best analysis of Nashe's style is David Kaula, 'The Low Style in Nashe's *The Unfortunate Traveller*', *SEL* 6 (1966), 43–57; see also A. K. Croston, 'The Use of Imagery in Nashe's *The Unfortunate Traveller*', *RES* 24 (1948), 90–101; Reinhard H. Friederich, 'Verbal Tensions in Thomas Nashe's *The Unfortunate Traveller*', *Language & Style*, 8 (1975), 211–19.
[19] Neil Rhodes, *Elizabethan Grotesque* (London, 1980), Chaps. 1–4.
[20] Ibid., p. 4 and p. 10.
[21] Ibid., p. 41.   [22] Ibid., p. 51.
[23] Margaret Ferguson builds her interpretation of the narrative on this sentence in 'Nashe's *The Unfortunate Traveller*: The "Newes of the Maker" Game', *ELR* 11 (1981), 165–82.

person narration: 'euerie man of you take your place, and heare
Iacke Wilton tell his own Tale' (p. 208).

Jack's speaking voice immediately holds the reader in its spell;
it is witty, colloquial, always indulging in a sense of display, like a
proud peacock, and always aware of its audience:

Bee it knowen to as many as will paie mony inough to peruse my storie,
that I followed the court or the camp, or the campe and the court, when
Turwin lost her maidenhead, and opened her gates to more than *Iane
Trosse* did. There did I (soft, let me drinke before I go anie further)
raigne sole King of the cans and blacke iackes, prince of the pigmeis,
countie palatine of cleane straw and prouant, and, to conclude, Lord
high regent of rashers of the coles and red herring cobs. *Paulo maiora
canamus*. Well, to the purpose. (p. 209)

Walter Davis has pointed to some similarity between Jack and
Ned Browne, the narrator in Robert Greene's *Black Book's
Messenger* (1592).[24] Browne is, however, much more of a
mouthpiece than a character. The similarity is perhaps most
evident in the early pages of *The Unfortunate Traveller*, when Jack
plays a number of tricks reminiscent of jest-book incidents.[25]

Unlike Ned Browne, Jack's speaking voice partakes of Nashe's
learning—it is sprinkled with classical tags. In this sense it is a
'university wit' style, as well as being vivid and colloquial.
Speaking about the style of *The Unfortunate Traveller* in this way
indicates that it is often difficult to separate Jack as a character
from Nashe.[26] Jack is much more of an independent character
than Pierce Penilesse, but, as we shall see, he is not consistent. We
first see Jack playing an elaborate trick on a nobleman who runs
an alehouse in the camp—the first of a number of comic figures
and incidents which are treated in the grotesque style outlined by
Neil Rhodes. The description of the alehouse Lord stresses a
disgusting yet comic array of physical details: he 'thought no
scorne . . . to haue his great velvet breeches larded with the
droppinges of this daintie liquor . . .' (p. 210); 'after he had spitte
on his finger, and pickt of two or three moats of his olde moth
eaten velvet cap, and spunged and wrong [*sic*] all the rumatike
driuell from his ill favored goats beard . . .' (p. 211). The

---

[24] Davis, p. 215.
[25] For an analysis of the jest-book, see below, Chap. 13, Sec. I.
[26] See Richard A. Lanham, 'Tom Nashe and Jack Wilton: Personality as Structure in
The Unfortunate Traveller', *Studies in Short Fiction*, 4 (1966), 201–16.

grotesque features in a number of descriptive passages: the sweating sickness (pp. 228–30); the 'bursten belly inkhorne orator called *Vanderhulke*' (p. 247); the elaborate parody of a joust, which relies on absurd armour and impresas;[27] Doctor Zachary's miserliness (pp. 305–6); Zadoch's anger (p. 310); and Cutwolfe's execution (p. 327). The description of Zadoch when he is told of the Pope's proclamation against the Jews is a good example of grotesque comedy forced from a potentially serious situation. This is achieved by an almost surrealistic description of physical details:

There is a toad fish, which taken out of the water swels more than one would thinke his skin could hold, and bursts in his face that toucheth him. So swelled Zadoch, and was readie to burst out of his skin and shoote his bowels like chaine-shot full at Zacharies face for bringing him such balefull tidings; his eies glared & burnt blew like brimstone and *aqua vitae* set on fire in an egshell, his verie nose lightned glow-wormes, his teeth crasht and grated together, like the joynts of a high building cracking and rocking like a cradle, when as a tempest takes her full but against his broad side. (p. 310)

The snowballing similes create an inhuman figure. This is the comedy of dehumanization, of distance. It is related to the violence which is so prevalent in *The Unfortunate Traveller*— violence whose intensity has disturbed a number of scholars.[28] This violence is also characteristic of the grotesque, as is the comic treatment of potentially repugnant incidents.[29]

There has, however, been some disagreement over incidents such as Cutwolfe's execution and the rape of Heraclide, since Agnes Latham put forward the notion that the main thrust of the book is satirical, and these two incidents are part of Nashe's general literary satire.[30] One of the most difficult features of the narrative is its shifting tone, and in the two incidents in question, no firm evidence can be found for any single interpretation. Nashe packs so much into the narrative—jest-book tricks; a

[27] See Katherine Duncan-Jones, 'Nashe and Sidney: The Tournament in *The Unfortunate Traveller*', *MLR* 63 (1968), 3–6.
[28] See Charles Larson, 'The Comedy of Violence in Nashe's *The Unfortunate Traveller*', *Cahiers Elisabethains*, 11 (1975), 15–27.
[29] Rhodes, Chap. 3.
[30] Agnes M.C. Latham, 'Satire on Literary Themes and Modes in Nashe's "Unfortunate Traveller"', *Essays and Studies*, New Series, 1 (1948), 85–100.

sermon; satire directed at Petrarchan poetry and courtly love;[31] religious satire; the attractions of popular travel literature *and* a didactic speech condemning travel; a revenge tale; accounts of historical characters and events; tragedy; averted tragedy (Jack's hair's-breadth escape from execution)—that one must allow for the possibility of violence being treated seriously *and* comically. In addition to its grotesque elements, *The Unfortunate Traveller* is very much a product of the interest in mixed modes; it is satirical-comical-tragical. Nashe likes to wring as much out of an event as possible, and then quickly move on to another, usually contrasting, event. His stylistic energy is an important element in this kaleidoscopic effect.

Cutwolfe's confession is a blood-curdling revenge story, which depends upon the Elizabethan stereotype of Italian behaviour:

therewith made I no more ado, but shot him full into the throat with my pistoll: no more spake he after; so did I shoot him that he might neuer speake after, or repent him. His bodie being dead lookt as blacke as a toad: the deuill presently branded it for his owne. This is the falt that hath called me hether; no true Italian but will honor me for it. Reuenge is the glorie of armes, & the highest performance of valure: reuenge is whatsoeuer we call law or iustice. (p. 326)

The death of Esdras is presented coldly and with some power. Cutwolfe's attitude to revenge is what one would expect from an Italian; it provides a *frisson* for the reader, who is half repulsed and half fascinated by this bold justification. Jack then dwells on the details of Cutwolfe's execution, enjoying the skill of the executioner: 'olde excellent he was at a bone-ach' (p. 327). G. R. Hibbard reminds us that public executions were enjoyed by Elizabethans.[32] But after the relish he takes in the scene, Jack is suddenly frightened into rapid repentance and a swift departure from Italy:

Vnsearchable is the booke of our destinies. One murder begetteth another: was neuer yet bloud-shed barren from the beginning of the world to this daie. Mortifiedly abiected and danted was I with this truculent tragedie of *Cutwolfe* and *Esdras*. (p. 327)

For the reader's delectation, and to display his own versatility,

---

[31] See Dorothy Jones, 'An Example of Anti-Petrarchan Satire in Nashe's "The Unfortunate Traveller"', *YES* 1 (1971), 48–54.
[32] Hibbard, p. 174.

Nashe packs into this incident the thrill of revenge and its condemnation; the sadistic pleasures of an execution and its moral lesson; a fascination with and condemnation of violence, which exemplifies the clash between the religious or didactic and the Festive, seen by Rhodes as an essential aspect of the grotesque.[33]

The rape of Heraclide is a similar example of the close juxtaposition of contrasting attitudes. On the one hand, Jack's role is comic; when Esdras drags Diamante away, Jack cries out 'Saue her, kill me, and Ile ransome her with a thousand duckets' (p. 287). Then Nashe extracts the maximum of horror and lasciviousness from Heraclide's predicament. Her elaborate rhetoric is, I think, a fitting response to the situation, rather than satire on Nashe's part.[34] She provides a moral commentary on the deed, but at the same time Nashe emphasizes the ravisher's vision, stressing Heraclide's 'yuorie throat', 'lilly lawne skinned necke', and 'bare snowy breast' (p. 291). Again Nashe provides a multi-faceted *frisson* for the reader:

On the hard boords he threw her, and vsed his knee as an yron ramme to beat ope the two leaud gate of her chastitie. Her husbands dead bodie he made a pillow to his abhomination. (p. 292)

The voyeurism is emphasized by Jack's later explanation that he has been watching the scene 'thorough a crannie of my vpper chamber unseeled' (p. 295). After an elaborate speech, Heraclide stabs herself. But when she falls upon her husband's apparently dead body, he revives, in an unsettlingly comic manner. The abrupt change in tone is continued by Jack's light-hearted account of his own near-execution for the rape – a display, on Nashe's part, of sheer literary agility:

Vppon this was I laid in prison, should haue been hanged, was brought to the ladder, had made a Ballad for my Farewell in a readines, called *Wiltons wantonnes*, and yet for all that scapde dauncing in a hempen circle. He that hath gone through many perils and returned safe from them, makes but a merriment to dilate them. (p. 295)

The shifting tone of *The Unfortunate Traveller* is relevant to two further questions which have been debated by critics: Jack's

---

[33] Rhodes, p. 37 and Chap. 3, *passim*.
[34] *Pace* Latham, see Hibbard, pp. 168–70.

characterization, and the book's structure (or lack of structure).
Jack has been seen both as a mere mouthpiece for Nashe and as
an independent character. G. R. Hibbard puts forward the idea
that there is such an *ad hoc* quality to the narrative that Jack
cannot be said to exist as a true character at all: 'The mischievous
page of the beginning and the courageous robber of the end
belong together, but they are wholly irreconcilable with the
ferocious preacher who lambasts the Anabaptists and the stern
moralist who tells the tale of Heraclide. . . .'[35] Richard
Lanham attempts to counter this view in a rather confusing
article, which sees the narrative as 'pseudobiographical', and
Jack as a 'truly neurotic personality'.[36]

   This misleading attempt at psychoanalysis of a character so
inconsistent is continued by Margaret Ferguson in a much more
challenging recent article. Ferguson's interpretation depends
upon a view of Jack as a rebel against authority, a projection of
Nashe's 'ambivalent attitude not only toward transgressors,
artists or children, but also toward the social and religious
authorities invested with punitive powers'.[37] Much of this
argument relies on teasing ambivalent meanings out of key
phrases, such as 'newes of the maker', and some unsettling
assertions about psychological symbols (for example, cider is 'a
forbidden oral gratification midway between milk and blood').[38]
Jack is something of a rebel, but he should be observed in the
context of Nashe's satire and humour, rather than merely as
someone with ambivalent feelings against authority. Jack's
attack on the Anabaptists stems from the satirist's typically
conservative attitude.

   Any search for a consistent world-view or a psychology of Jack
Wilton is certain to be undermined by the constant shift in his
nature as Nashe's literary display moves from one area of interest
to another. One solution to this problem is to accept Jack as a
partial creation, a character who at times assumes independence
but at other times seems to be a very thin mask for the author.
Certainly Jack is much more a true character than, say, Robert
Greene's Ned Browne. The exuberant style in which the
narrative is written, while often very elaborate, is colloquial and
full of snippets of self-dramatization on Jack's part—features

---

[35] Hibbard, p. 177.   [36] Lanham, pp. 216 and 215.
[37] Ferguson, p. 177.   [38] Ibid., p. 168.

which lead the reader to believe (for the moment) in the speaker: 'Heeres a stir, thought I to my self after I was set at libertie, that is worse than an vpbraiding lesson after a britching . . .' (p. 303). I think that most readers do accept that there *is* a Jack Wilton, but if one freezes the narrative and searches for consistent characterization one will be disappointed.

Because *The Unfortunate Traveller* mixes so many modes together, it is essentially episodic. Nashe, as Hibbard rightly emphasizes, 'works in terms of what may be described as scenes'.[39] The scenes in the early part of the work are quite distinct, but by the time Jack reaches Italy in the service of Surrey the narrative becomes more connected, the individual scenes more substantial. Alexander Leggatt has undertaken a search for 'artistic coherence' in the narrative.[40] He has noted 'a coherent pattern of images (centered here on the frailty of the flesh)'.[41] He also feels that in the last third of the narrative Jack may be seen as a rogue who, through becoming a victim, is led to reform. This argument once again relies on seeing some consistency in Jack. After the rape of Heraclide, Jack barely escapes from being hanged through the intervention of 'a banisht English Earle' (p. 296). The Earl delivers a diatribe against the dangers of travel—and Jack is left quite untouched by the advice offered to him. Jack's eventual repentance after the execution of Cutwolfe is very cursory, at least in the narration, and seems to be nothing more than an easy way to end a narrative which might have continued indefinitely: 'And so as my storie began with the king at *Turnay* and *Turwin*, I thinke meete heere to end it with the king at *Andes* and *Guines*' (p. 328). This is not very different in effect from the end of *Pierce Penilesse*: 'And so I breake off this endlesse argument of speech abruptlie' (i. 245).

Violence may be part of the grotesque, but it is much more pronounced in *The Unfortunate Traveller* than it is in Nashe's other works. This may partly be explained by the location of a large part of Jack's narrative in Italy—the violent Italy of the novella (and Jacobean tragedy). Jack is, like the reader, always off

---

[39] Hibbard, p. 147.

[40] Alexander Leggatt, 'Artistic Coherence in *The Unfortunate Traveller*', *SEL* 14 (1974), 31–46.

[41] Ibid., p. 46; this notion is expanded by Rhodes, but not in any detailed account of *The Unfortunate Traveller*.

balance, now serious, now jesting, as he describes scenes of violence: 'It was my good lucke or my ill (I know not which) to come iust to the fighting of the Battel; where I saw a wonderfull spectacle of blood-shed on both sides . . .' (p. 231).

Nashe's satire constantly cuts through any attractive surface to reveal absurdity or worse. After describing the elaborate devices used by the participants in the joust with Surrey, Jack says

To particularize their manner of encounter were to describe the whole art of tilting. Some had like to haue fallen ouer their horse neckes and so breake their neckes in breaking theyr staues. (p. 278)

The reality belies the ornate display. A more light-hearted example of such debunking is the treatment of Surrey, particularly when he and Jack are imprisoned in Venice. Surrey, in a scene reminiscent of *As You Like It*, pretends that Diamante is his love Geraldine, and courts her with ceremony. His sonnet is actually full of images of harsh passion—'Let our tongs meete and striue as they would sting' (p. 263)—and Jack quickly explodes the Petrarchan bubble:

Sadly and verily, if my master sayd true, I shoulde, if I were a wench, make many men quickly immortall. What ist, what ist for a maide fayr and fresh to spend a little lipsalue on a hungrie louer? My master beate the bush and kepte a coyle and a pratling, but I caught the birde. (p. 263)

This is a world in which lust mocks love; comedy undercuts nobility; plague, horrific punishments, and massacres assault mankind. Very little respite is offered. One isolated instance is Jack's description of 'a summer banketting house' in Rome (p. 282). Full of elaborate artifice, it is presented as an eden, an oasis of innocence:

the Wolfe glad to let the Lambe lye vppon hym to keepe him warme, the Lyon suffering the Asse to cast hys legge ouer him, preferring one honest vnmannerly friende before a number of croutching picke-thankes. No poysonous beast there reposed, (poyson was not before our parent *Adam* transgressed.) (p. 284)

Alexander Leggatt, however, sees this description as part of the grim vision of Nashe: 'The outside world is real but horrible; the garden is beautiful but unreal: each world mocks the other.'[42]

[42] Ibid., p. 33.

The narrative moves too swiftly to permit any emphasis on the symbolic significance of a single scene. The traveller only stops moving when he ends his narrative. It is, in the end, Nashe's effervescent style which maintains our interest, giving the narrative an energy which leads to wonder rather than revulsion. The reader, while he watches surfaces being peeled back by Nashe's comic vision, is paradoxically forced to pay more attention to the stylistic surface of the narrative, to its virtuosity, than to what is being described.

Chapter 8

Thomas Deloney and Popular Fiction

I. The Popular Chivalric Romance

The new Renaissance romances by Sidney, Greene, and Lodge did not drive out the older romance forms, but they precipitated a shift in the reading public. Throughout the last quarter of the sixteenth century the demand for prose fiction increased markedly, and this demand existed at all levels of society, from those who paid shillings for the *Arcadia* to those who paid pennies for *Tom a Lincoln* or *Valentine and Orson*. The Spanish and Portuguese chivalric romances of the early sixteenth century achieved their greatest success in England during the late sixteenth and early seventeenth centuries. The long cycles of *Amadis* and *Palmerin*, and similar romances such as *Don Bellianis*, were published in Spain and Portugal between 1508 and 1550.[1] While they were available to English readers in French, most were not translated into English until the late 1590s.[2]

Just when the sophisticated romance was rejecting the marvellous in favour of verisimilitude, and exploring, through the influence of Greek romance and the drama, a complex structure for romance rather than an endlessly proliferating narrative, the outmoded chivalric romance was eagerly accepted by a new group of readers. The influence of *Amadis*, as John O'Connor has shown, may be found in a very wide range of Elizabethan literature from *The Faerie Queene* to Donne's 'The Ecstasy', but it was not regarded as a serious model for fiction.[3] Sidney noted that it may move men to exercise 'courtesy, liberality, and especially courage', but it 'wanteth much of a perfect poesy'.[4]

---

[1] See Henry Thomas, *Spanish and Portuguese Romances of Chivalry* (1920, rpt. New York, 1969), pp. 147–8.

[2] See John J. O'Connor, *Amadis de Gaule and Its Influence on Elizabethan Literature* (New Brunswick, N.J., 1970), pp. 15–18.

[3] Ibid., *passim.*

[4] *Miscellaneous Prose of Sir Philip Sidney*, ed. K. Duncan-Jones and J. Van Dorsten (Oxford, 1973), p. 92.

Francis Meres, admirer of the *Arcadia*, censures the chivalric romances in *Palladis Tamia*.

During the 1590s English chivalric romances were written to satisfy the rising demand, and these reflect the interests of their readers. The readers themselves are elaborately mocked in Francis Beaumont's *The Knight of the Burning Pestle* (1613), in which Rafe the apprentice acts out the role of knight errant to the delight of the Citizen and his wife. The play not only laughs at the unfashionable chivalric romance but also at its new readers, the merchants, shopkeepers, tradesmen, and apprentices. In some respects the life of the London citizen mirrored (albeit with some distortion) the sophisticated, allegorized, and ceremonial chivalry of Elizabeth's court—as was particularly apparent in the Lord Mayor's Pageants.

The three most important writers of these chivalric romances were Richard Johnson, Henry Robarts, and Emanuel Forde, who, together with the numerous translations from the *Amadis* and *Palmerin* series made by Anthony Munday, met a demand which existed for well over a century.[5] Munday's workmanlike translations were well received, but astute popular writers realized that the audience which bought Munday's books had certain ideals which could be reflected in native romances. Emanuel Forde (whose *Ornatus and Artesia* has already been discussed as a popular romance influenced partly by the *Arcadia*) produced three chivalric romances: *Montelyon* (*c.* 1599), *Parismus* (*c.* 1598), and *Parismenos* (*c.* 1599). John O'Connor points out that Forde 'often writes in a manner which comes very close to that of chivalric romances in English translation'.[6] Forde is best described as a very effective formula writer, a manipulator of expected characters and events.

Henry Robarts is more a conveyor of an ideology than a disinterested entertainer like Forde. Louis Wright has described him as a 'patriotic propagandist', a writer who 'gives expression to the new class pride which fostered the virtues described in his own citizen-heroes . . .'.[7] Robarts's didactic bent is reflected not

---

[5] See Celeste Turner Wright, *Anthony Munday: An Elizabethan Man of Letters* (Berkeley, 1928), *passim*.

[6] O'Connor, p. 222.

[7] Louis B. Wright, 'Henry Robarts: Patriotic Propagandist and Novelist', *SP* 29 (1932), 199.

only in his productivity as a pamphleteer, but also in the gradual shift away from the pedestrian and formulaic and towards the more idiosyncratic expression of his own political and historical preoccupations, which is apparent in his four works of fiction. *A Defiance to Fortune* (1590) is an undistinguished chivalric romance. *Pheander The Maiden Knight* (c. 1595) is close to the work of Emanuel Forde. His third romance, *Honours Conquest* (1598), concentrates on what Louis Wright describes as the exaltation of 'national bravery and English virtues'.[8] What the romance basically invokes is national pride through the exploits of Edward of Lancaster. Robarts was quick to follow Thomas Deloney's lead with his final work of fiction, *Haigh for Devonshire* (1600), which was influenced by *Thomas of Reading*.

The writer who most successfully infused the chivalric romance with the spirit of citizens' aspirations was Richard Johnson. Johnson himself was evidently an apprentice when he began writing, and he later became a freeman of London.[9] His first substantial work, *The Nine Worthies of London* (1592), is not fiction, but it is closely related to his most popular work of fiction, *The Seven Champions of Christendome*. *The Nine Worthies*, which Johnson describes as proceeding from the 'barren braine of a poore apprentice' (A2ᵛ), is dedicated to William Webbe, the Lord Mayor of London. Each of the 'worthies' is the subject of a poem and a short prose reflection. They are all notable citizens: 'Sir William Walworth Fishmonger', 'Sir Henry Pritchard Vintener', 'Sir William Seuenoake Grocer', 'Sir Thomas White Marchant-tailer', 'Sir John Bonham Mercer', 'Sir Christopher Croker Vintener', 'Sir John Hawkwood Marchant-tailer', 'Sir Hugh Cauerly Şilke-weauer', 'Sir Henrie Maleuert Grocer' (A4).

Johnson's chivalric equivalent to this collection appeared four years later: *The Seven Champions of Christendome* (part i, 1596; part ii, 1597). The champions are headed by St George; and the title-page of the first part summarizes the nature of the contents:

Shewing their Honourable battailes by Sea and Land: their Tilts, Iousts, and Tournaments for Ladies: their Combats with *Giants*, *Monsters* and *Dragons*: their adventures in forraigne Nations: their

---

[8] Ibid., p. 196.

[9] Richard Johnson, *Tom a Lincolne*, ed. Richard Hirsch (Columbia, Sth. Carolina, 1978), p. xx.

Inchauntments in the holie Land: their Knighthoods, Prowesse, and Chiualrie, In Europe, Africa, and Asia, with their victories against the enemies of Christ.

Johnson is particularly fond of astounding, supernatural events which were evidently appreciated by the readers of the romance. A typical example occurs in Chapter Four:

How Saint Dennis the Champion of France, liued seuen yeares in the shape of a Hart, and howe proud Eglantine the Kings Daughter of Thessalie, was transformed into a Mulberie Tree, and how they both recouered their former shapes by the meanes of Saint Dennis his horse. (p. 34)

His *Tom a Lincolne* (part i, 1599; part ii, 1607?) intertwines Tom's story with Arthurian characters, portraying a fairly uninviting Arthur who, as Richard Hirsch points out in his edition, 'ends by wrecking his kingdom'.[10] Johnson takes care to use London as a locale for a number of episodes and, like Robarts, he infuses the chivalric romance with a nationalistic spirit. While the popular chivalric romance is perhaps the least interesting of all the modes of Elizabethan fiction for the modern reader, it is an important part of the milieu which nourished Deloney's fiction— the one area of popular Elizabethan fiction still accorded high praise.

II. Thomas Deloney

A silk-weaver, Deloney was bold enough to abandon the fantasy world of the chivalric romance and instead depict the world of the skilled artisan and successful merchant. He creates a fictional equivalent of Richard Johnson's *Nine Worthies of London*. Like Nashe, he sets his fiction in the past and introduces historical figures such as Henry VIII to stand beside fictional and semi-fictional characters like Jack of Newbury and Long Meg. Deloney's intention was to hold up notable examples of honourable and successful tradesmen for the admiration and emulation of his readers; in the dedication of *Jack of Newbury* 'To all famovs Cloth workers in England', he writes:

Wherefore to you most worthy Clothiers doe I dedicate this my rude

[10] Ibid., p. xi.

worke, which hath raised out of the dust of forgetfulnesse a most famous
and worthie man . . . of whose life and loue I haue briefly written, and
in a plain and humble manner, that it may be the better vnderstood of
those for whose sake I take paines to compile it, that is, for the well
minded Clothiers, that herein they may behold the great worship and
credit which men of this trade haue in former times come vnto. (p. 3)[11]

Similarly, *The Gentle Craft* honours the shoemakers.

Deloney's work is generally associated by scholars with the so-
called Elizabethan 'middle-class'.[12] Literary scholars are often
unaware of developments in historical scholarship, and in this
particular case the idea of a rising Elizabethan middle-class has
been questioned by historians. This is not to deny Deloney's
interest in tradesmen and his undoubted audience of shoemakers,
weavers, and merchants. However, a number of assumptions
have been made in order to link Deloney with eighteenth-
century novelists, particularly Defoe, and with the 'realist' novel
in general. If Deloney is a 'middle-class' novelist, then he may
easily be associated with the 'rise' of the novel in the eighteenth
century under the impetus of the new middle-class reading
public. This view of Deloney emphasizes some aspects of his
work (his use of realistic dialogue, and of characters from the
commercial world) while ignoring other less 'progressive' aspects
(the use of euphuism for aristocratic characters, fragmentary
structure, the influence of the jest-book). It also overstates the
position of the middle-class at the time when Deloney was
writing.

J. H. Hexter has criticized the excessively broad definition of
the Tudor and Elizabethan middle-class, which was a much less
coherent and assertive group than has been claimed by literary
historians like Louis Wright.[13] Hexter firmly states that the
group's 'new riches evoked from it no new social pretensions, no
new unrest, no new ideology'.[14] Deloney's work does indicate the

---

[11] All references are to Merritt E. Lawlis, ed., *The Novels of Thomas Deloney*
(Bloomington, 1961).

[12] See in particular Louis B. Wright, *Middle-Class Culture in Elizabethan England*
(Chapel Hill, Nth. Carolina, 1935); Walter R. Davis, *Idea and Act*, Chap. 7; Merritt E.
Lawlis, *Apology for the Middle Class: The Dramatic Novels of Thomas Deloney* (Bloomington,
1960).

[13] Wright, *Middle-Class*, Chap. 1; J. H. Hexter, *Reappraisals in History* (London, 1961),
Chap. 5, 'The Myth of the Middle Class in Tudor England'.

[14] Hexter, p. 113.

arrival of a reading public which appreciated literature written
about their own lives (or lives to which they aspired). In some
respects Deloney's rags-to-riches heroes are as much wish-
fulfilment figures as chivalric romance heroes, but their success
stories did occur in real life. The 'rising middle class' which
Merritt Lawlis sees in Deloney's fiction was evidently a projection and expansion of a few successful figures, rather than an
accurate picture of the social situation.[15] Deloney's tradesmen
are highly idealized figures, and their activities are not always
particularly convincing in terms of documentary realism. The
picture of Jack of Newbury's weaving factory would have been
greeted with awe and admiration by most readers, rather than
with familiarity:

> Within one roome being large and long,
> There stood two hundred Loomes full strong:
> Two hundred men, the truth is so,
> Wrought in theese Loomes all in a rowe . . . (p. 26)

Deloney's first published work of fiction was *Jack of Newbury*.
Early editions were read until they fell to pieces, and the first
surviving edition is that of 1619. *Jack of Newbury* was entered in
the Stationers' Register on 7 March 1597, and probably
appeared in print a few months later. It is based on the fairy-tale
rags-to-riches plot: Jack is courted by his Master's widow and
rises from foreman to become Master himself. He quickly reaches
a position of eminence, and then his wife dies, leaving him free to
marry a young servant. Jack then steps beyond his initial sphere
of success by sending a contingent of 150 men to the Queen in
support of Henry's French campaign. The 'poore Clothier'
(p. 31) outdoes the nobility not simply by the number of his men
but by his natural gentility: 'Welcome to mee, *Iacke of Newberie*,
saide the Queene, though a Clothier by trade, yet a Gentleman
by condition . . .' (p. 32).

Jack's next encounter with royalty involves Henry himself.
Jack's opponent is Cardinal Wolsey, who is both personally and
ideologically antipathetic to the tradesman-hero: 'note the vaine
glory of these Artificers', he exclaims (p. 39). Jack stages a small
allegorical show for the King, pretending to be the Emperor of
the Ants (as indeed he is King of the Clothiers). Max Dorsinville

[15] Lawlis, *Apology*, p. 8; see Hexter, *passim*.

has placed great emphasis on this aspect of *Jack of Newbury*. He
sees the central design as a new kingdom set up in the novel, with
Jack as its ruler.[16] Unlike Henry's realm, Jack's is orderly and
efficient; it is a 'middle-class kingdom',[17] with quite different
values from Henry's. We have already seen that it is dangerous to
assume an increasing rise to power of the Elizabethan middle-
class, and part of Dorsinville's argument depends upon such an
assumption: 'he [Jack] is the epitome of the rising Elizabethan
mercantile class that wishes to counterbalance the power of the
Courtiers'.[18] Dorsinville takes very seriously what Constance
Jordan, in a recent article, sees as a mock-kingdom, in accordance with her view of Deloney's characters as essentially role-
players.[19] Jack certainly does not want to leave his kingdom in
order to enter the world of the court. From this point of view, one
of the most important moments in *Jack of Newbury* (its importance is underlined by the existence of a similar scene in *Thomas of
Reading*, pp. 269–71) is Henry's recognition of the inter-
dependence of his kingdom and Jack's: 'no Trade in all the Land
was so much to bee cherished and maintained as this' (p. 47). The
King decides to recruit younger members of Jack's 'kingdom',
placing the ninety-six poor children pointed out to him by Jack in
the service of members of the court (p. 49).

Deloney does not approach his theme with unrelieved gravity.
He is always ready to turn to the jest-book antics of Will
Summers, and indeed the jest-book was a constant influence on
his fiction.[20] But in *Jack of Newbury*, Will is the victim rather than
the trickster. Jack's bevy of spinning Maids take their revenge on
Will when he insults them—like the rest of the court he must bow
to the superiority of Jack's world. Deloney further reinforces
Jack's rise to prominence with a guided tour of Jack's picture-
gallery, which contains fifteen paintings depicting famous men of
humble origins (pp. 52–5). The final triumph which concludes
the book is Jack's manipulation of Sir George Rigley into
marriage with the maid who is pregnant by him.

Jack of Newbury does not reach a true *dénouement*, it simply ends

[16] Max Dorsinville, 'Design in Deloney's *Jack of Newbury*', *PMLA* 88 (1973), 233–9.
[17] Ibid., p. 236.   [18] Ibid.
[19] Constance Jordan, 'The "Art of Clothing": Role Playing in Deloney's Fiction', *ELR*
11 (1981), 183–93.
[20] See Kurt-Michael Patzold, 'Thomas Deloney and The English Jest-Book
Tradition', *English Studies*, 53 (1972), 313–28.

rather than concludes. The two parts of *The Gentle Craft* which
followed it are much more fragmented. Once again Deloney's
purpose is to demonstrate the merits of tradesmen, in this
instance of shoemakers. But he turns to romance motifs to flesh
out his series of stories about successful shoemakers. Part One of
The Gentle Craft begins with the story of Sir Hugh's love for
Winifred (who becomes Saint Winifred). The opening phrases
are reminiscent of many a romance beginning:

Conquering and most imperious Loue, hauing seized on the heart of
young sir *Hugh*, all his wits were set on worke, how for to compasse the
loue of the faire Virgin *Winifred*, whose disdaine was the chiefe cause of
his care . . . (p. 93)

Both lovers die, and Hugh's time as a shoemaker lends that trade
the name 'gentle craft'. The story is a piece of mythologizing, as
well as a saint's life; it grants the shoemakers an ancestry, a
dignity, and by implication a historical legitimacy.

Deloney continues in this romance vein with the story of
Crispine and Crispianus, 'the two sons of the King of Logria'
(p. 115). The story is intertwined with the glory of shoemaking,
but in this particular case Crispine really is of noble blood—
although he is a shoemaker when Ursula, the Emperor's
daughter, falls in love with him. After the happy conclusion of
this story Deloney returns to a successful tradesman: Simon Eyre,
who became Mayor of London.

The second part of *The Gentle Craft* is even more of a pot-pourri,
although the dominant theme is still the same. It contains a large
amount of comedy, including Deloney's account of Long Meg.
Deloney intended to write a third part but this never appeared
(p. 173). In his dedication of the second part to the Company of
Cordwainers he admits that sheer entertainment was his principal aim:

And albeit this pamphlet doth not minister matter worthy your grave
view: yet in regard of the subject, I trust you will deigne to esteeme it,
sith so well as I could, though not so well as I would, I haue sought
herein to procure your delight . . . (p. 173)

Deloney's last work of fiction, *Thomas of Reading*, is a startling
contrast to *The Gentle Craft*. Its mood, particularly in the last four
chapters, is sombre, its conclusion tragic. The suddenness of this
shift precludes much emphasis on any over-all development in

Deloney's work from comedy in *Jack of Newbury* to tragic despair in *Thomas of Reading*. Deloney's output cannot be dated exactly, but all his fiction was produced within a few years. However, the successful individuals of the earlier works are now in a good deal of trouble. Deloney's previously optimistic vision of commercial success has changed. We do see Henry VIII admiring the wealth of Thomas Cole of Reading and Sutton of Salisbury (pp. 269–71), and granting the clothiers' requests. One demand is for the punishment of hanging to be instituted for cloth-stealing in Halifax. This grim piece of commercial legislation fails when no one in Halifax can be found to perform the office of hangman, but the problem is solved by an enterprising friar who invents a guillotine!

Deloney's comedy, which under the influence of the jest-book is always rather crude, becomes almost menacing in the incident of the womanizer Cuthbert, who is hung in a basket and smoked over a fire almost to the point of death as a punishment for cuckolding Hodgekins. Deloney also seems to be aware of the less admirable, indirect effects of increased wealth and influence. The wives of Simon and Sutton are portrayed as proud and greedy, envious of the fine clothes worn by the wives of the city merchants (p. 295). Simon's wife feigns a fatal illness to get her own way:

But you shall understand, that her husband was faine to dresse her London-like ere he could get her quiet, neither wold it please her, except the stuffe were bought in Cheapside . . . And hauing thus won her husband to her will, when the rest of the Clothiers wiues heard thereof, they would be suted in the like sort too: so that euer since, the wiues of South-hampton, Salisbury, of Glocester, Worcester, and Reading, went all as gallant and as braue as any Londoners wiues. (pp. 302–3).

The wives show their frivolous vulgarity again after Thomas Cole's death, which is simply a topic for them to include in their gossip (and they compare completely inaccurate accounts as well): 'some talkt of their husbands frowardnes, some shewed their maids sluttishnes, othersome desciphered the costlines of their garments, some told many tales of their neighbors . . .' (p. 328).

Thomas of Reading contains two tragic stories which are skilfully interwoven by Deloney: an upper-class romance story (no longer a happy one, as in previous works; Robert is blinded and

Margaret enters a nunnery, and the association with tradesmen does not lead to success as it does in *The Gentle Craft*); and the death of Thomas Cole, murdered by the host and hostess of an inn—a pair who have murdered many for their money. The atmospheric scene is powerfully presented, and once again Deloney shows the darker side of prosperity:[21]

Then shewing him a great deale of gold which *Cole* had left with her, she said, Would it not grieue a bodies heart to loose this? hang the old churle, what should he do liuing any longer? he hath too much, and we haue too little . . . (p. 325)

Wealth and influence, no matter how substantial, are overshadowed by death:

Coles substance at his death was exceeding great, he had daily in his house an hundred men seruants, and xl. maids; he maintained beside aboue two or three hundred people, spinners and carders, and a great many other housholders. (p. 327)

The impact of this account is scarcely diminished by the more optimistic story of Tom Dove, who is rescued from his financial difficulties by his fellow clothiers.

Much of the attraction of Deloney's fiction stems from what Merritt Lawlis has called his 'dramatic' style, his intention 'that characters should explain themselves in terms of dialogue and action'.[22] Deloney's extensive use of dialogue which can be called colloquial is unusual in early fiction, and it is largely responsible for the 'realism' which has been ascribed to his work. Merritt Lawlis carefully distinguishes Deloney's 'realistic' style from other styles which he utilizes, such as euphuism.[23]

Deloney is capable of infusing his naturalistic dialogue with a symbolic subtext. A good example occurs when Meg and Gillian are sent on a wild goose chase by Richard Castler's servant. Both women pretend to be gathering herbs when they meet each other:

Nay what doe you here (quoth she)? for my owne part I was sent for to seeke Harts-ease, but I can find nothing but sorrel.

---

[21] See the excellent analysis in Lawlis, *Apology*, pp. 61–6.   [22] Ibid., p. 3.
[23] Ibid., p. 8, and see also T. Dahl, *An Enquiry into Aspects of the Language of Deloney* (Copenhagen, 1951) and O. Reuter, 'Some Aspects of Thomas Deloney's Prose Style', *Neuphilologische Mitteilungen*, 40 (1939), 23–72.

Alack good soule (quoth *Meg*) and I come to gather thrift, but can light on nothing but thistles, and therefore I will get my waies home as fast as I can.

In doing so you shall doe well (quoth *Gillian*) but I mean to get some Harts ease ere I goe away:

Nay *Gillian* (quoth she) I am sure I shall find thrift as soone as you shall find Harts-ease, but I promise you I am out of hope to find any to day.

I pray you get you gone then (quoth she).

What would you so faine be rid of my company (quoth *Meg*)? for that word I meane not to be gone yet: Ifaith *Gill* I smell a rat. (pp. 199–200)

In the account of Thomas Cole's murder, dialogue is used to heighten tension, particularly the brief exchange between Thomas and the hostess when he decides to make out his will:

Doubt not, Master *Cole*, you are like enough by the course of nature to liue many yeeres.

God knowes (quoth he) I neuer found my heart so heauy before. (p. 323)

Deloney structures his fiction in scenes, often using each chapter as a separate narrative unit.[24] Individually each scene is vivid, but often the end result is fragmentary, particularly in the two parts of *The Gentle Craft* and much of *Jack of Newbury*. Deloney lacks the sophisticated sense of structure present in the Renaissance romance, and even in *Thomas of Reading* he interposes tales rather than developing anything that could accurately be called a plot. The diffuse structure of the fiction may also be attributed to the influence of the jest-book; Deloney 'stages' each chapter as an entertainment. He includes songs and ballads (he wrote a number of broadside ballads before he turned to fiction), which enhances the reader's sense of an improvisatory structure, a spontaneous occurrence of events which are sometimes connected in a very tenuous fashion.

This variety was appreciated by his readers: the first part of *The Gentle Craft* promises 'many matters of delight, very pleasant to be read' (title-page). *Thomas of Reading*, Deloney's most unified work of fiction, was less popular than *The Gentle Craft*, judging by the number of editions which appeared in the

---

[24] See Lawlis, *Apology*, p. 38.

seventeenth century. Despite his enormous popularity, Deloney had a surprisingly small influence on the fiction written during the century after his death, although the audience of apprentices and tradesmen was growing. They still devoured chivalric romances just as avidly as Deloney's new fiction, and the most interesting and original fiction of the seventeenth century owed nothing at all to Deloney's attempt to shape a new form.

Chapter 9

The Nature of Seventeenth-Century Fiction

The fiction of the seventeenth century is, in comparison with the works discussed in the preceding chapters, relatively uncharted. No very dramatic change occurred immediately after 1600— imitations of the *Arcadia* were the norm for fashionable romance, while the lower ranks of the reading public had a continuing supply of translations and redactions of chivalric romances, and frequent editions of Thomas Deloney's works. However, the amount of prose fiction published for all levels of the reading public increased steadily year by year, and quite a large number of new forms eventually developed.

I. Audience

H. S. Bennett has pointed to 'a growing demand for books' during the first forty years of the seventeenth century, covering a notable 'range of interests'.[1] The growth of literacy, which began in the sixteenth century, continued unabated, and the different types of prose fiction available provide evidence for the varied nature of the reading public.[2] Chapbook fiction, either in the form of redactions or of original works such as Richard Johnson's *The Pleasant Conceits of Old Hobson the merry Londoner* (1607), was aimed at the very poorest readers.[3] The chivalric romances, which have been discussed in relation to Deloney (see above, Chapter 8), were aimed at artisans, merchants, tradesmen, apprentices—people who could afford to pay a shilling or more for a book. At a level above these works we find the sophisticated

[1] H. S. Bennett, *English Books and Readers 1603 to 1640* (Cambridge, 1970), pp. 1 and 2.
[2] Ibid., Chap. 6.
[3] For an extensive study of the chapbook audience, see Margaret Spufford, *Small Books and Pleasant Histories: Popular Fiction and Its Readership in Seventeenth-Century England* (London, 1981), which concentrates on the mid- to late seventeenth century, and see the discussion in Chap. 15 below.

romances of Greene and Lodge, and then the still more expensive folios such as the *Arcadia*. The different audiences are clearly reflected in book prices: during the early years of the century, a bound copy of the *Arcadia* cost nine shillings, *Tom a Lincolne* cost sixpence, while a chapbook cost twopence.[4]

The female reading public also continued to grow during the seventeenth century, and writers maintained the practice of addressing women readers directly, as Lyly did in *Euphues*. Robert Baron's *Erotopagaion* (1647) has an address to 'the ladies' in imitation of Lyly, and Sir George Mackenzie's *Aretina* (1660) has a preface directed 'To All the Ladies of this Nation'. However, if the romance was written for women, in England it was written by men, with only a few notable exceptions. Men regarded the romance very seriously—Sir George Mackenzie asks 'who should blush to trace in these paths, which the Famous Sidney, Scuderie, Barkley, and Broghill hath beaten for them . . .'.[5] Roger Boyle discovered during his exile in France that a knowledge of romances was essential for a man of fashion:

Making some Residence in France, I assotiated my selfe with Persons of my owne Age, where I soone found, that he who was Ignorant of the Romances of those Times, was as fitt an Object for Wonder, as a Phylosopher would be, who had never heard of Aristotle . . .[6]

The respect for the romance form was inspired by the intense admiration (examined at length in the following chapter) for Sidney and his *Arcadia*. Sir William Alexander may stand as a representative for numerous adulatory comments made throughout the century:

The *Arcadia* of S.P. *Sidney* (either being considered in the whole or in several Lineaments) is the most excellent Work that, in my Judgement, hath been written in any Language that I understand, affording many exquisite Types of Perfection for both the Sexes . . .[7]

---

[4] See Frances R. Johnson, 'Notes on English Retail Book Prices 1550–1640', *The Library*, V. 2 (1950), 104 and 110, and Bennett, p. 228.

[5] Sir George Mackenzie, *Aretina* (1660), p. 6.

[6] Roger Boyle, *Parthenissa* (Part One, 1655), A[v].

[7] William Alexander, *Anacrisis* (1634?), *Critical Essays of the Seventeenth Century*, ed. J. E. Spingarn (Oxford, 1957), Vol. 1, p. 187.

II. Political and Social Influences

The romance in particular is often assumed to be a highly stylized form of fiction, unresponsive to events taking place in the 'real world'. But in fact, some forms of romance in the seventeenth century have a much closer relationship with the social and political turmoil of the period than many modern critics have realized. The Renaissance romance at times has a *roman à clef* element: Sidney may appear in the *Arcadia* as Philisides, for example. This element becomes much more important in some later Sidneian romances, especially Lady Mary Wroth's *Urania* (1621, discussed in detail in the following chapter).

But one particular form of romance established in the seventeenth century was directly concerned with the political events and arguments of the day: the hybrid form which I have designated 'political/allegorical romance'. By portraying the events of the Civil War in romance guise, complete with the allegorical depiction of historical figures such as King Charles and Cromwell, this form of romance becomes a serious, imaginative exploration of pressing dilemmas. Sidney's example was seen, influentially, by Fulke Greville as being wholly serious: 'in all these creatures of his making, his intent, and scope was, to turn the barren Philosophy precepts into pregnant Images of life.'[8] After John Barclay's *Argenis* (1621), the romance was frequently seen as a vehicle for the portrayal of contemporary thought about numerous subjects:

> *Romances* are not always farc'd with *Love-stories* and toyes, though those are intertexted for delight, and that things *Oeconomical, Ethical, Physical, Metaphysical, Philosophical, Political,* and *Theological* as well as *Amatory,* may be, not unaptly, nor unfitly exhibited.[9]

King James's interest in *Argenis* was indicative of the new respect gained by romance; Nahum Tate introduced his translation of Heliodorus with the aside: 'The Philosophy and Politicks deliver'd in the Romance of *Barclay* have render'd it worthy the perusal of the greatest Statesmen . . .'.[10] Previously, romance had relied for its justification on the notion that it

---

[8] Fulke Greville, *The Life of the Renowned Sir Philip Sidney* (1652), ed. N. Smith (Oxford, 1907), p. 15.

[9] *Eliana* (1661), A3ᵛ.

[10] Heliodorus, *The Triumphs of Love and Constancy*, trans. Nahum Tate (1687), A3.

presented images of virtue and vice to be, respectively, imitated and abhorred—but it shared this formula even with cony-catching pamphlets. This formula continued to be used in the seventeenth century ('the true ground and scope of these Kind of Writings . . . is to depaint vertue and vice in their natural and genuine colours'[11]), but a much more impressive justification was now available.

Picaresque fiction questions society, and may have appealed to the apprentices who are seen cheating their masters in *The English Rogue*. But the new seriousness of romance encountered, in the Civil War, an extremely difficult social and political situation to deal with. Cowley abandoned his poem on the Civil War in 1643, even before the death of Charles seemed a possibility. He suppressed it, not wanting to 'rip up old wounds', and it was (except for a small portion published in 1679) thought to have been destroyed until very recently.[12] But the romance was able to deal with the Civil War, by absorbing it into fiction. It most certainly did not turn its back on the tumult, but came to terms with the most important political event in England during the century.

III. Form and Change

Much of the popular fiction seems to indicate that its authors were quite unconcerned with form, and the picaresque novel actually rejoices in its unconstrained, episodic approach to narrative. But critics who see the whole of seventeenth-century fiction as formless ignore one of the most ambitious attempts to provide a structure for a long prose narrative: the heroic romance. Diana Spearing, in her analysis of the eighteenth-century novel, dismisses the heroic romance as 'episodic',[13] but the epic form of the heroic romance (outlined at length in Chapter 12, below) indicates how both theory and practice aimed at careful control over narrative form.

The quest for a structure which embraces variety as well as unity tends to produce romances of exceptional length. The modern reader may be more appreciative of the simpler structure

---

[11] *Eliana*, A3^v.

[12] Abraham Cowley, *The Civil War*, ed. Allan Pritchard (Toronto, 1973), p. 4.

[13] Diana Spearman, *The Novel and Society* (London, 1966), p. 106.

used by Sidney for the *Old Arcadia*; but with the emergence of the Restoration novel, the seventeenth century produced a more concise form, and one which has a dramatic structure: the plot of a play, rather than an epic, retrospective narration. In the preface to his *Incognita* (1692), Congreve states that his aim was to 'imitate Dramatick Writing . . . in the Design, Contexture and Result of the Plot'.[14]

The fiction of the period is far from being stagnant, for its authors constantly explored new forms. The eclectic approach to fiction produced some ungainly experiments, but they testify to writers' interest in searching for an effective structure for a prose narrative.

IV. Translation

This sense of experiment is also evident when one considers the foreign influences on seventeenth-century fiction. During the century, English readers were quickly introduced to the prose fiction of the continent: the Spanish novella and picaresque novel; the French heroic romance and anti-romance. But while numerous translations (and original works) were available, English taste often demanded changes in foreign fiction before it was accepted. A native taste and tradition balanced the foreign influence—as we shall see when picaresque fiction is examined.

Of the 450 new works published in England during the century, 213 were translations. The most striking fact is the complete domination of French authors: 164 were translations from French, only 22 from Spanish and 13 from Italian. This represents a dramatic change from the previous century, when the bulk of translations had been from Italian.[15] One should not jump to the conclusion that the French taste of Queen Henrietta Maria and her followers was solely responsible for this. While they may have stimulated fashionable interest in the French romance, French translations were already dominant before Charles married Henrietta Maria. The Civil War drove a number of royalists to France, and one can see from Boyle's

---

[14] William Congreve, *Incognita*, ed. A. Norman Jeffares (London, 1966), p. 33.
[15] See E. A. Baker, *The History of the English Novel* (1936, rpt. New York, 1963), Vol. 2, Chap. 2.

remark quoted above (p. 111) that this increased the fashionable courtier's interest in romance.

However, there is also a literary explanation: Spain and France produced the most important new forms of fiction during the century. Translations from both these languages indicate that the reading public was eager to keep up with the new developments: the new genres of Spanish picaresque, heroic romance, and, later in the century, the French *nouvelle*.

The dominance of French translations was noticed throughout the century:

Whereas our Nation hath been so profusely entertain'd, and perhaps by this time in a manner Satiated by the fluency and luxuriance of the French Gallantry; it will not be amiss to give a taste of the Spanish Reserve and Gravity.[16]

The fashion for all things French reached its peak after the Restoration: 'Booksellers are grown men of mode too, they scorn any thing of this Kind below an *Originally in F——* in the Title Page, with a *Made English*.'[17] These claims should not blind us to the equally large amount of original fiction written at the time. A close examination of the translations indicates that often quite substantial changes were made by translators, at times only for commercial reasons, but frequently in order to naturalize a foreign work.

For example, *A Tragi-Comical History of Our Times Under the Borrowed Names of Lisander and Calista* (1627), translated from the French of Vital D'Audiguier, alters the conclusion of the romance to what has been described as a 'tidy English conclusion'.[18] A translation of Scarron's *Roman Comique* appeared in 1676, as *Scarron's Comical Romance*, in which French names and locations have been carefully changed to English ones. Changes did not always occur solely for artistic reasons. Leonard Digges, in his translation of Gonzalo de Céspedes y Meneses' *Gerardo the Unfortunate Spaniard* (1622), leaves out 'One by-discourse . . . as superstitiously smelling of Papisticall Miracles'.[19] Dale Randall,

---

[16] Perez de Montalvan, *The Illustrious Shepherdess* (1655), B4.

[17] *Evagoras*, by L. L. (1677), A3ᵛ.

[18] See F. W. Vogler, *Vital D'Audiguier and the Early Seventeenth Century French Novel* (Chapel Hill, Nth. Carolina, 1964), p. 118.

[19] Dale B. J. Randall, *The Golden Tapestry: a Critical Survey of Non Chivalric Spanish Fiction in English Translation 1543–1657* (Durham, Nth. Carolina, 1963), p. 33.

in his excellent study of translations of non-chivalric Spanish fiction until 1657, notes the ' "adapting to the English taste" ' which went on in, for example, the translation of Lope de Vega's *Pilgrim of Casteele* (1621).[20] Translation and imitation enriched English prose fiction throughout the century, but neither activity was unthinkingly slavish.

V. Style

Scholars studying the prose styles of the seventeenth century have tended to ignore fiction. Any close study of changing style in fiction complicates the received view of its concerns, and its relationship with the style of non-fictional prose. Some disagreement still surrounds the question of changing prose styles during the century: Morris Croll's analysis of the anti-Ciceronian movement behind two major styles of the century, the Lipsian *style coupé* and the loose, meditative style,[21] has been challenged by R. F. Jones as being too far-reaching.[22] Jones emphasizes the 'attacks of science upon rhetorical prose'.[23]

Less controversy has arisen over the importance of a new plain style in the second half of the century.[24] George Williamson states that 'the tendency both in poetry and in prose during the seventeenth century was towards the conversational norm', and that the prose of the later part of the century 'feels and manifests the pressure of the social scene'.[25] Fiction was certainly influenced by these stylistic changes, but it also had its own stylistic tradition and development.

According to Ian Watt,

The previous [i.e. pre-eighteenth-century] stylistic tradition for fiction was not primarily concerned with the correspondence of words to things, but rather with the extrinsic beauties which could be bestowed upon description and action by the use of rhetoric.[26]

[20] Ibid., p. 34, see pp. 102–12.
[21] Morris W. Croll, 'The Baroque Style in Prose', in *Seventeenth Century Prose: Modern Essays in Criticism*, ed. Stanley Fish (New York, 1971), p. 48.
[22] R. F. Jones, 'Science and Language in England of the Mid Seventeenth Century', in Fish, *Seventeenth Century Prose*, pp. 94–107.
[23] 'Science and English Prose Style', in Fish, p. 77.
[24] See Robert Adolph, *The Rise of Modern Prose Style* (Cambridge, Mass., 1978), Chaps. 4 and 5, and James Sutherland, 'Restoration Prose', in *Stuart and Georgian Moments*, ed. Earl Miner (Berkeley, 1975), pp. 109–26.
[25] George Williamson, *The Senecan Amble* (London, 1951), p. 341.
[26] Ian Watt, *The Rise of the Novel* (London, 1963), p. 28.

This statement may apply to dominant styles in Elizabethan fiction: to euphuism and to Sidney's style. During the seventeenth century, however, a new style appeared in numerous romances, which can be seen to have many of the aspects of the 'loose' anti-Ciceronian style described by Croll, and which could, for convenience, be called a plainer style in prose fiction.

This style is particularly prevalent in the political/allegorical romance, but it can be found in many other types of romance too. Some idea of the changes may be indicated by a comparison with Sidney. Here is a passage from the *New Arcadia*:

But (said he) when they were with swordes in handes, not turning backs one to the other (for there they knew was no place of defence) but making that a preservation in not hoping to be preserved, and now acknowledging themselves subject to death, meaning onely to do honour to their princely birth, they flew amongst them all (for all were enimies) & had quickly either with flight or death, left none upon the scaffolde to annoy them. Wherein *Pyrocles* (the excellent *Pyrocles*) did such wonders beyond beliefe, as was hable to leade *Musidorus* to courage, though he had bene borne a coward. But indeed, just rage & desperate vertue did such effects, that the popular sorte of the beholders began to be almost superstitiously amazed, as at effectes beyond mortall power. But the King with angry threatnings from-out a window (where he was not ashamed, the worlde should behold him a beholder) commaunded his garde, and the rest of his souldiers to hasten their death. But many of them lost their bodies to loose their soules, when the Princes grew almost so weary, as they were ready to be conquered with conquering.[27]

I have intentionally chosen a relatively unadorned passage, but some of Sidney's characteristic stylistic features are apparent. This is a narrative passage which avoids metaphor; Sidney concentrates on balance and antithesis of words and thoughts, together with the repetition of key words. One immediately notices the repetition: 'preservation/preserved', 'beholde/beholder', 'conquered/conquering'. This is, strictly speaking, a use of the figure known as polyptoton—the repetition of words with identical roots, but changed endings (and of course meanings). Sidney adds antithesis: 'birth/death' (in the first sentence), 'courage/coward' (in the second). Reinforcing these devices is a more complex figure, still emphasizing the antithesis, but also using polyptoton: 'lost their bodies to loose their soules'.

These figures relate directly to the scene described: a paradoxical conflict, where two battle against a multitude; their modesty (in part the modesty of the speaker—Musidorus—who naturally gives the credit, with another use of repetition, to '*Pyrocles* (the excellent *Pyrocles*)') is belied by their victory. Instead of metaphor, we have what may be called subdued simile—the beholders amazed 'as at effectes beyond mortall power', the princes so weary 'as they were ready to be conquered with conquering'. The passage skilfully reflects this antithesis as it moves between alternating long and short sentences. As always, Sidney's style is intricate but carefully controlled; ornate, but fully in accord with its subject. A good comparison, an example of the plainer style in romance, is provided by Roger Boyle's *Parthenissa* (Part I, 1651):

This relation (my deere *Artabanes*, continued *Artavasdes*) gave me as much Horror as Amazement, and while I was enquiring what might be the cause that *Palisdes* was not come, one of my Scouts came galloping in and told me, he discover'd a body of about 500. Horse, not eight furlongs off, that came on a round trott almost the same way we had marched. This Troope we easily imagined was *Palisdes*, whom I resolved to Charge, But first of all dispatch'd away an Expresse to my Father to acquaint him with what I had learn'd, and to conjure him to send out as many Horse as possibly he could spare under some good commander, but not lead them himselfe, lest the Towne might be betrayed in his absence. *Evaxes* had assur'd me thereupon, that *Artaxata* would be lost if he were once out of the Walls, for *Celindus* had many Partisans there that waited onely such an opportunity to betray it. This being done; I began to order my Troope which consisted of 150. but of so cleere Valours and resolutions, that those vertues supply'd the defects of their Numbers.[28]

Boyle's style is clear and restrained; he avoids Sidney's use of figures—we have only the simple antithesis 'as much Horror as Amazement'. Boyle's periods are not balanced, but move forward with the narrative; we move from two sentences of equal (and considerable) length, to two sentences half that length, as Artavasdes proceeds. The narrative is easy to assimilate, and. Boyle signposts its progression: 'This being done'. A military exactness is apparent, and an attention to detail. Sidney focuses

[28] Roger Boyle, *Parthenissa* (1654), Part I, Bk. 2, p. 46.

on the two desperate princes and, to signify their enemies, on the cowardly King watching from a window. Boyle's perspective remains that of Artavasdes as he beheld the scene; the troops are carefully numbered.

However, this is only one style found in the fiction of the period. Many romances ignore the plain style, and either continue to imitate Sidney, or develop an ornate style of their own (see Chapter 10). The ornate style survived into the 1660s, existing alongside the new plain romance style; its persistence cautions the scholar against any over-simplification of changes in prose style during the period, at least as far as fiction is concerned.

Also important was the development of a style for picaresque fiction. The picaresque style borrows some of its vigour from Nashe and the Elizabethan pamphleteers, but is also moving towards the more subdued style of Defoe. The openings of *The Unfortunate Traveller* (1591), *The English Rogue* (1665), and *Robinson Crusoe* (1719) illustrate this:

About that time that the terror of the world and feauer quartane of the French, *Henrie* the eight (the onely true subiect of Chronicles), aduanced his standard against the two hundred and fifty towers of *Turney* and *Turwin*, and had the Emperour and all the nobilitie of *Flanders, Holand, & Brabant* as mercenerie attendants on his ful-sayld fortune, I, *Iacke Wilton*, (A gentleman at least,) was a certain kind of an appendix or page, belonging or appertaining in or vnto the confines of the English court; where what my credit was, a number of my creditors that I cosned can testifie: *Coelum petimus stultitia*, which of vs al is not a sinner?[29]

After a long and strict inquisition after my fathers Pedegree, I could not finde any of his Ancestors bearing a *Coat*; surely length of time had *worn* it out. But if the *Gentlemen Craft* will any ways ennoble his Family, I believe I could deduce several of his Name, Professors of that *lasting Art*, even from *Crispin*. My Fathers Father had by his continual labour in Husbandry, arriv'd to the height of a Farmer, then the head of his kindred: standing upon one of his own Mole-Hills, Ambition so swell'd him, that he swore by his Plow-share that his eldest Son (my Father) should be a *Scholliard* . . .[30]

I was born in the Year 1632, in the City of *York*, of a good Family, tho'

---

[29] *The Works of Thomas Nashe*, ed. R. B. McKerrow, rev. F. P. Wilson (Oxford, 1958), Vol. 2, p. 209.
[30] Richard Head, *The English Rogue* (1665), pp. 1–2.

not of that Country, my Father being a Foreigner of *Bremen*, who settled
first at *Hull*: He got a good Estate by Merchandise, and leaving off his
Trade, lived afterward at *York*, from whence he married my Mother,
whose Relations were named *Robinson*, a very good Family in that
Country, and from whom I was called *Robinson Kreutznaer*, but by the
usual Corruption of Words in *England*, we are now called, nay we call
our selves, and write our name *Crusoe*, and so my Companions always
call'd me.[31]

These three passages indicate a more uniform movement of
style in picaresque fiction than in the romance. Nashe's single,
sprawling sentence reflects the exuberance of the speaker, Jack
Wilton; its audacious, perhaps even raucous, alliteration reflects
the speaker's irrepressible energy. The tone changes rapidly—
the narrator is in a moment brash ('the onely true subiect of
Chronicles'), boastful ('A Gentleman at least'), and even
moralistic, if in a clichéd fashion ('which of vs al is not a sinner?').

Richard Head still reflects some of Nashe's exuberance in his
fondness for puns ('worn it out/*lasting Art*'), and in his humorous
tone. Parts of *The English Rogue* are very reminiscent of Nashe in
style. Head inherits Nashe's delight in a detail which may be
pushed to a point of comic, vivid exaggeration, as in Meriton's
father standing 'swell'd' with ambition on a mole-hill, swearing
by his plough-share. But Nashe's expanding sentence has been
subdued, and his populated world ('all the nobilitie of *Flanders*,
Holand & Brabant') thinned.

Defoe's style avoids figures, and reflects the narrator's assured
stance. Direct statement ('I was born in the Year 1632') replaces
the circumlocutory speculation of Head and Nashe. Defoe
ensures that each clause is firmly and visibly linked to its
predecessor ('from whence', 'from whom', 'and so').

In the second half of the century, four major styles in fiction
coexisted: the plain and the ornate romance styles; the picaresque style; and, finally, the Restoration novel style, which is closer
to the polished, epigrammatic style of Restoration comedy
(making much use of urbane dialogue, and often of a witty, self-
conscious narrator). No single style dominated, at least until the
1680s (when the Restoration novel was in the ascendancy), and
so fiction both embraced the major changes in prose style during

[31] Daniel Defoe, *Robinson Crusoe*, ed. J. D. Crowley (Oxford, 1972), p. 3.

the century, and also carried its own stylistic tradition, some elements of which ran counter to the general movement of prose style.

VI. Characters

While John Hoskyns maintained that Sidney was influenced by Theophrastus in the creation of his characters,[32] the Character as a literary form first appeared in England in 1608, when Joseph Hall published his *Characters of Vertues and Vices*. Theophrastus had been edited by Isaac Casaubon only a few years earlier, in 1592, but it was Hall's collection which stimulated the eager interest in Character collections during the early seventeenth century. The extremely popular collection by Sir Thomas Overbury first appeared in 1614, but the initial twenty-two characters were expanded by others (notably John Webster) until there were eighty-three in the 1622 edition.[33]

Benjamin Boyce has shown that the Character, while a distinct literary genre, was closely connected to both the Essay and the Epigram in its early growth.[34] Boyce sees little interaction between the Character and prose fiction, pointing out that the Character is 'a highly artificial form', and that it is 'a literary form that did not naturally develop in the art of story-telling'.[35] Certainly the Character is a static set-piece, building up what is usually a type-figure—a Constable, a grave Divine, an idle gallant, a forward man, to take some examples from John Earle's *Micro-Cosmographie* (1628)—through small details of appearance, habit, or attitude. Narrative is of little concern to the Character-writer, but one might well ask whether the Character made any substantial contribution to characterization in prose fiction.

Boyce points out that the Character itself has a number of limitations as a form, and that after 1614 only two lines of development seemed possible: writers could produce variations on the obvious subjects already exploited, or they could turn to more unusual subjects.[36] The Character proper did make an

---

[32] John Hoskyns, *Directions for Speech and Style*, ed. H. H. Hudson (Princeton, 1935), p. 42, and see John Buxton, 'Sidney and Theophrastus', *ELR* 2 (1972), 79–82.

[33] See Benjamin Boyce, *The Theophrastan Character in England to 1642* (1947, rpt. London, 1967), p. 136.

[34] Ibid., pp. 93–111 and Chap. 7.

[35] Ibid., pp. 19 and 88.   [36] Ibid., pp. 165–6.

appearance in prose fiction in *The English Rogue* (see below, Chap. 13, Sec. VI). Richard Head stole a good deal of his material, including a Character of a bottle of canary wine—the idea of writing Characters of numerous inanimate objects was fully exploited in *A Strange Metamorphosis of Man* (1634), following some hints in Donald Lupton's *London and the Country Carbonadoed* (1632).[37]

The Character tends to produce a static, external view of a representative type rather than an individual. Renaissance romances, notably Sidney's, owe something to the general notion of type-characters. Sidney's names often represent a character's qualities—Euarchus, for example, epitomizing good rule. In almost every mode of Elizabethan fiction characters fall into one of two categories: either they remain exemplars of a single quality, or like Jack Wilton they lose virtually all consistency and are animated only by their creator's style. Exceptions may be found, of course, most notably in Gascoigne's *Master F.J.* But these two strains of characterization run right through to the eighteenth-century novel, to Fielding's type-characters who keep decorum, and Defoe's Moll Flanders, whose lack of 'consistency' has troubled critics as much as Jack Wilton's.

Most areas of seventeenth-century fiction show little change in their approach to characterization as compared with Elizabethan fiction. The one area where the Character might have had at least an indirect influence is the use of the portrait in the French heroic romance and its English imitations (see below, Chap. 12, Sec. VI). These often quite complex set-pieces of character description do go some way towards describing individuals rather than types. The portrait is only a distant cousin of the Character, but the general interest in Character-writing in the seventeenth century may have encouraged the interest in portraits.

[37] Ibid., pp. 292–4.

Chapter 10

Sidney and the First Generation of Seventeenth-Century Fiction

I. The *Arcadia* and Its Imitators

With the absence of skilled writers like Greene and Lodge, the romance did not have a very clear sense of direction in the early years of the seventeenth century. The most overwhelming influence on the romance at this time was Sidney's *Arcadia*, which was, as John Buxton points out, 'the best-loved book in the English language' until 1745.[1] The composite 1593 version of the *Arcadia* went through nine editions between 1605 and 1638, and was the model for numerous writers. Its influence was not confined to England: Jean Baudoin's French translation appeared in 1624; Giovanni Francesco Biondi translated Sidney into Italian, and three of his own romances, influenced by Sidney, appeared in English translations: *Eromena* (1632), *Donzella Desterrada* (1635), and *Coralbo* (1655). Biondi, or at least his translator, utilizes a very tortured style, presumably in an attempt to mimic Sidney, although one immediately agrees with an honest couplet prefixed to *Eromena*: 'If Language thou expects, then pore not here/But *Sidney* read, whose Pen ne're yet found peere' (b).

The 1593 version of the *Arcadia* left a hiatus between the 1590 *New Arcadia* which ends in mid-sentence in Book Three, and the remaining books of the *Old Arcadia*, which were simply added on to complete the romance. The hiatus is readily acknowledged:

[1] John Buxton, *Elizabethan Taste* (London, 1963), p. 246. For Sidney's influence on the drama see Hardin Craig, 'Motivation in Shakespeare's Choice of Materials', *Shakespeare Survey*, 4 (1951), 32–3; Irving Ribner, 'Sidney's *Arcadia* and the Structure of *King Lear*', *Studia Neophilologica*, 24 (1952), 63–8; Kenneth Muir, ed., *King Lear* (London, 1952), pp. xxxvii–xlii; R. W. Dent, *John Webster's Borrowing* (Berkeley, 1960); O. Bruckl, 'Sir Philip Sidney's *Arcadia* as a Source for John Webster's *The Duchess of Malfi*', *English Studies in Africa*, 8 (1965), 31–55; Michael Cameron Andrews, 'Sidney's *Arcadia* on the English Stage', (unpublished Ph.D. dissertation, Duke University, 1966); Felicia Rota, *L'Arcadia di Sidney e il teatro con un testo inedito* (Bari, 1966).

How this combate ended, how the Ladies by the comming of the discovered forces were delivered, and restored to *Basilius*, and how *Dorus* againe returned to his old master *Dametas*, is altogether unknowne. What afterward chaunced, out of the Authors own writings and conceits hath bene supplied, as foloweth. (ii. 218)[2]

This challenge was met by Sir William Alexander, whose 'supplement' was first added to the 1621 edition of the *Arcadia*, although it had been written a few years earlier.[3] The supplement was a success, and appeared in all succeeding editions. Alexander competently brings the fight between Zelmane and Anaxius to an end, concludes the captivity episode with the appearance of Musidorus and a troop of knights, and effectively places Musidorus back in Dametas' service. Although the style may be a 'poor imitation of Sidney's', it does not jar.[4] A. G. D. Wiles praises Alexander's success in handling 'plot and characters';[5] in the space of thirty pages Alexander has little scope for development, but he remains true to Sidney's purpose.

A tribute to Sidney is the introduction of Philisides as the Knight of the Sheep, who dies after being wounded, like Sidney, in the thigh: 'Hee died as joyfully as he left them sorrowful, who had knowne him a mirror of courage and courtesie; of learning and armes; so that it seemed that Mars had begotten him upon one of the Muses' (1638 edn., p. 338). Wiles further praises Alexander for identifying the Knight of the Sheep (whose *impresa* is described by Sidney, i. 462) as Philisides;[6] the similar supplement provided by James Johnstoun identifies the Knight as Plangus (bb3ᵛ).[7] However, a marginal comment found in the

---

[2] References are to Albert Feuillerat, ed., *The Prose Works of Sir Philip Sidney* (Cambridge, 1912).

[3] See A. G. D. Wiles, 'The Date of Publication and Composition of Sir William Alexander's Supplement to Sidney's "Arcadia"', *Publications of the Bibliographical Society of America*, 50 (1956), 387–92; Alison Mitchell and Katherine Foster suggest that the supplement was first printed some time between 1616 and 1618, see their 'Sir William Alexander's Supplement to Book III of Sidney's *Arcadia*', *The Library*, 24, series 5 (1969), 235. The supplement can be most conveniently consulted in Maurice Evans's edition of the *Arcadia* (Harmondsworth, 1977), which is not, however, a very reliable text.

[4] A. G. D. Wiles, 'Sir William Alexander's Continuation of the Revised Version of Sidney's *Arcadia*', *Studies in Scottish Literature*, 3 (1966), 223.

[5] Ibid., p. 229.   [6] Ibid., p. 227.

[7] References are to *A supplement to the third Booke of Arcadia* by James Johnstoun in the 1638 edition of *Arcadia* (sigs. aa–bb4), signed dedication and running title, but no separate title-page.

Cambridge University Library copy of the 1621 *Arcadia* observes, when Sidney first introduces the Knight of the Sheep, that 'The Preference is here plainly given to the Knight of the sheep, from whence, if there were no other Reason we may be very sure the Author does not mean *Himself*, but rather his particular friend *Sr Fulke Greville*, to whom he here makes a Handsome Compliment' (p. 296). This is pure speculation; but Sidney's description of the Knight of the Pole (the companion of the Knight of the Sheep) contains evidence for *his* identification as Philisides. The Knight of the Pole's 'device was the very Pole itselfe, about which many starres stirring but the place itselfe lefte void. The word was, *The best place yet reserved*' (i. 462). One might speculate that the space is reserved for Philisides' '*Star*' (see i. 285). Even if one admires Alexander's identification, his depiction of Philisides as having been in love with Philoclea is unfortunate, rather than effective; he fails to associate Philoclea with Philisides' star, so that we appear to have an unfaithful Sidney before us. However, Alexander's presentation of Philisides' death certainly stands as a touching tribute to his admired literary master.

Johnstoun's supplement appeared in the 1638 edition, although its dedication to King James indicates a much earlier date of composition. Again tribute is paid to Sidney, who appears this time in the guise of the Knight of the Star, dying when he refuses to have his wounded leg amputated (bb). Johnstoun provides a comic account of Musidorus' return to Dametas. He is accused of cowardice by Mopsa and Pamela, and returns to favour by curing Dametas and Miso after they have eaten hemlock in mistake for parsnips. Johnstoun's bridging passage does close the gap between the *New Arcadia* and the *Old Arcadia*, but it is not quite as convincing as Alexander's, although Wiles praises its style.[8] These supplements indicate the admiration and attention bestowed on the *Arcadia*; the small rent in the seam of the century's best-loved book was, if not invisibly mended, at least carefully sewn together.

If the unfinished sentence at the end of the *New Arcadia* implicitly invited those who desired to imitate Sidney to join in the

<hr>

[8] Wiles, 'Continuation', p. 114.

expansion of his romance, the *Arcadia*'s concluding sentence is quite explicit:

> But the solemnities of these marriages, with the *Arcadian* pastoralles, full of many comicall adventures, hapning to those rurall lovers; the straunge stories of *Artaxia* and *Plexirtus*, *Erona* and *Plangus*; *Helene* and *Amphialus*, with the wonderfull chaunces that befell them: The shepheardish loves of *Menalcas* with *Kalodulus* daughter; the poore hopes of the poore *Philisides* in the pursuite of his affections; the strange continuance of *Klaius* and *Strephons* desire; Lastly the sonne of *Pyrocles*, named *Pyrophilus*, and *Melidora*, the faire daughter of *Pamela* by *Musidorus*, who even at their birth entred into admirable fortunes; may awake some other spirite to exercise his penne in that, wherewith mine is already dulled. (ii. 206–7)

Three writers took up the challenge: Gervase Markham, Richard Beling, and Anne Weamys. As over fifty years separate the work of Markham from that of Weamys, these two substantial continuations provide an interesting contrast: indicative of changes in the response to Sidney, and to the romance in general.

Richard Beling's *Sixth Book To the Countesse of Pembrokes Arcadia* first appeared at the end of the 1628 edition. It is a modest thirty-four folio pages in length, but Beling responds to a number of possibilities left open by Sidney. Beling's interest lies with the first three pairs of lovers mentioned by Sidney: Artaxia and Plexirtus, Erona and Plangus, and Helen and Amphialus. After the marriages of Pamela, Musidorus, Philoclea and Pyrocles are celebrated, we hear how Amphialus left Helen's care after his wounds were cured. But his feelings begin to change when he believes that she is dead; eventually they meet and are married. Within this account, Beling completes the tragic story of Plangus and Erona. Although Plangus defeats Plexirtus, Erona does not realize this, and so drinks poison. Plangus, when he finds her, does the same. Plexirtus hangs himself, while Artaxia dies of remorse.

Beling is able to provide an appropriate happy ending (we are told that, one year after their marriage, Helen and Amphialus produced a son, who bears the unfortunate portmanteau name of Haleamphilus), while also exploiting the tragic potential of Plangus and Erona. All three sequels revive Amphialus and marry him to Helen. Beling's continuation is neat and efficient, but still strikes the reader as being, like the supplements of

Alexander and Johnstoun, a not particularly original act of homage, admirable more as an indication of the esteem in which the *Arcadia* was held than as an independent romance.

Very different is Gervase Markham's *English Arcadia*: a romance in the style of Sidney, which is a continuation of the *Arcadia* but in a more individual, imaginative manner than the works discussed so far. *The English Arcadia* appeared in two parts, in 1607 and 1613. Markham's statement in the preface to Part One, that he retained the romance 'any time this half-score yeares from . . . publication' (I. A2), indicates an earlier date of composition, perhaps 1597.[9]

Once again, we hear of Amphialus' marriage to Helen, after his miraculous recovery. But in Markham's romance a generation has passed. Amphialus has grown suspicious of Helen's constancy; at the beginning of the romance she is spared, but only for a brief respite, from being put to sea in an open boat, a punishment ordained in Amphialus' absence. As in Sidney's *Arcadia*, we see a kingdom in disorder, owing to the ruler's withdrawal (in this case, Amphialus has left the kingdom completely). This situation is still unresolved when the romance ends. It grows into a work which, if finished, would have been as large and complex as the *Arcadia* itself.

Walter Davis has described the action of *The English Arcadia* as 'curiously literary'.[10] Markham opens his romance in imitation of the *Arcadia*, with the two shepherds, Credulo and Corino, mourning the loss of Cynthia, just as Strephon and Claius mourn for Urania:

At such time as the flowers appearing vpon the earth, had summoned the ayrie quiristers to entertaine the first Embassadors of the Spring, and that Nature (deliuered from the barraine wombe of Winter) had shewed herselfe lyuelie as the morning, faire as the nightes Gouernesse, pure as the Sunne, and as almighty as an armye of inuincible fortune: The vnhappy and forlorne Shepheard *Credulo* being come to the foot of the mountain *Tagetus*, from whose large distributed skirts, ranne an euen and wel leuiled plaine . . . (I. 1)

Certainly the *Arcadia* is always in our minds as an antecedent, but Markham's Tempe is not Sidney's Arcadia—it is a world with rather different symbolic qualities.

    [9] References are to Gervase Markham, *The English Arcadia* (1607) and *The Second and Last Part of the First Booke of the English Arcadia* (1613).
    [10] Walter R. Davis, *Idea and Act*, p. 72.

There are two buildings at the centre of Tempe. One is Diana's temple, the centre of the traditional 'inner pastoral circle' of pastoral romance.[11] The other, however, is the enchanted mansion of Mysantropos, an evil magician (II. 14). He may be contrasted with the wise and good Eugenio, who also has magical powers; but Eugenio stands outside Tempe. He sees all that occurs, but can only explain the events he sees and their significance to Pyrophilus. Mysantropos operates within Tempe itself—at its very heart, in fact. He stands at the centre of a vast illusion, through which Mellidora must pass in order to reach the captive Thirsis.

Mysantropos' valley is

bordered on each side with all manner of flowers, whom Winter neuer toucht, but flourished farre beyond the works of best industry; onely they were full of pollution when they were handled, and noysome to smell to when indiscretion had gathered them. (II. 21)

The fair exterior with a foul heart is a warning to those lured on by the fair form of Tempe, or even by love—for Mysantropos' favourite victims are lovers:

he holds in prison, with torments most vnspeakable, all that euer set their feet within his charmes; especially louers, whose howling lamentations he vowes to exceed all musick whatsoeuer. (II. 14)

Remembering the usual torments and lamentations of Arcadian lovers, one can see Mysantropos' mansion as a projection of their emotional tribulations, which are all too often self-induced. When Mellidora meets Mysantropos, she is overcome by his illusions. She has been warned about them more than once, but Markham implies that love and faith are unable to conquer guile. It is Diatassan (with the help of Elpyno's music) who destroys the illusion: an act motivated by his perverted desire for Mellidora, not by a pure love such as that of Thirsis (II. 25ᵛ–26ᵛ).

Markham questions a number of idealizations, and submits certain pastoral motifs to an ironic treatment. For example, when the two shepherds, Opicus and Mopsus, discuss the court and the country, Mopsus puts the traditional pastoral case against courts, warning Opicus to 'liue securelye in thy countrye habitation' (I. 59ᵛ). But Opicus then explains how his visit to the city and the

---

[11] Ibid., p. 57; see pp. 57–9.

court completely disproved the pastoral contrast: 'I beheld more
excellent obiects then I could imagine' (I. 60), and the city is
ruled by 'a God or man, or at least a moste Godly man' (ibid.).

More evils seem to lurk in 'innocent' Tempe than in Opicus'
city. Tempe is haunted by Mysantropos, and also by the
renegade Demagoras, who almost rapes Mellidora (I. 53). *The
English Arcadia* is more purely pastoral than Sidney's *Arcadia*; the
chivalric element is largely abandoned. In each part, an
elaborate hunt is held. In Part One, Mellidora, who has
outdistanced everyone else, is identified with the prey:

this absolutely worthy Princesse, her too much earnestnes to pursue her
sportes (being arrested by wearynes) made her now begin to distaste
sporte and not shee alone was wearie, but euen the poore hunted beast.
(I. 51–51ᵛ)

In the tiger hunt described in Part Two, Mellidora is indeed the
prize (whoever kills the tiger will gain Mellidora's hand), and the
victim of Diatassan's scheme. Mellidora recognizes the degradation to which she is subjected: 'what shall I be that day, more
then a Sommer-games prize' (II. 11ᵛ).

Markham emphasizes this dangerous side of his Arcadian
landscape by invoking the image of uncertain Fortune, an image
which is related to a series of paradoxes. Part Two opens with an
aphoristic comment reminiscent of some of Sidney's own ideas:

The infinite varieties wherewith the hand of Fortune feedeth the
hungry cares of change-desiring-man; are so full of honey-poysons, that
with our vncloid appetites wee seeke to swallow that with delight, which
with greatest earnestnesse wee haue fled from . . . (II. 1)

In this illusory world, the image of Thirsis, who appears before
Mellidora, is in fact Mysantropos (II. 22ᵛ). In Eugenio's magic
mirror, Mellidora sees a vision of Fortune's wheel:

about this Wheele she sawe swarming all sortes of people, euen from the
Throne of Maiestie, to the stoole of earth, which is much lower then the
Cottage, some hanging by the heades, some by the handes, and some by
the feete, some by the eyes, some by the eares, and some by
imagination. . . . (I. 69ᵛ–70)

In this same mirror, Thirsis sees 'nothing but a weather-wrackt
ship' (II. 4ᵛ). These forbidding images undercut Thirsis' naïve
claim to Opicus: 'I tell thee Shepheard *Mellidora* liues not within

the reach of *Fortune*, neyther can *Time* (were his power re-doubled) make her immortall flower shedde one leafe from her braunches' (I. 58ᵛ). The irony is increased if we recall that those two eternal lovers from the *Arcadia*, Mellidora's parents Musidorus and Pamela, are dead in *The English Arcadia*.

This bitter Arcadia even refutes the pathetic fallacy: Thirsis wanders hopelessly, 'casting forth vnto the ecchoing rockes, the grieuous accents of vnsupportable calamities, striuing to make insensible things sensible of his anguish . . . ' (II. 14ᵛ). Markham's Tempe thus has an intermittent, refreshing as-tringency. This is enhanced by the relatively uncomplicated narrative structure, closer to the *Old Arcadia* than to the *New Arcadia*. Eugenio's single, retrospective narration to Pyrophilus moves smoothly into Pyrophilus' own participation in the action.[12] Markham produced a sequel which we might well wish extended.

In 1651 Anne Weamys, a 'young Gentlewoman', produced *A Continuation of Sir Philip Sidney's Arcadia*.[13] Weamys's *Continuation* is scarcely comparable to Markham's in terms of literary merit, but it enables us to see how the approach taken to the imitation of Sidney changed in half a century. B. G. MacCarthy emphasizes the qualities of Weamys's style, which she describes as 'clear, straightforward and economical'.[14] Sidney's elaborate, complex sentences have been shortened, and a plainer style is evident. Weamys prefers three short sentences to one long one:

Now I have finished my message, and I must be gone. So with less reverence than he used when he came, he hastily went his way. *Plangus* being cast into such an astonishment, that he let him go at his pleasure, without so much as enquiring after *Eronas* welfare. (p. 8)

But this does not appear to be a conscious modification, in the manner of Mrs Stanley's modernization of Sidney's style in her reworking of the *Arcadia* (1725), for Weamys is attempting to be as faithful to Sidney's style as possible. The stationer informs the reader that 'no other than the lively Ghost of Sydney, by a happie

---

[12] See ibid., p. 73.

[13] Anne Weamys, *A Continuation of Sir Philip Sidney's Arcadia* (1651), title-page.

[14] B. G. MacCarthy, *Women Writers: Their Contribution to The English Novel* (Cork, 1944), p. 65 and see pp. 65–7.

transmigration, speaks through the organs of this inspired Minerva' (π_4). By 1651, the direct imitation of Sidney's style was a difficult task, and the inspired organs distort Sidney's voice somewhat. Sidney's characters are 'transmigrated' almost unrecognizably; for example, Pamela's 'majestie' and 'high thoughts'[15] are no longer evident. The reader is disturbed to see her so distraught, when Musidorus has to leave to aid Plangus, that Philoclea has to calm her (p. 98). Yet the stationer has assured us that we will see 'both Pamela's Majestie, and Philoclea's Humilitie exprest to the life' (π_4).

I cannot detect the undefined 'realism' found in Weamys's work by Dr MacCarthy.[16] Mopsa is indeed treated with humour, but no more so than in the *Arcadia*. Weamys, like Markham, uses a narrative structure which avoids digressions, but she is forced into a certain amount of clumsy retelling of events already depicted in the *Arcadia*. Unlike Markham's work, Weamys's romance had a second edition, in 1690. It is evident that we are drifting away from pure imitations of Sidney; the understanding of Sidney's purposes that was shown by Alexander, or even Markham, is no longer present. Shorter romances increased in popularity during the Restoration, in reaction to the long French heroic romances, and the second printing of Weamys's *Continuation*—lighter and simpler than other, earlier works influenced by Sidney—may well have appealed to readers of Restoration novels.

II. Argalus and Parthenia

A. C. Hamilton has recently summed up Sidney's depiction of Argalus and Parthenia as 'a story to be planted in the reader's imagination and worn upon his memory in order to move him to virtuous action'.[17] The tragic story of these two faithful lovers exerted a strong attraction in the seventeenth century. In 1629 Francis Quarles produced his long poem in couplets, 'Argalus and Parthenia', which he called 'a *Siens* taken out of the Orchard of Sir Philip Sidney, of precious memory'.[18] While Quarles includes the details found in the *Arcadia*, the story of Argalus and

---

[15] Kalander's words, Feuillerat, I. 20.   [16] MacCarthy, p. 68.
[17] A. C. Hamilton, *Sir Philip Sidney: A Study of His Life and Works* (Cambridge, 1977), p. 137.
[18] Francis Quarles, *Complete Works*, ed. A. B. Grosart (n.p., 1891), Vol. 3, p. 240.

Parthenia is slightly expanded, so that, for example, he can include an elaborate account of their wedding.[19]

The popularity of Quarles's poem perhaps paved the way for a prose version of the story. A chap-book version appeared in 1672 or 1673; then in 1683, 1691, 1692 and 1700.[20] These provided the very poorest section of the reading public (the 1673 edition, printed in black-letter gothic type, is only twenty-one quarto pages long) with what was evidently considered to be the most touching story in the *Arcadia*. Here is evidence that the *Arcadia* really was a widely-loved book, for while the most refined members of the reading public consulted their folios, anyone who had a few pence could read at least one of Sidney's stories, in more or less his own words.

In 1703 another version of the Argalus and Parthenia story appeared, entitled *The Unfortunate Lovers: Or, The Famous and Renowned History of Argalus and Parthenia*. This work returns to Quarles in order to expand the story, and it too includes an elaborate account of the lovers' wedding (Book III). When Sidney's words are evoked, they suffer a sea-change into something strange, if not rich. Kalander's well-known description of Arcadia (originally the opening of the *Old Arcadia*) is altered, although the source is still recognizable. Sidney's words are:

This countrie Arcadia among all the provinces of Greece, hath ever beene had in singular reputation: partly for the sweetnesse of the ayre, and other natural benefites, but principally for the well tempered minds of the people, who (finding that the shining title of glorie so much affected by other nations, doth in deed helpe little to the happinesse of life) are the onely people, which as by their Justice and providence geve neither cause nor hope to their neyghbours to annoy them, so are they not sturred with false praise to trouble others quiet, thinking it a small reward for the wasting of their owne lives in ravening, that their posteritie should long after saie, they had done so. (i. 19)

In *The Unfortunate Lovers* we find:

Nor was it fam'd for the Sweetness of its Air, and other Benefits of Nature, with which it was so plentifully stor'd, than for the well-

---

[19] Ibid., pp. 269–76.

[20] The dates are taken from Charles C. Mish, *English Prose Fiction 1600 to 1700: A Chronological Checklist* (Charlottesville, 1967); Mish takes the date 1672 from a copy cited by Esdaile which is no longer available, but the copy from the Huntington Library which I have consulted is dated 1673.

temper'd Mind of its Inhabitants, who finding the shining Title of
Glory, which is so eagerly thirsted after by other Nations, does yet
contribute but little to the Happiness of Life, did by their Justice and
Moderation give no Temptations to their Neighbours to disturb
them . . . (I. 1–2)

But however much Sidney's style might be simplified, the true
pathos of the story is still apparent in these popular versions.

III. Mrs Stanley's Modernization

When the thirteenth edition of the *Arcadia* appeared in 1725,
it competed with *Sir Philip Sidney's Arcadia, Moderniz'd by
Mrs Stanley*. The unknown Mrs Stanley (her preface is signed
D. Stanley) performed an astonishing and, one is forced to
conclude, unfortunate labour of love. One must be wary of
generalizing about Augustan taste and eighteenth-century attitudes to the *Arcadia* from this single piece of evidence. It is true,
however, that only one eighteenth-century edition of the *Arcadia*
was to follow that of 1725. Our evidence has already indicated
that the *Arcadia* may have remained loved, but not always
understood. Mrs Stanley certainly regarded it highly enough to
spend some time in refashioning it to suit 'modern' tastes.

Unfortunately, the product of this effort cannot stand, in
quality, as the prose equivalent of Dryden's Chaucer, or Pope's
Donne, although its intentions are similar. Mrs Stanley explains
her method in the preface:

I have been very careful not even in the minutest Point to vary from his
Tract, either in the Thought or in the Story, and have followed him so
closely as entirely to pass over any Additions that have been made to
him, how necessary soever a Supplement to Part of the Third Book may
be thought, it being my Opinion, that Sir Philip Sidney alone was
capable of finishing what Sir Philip Sidney began: As to the leaving out
of the Eclogues, I have the opinion of most of my Subscribers for
it . . . (b^v)

In fact, every poem has been excluded. Sidney's poetry, one
may speculate, would resist 'modernization' even more than
Donne's: one cannot simply smooth out hard lines. Sidney's prose
is a very different matter. Mrs Stanley follows him sentence by
sentence, leaving no sentence unchanged, but adding very little
new material. Her opening sentence may serve as an example:

The Season of the Year was just returning, when all the Ornaments which adorn our Earth, and deeper strike the Senses with our great Creator's Power, shone with a double Lustre; the Sun forgot his Partiality, and Night and Day succeeded equally; when the young Strephon, regardless of the flocks, and full of self-consuming care, and hopeless Love, came to the Sands which just oppose the well-known Isle of Cythera. (p. 1)

A rationalization has occurred; rich personification ('It was in the time that the earth begins to put on her new apparel against the approach of her lover') has been impoverished. Mrs Stanley's alterations actually alert us to the latent images in Sidney's prose; the unobtrusive image of 'the sands which lie against the island of Cythera' is flattened and tamed.

Figures such as oxymorons are seen as paradoxes, and are broken up and explained: Claius is not Strephon's 'friendly rival', but 'his only Friend, though Rival' (p. 1). The specific disconcertingly becomes general, as the famous image:

. . . each pasture stored with sheep feeding with sober security, while the prety lambs with bleating oratory craved the dams comfort; here a shepheards boy piping, as though he should never be old . . . (*Arcadia*, I. 13)

becomes:

. . . the harmless Sheep were feeding on the Pasture, their wanton Lambs sporting and frisking by, moving with bleating Oratory the Notice of their Dams; the Shepherd-Boys were playing on their Pipes, as they were ignorant they lost the Hours they soothed . . . (p. 7)

Mrs Stanley always maintains an Augustan decorum; thus Sidney's avoidance of jarring theological anachronisms is metamorphosed into an almost slavish acknowledgement of 'our great Creator's Power'. Disapproving of the tone of Philinax's letter of advice to Basilius (*Arcadia*, i. 80–2), she adds, at the end, a salutation quite out of character:

So recommending your Highness to the Protection of the Almighty, and once more conjuring you entirely to confide in Him, who is alone sufficient to guard you against all future Evils, I remain your Highness' *Most faithful*, *Most Devoted*, *and Most Obedient Servant*, Philinax. (p. 17)

Also in the interest of decorum, Mopsa's tale only reaches as far as

'one hair of Gold and another of Silver' before it is interrupted
(p. 176; compare with *Arcadia*, i. 241).

Mrs Stanley's interpretation of the *Arcadia* may be found in the
sentence which she substituted for Sidney's final paragraph:
'Time and Assiduity (at least in love) will conquer every
difficulty, and pay us double Interest for every Disappointment
which we have or can endure' (p. 511). The *Arcadia* is seen as a
simple story of love's triumph. However, one can hardly use
Mrs Stanley's modernization to characterize all eighteenth-
century responses. Clara Reeve, looking back some fifty years
later, tartly places her: 'In 1725 [the *Arcadia*] underwent a kind of
Translation by Mrs Stanley, by which it was thought to lose
more beauties than it gained.'[21] Clara Reeve herself defended
Sidney against Walpole's criticism, although she considered the
Arcadia to be only 'equal, but not superior to any of the Romances
of the same period'.[22]

IV. Sidney's Stylistic Influence

Sidney's style, like Lyly's, attracted a large amount of attention,
although it was less easily imitated than Lyly's. Romance writers
in the early seventeenth century might even draw on both styles.
Such a combination is present in John Hind's *Eliosto Libidinoso*
(1606), where the reader will find a virtuous queen named
Philoclea, and also a wicked maid called Lucilla who acts as a go-
between. Hind's style constantly combines echoes of Sidney
('Amasias offred her gentle violence, and violent gentleness', C4)
and of Lyly ('as the stone of *Thracia* which dipped in water to be
cooled, waxeth most fervent . . .', ibid.), although Lyly's influence does predominate.

Euphuism faded away in the course of the century (although
Euphues continued to be read), and Sidney's stylistic influence
predominated. For example, in *The History of Trebizond* (1616),
by Thomas Gainsford, Sidney's influence has been completely
assimilated. *Trebizond* is a pastoral romance, but Book Three
contains a number of chivalric elements. Despite the fact that
Sidney is absorbed rather than directly imitated in *Trebizond*, one
cannot point to a gradual development in this direction during

[21] Clara Reeve, *The Progress of Romance* (1785), Vol. 1, p. 79.
[22] Ibid., p. 78.

the century. Individual writers always had a new edition of the *Arcadia* to spur them on, particularly in the period through to 1674. The only long pause in its publication, caused by the Civil War, was from 1638 to 1655.[23]

Clidamas (1636), by J.S., has, as one pair of heroes, Cleanthes and Polidore—who, like Pyrocles and Musidorus, fall in love with two sisters. J.S., like Sidney, concludes with an impressive trial scene (pp. 125–41). J.S., however, has an attractive personal style which owes little to Sidney. One cannot say the same for the two works of Robert Baron: *Erotopagaion or The Cyprian Academy* (1647) and *An Apology for Paris* (1649). Baron's plagiarism ranged far and wide, and Sidney is in good company in his works.[24] One may excuse Baron with the words intended as praise by J. Quarles in his commendatory poem attached to *Erotopagaion*, for Baron was 'scarce seventeen' (a5^v) when he wrote it. In another poem, one Thomas Bradford urgently asks, 'Is this not Sidney; marke his Veine in verse/His stile in prose' (a2^v). While sections are taken from Sidney (see II.20, 37), Lyly has also been ransacked (see II. 8). Sidney is less in evidence in *An Apology for Paris*. The *Arcadia* is beginning to take on the appearance of a world, from which later romance writers may even draw their comparisons: 'as the *Arcadian* Fishermen were when they saw that brave *Triton*, the incomparable Prince *Pyrocles* . . . ' (*Paris*, p. 4).

Baron may also serve to illustrate a style for which one cannot blame Sidney, although writers who practised it may have thought that they were displaying his 'stile in prose'. Sidney's delicate metaphors are hardened, an easy personification is evident, and writers strain to produce periphrastic expressions. This style all too often produces a postured attempt at elegance, arising from a misapprehension of the nature of Sidney's prose. So Baron describes 'a Damsell of exquisite formosity' (*Erotopagaion*, p. 8), and explains that 'After this, I with my Orphan Sister *Andronica*, retir'd to our Castle, (towards which we now equitate)' (ibid., p. 11).

Other styles may be found in romances during the century, but

---

[23] See the detailed bibliography by Bent Juel-Jenson, 'Some Uncollected Authors XXXIV: Sir Philip Sidney', *The Book Collector*, 2 (1962), 468–79.

[24] See Charles R. Forker, 'Robert Baron's Use of Webster, Shakespeare and Other Elizabethans', *Anglia*, 83 (1965), 176–98.

this particular extension of Sidney into preciosity was quite
persistent. After the relatively early work of Alexander,
Johnstoun, Markham, and Beling, no effective imitation of
Sidney's style seems to have occurred. John Crowne's *Pandion
and Amphigenia* (1665) indicates the persistence of the style
illustrated by Baron. Crowne also has the excuse of youth: 'I was
scarce twenty years of Age' (A2). The romance opens with
familiar conceits:

No sooner were Nights Sable Curtains drawn, and *Aurora* had opened
her Rosie Courts, but fair *Cleodora* arose, and dispossessed her downy
Bed of those perfections, which that Night had been a treasure of: And
looking forth out of a window, to see whether the season would permit
her usual Custom, which was early while others were fettered with
Morpheus his chains, and wrapped in Sleeps *care-charming* Mantle to
walk forth, sometimes into the Gardens, sometimes into the [o]pen
Fields . . . (p. 1)

Crowne is much more indebted to the *Arcadia* than Baron. He
borrows the false-beheading trick from the captivity episode
(p. 296); phrases from Sidney appear from time to time; and he is
also not shy of borrowing the odd line from George Herbert to use
in a poem (see the use of 'a box, where sweets compacted lye',
borrowed from 'Virtue', p. 93). The familiar description of
Arcadia by Kalander makes its due appearance, altered to fit
Crowne's romance: 'This Country of *Thessalia*, as it hath been
ever famous for pleasure and delight . . .' (p. 95). Figures used
with great restraint by Sidney are thrown about with gay
abandon by Crowne: 'his sences sensible of insensibility, grew
weary of being sensible' (p. 30, see also p. 92).

Sidney's influence continued, even after the establishment of
the Restoration novel. *Evagoras* (1677) has some of the colloquial
vigour of the Restoration novel (note especially the preface), but
the opening scene is indebted to Sidney, as is Coriander's speech
against love (pp. 9–10), and also the situation of Clarinda,
disguised as Theocles, who loves Coriander/Clidamant, who in
turn loves Emilia, who in turn (thinking her to be a man) loves
Clarinda/Theocles (see p. 136).

Of course the fame of the *Arcadia* lured booksellers, who were
not beyond exploiting it dishonestly. The extremely didactic
Arcadian Princess (1635), by Richard Brathwait in the disguise of
'Mariano Silesio', is in no way related to Sidney's *Arcadia*. In

1678 a translation from the French of La Roche Guilhem, entitled *Almanzor and Almanzaida*, was published bearing the enticing sub-title, *A Novel: Written by Sir Philip Sidney, And found since his Death amongst his Papers*. Despite the bookseller's circumstantial preface, explaining how 'A Gentleman who came in the Train of the Prince of *Orange* when he was last in *England*, brought this *Novel* in an old Manuscript, and presented it to a Lady as a great Rarity of that excellent Author *Sir Philip Sidney*, and supposed he wrote it when he was Governor of *Flushing*, for soon after his Death it was found amongst his Papers' (A4ᵛ–5), this tale of the seraglio is in no way connected with Sidney, or influenced by the *Arcadia*.[25]

V. *Urania* and the Tyranny of Love

In 1621 Sidney's niece, Lady Mary Wroth, published *The Countesse of Montgomeries Urania*—the first work of fiction written in English by a woman (or at least, the first to appear in print). *Urania* was certainly the most controversial seventeenth-century romance, as well as one of the most original. Ben Jonson praised Lady Wroth as the 'fair crown of your fair sex',[26] and politely wrote that 'Since I exscribe your sonnets, [I] am become/A better lover, and much better poet.'[27] Her literary endeavours ceased being merely part of an elegant exchange of sonnets when she was left in financial difficulties following the death of her husband, Sir Robert Wroth, in 1614.[28] The *Arcadia*'s popularity was still at its height, and Wroth endeavoured to produce a romance which would, at least by its title-page, attract admirers of her famous uncle. *The Countesse of Montgomeries Urania* echoes *The Countesse of Pembrokes Arcadia*.[29] The author's relationship to the Sidney family also figures prominently:

Written by the right honourable the Lady Mary Wroath. Daughter to

[25] The bookseller has evidently fooled Professor Buxton, *Elizabethan Taste*, p. 251; the work may be found, accurately introduced, in Charles C. Mish, ed., *Restoration Prose Fiction 1660–1700: A Representative Anthology* (Lincoln, Nebraska, 1970).

[26] Epigram CIII, Ben Jonson, *The Complete Poems*, ed. George Parfitt (Harmondsworth, 1975), p. 71; see also Epigram CV.

[27] 'A Sonnet, to the Noble Lady, the Lady Mary Wroth', ibid., p. 165.

[28] See *Letters of John Chamberlain*, ed. N. E. McClure (Philadelphia, 1939), Vol. 1, p. 519.

[29] Susan, Countess of Montgomery, was married to Mary Wroth's cousin, Sir Philip Herbert, the son of Sidney's sister Mary.

the right Noble Robert Earle of Leicester. And Neece to the ever famous, and renowned Sr. Philip Sidney knight. And to ye most exalt[ed] Lady Mary Countesse of Pembroke late deceased.

Despite these nods in the direction of the *Arcadia*, Wroth produced a dramatically different kind of romance. She decided to use the romance form as a *roman à clef*, and depicted a number of contemporary individuals and incidents in the guise of romance characters and stories. Her inspiration may have been Sidney's brief depiction of himself as Philisides in the *Arcadia*, but the character of Philisides only glances in an elegant fashion at Sidney's pursuit of his star (Stella), while Wroth chose scandalous stories which she related in detail. This aspect of *Urania* created a stir when Edmund Denny reacted violently to events concerning his family and himself which were portrayed in it.[30] Mary Wroth had some cause to dislike Denny, as Denny's son-in-law, James Hay, had a long, violent quarrel with Mary's brother Robert (Robert was married to Dorothy Percy, the sister of Hay's second wife, Lucy Percy). Wroth depicted Honora Denny's marriage to Hay, her supposed adultery and her father's brutal reaction to this, and Hay's second marriage after Honora's death.

Denny was undoubtedly infuriated by the fairly accurate depiction of his nature: 'her father, a phantastical thing, vaine as Courtiers, rash as mad-men, & ignorant as women . . .' (I. ii.2^v–3).[31] He sent a bitter poem to Wroth, calling her a 'Hermaphrodite in show, in deed a monster', to which she wrote a clever poem in reply, while vehemently denying that she intended to portray Denny in *Urania*.[32]

Despite her protestations of innocence, which included a letter written to Buckingham in an attempt to clear her name with King James, Wroth was forced to withdraw *Urania* from sale, and an extensive continuation which she had written was never published. The scandal surrounding its publication had become quite a talking-point: John Chamberlain wrote to Dudley Carleton on 9 March 1621, outlining Denny's claim that 'in her

[30] For a detailed account, see Josephine Roberts, 'An Unpublished Literary Quarrel Concerning the Suppression of Mary Wroth's "Urania"', *N&Q* 24 (Dec. 1977), 532–5; Paul Salzman, 'Contemporary References in Mary Wroth's *Urania*', *RES* 24 (1978), 178–81.

[31] References are to the 1621 edition of *Urania*.

[32] For the poems, see Roberts, pp. 533–4.

booke of Urania she doth palpablie and grossely play upon him and his late daughter the Lady Hayes, besides many others she makes bold with, and they say takes great libertie to traduce whom she please, and thincks she daunces in a net.'[33]

Chamberlain's comment indicates that *Urania* glances at more individuals than just Denny and his daughter and son-in-law, but the tangled web of stories and large cast of characters make it difficult to determine what other long-forgotten scandals are present. By addressing his verses to 'Pamphilia', the female protagonist of *Urania*, Denny indicates that he regards Pamphilia as a self-portrait of Mary Wroth. This hint is generally supported by an examination of Pamphilia's siblings. Like Wroth, Pamphilia has two brothers—one of whom is named Rosindy, which is obviously a play on the name of Wroth's brother Robert Sidney. Parselius, Pamphilia's second brother, is less likely to be a portrait of Wroth's brother William, who died in 1612 aged 22; Parselius marries and fathers children before he dies, while William died unmarried. However, Pamphilia's sister Philistella is probably Wroth's younger sister Philip Sidney—not only is the name Philistella a play upon that of Philip Sidney, but it also refers to the female Philip's famous namesake, and his Stella.[34] Mary describes Philistella's death at the beginning of the manuscript continuation of *Urania*, and her sister Philip died in 1620. In a more speculative spirit, it is possible that Urania is Susan, Countess of Montgomery, to whom the romance is dedicated. After Pamphilia's husband and son die (just as Mary's own husband and 3-year-old son died, in 1614 and 1616 respectively), she is courted again by her old lover, Urania's brother Amphilanthus. Rumour had it in 1619 that the young Earl of Oxford, the Countess of Montgomery's brother, might marry Mary.[35]

Wroth did not, by any means, simply alter names and transcribe real events: there is a good deal of invention in *Urania*. But her quite extensive use of material from the world of James's court and aristocracy marks a significant departure for the

---

[33] *Letters*, Vol. 2, p. 427.

[34] For information on Mary's sister Philip, subject of Ben Jonson's Epigram 114, see Lisle Cecil John, 'Ben Jonson's Epigram cxiv To Mistress Philip Sidney', *JEGP* 45 (1946), 214–17.

[35] See *DNB*, Wroth, Lady Mary.

sophisticated romance. The pressure of reality upon the romance in the seventeenth century has not been examined by scholars, perhaps owing to preconceptions about the romance form becoming outmoded at this time. Wroth's motivation for depicting Denny's family scandals may have been simply spite, but her depiction of her own family is a utilization of the sophisticated romance form to explore personal problems, and to examine the people and events within the author's own milieu. The following two chapters outline an increasing interaction between the romance and political events. *Urania* is concerned with personal rather than political crises, but it represents a new engagement with the minutiae of contemporary life, which makes it possible for the later political romances to encompass the events of the Civil War in detail rather than to look at political issues in a more abstract way, as Sidney did in the *Arcadia*.

Urania is not structured in the epic manner of the *Arcadia*, but is more like an old-fashioned chivalric romance. It has a very large cast of characters, and the narrative moves from one group of them to another, while including a substantial number of subsidiary stories. The characters and stories are in fact so numerous that the reader is hard pressed to keep track of them, and without a firm structure, the narrative tends to become increasingly fragmented. However, a clear thematic interest runs through the romance: the destructive power of 'Vncertaine Tyrant Loue' (p. 102). Story after story is concerned with 'the spider loue' (p. 149), which entraps the innocent in its web. Mary Wroth's own emotional situation may be behind this view, on the evidence of Ben Jonson's remark to Drummond that 'My lord Lisle's daughter, my Lady Wroth, is unworthily married on a jealous husband.'[36]

Wroth creates a feminist reading of the romance form by directing her attention at the less salubrious underside of the heroic and courtly code. *Urania* has its valiant heroes, but the reader's attention is directed to the women who are left behind by the questing men, or whose paths cross the heroes' with invariably miserable results. Wroth breaks romance convention by depicting marriage rather than courtship: the major charac-ters marry in the middle of the romance. These marriages are

---

[36] 'Conversations with Drummond', ll. 359–60, in Jonson, *Poems*, ed. Parfitt, p. 470.

seldom happy; adultery, or at least the love for someone other than one's spouse, is the norm. Faithful women are rewarded by unreasoning jealousy from their husbands—for instance, the story of Perissus and Limena details the vicious punishment meted out to the faithful Limena by her mistrusting husband.[37] Women pursue lovers who spurn them, and Wroth presents numerous vivid vignettes of women in a state of impassioned degradation. A good example is this scene recounted by Pelarina, who is on an outing with her inconstant lover and his new mistress:

I haue gone (as one day I must needs remember aboue the rest) a Fouling with them, where so much fauour I receiued from him who was once mine, as she being a little parted from vs to shoote at a Fowle, he went as fast from mee as hee could without running, while his scorne rann to me. An other Gentleman was there, and none els, he was of his Family and kindred, and as true a louer of me, as I was of his cousens, but him I as much shunn'd, and rather then goe softly with him I went apace after my flyer, the way of necessity leading me to follow my disdainer. When they met, with what loue did he take her hand and kisse it? I following vnmarckt, but weary, and dabled like a hunted Hare in Winter, tyred with my disgrace, and weary of my wrongs, sweeting with passionate paine, and durted in despaire, yet loued I still. (p. 452)

Urania, through a multiplication of such stories, fulfils the request made by the sorrowful Pamphilia (i.e. Mary Wroth) to Limena:

let me but vnderstand the choise varieties of Loue, and the mistakings, the changes, the crosses; if none of these you know, yet tell me some such fiction, it may be I shall be as luckless as the most vnfortunate; shew me examples . . . (pp. 188–9)

Women's vulnerability to the entrapment of love, and the passive role which they are forced to play in a heroic (masculine) world, are portrayed symbolically in the enchantments which capture the characters. The castle of love, its three towers representing Cupid, Venus, and Constancy, is featured on the frontispiece of the book.[38] Urania is trapped alone in the third tower,

---

[37] Discussed by MacCarthy, pp. 60–2.
[38] See Graham Parry, 'Lady Mary Wroth's *Urania*', *Proceedings of the Leeds Philosophical and Literary Society*, 16 (1975), 55–6.

Constancy: 'Thus were the women for their punishment, left prisoners in the throne of *Loue*: which Throne and punishments are daily built in all humane hearts' (p. 41). The enchanted theatre in Book Three serves a similar symbolic purpose.

Wroth is not just overturning romance conventions, but also using the romance form to explore the situation of women in the courtly society which she knew so well. This is the perspective not of the noble Philip Sidney, who could sacrifice his life in a heroic gesture at Zutphen, acting out the role of a Pyrocles or Musidorus, but of the wife and family left behind. The un-published manuscript continuation is even more negative in its treatment of marriage. It begins with the death of Philistella in childbirth, before turning to Pamphilia and Amphilanthus (I. 27).[39] Pamphilia's marriage to a man she does not love is treated as a common situation by her female friends, who advise her to 'obey your husband with discretion, and no farther' (II. 48).

The major characters of the published part of *Urania* are in decline; we read more often of unheroic deaths than of noble deeds. When Parselius' wife Dalinea dies, a match between him and the widow of Ollorandus is proposed, but it takes two years for the marriage treaty to be drawn up, 'in wch time Parselius full of blood and wth laisiness grown somewhat fuller then ordinary fell sick' (II. 133). He soon dies. Our 'heroes' are mortal; 'life is a moment, death a certaintie' (II. 102) is the solemn message from Mary Wroth, whose brother, husband, son, and sister all died in the space of eight years.

Magic features quite extensively in *Urania*. It is used as a plot device in order to gather characters together and then scatter them again. The female magician Melissea presides over the characters and events of the romance. She often explains to the characters, and the reader, the course of future, pre-ordained events. She thus provides a positive balance to the passive role forced upon most of the female characters. However, Wroth also provides a curious, negative figure, who seems to undermine her

---

[39] I am indebted to Katherine Duncan-Jones, who has generously allowed me to consult her microfilm of the manuscript, which is in the Newberry Library. The manuscript is in two parts. While leaves and gatherings are numbered, pagination is not always consistent or legible, and therefore I have numbered the pages of each part consecutively: the first part consists of 141 pages, the second of 122 pages.

own position as a woman writer. This is Antissia, who changes from the powerful captor of Amphilanthus in Part One to a mad writer of 'fustian poetry' (I. 30) in Part Two. Her eccentric dress is described at length:

She was neither dressed, nor undrest, butt a strange Vaile she had on, and a strawe hatt on the top of that wth a feather in itt, she had ne[i]ther a ruff, nor a falling band on, but partly a band, wth a little ruff instead of a lace on itt, and round about itt, she had a kinde of thing on her body . . . (I. 21)

Antissia sees her literary ambitions as part of her insanity, stating after Melissea cures her: 'I was possest with poettical raptures, and fixions able to turn a world of such like woemens heads into the mist of noe sense' (II. 31). This may have been written after the publication of the first part of *Urania* brought scandalous notoriety to Wroth, instead of much-needed money. Antissia also bears some resemblance to the eccentric Margaret Cavendish, Duchess of Newcastle.[40]

Whatever misgivings Wroth may have had about women's literary ambitions, her own achievement is impressive. She may have set out to write an imitation of the *Arcadia*, but she approached romance conventions in a wholly original way. Her prose style is also far from being imitative of Sidney's.[41] It is a much plainer style, a style which became a feature of sophisticated romance in the seventeenth century. Against the idealizing conventions of romance, which, for all the conflict that may ensue between beginning and end, promote a sense of trust, Wroth sets a knowledge of the disappointment in store for women who believe in the heroic stories which men tell. 'Credit noe thing' (I. 7) is her warning to her readers.

VI. The Didactic Impulse

The didactic impulse, a characteristic of fiction throughout the seventeenth century, is seen in what Professor Mish calls the 'moral tale' as well as in the romance. Of course a didactic purpose was proclaimed by numerous Elizabethan writers, who echo Sidney's formula that the aim of poetry is to 'teach and

---

[40] See below, Chap. 16.
[41] *Pace* McCarthy, pp. 58–62.

delight'.[42] This became a truism to be seen on numerous title-pages, not only of romances, but even of cony-catching pamphlets.[43]

In the following century, the moral aim of fiction achieved more than a mere catch-phrase on a title-page. Religious allegory was in evidence well before Bunyan (with an emphasis on static moral allegory, rather than plot and character), notably in Richard Bernard's extremely popular *Isle of Man* (1627). But the interests of prose fiction were best served by an equally popular and much more lively work by John Reynolds.

In 1621 the first book of Reynolds's collection of tales appeared. Further books followed in 1622 and 1623, and in 1635 six books, each containing five tales, were published as *The Triumphs of Gods Revenge against The Crying and Execrable Sinne of (Willfull and Premeditated) Murther*. The series of prefaces indicate a highly moral purpose:

Christian Reader, we cannot sufficiently bewaile the Iniquity of these last and worst dayes of the world, in which the crying and scarlet sinne of Murther makes so ample, and so bloody a progression. (A3)

The tales will correct this vice:

My intent, desire, and prayer is, that if thou art strong in Christ, the perusing and reading of these Histories may confirme thy faith, and thy defiance of all sinnes in generall, and of Murther in particular. . . . (A5)

The tales will 'show thee Gods sacred Iustice, and righteous Iudgements' (A6ᵛ). One is prepared for a moralistic but perhaps rather sensational compilation of incidents, such as Samuel Clarke's *Mirror or Looking Glass for Sinners* (1646).

Reynolds, however, is a most convincing story-teller.[44] His style is plain and effective and his organization is economical, with each tale averaging about twenty folio pages. The summaries provided by Reynolds bring to mind the violent plots of Jacobean tragedy; in fact, Book Two, History Three, is a source for *The Changeling*:

Beatrice-Ioana, to marry Alsemero Causeth de Flores to murther

---

[42] *A Defence of Poetry, Miscellaneous Prose of Sir Philip Sidney*, ed. K. Duncan-Jones and J. Van Dorsten (Oxford, 1973), p. 80.

[43] See, for example, Greene's *Pandosto* (1588), and *A Disputation Between a Hee conny-catcher and a Shee Conny-Catcher* (1592).

[44] See the discussion in Mish, *Short Fiction*, pp. 195-7.

Alonso Piracquo, who was a sutter to her. Alsemero marries her, and finding de Flores and her in adultery, kills them both. Tomaso Piracquo challengeth Alsemero for his Brothers death. Alsemero kills him treacherously in the field, and is beheaded for the same, and his body throwne into the Sea: At his execution hee confesseth, that his wife and de flores Murthered Alonso Piracquo: their bodies are taken out of their graves, then burnt, and their ashes throwne into the ayre.[45]

Reynolds may simply pile one death on top of another, each more violent and grotesque than the last—in which case he may be accused of a sensationalism which runs counter to his asseveration of morality. But a number of tales concentrate on the psychological effect of murder upon one or two characters (see, for example, Bk. 6, Hist. 27). The powerful stories resulting from this concentration approach the tragic force of Jacobean drama. Reynolds's collection was extremely popular, reaching ten editions in the course of the century. The didactic impulse motivates a number of impressive stories, whether we accept their stated moral purpose, or believe it to be a disingenuous justification.

Later in the century, two French writers experimented with didactic romances: Jean-Pierre Camus and René de Ceriziers. Their works were readily translated in England, and Camus in particular was a prolific writer. But such overt didacticism palls during a long romance, or even in the briefer tales of Camus. Reynolds's narrative verve is missing. Camus advises the reader that 'The enterprise which I have taken in hand, is to wrastle, or rather to encounter with those frivolous books, which may all be comprised under the name of Romants.'[46] His aim is 'setting relations true and beneficiall, in the place of those that are prophane' (a^v). While he may be 'strictly tyed to the bounds of probability' (a2), excessive preaching mars his works. The one exception is *Elise, Or Innocencie Guilty* (1652), which is serious without buttonholing the reader and delivering a sermon.

VII. Conclusion

The first generation of seventeenth-century fiction offers a bewildering variety of approaches to narrative form. Despite the

---

[45] 1635 edition, I. iv. 45.
[46] *Admirable Events* (1639), A8; references in parentheses are to this work.

dominance of Elizabethan writers, particularly Sidney, a number of new modes developed in this period. Not all were successful, but their very existence attests that prose fiction did not stagnate after Sidney, Greene, Nashe, and Deloney ceased to write; and Mary Wroth's *Urania* stands as a work of enduring interest.

Chapter 11

The Political/Allegorical Romance

The most dramatic change in the romance form during the seventeenth century was precipitated by the tumultuous effects of the Civil War.[1] The audience for the sophisticated romance was confronted with a political crisis which overshadowed the use of personal, scandalous detail in a book like *Urania*. The elegant world of Charles I's court, in which all things French were fashionable, such as the refined pastoral romance *L'Astrée*, by D'Urfé (1607, translated in 1620), was swept away by the forces of Parliament. The accepted picture of the Cavaliers' literary response to their defeat is an image of retreat mirroring their necessary withdrawal from action. Despite his great sympathy for the Cavalier mode, Earl Miner still believes that 'the most distinctive feature of the Cavalier response to the times was retreat'.[2] This idea, echoed by numerous critics, is reinforced by historians, who paint a picture of the royalists in a state of malaise during the Interregnum. David Underdown's book on royalist conspiracies is largely a record of humiliating failure, and Paul Hardacre supports Professor Miner when he claims that 'the royalists tended to withdraw from the world'.[3]

However, Richard Lovelace's grasshopper, frozen by the 'Cavalier winter'[4] into 'green ice', was not the only literary response made by the royalists. They also took the romance form and used it in the manner of a *roman à clef* to explore their experience of the Civil War. The sustained presentation of historical events in disguised, romance form was brought into prominence by John Barclay's *Argenis* (1621) which was ex-

[1] Some material in this chapter was first presented in my article '*The Princess Cloria* and the Political Romance in the 1650's: Royalist Propaganda in the Interregnum', *Southern Review* (Adelaide), 14 (1981), 236–46.

[2] Earl Miner, *The Cavalier Mode From Jonson to Cotton* (Princeton, 1971), p. 179.

[3] David Underdown, *Royalist Conspiracy in England 1649–1660* (New Haven, 1960), *passim*; Paul H. Hardacre, *The Royalists During the Puritan Revolution* (The Hague, 1956), p. 81.

[4] Miner, p. 177.

tremely popular in England during the years leading up to the Civil War. Political allegory surfaced in a number of literary forms at this time. James Howell wrote two dialogues, with some narrative interest, which portray political events through allegorical trees in *Dendrologia or Dodona's Grove* (I, 1640, II, 1650), and through allegorical animals in *The Parly of Beasts* (1660).[5]

A number of political/allegorical plays also contributed to the general literary interest in current political events. Mildmay Fane's *Candy Restored* (1641) and *The Change* (1642) were privately performed. Clifford Leech, the editor of *Candy Restored*, points out that Fane's play, written three months after the initial sitting of the Long Parliament, is optimistic about Candy's (England's) 'return to health'.[6] This political interest continued when the sophisticated romance was superseded by the Restoration novel. Some novels were written in response to the political controversies of the 1680s and 90s. Dryden's *Absalom and Achitophel* was adapted in a novel entitled *The Fugitive Statesman*.[7] *The Perplex'd Prince* (1682) virulently put the Whig case with an account of Charles's flight to the continent and the 'legitimacy' of Monmouth. James II is the subject of the amusing burlesque *Pagan Prince* (1690) and Peter Bellon's more serious *Court Secret* (1689).

The political/allegorical romance is a much more ambitious form than the preceding drama, or the Restoration novels which superseded it. The ease with which the romance form embraced history and politics may be demonstrated by a brief consideration of *Argenis*.

I. John Barclay's *Argenis*: 'the perfect Glass of State'

Argenis has rejoiced in the admiration of men as dissimilar as James I and Coleridge.[8] John Barclay, of mixed Scottish and

---

[5] The latter is not included in Charles C. Mish, *English Prose Fiction 1600 to 1700*; the two works seem to me to be similar, although *Dodona's Grove* may have a slightly stronger infusion of narrative interest.

[6] Mildmay Fane, *Candy Restored*, ed. Clifford Leech (Louvain, 1938), Materials for the Study of the Old English Drama, Vol. 15, p. 40; see also Alfred Harbage, *Cavalier Drama* (1936, rpt. New York, 1964), Vol. 2, Chap. 4.

[7] See my note '*Absalom and Achitophel* and *The Fugitive Statesman*', *Restoration*, 4 (1980), 11–13.

[8] For James, see note 9; Coleridge, in a note written in Southey's copy of *Argenis* (the Le Grys translation), calls it 'this great work', see Gerald Langford, 'John Barclay's Argenis: A Seminal Novel', *University of Texas Studies in English* (1947), pp. 75–6.

French parentage, wrote *Argenis* in Latin. After its appearance in
1621 a series of projected and actual translations followed, as well
as numerous editions in the original Latin. John Chamberlain's
letters reveal that in 1622 King James asked Ben Jonson to
translate *Argenis*.[9] This translation was entered in the Stationers'
Register on 2 October 1623, but was among those works
destroyed in the infamous fire of November in the same year.[10]
The first English translation to be published, in 1625, was by
Kingesmill Long, closely followed in 1628 by that of Sir Robert
Le Grys, which was proclaimed on the title-page to be 'published
by his Maiesties Command'.[11] Of these two rival translations
Long's was deservedly the more popular; a new illustrated
edition appeared in 1636. In 1734 John Jacob published an
abridged translation, and in 1772 Clara Reeve's translation was
published under the title of *The Phoenix*.

Argenis is a political allegory depicting the religious and
political turmoil in France under Henry III and Henry IV. The
narrative works on three levels: a 'romance' plot—the pursuit of
King Meleander's daughter Argenis by the evil Lycogenes and
Radirobanes and by the good, ultimately reconciled Poliarchus
and Archombrotus; an allegory—though one open to a variety of
interpretations—with Meleander representing Henry III,
Lycogenes the Duke of Guise or perhaps the whole house of
Lorraine, Radirobanes Philip II of Spain, and so on; finally
Argenis is a serious political fiction, aptly described by Long in the
dedication of his translation:

It is so full of wise and politique Discourses, and those so intermixed and
seconded with pleasing accidents, so extolling Vertue and depressing
Vice, that I haue sometimes compared it to a greater Globe, wherein
not only the World, but even the businesse of it is represented; it being
(indeed) such a perfect Glasse of State . . . (A3)

The allegorical targets of *Argenis* were the subject of some
speculation. The first key appeared in the Latin '*Editio nouissima*'
of 1627, and was translated in Long's second edition; and a short
key was printed with the 1628 Le Grys translation.

    [9] *Letters of John Chamberlain*, ed. N. E. McClure (Philadelphia, 1939), Vol. 2, p. 436.
    [10] See Ben Jonson, *Works*, ed. C. H. Herford and P. Simpson (Oxford, 1925), Vol. 1,
pp. 74–5, Vol. 11 (1952), p. 78.
    [11] References will be to *Barclay His Argenis*, trans. Kingesmill Long (1625), and *John
Barclay his Argenis*, trans. Sir Robert Le Grys 'And the Verses by Thomas May Esquire'
(1628); the versions of the poems are in fact identical in both translations.

Barclay includes many unambiguous references to contemporary ideas and events. He discusses, at some length, the
religious tenets of the Hyperephanians (Huguenots) and the
religious leader Usinulca (an anagram for Caluinus). While
Argenis is set in the sixteenth century, Barclay includes some more
recent Jacobean events, describing

the *Phrygian* couple . . . who lately for Sorcery were condemned to
dye, and taken from the Kings elbow, where they had been most
powerful! but the King mindefull of his former affection, saued their
liues, though condemned to perpetuall prison. (p. 15)[12]

This obvious reference to the Overbury scandal is confirmed in
the key to Long's second edition:

The other paire of married folkes, which came out of Phrygia, is meant a
paire of Noble Personages in England, which were condemned to Prison
for Poysoning: That is a story of our times, knowne well enough. (A7)

Beyond these easily identifiable details there is room for some
speculation. Barclay mostly writes an allegory, rather than a
simple *roman à clef*; as Le Grys notes:

[he] will in divers things raise imaginary names, onely to bear the
persons of vertues and vices, so as he shall as well mistake, that
concludes all things contained in it, to be nothing but meare fictions, as
hee that will not allow any part thereof, to be a description of things
indeed and really acted. (p. 485)

Argenis has a firm didactic purpose: 'to set forth a Royall
institution both of a King and his Kingdome, by Examples, and
Precepts' (Long, 2nd edn., A8). It is a 'perfect Glasse of State' in
two senses: it projects the perfect state, but also mirrors the flaws
of the existing state. Barclay achieves this by a strongly linear
narrative. Unlike the *New Arcadia*, which has a similar didactic
purpose, *Argenis* eschews retrospective narrative. The two main
locations are Sicily (France) and Mauritania (England). Within
the narrative Barclay includes a series of disquisitions by
characters on various moral and/or political topics. He may
present a balanced argument, as is often the case with the advice
given to Meleander by his counsellors; or he may guide an
argument to a particular conclusion, a good example being the
discussion between Hyanisbe (Queen Elizabeth) and Poliarchus

---

[12] Unless otherwise noted, references will be to the Long translation.

on the need to gain Parliament's assent in order to raise levies—
the fact that Poliarchus convinces Hyanisbe that this is a most
heinous custom may have been one of the reasons behind King
James's admiration of the romance.

The political world depicted in *Argenis* is not simply a neutral
picture of disguised historical events, but an interpretation of the
use and abuse of power. Like Basilius in the *Arcadia*, Meleander is
a weak ruler whose realm is overwhelmed by dissimulation.
Although not referred to directly, Machiavelli's shadow looms
over the romance; his precepts about the achievement and
maintenance of power are illustrated by the events which occur
in *Argenis*.[13] Meleander himself is a naïve ruler who relies on trust
rather than on clear-sighted enquiry into other peoples' motivation: 'not obseruing the times and dispositions of men [he]
putteth such confidence in others, that hee thinketh by his owne
goodness, all men to stand so affected to him' (p. 5). His daughter
Argenis, on the other hand, is skilled in the useful political art of
pleasing people through careful contrivance: 'shee did distribute
her smiles, lookes, and graces so cunningly, that the people, taken
with her courtesie, shouted for ioy . . .' (p. 25). This examination
of social guile extends to an interest in disguise and imperso-
nation. Poliarchus, for instance, disguises himself, and is also
impersonated by a madman.

Duplicity is seen simultaneously as necessary and morally
wrong—such a reaction is an understandable response to the
Court of King James, for example, which Barclay saw at close
hand between 1606 and 1616. The intense arguments over the
best form of government, which occur at Eurymedes' house in the
first book of the romance, reflect the uncertainty that an
intelligent person might feel when contemplating the contemporary political situation. Most speakers argue out of self-
interest; for example, Lycogenes' nephew argues against monarchies, hoping to please his uncle, but Lycogenes, who 'did not
striue to abolish, but to get a Kingdome', argues in favour of an
elected monarch (p. 51).

The narrative method itself reinforces the reader's uncertainty
about the interpretation of behaviour and analysis of motives.
For example, in Book One Argenis is seen by Poliarchus as she

[13] On the English reception of Machiavelli's thought, see Felix Raab, *The English Face
of Machiavelli* (London, 1964), *passim*, and especially Chap. 3.

presides over the Temple of Pallas as a High Priestess. In Book Three, however, the circumstances surrounding her appointment are explained. Poliarchus, while in disguise, had saved Meleander's life, and through the hysterical reaction of an onlooker, was thought to be Pallas. The solemn scene in Book One suddenly changes to an ironic one, when the reader realizes that Argenis has been worshipping not Pallas, but Poliarchus. The narrator will only speculate about ambiguous events, and seldom gives the reader a firm interpretation. For example, when Meleander's chariot is pulled into a lake by bolting horses, the narrator offers three possible reasons: 'the Kings Horses, whether of themselues affrighted, or chased with the stinging of the Marish Gnats, or lastly, by reason of the Coach-man' (p. 71). Eristhenes kills the coachman, so we never find out; nor do we even know if Eristhenes kills him out of love for the King or to hide a plot.

This world of deceit encourages paranoia in Meleander, and the narrative's opacity pushes the reader in the same direction. Barclay is particularly adept at portraying the effect of rumour and speculation on the general populace, who are removed from the centre of political power. Poliarchus' arrival in Mauritania provokes a flood of ill-informed speculation: 'Some said, the Queenes Sonne was come; some, that his dead body was brought in the Ship' (p. 102).

Englishmen who were plunged into Civil War not many years after the appearance of *Argenis* might have recalled the picture of chaos painted by Barclay in his treatment of sixteenth-century France:

Sicily now offers a sad spectacle to all men: Religion is banished, and the Lawes neglected: the wayes dangerous for Travellers; houses and streetes every where afflicted with Rapine, Fire and Fury: onely the Tents in the forlorne Fieldes, shew glorious with bright Armour. (p. 116)

The particularly senseless horror of civil war is stressed:

many innocent people suffered for the fury of a few; and which is the most pittifull mischiefe of warres, they did not fight and kill men for hatred and wrong done, but onely as fortune deuided them. (p. 308)

Meleander and his daughter Argenis are divided against each other, and this is reflected by the nobility, who are already adept at *real-politik*:

The rest of the Nobility begun [*sic*] now to bee more backward in their politique aduices, fearing the King, if they went about any harm to Archombrotus; and assuring themselues, that in the least wrong to Poliarchus, they should offend Argenis. (p. 388)

One of the most interesting aspects of *Argenis* is the elaborate consideration of the role played by the artist in such an imperfect society. Throughout the romance, poetry is used as an adjunct to political life; it commemorates every notable event. During a discussion condemning the use of panegyric poetry which 'may erre beyond the limits of truth, to please the itching eare', public poetry is mocked by the announcement that a series of elegies has been written on the death of Poliarchus' dog Aldina. In contrast to this use of poetry as propaganda, Nicopompus, Barclay's self-portrait, decries the present state of affairs, and announces that he will

freely vse a sharpe Stile: I will discouer, how the King hath done amisse . . . Then will I take off the maske from the factious subjects . . . Neyther will I hide from the people the folly of their owne credulity . . . (pp. 107–8)

Antenorus claims that 'It is long since that this kinde of wisdome grew stale' (p. 108), but Nicopompus projects a utopian vision of a new form of writing:

I will circumuent them vnawares, with such delightfull circumstances, as euen themselues shall be pleased in being taxed vnder strange names. . . I will compile some stately Fable, in manner of a History: in it will I fold vp strange euents. . . with many and various successes. The Readers will be delighted with the vanities there shewne incident to mortall men: and I shall haue them more willing to reade mee, when they shall not find mee seuere, or giuing precepts. I will feed their minds with diuers contemplations, and as it were, with a Map of places. Then will I with the shew of danger stirre vp pity, feare, and horrour: and by and by cheere vp all doubts, and graciously allay the tempests . . . because I seem to tell them Tales, I shall haue them all: they will loue my Booke aboue any Stage-play, or spectacle on the Theater . . . I will figure vices, and vertues; and each of them shall haue his reward. While they reade, while they are affected with anger or fauour, as it were against strangers, they shall meete with themselues; and finde in the glasse held before them, the shew and merit of their owne fame. It will perchance make them ashamed longer to play those parts vpon the stage of this life, for which they must confesse themselues

iustly taxed in a fable. And that they may not say, they are traduced, no
mans Character shall be simply set downe: I shall finde many things to
conceale them, which would not well agree with them, if they were
made knowne. For, I, that binde not myselfe religiously to the writing of
a true History, may take this liberty . . . I will haue heere and there
imaginary names, to signifie seuerall vices and vertues; so that he may
be as much deceiued, that would draw all in my writing, as he that
would nothing, to the truth of any late or present passage of State.
(p. 109)

Here is a perfect critical exposition contained within the actual
work it projects. When Nicopompus' outline meets with ap-
proval, he says

I will goe forward vpon your warrant. While my matter is fresh, and my
mind yet on fire . . . I will let fly my rais'd conceit, and weaue a
fabulous Storie. Neither will I leaue thee out, Gelanorus, nor
Poliarchus . . . he call'd for paper, and euen then begun his most
vsefull and delightfull Story. (p. 109)

For a moment, *Argenis* takes on some of the self-conscious
nature of *Don Quixote*, as its creator discusses the writing of the
romance within the romance itself. While Barclay mirrors the
imperfect state, the deceit-ridden and war-plagued present, he
also projects a perfect state which may become a possibility in the
future. *Argenis* was also the model for English writers searching
for a genre which would encompass the events of the Civil War.

II. Political/Allegorical Romance in England, 1645-1661

Barclay's influence is first seen in a romance entitled *Theophania*,
written by Sir William Sales in 1645, although not published
until 1655.[14] It focuses on a fictional nobleman called Synesius,
who has retreated from the chaos of the Civil War to his country
estate. Events catch up with him, however, and the romance
depicts a largely imaginary wooing of Charles's daughter Mary
by William II, and gives a very accurate account, narrated in the
first person, of Essex's involvement in the war, culminating in his
downfall during the army reforms of 1644-5. The portrayal of

---

[14] See Augustus Hunt Shearer, 'Theophania: An English Political Romance of the
Seventeeth Century', *MLN* 31 (1916), 72-3.

Essex (Cenodoxius) is a detailed and penetrating exploration of the reasons behind his alliance with Parliament. *Theophania* is unfinished, and ends on the note of uncertainty which one might expect from a royalist romance written in 1645.

Only five political romances are now extant: *Theophania*; *Cloria and Narcissus* by Sir Percy Herbert, published in two parts in 1653 and 1654, and in five parts as *The Princess Cloria* in 1661; *Panthalia* by Richard Brathwait, published in 1659; *Aretina* by Sir George Mackenzie, published in 1660; and *Don Juan Lamberto*, possibly by John Phillips or Thomas Flatman, published in 1661. A number of other examples of this genre have undoubtedly been lost. Dorothy Osborne makes a most enticing remark in one of her letters to William Temple:

My Lord Saye I am tolde has writ a Romance Since his retirement in the Isle of Lundee, and Mr Waller they say is makeing one of Our Warr's, wch if hee do's not mingle with a great deal of pleasing fiction cannot bee very diverting sure, the Subject is soe sad.[15]

Alas, no trace of Waller's romance has survived.

Individually, the romances are quite distinct. *Panthalia* has been discussed in an article by Benjamin Boyce, who praises its realism.[16] It has some strong picaresque elements, and may be seen as a popular royalist romance, intended for less sophisticated readers than the large, complex *Princess Cloria*. Brathwait's lively style adds considerably to *Panthalia*'s appeal, particularly for a modern reader.

Aretina is loosely constructed and digressive; Mackenzie, however, does provide an unusual view of the Civil War from a Scottish perspective.[17] *Don Juan Lamberto* is a burlesque anti-romance which concentrates on the decline of the parliamentary cause following Cromwell's death, and has a great deal of fun with figures like 'Sir Fleetwood the contemptible knight' and the 'grim Gyant Desborough'.[18]

---

[15] *The Letters of Dorothy Osborne to William Temple*, ed. G. C. Moore Smith (Oxford, 1928), p. 91 (letter 40).
[16] Benjamin Boyce, 'History and Fiction in *Panthalia: Or the Royal Romance*', *JEGP* 57 (1958), 477-91.
[17] *Aretina* is dismissed, too harshly, as 'no longer readable', in Andrew Lang's *Sir George Mackenzie* (London, 1909), p. 27.
[18] *Don Juan Lamberto*, 2nd. edn. (1661).

III. *The Princess Cloria*

The most impressive of these romances is *The Princess Cloria* by Sir
Percy Herbert.[19] Sir Percy was a member of the recusant branch
of the Herbert family, all strong supporters of King Charles. He
was MP for Shaftesbury in 1620 and for Wilton in 1624–5 (this
was the Parliament in which George Herbert represented the
borough of Montgomery).[20] In 1639 he was the Collector in the
County of Montgomery of Catholic contributions for the war
with the Scots. In 1641 he was called before the Committee for
Recusants Convict and, though he was bailed at that time, his
estates were sold in 1651. In 1650 he published the first fruits of
his involuntary retirement, a series of essays addressed to his son
entitled *Certaine Conceptions, Or, Considerations*. These expound a
moderate, stoic *via media*, not at all blatantly Catholic, full of
commonplaces on atheism, pride, and dissimulation.

The Princess Cloria, Herbert's next work, is an elaborate
romance, best summarized by its own sub-title: 'Imbellished with
divers Political Notions, and Singular Remarks of Modern
Transactions. Containing the Story of most part of Evrope, for
many Years last past.' The romance focuses on the period from
1640 to 1660, but retrospective accounts of the reigns of King
James and Queen Elizabeth are included. The political events
themselves are presented with considerable accuracy, and reveal
the author's quite intimate knowledge of the machinations which
occurred behind the scenes in seventeenth-century Europe. The
narrative relies on an indirect presentation of events through the
speeches of a wide range of observers.

Like *Argenis*, *The Princess Cloria* is not a schematic allegory;
fiction and history combine. The preface to the reader provides
an interesting account of this method. We are warned not to 'look
for an exact History, in every particular circumstance' (a).[21] No
key is provided, but 'the Story is no way difficult to be understood
by any, who have been but indifferently versed in the Affairs of
Europe.' We are told that fiction must be added to history,
because

the common Occurrances of the World, do not arrive alwayes at a pitch

[19] I am indebted to Katherine Duncan-Jones for assistance in the identification of Sir
Percy.

[20] See Amy M. Charles, *A Life of George Herbert* (Ithaca, 1977), p. 106.

[21] All references are to the second edition (1661).

high enough for example, or to stir up the appetite of the Reader, which
things feigned may do under the notion of a *Romance*. (A2ᵛ)

This is the traditional moral apology for fiction, but it does not
quite explain the particular effect achieved within *The Princess
Cloria*.

Cloria herself, as a character, exemplifies the allegorical
approach to history. The preface emphasizes that 'Princess
Cloria, is not onely to be taken for the Kings Daughter, but also
sometimes for his National Honour' (A2). Her role is obviously
modelled on that of Argenis in Barclay's romance. Thus while
Narcissus is William II, and the correct date of his death is
observed (1650), the marriage between Cloria and Narcissus
occurs after the death of Euarchus (Charles I), while Mary
actually married William in 1641. Cloria's activities in England
are fictional, while the death of Narcissus and his son's struggle to
assume his rightful position are historical. The preface bears out
the claim that the Civil War can best be explained within the
conventions of an allegorical romance:

the Ground-work for a *Romance* was excellent . . . since by no other way
almost, could the multiplicity of strange Actions of the Times be
exprest, that exceeded all belief. (Aᵛ)

For this reason, history and romance do not conflict in *The
Princess Cloria*.

The historical events are enlivened in the romance primarily
because the reactions of characters to these events are explored.
This may involve a set speech, a soliloquy, or simply a brief but
effective impression that individuals are emotionally involved in
historical situations. For example, the first battle of the war is
described concisely and accurately, but the whole account is
coloured by its concentration on Euarchus, and his responses:

they met the Senates Forces upon an ample plain, spacious enough to
have decided the controversie for the Worlds Empire: The Conflict of a
sudden grew so desperate, that it was a question whether they sought
more to satisfie their own spleens, or to gain a beneficial Victory; which
however was prosecuted for some hours with doubtful fortune; for
although the Kings Horse commanded by *Thyasmus* in person, at the
first charge defeated their Enemies, insomuch as for many furlongs they
had the chace of their Troops, yet the Foot Forces in their absence, that
for the most part wanted Arms, had sufficient imployment to sustain the

fury of the Senates Souldiers, being better provided: Which however was bravely supplied by the noble valour of the King himself, insomuch as he sustained the violence of the tempest, until his own Horse again came in to his rescue: though with such a slaughter of his poor Subjects, that it created a most passionate compassion in his Royal Breast . . . (p. 165)

Many events are presented through the narration of characters such as Cloria or Creses, who comment on the events they relate.

On a less serious level, certain 'romance' passages serve to give the reader some respite from the harrowing historical events. These passages are mainly concerned with love, although there is surprisingly little attention paid to this sense of the word 'romance' in *Cloria*. One example, which appeals because of its tone of mock-naïvety, is Cloria's first meeting with Narcissus:

taking her by the fair hand to perform the office, *Cloria* suddenly feeling the touch, which her modesty had scarce ever been acquainted with from any other person, with a quick violence pluckt it from him, and hid it in her Muff. He too much apprehending the action, had hardly power with trembling steps, to carry himself up into the room; yet, by that time having recovered some breath, and considering this last part of Courtship was to be played, since she was shortly to be inclosed in her Chamber from his sight, approached her ears with a few distracted complements, which she answered no otherwise then with a smile, and presently seemed to flie to the protection of her Mother . . . (p. 53)

The depiction of Euarchus' imprisonment, trial, and execution is a useful example of the way in which *Cloria* dignifies history. Once again, Charles's trial is an event which lends itself to just this method of elevation. When Euarchus falls into the hands of the Lydian army, he is taken to a remote castle:

The Castle designed for the Kings new imprisonment, was seated upon a Rocky Isthmus, that afforded it almost no more ground, then was necessary for the building thereof; so that the continual beating of the waves of the Sea, upon the ragged sides of the Cliffs in the night season, gave a most melancholly horrour to the thoughts and apprehension of the people, which allowed the King scarce any other recreation, then what proceeded from the daily exercize of his own pen, that in a manner he imployed continually, in setting down all the unfortunate passages of his life [he is, in fact, writing *Eikon Basilike*]; though sometimes he mixed his studies, with divers contemplations of the uncertainty of worldly affairs. (p. 311)

The poignancy of the King's situation is reinforced by Herbert's very effective use of setting:

Whilst the King had liberty enough, both for these complaints and other devotions, (since for the most part his conversations, were onely the solitary whisling of the winds from the vast body of the Sea, that in a manner incompassed the melancholly Castle round about, and the violent beating of the Waves upon the sides of the Rocks, that lay under his Chamber window, which often afforded his sorrowful eare un-welcome noises) . . . (p. 315)

While Charles was, in fact, prevented from delivering his final speech,[22] Euarchus delivers a moving oration when he is condemned, which provides a good example of the dignified style found in many parts of the romance:

I hope there are some here (said he) that are rather sorry for my misfortunes, then contemners of my dignity, wherefore less perswaded of these my crimes then others, to whom I shall onely address those few words I have to say, since I neither can nor ever will, acknowledge this jurisdiction, that seems to claim an unheard of authority over my person: You see your King, not onely brought before I know not what Tribunal as a Malefactor, but condemned to die, by a Law never yet put in practice by any power . . . You may behold also a liberty extraordinary given to these men, rather by violence to execute what they please, then justly to proceed in what they should . . . O you Gods, it is the Sword onely (that never was ordained for Government, but Execution) by which *Euarchus* must fall: Alas, alas, my friends, (said he) to what a pass are your Rights come, when the Father of them all must perish, because he desires still to make them good to your posterity? (p. 333)

Here, as frequently elsewhere in *Cloria*, Herbert constructs the appropriate response to a historical situation. The allegorical element provides a framework for a series of very disturbing situations. Unlike *Argenis*, *Cloria* presents reactions to a political situation, rather than exempla intended to reform a political situation.

The central action in *Cloria* is the execution of Euarchus, and the events of the Civil War in Lydia (England) are grouped around his death. When we move to Asia (Europe) we are presented with an equally anarchic (or potentially anarchic)

[22] See C. V. Wedgwood, *The Trial of Charles I* (London, 1967), pp. 185–6.

situation, even if it is not quite so horrifying at first sight. *Cloria*
considers the possibility of political chaos, of the world turned
upside down.²³ The destruction of Lydia's King is only the
extreme example of destruction in a world beset by war and
political manipulation, by dissimulation and the disruption of
stable government. The effect of this situation is portrayed with
considerable subtlety. Intimations of Euarchus' fate appear in
the first two parts of the romance, creating an ominous
reverberation in the mind of the reader, who knows in advance
what that fate is to be. Some examples may serve to convey the
over-all impression of potential political and moral dissolution.

At the very beginning of the romance, Cassianus explains how
his father was driven out of Iberia (Bohemia), setting the
romance in the context of the confusion caused by the Thirty
Years' War.²⁴ His address to Euarchus conveys the effects of this
European conflict, and is also extremely ironic in its depiction of
Euarchus' safe and happy situation:

Mighty King, said he, although your Emperial Diadems [*sic*] seems to
flourish with Olive Branches, whilest the ambition of other Princes
make but the Prerogative of their Crowns nourish the lusts of their own
tyranny . . . yet certainly the Gods have not onely placed you upon a
Throne, to be happy yourself by a lasting peace, but to render others
satisfied by your Power and Justice . . . (p. 4)

His friend Eumenes tells Euarchus about the long struggle
between Cyprus (United Dutch Provinces) and Egypt (Spain).
Although Cyprus is to achieve some order, Narcissus will face
revolt, and will die, leaving his country in tumult. It is after
Eumenes' speech that Euarchus reveals his own fears:

I finde my owne Subjects begin already, to be weary of those
happinesses under a peaceful Monarch, that other Kingdoms can but
onely hope for, after a long and bloody experience: The King at these
very words, as if he felt something inwardly at the soul, rested silent for a
pretty space . . . (p. 16)

The story of Philostros' (Richelieu's) control over affairs in

²³ For a consideration of this theme during the Civil War, see Christopher Hill, *The
World Turned Upside Down* (London, 1972).
²⁴ C. V. Wedgwood notes that 'The breakdown of social order, the perpetual changing
of authority and religion in so many districts, contributed to that disintegration of society
which was more fundamentally serious than the immediate damages of war'; *The Thirty
Years War* (London, 1938), p. 516.

Syria (France) indicates how kings may be subverted, even if their thrones are not directly threatened. The vignette of Philostros cunningly pulling the strings is a powerful image of his frightening control over events:

Philostros plaid with him like a huge Fish intangled with an Angle, too great suddenly to pull out of the water; letting him by degrees work himself out of breath, that at last he might deal with him according to his pleasure . . . (p. 31)

This aspect of French government is later represented by Mazarius (Mazarin). In Books Four and Five particularly, we see how the states of Asia (Europe) intrigue, as well as fight, against each other. Political intrigue overrides considerations of the rights of individuals, just as it stems from self-interest. Philos, Philostros' nephew, expresses his view of marriage in these words: 'the Gods do but unite hearts in nuptial tyes, for the commodity of men, and certainly all generals, are to be preferred before particular interests . . .' (p. 93). This is a sentiment directly opposed to the care for individuality shown by the romance itself. Mazarius, in the course of a long oration, makes the following statement:

Gratanus my friend, said he, secrets of State to the common people, resemble Speculative Divinity, onely known to the learned studiant, and not to be debated without an interpreter, lest outward sense, turn all rather to Atheisme then sollid Doctrine; because what they understand not fully they think impossible to be, for that they cannot conceive the manner how; and so by consequence, either think it fiction or imposture. (p. 568)

What we cannot understand, we believe to be 'fiction or imposture', and a political manipulator like Mazarius relies on this lack of vision. The religious image indicates that political 'doctrine' is convincing because its roots are hidden from the sight of the common people.

The prevalence of political confusion may be indicated by glancing at the history of Lydia (England), as portrayed in *Cloria*. This history is presented retrospectively by various characters, as the events of the Civil War and its aftermath unfold. The presentation ensures that the reader is struck by connections between the past and the present. The political uncertainty of yesterday is not simply a prelude to the political uncertainty of today: crises of the past and the present seem to occur at the same time. The history of Crete (Ireland) provides a telling example. When Cloria and Roxana reach Crete, at the end of Part One, they find Pergame (Dublin) under threat, and the whole country almost literally torn apart by factions. The Governor Dedalus (Ormonde) outlines the history of Crete, beginning with its initial subjection to Lydia. The tale he tells is a balanced one: the Lydians were often cruel, but the Cretans were 'lazy and proud' and rebellious. Against this background, Dedalus presents the details of the revolt, lamenting 'the outrageous violence committed of both sides' (p. 115). Added to this picture of destruction is the present intrigue: Euarchus is trying to reach some agreement with the natives, but a messenger from Delphos (Rome) is undermining the negotiations. The whole account is an exact historical picture, but the presentation greatly increases the sense of past and present chaos as coexisting.

The history of Myssia (Scotland) is presented in much the same way, although at greater length. An old priest tells Narcissus about the death of Minerva (Mary Queen of Scots). Again the emphasis is on intrigue (the machinations of Leonatus), and the repercussions of past violence. Elizabeth does not fare well in the romance , nor does James. This may be due to the author's political bias, but it also underlines Euarchus' inheritance of a cankered state. One should note that the account of Myssia also stresses its religious history. Creses (Clarendon?) emphasizes the destructive tenets of Herenzius (Calvin), who managed to have his doctrine accepted in Myssia. Events of the past and of the present are both conveyed indirectly, so that the present is not imbued with an immediacy that the past lacks.

This narrative method begins to bring out the reasons behind individual acts, or the motivation behind one person's behaviour. The Myssian general Arranus explains how he came to oppose Euarchus out of self-interest, spurred on by an oracle promising Euarchus' downfall and his own success. Joyela provides a similar, although much more detailed, account of her half-brother Argylius (Argyll). Argylius' opposition to Euarchus is explained, in part, by the fact that he was raised by 'factious Priests' (p. 396). Joyela's account emphasizes, once again, the influence of the past on the present. As these various accounts multiply, the history of Lydia and the surrounding countries becomes a picture of unrelenting intrigue and political unrest. The indirect presentation of past and present events produces the impression of Lydian history following a similar course, regardless of the differences between particular events. This technique also emphasizes that *Cloria*, far from being a thin, allegorical cloak draped over the shoulders of history, arranges the events of history, or at least arranges the order in which we perceive them.

Chaos and potential anarchy do not only exist on the level of politics in *Cloria*. The landscape of the present, both in Lydia and in many other countries, is ravaged by war and unrest. We are not only shown the plight of kings, but also the plight of ordinary people. This pervasion of destruction becomes clear when the principal characters travel through wasted countryside, and also in the depiction of the aftermath of the Civil War. When Creses and Arethusius (Charles II) pass through countryside ravaged by the conflict between Egypt (France) and Syria (Spain), Arethusius immediately thinks of his own country. A bitter irony is apparent when the host of a poor inn tells them that this region rebelled against heavy taxes, but the rebellion was put down, and now the taxes are even heavier. Cloria sees how Lydia has fared during the Civil War when she escapes at the end of Part Three. She travels 'through a Countrey that began something to taste of devastation, by reason of the late Wars between the King and the Senate' (p. 344). A subtle loading of the dice against the Roundheads is achieved through this picture of the suffering of the common people after the revolution.

The depiction of Cromwell in the romance is a less subtle piece of propaganda. Named Hercrombrotus, he is dramatically portrayed as an arch-villain. He is upbraided by his daughter Clelia (presumably Cromwell's daughter Elizabeth) before she dies: 'the Gods cannot forget (I fear me) ever the injury, by remarkable testimonies of their wrath' (p. 533). After Clelia's death, the violence that by now seems universal manifests itself forcefully in Hercrombrotus' own death. The significant fact that he vomits 'corruption' underlines the religious nature of this particular vision of chaos:

being frighted in his dreams, and tormented in his sleep, [he] started out of his bed, calling for his Sword to maintain his own Dominions (as he said) against his great enemy Prince *Arethusius* . . . after he had been often called upon by the Ghost of his deceased Daughter, whereby to render an account concerning her demands, was suddenly in his own Chamber, taken with a most horrid extasie; where voiding of blood, and vomiting of corruption, he at last expired, in the very height of all his glory and prosperity. (p. 534)

Both the political and the physical manifestations of chaos are found everywhere in Parts Four and Five. When Euarchus is dead, confusion reigns, not just in Lydia but throughout Asia. This bears out the warning of Queen Hiacinthia (Henrietta Maria) in Part One: 'the consequence of any Rebellion or change of Government in this nature, cannot be, but a most dangerous president to the kingdom of *Syria* it self' (p. 48). After Narcissus' death, the disruption in Lydia seems echoed in Cyprus, where the assembly considers a new form of government:

it now became a main question in this general, if not ungrateful assembly, whether or no they would have any more Princes of the family to succeed in after ages? since they had happily as they said, freed themselves from a dangerous bondage . . . (p. 469)

After Euarchus' death, Cloria cries 'Is it possible that all Princes of *Asia* will still sleep in a false security, when such examples are permitted to threaten new dangers to their Dignities?' (p. 334). We are ultimately presented with the threat of anarchy in both the public and private spheres.

This begins as early as Part One, when Cloria is captured by pirates. The pirates revolt against their captain, and provide a frightening premonition of Lydia's political future, and Euarchus' death: 'the Conquerours . . . putting the Head of their late Lord upon a Spear, crying Liberty, shewed it to the people of the other Vessels' (p. 64). The increase in the power of intrigue is also evident after Euarchus' death. When Arethusius discovers that he is harbouring a treacherous servant, Dolan, he exclaims:

Cannot the calms and private retirements of the *Daphenine* Groves, afford so much secure content to the thoughts of a banished Prince, as to suffer him to rest free from the dangers and treasons of his own private Family and Servants? (p. 485)

Much of Part Five is taken up with the intrigue of Locrinus, who has worked against the cause of Euarchus *and* the cause of the Lydian Senate. As Locrinus dons and sheds disguises, following now the Syrian court, now the Lydian Senate, we are presented with the final breakdown of personal loyalty.

Cloria does not just present a picture of political anarchy and physical destruction. There is a very strong emphasis on certain moral and religious dilemmas arising from Euarchus' death and the political situation in Asia. *Cloria* again differs from *Argenis* in that it presents questions rather than answers, and considers the problems arising from the Civil War, rather than offering any solutions.

King Charles's death is seen as a paradox. His character is favourably contrasted with that of his father, which implies the question, 'how could such a good (that is, a *moral*) King be executed?'. Why did his subjects rebel against him, when his character was so commendable? Questions which modern historians may find irrelevant were all-important in the seventeenth century. *Cloria* explores the dilemma posed by rebellion against a good king, a dilemma which perplexes characters throughout the romance. Creses makes the following telling observation in a speech to Roxana:

Euarchus not many years ago, appeared so glorious and fortunate in his Government, crowned with a flourishing prosperity, in Wife, Children, Peace, and Power, that he was not onely the absolute envy of all *Asia*, but seemed to carry in his hand the arbitration of the world; being now cast down into so low, and I may call it miserable condition by a little faction of his own people, that he is not onely denyed to be a King, but deprived of the comfort of all that ever was his; with the addition of a sharp and lasting captivity, according to the discretion sometimes of his meanest Subjects; whilest in the interim, Honour, Love, Justice, and Gratitude seem to be laid asleep in the deep center of the earth: other Princes onely watching to their own preposterous spleen, not considering how soon it may be their fortunes, to fall under the same Fate, for that all men naturally covet liberty . . . (p. 199)

The superb image of justice and gratitude 'laid asleep in the deep center of the earth' emphasizes the uncertainty resulting from revolt against a good king.

In Part Two, Narcissus meets an old priest, who shows him a picture of Euarchus and offers a 'Lecture concerning his life and disposition' (p. 168). Euarchus' father is characterized as a man 'wholly given, as I may say, to his own pleasure'. Euarchus, on the other hand, is 'a Prince given to no manner of vice'. He is modest, temperate, and a good husband. One is forced to ask why the virtuous Euarchus is threatened, while his self-indulgent father ruled in security. This is, one should again stress, a moral question, not a request for historical causes. Euarchus urges his subjects to

Remember but your past delight, and compare it with the present distraction, and I am assured you will find a difference; wherefore if these be but the beginnings of evils, consider what the end will be: Alterations of Government are like desperate purges, that at the best exceedingly distemper, and at the worst are deadly. (p. 84)

His description of the sickness which may be brought about in the body politic is to prove accurate, and it stems directly from the perverse rejection of 'past delight'.

The paradox echoes throughout *Cloria*. After he has lost the war, Euarchus replies to the Senate's demand that he should acknowledge himself to be guilty of causing the war:

Why should my unkinde Subjects, thought he, put me upon these straights, that either I must confess my self guilty of those crimes I never intended to commit, or quit my interest to those Crowns, that have for so many lasting ages, been worn by my predecessors . . . when my Reign hath been gentler then former Kings and Princes of the same line that could challenge by right no greater prerogative then my self. (pp. 303–4)

Even Locrinus the intriguer is struck by this: 'You Gods, when I think of these circumstances, I cannot but condemn, either your Justice or your Power . . .' (p. 555).

The result of this paradox is a constant doubt felt by characters as to the nature of providence. This religious uncertainty is meditated upon by individual characters, and discussed in a series of debates. At times Herbert reveals a certain sympathy for Catholicism, but this is rarely presented as an answer to the dilemma posed by Euarchus' fate. The questions take precedence over any simple answer. Cassianus opens the debate at the beginning of the romance, well before Euarchus' troubles begin, although his own plight is explanation enough for his perturbation. He can accept without trouble the notion of God's existence, but he wonders whether God actually concerns

Himself with the affairs of man. The priest he talks to is forced to present a traditional stoical argument in reply:

man onely takes no constant content here, his minde being still full of perturbations, having always a kind of longing in himself, to have that which he hath not, and a wearisomness of what he possesseth, let his condition be never so seeming prosperous; whereas all other Creatures, are never perplext with the fear of change, or desire of alteration; so that of necessity, man must except [*i.e.* accept] something to countervail the miserableness of his condition, since it is his meer knowledge, that renders him unfortunate, and the want of it makes Beasts happy. (p. 26)

He presents Cassianus with a poem 'against the alluring vanities of present delights', which contains one impressive image of man's plight: 'The heart of man is angular, the earth/Being round, must not afford a constant birth/Of such delights' (p. 27). This is not particularly consoling, and the debate serves to bring out man's perplexity, rather than any possibility of happiness.

Before his trial, when he is subjected to rude treatment by his captors, Euarchus calls for the attendance of the old priest Hephestion (Juxon). He reveals his own uncertainty: 'what assurances (said the King) have we . . . when every one pretends to be in the right, both in his belief and proceedings' (p. 319). This question does not stem from Euarchus' doubt of his own actions, so much as from the paradox of his present position. Hephestion replies that we must obey the Gods, but the King asks how we may recognize their commands. Once again, Hephestion's final comment that we must 'observe in a manner continually, both a perfect charity, and an entire patience' (p. 320), is perfectly sound, but does not solve the problems raised by Euarchus' question. Euarchus continues to be puzzled by the incongruity of his treatment:

oftentimes would he be contented to perswade himself, that it was impossible for humanity, to use him with too much rigour, since he knew his own resolutions were alwayes, to shew what mercy and forgiveness could be desired to his greatest enemies. (p. 320)

This is not simply a naïve trust in the power of goodness, but a faith in moral logic which has been shattered in the course of the romance.

After Cloria has escaped, Roxana and Cloria's page are cast adrift by the Senate as punishment for abetting her flight. During a storm, when they appear to be doomed, the page puts the familiar question in an acute form. Why, he asks, do the Gods allow us to suffer, and our evil enemies to triumph? The existence of a divine power is accepted without question, but this only increases the horror inherent in the query:

whether this power have any consideration or regard to our actions, otherwise then to maintain a succession and increase upon earth, onely for the continuation of the world, as it fareth with Birds, Beasts, Plants and the like? (p. 365)

Although Roxana replies that God created the world for a particular purpose, and that His interest is constant, an over-whelming number of events seem to contradict this idea.

The bewilderment induced by a multiplicity of religious persuasions is discussed by Joyela with Arethusius:

since the first appearing of *Herenzius* [Calvin], in the confines of *Arabia*, the world hath been filled in a manner with nothing but Slaughters, Rebellions, and Impiety, altering their opinions (at leastwise the exercise of their Rites) as often as the Moon doth her garment. (pp. 442–3)

Her purpose (and evidently that of the author) is to indicate the strengths of the religion of Delphos (Rome), but Euarchus' question as to how we may distinguish between apparently sincere adherents remains pertinent.

Euarchus' son Arethusius (Charles II), in his travels abroad, finds himself faced with the same doubts. He encounters a tangled web of political scheming, intertwined with religious questions. The power of favourites in Syria and Egypt, debates between the adherents of Delphos and Herenzius, policy which sees both Arethusius and the Lydian Senate as pawns to be manipulated—these aspects of the situation in Asia provoke Arethusius' question:

Is it possible, said he, that all this can be done for Religion, when the world seems to be so stupified in that particular, that scarce can it be believed, there are any Gods in Heaven, or at the most that minde our actions upon earth? (p. 463)

Cloria is caught up in the secular counterpart of this religious uncertainty. Without Narcissus, she must struggle for her son's rights, while she is pursued by, amongst others, Mazarius' son Manchinus:

Cloria, Cloria, said she, the most unfortunate creature of all thy generation, since no region can bring settlement to thy thoughts, or pretended friendships true enough to secure thy actions; Mothers being won by ends from their natural indulgencies, and Servants never so much obliged to be trusted in resolutions. (p. 503)

Lydia itself suffers from an uncertainty which is eventually seen in religious terms. The period after Hercrombrotus' death is only the culmination of a series of changes in government which can scarcely be comprehended by the inhabitants. Locrinus explains how 'the Armies insolency, and the Senates arbitrary Government, leaves no man a certainty, either in his being or his possession' (p. 538). To less speculative minds than those whose thoughts we have been considering, this uncertainty can only be interpreted as a providence which punishes mankind. This period of disorder 'certainly hath been acted rather, by predominate fate and providence, conducing to some strange period (ordered by the heavens, for the punishing of wickedness)' (pp. 539–40). This, of course, begs the question, unless we assume that a universal wickedness is being punished.

It is not surprising to find this dilemma reflected elsewhere in the romance. Certain incidents portray a natural world which is cruel or violent, and which seems to mirror the political world. Some traditional use is made of a pastoral setting as a peaceful alternative to the violence of war and politics, but a much more telling presentation of a harsh environment predominates. Philos and Narcissus, rivals for Cloria's hand, save each other from a singularly vicious panther, which is very reluctant to die:

as if he yet retained some vigour or malice in his heart, notwithstanding for a long time there appeared no life at all in him, whilst the company were discoursing severally of the accident and encounter . . . the *Panther* of a sudden, not onely again revived, but flew violently upon one of the Dogs lying near him, and bit him so, that the blood followed . . . (p. 100)

When enemies save each other from a wild beast, or when an enemy is saved by the man he is persecuting, a reconciliation usually follows, as, for example, in *As You Like It*. Here no reconciliation occurs, and we are left with an image only of the senseless cruelty of nature.

The connection between the world of man and the world of nature is emphasized when a pair of falcons are taken out. The description of the falcons pursuing the 'Hearn' (heron) is impressive in its evocation of the scene itself, and in its implicit commentary on the significance of the hunt:

> the fowl was presently put to the Mount, who within a quarter of an hours space, having in the interim almost hid her body in the clouds, a dainty cast off [*sic*] Jerfaulcons were loosed to the chase: It was a delectable sight to see, with what a courageous industry, the two Royal Birds sought to get the winde, whereby to become the better masters of their prey: Whilst the poor Hearn on the other side, with as much labour and craft as nature had bestowed upon her, strived to avoid her own destruction: But as soon as the Hawks had fully attained to their pitch, then was the combate to be admired in perfection, since whensoever the Hearn found her self ready to be assailed, by her deadly though gallant enemies, she would turn her body in the air suddenly upon her back, and with her long beak, and both her feet defend her life to the best advantage, seeing those pointed weapons were more then dangerous to be attempted: Then . . . she would take a new flight, wherein as her prosecutors followed her with violence, she would slice out behinde, whereby to blind their eyes with her excrement, that they might be the more discouraged to pursue: Then the gallant Falcons finding her stratagem, endeavoured by dent of wing to get above her, that in their several stoopings, they might have the more power to become victorious; until at last the poor Bird, having altogether lost her strength by often combating, was made an intire Trophey of their conquest, falling with her enemies half dead at the feet of the Royal spectators, as a sacrifice both to cruelty and delight . . . (p. 381)

The hunt is viewed, aesthetically, as a 'delectable sight', and certainly sentiment would be out of place in the world of nature. However, the telling conclusion, seeing the death of the heron as 'a sacrifice both to cruelty and delight', encompasses the tragedy inherent in this aspect of nature when it interacts with the life of man. There is, perhaps, even another image here of Euarchus' death. It is as difficult to explain this aspect of the natural world as it is to explain the effects of providence in a world overwhelmed by chaos. The author at times deliberately shocks the reader by presenting characters' reactions to natural forces in a

violent manner. Storms at sea are a feature of romance, but they
rarely produce a sickness as extreme as Joyela's:

Joyela who had not been much accustomed to those churlish tossings of
the water, began after a while to be extream sick . . . until at last the
young Lady being in a manner overcome by her distemper, began to
vomit blood in place of other superfluities, that had for some hours
defended her from danger. (p. 447)

Characters are often unable to cope with the senseless violence
manifested all round them, leading to a mental, as well as
physical, disturbance.

These problems lead to a number of important statements by
characters, or meditations upon the situations in which they find
themselves. The question of the characteristics of an individual
soul is vital when one is surrounded by a violent world. Cloria,
held captive by Osiris, who tries to seduce her, delivers this
eloquent speech to him:

My Lord said she, although I cannot but thank my fortune, for having
delivered me into so noble hands, where honour and vertue seem to be
partners, in the making up an absolute greatness in your person; yet I
must needs believe, liberty would have offered me much more cause of
content, since it is a humane misery to be imprisoned, though it be in a
golden Tower; for nothing endued with life and motion, but certainly
covets a freedom in its own dispose, rather than be captied [*sic*] at any
rate; and especially man, that is inspired with a reasonable soul, whose
apprehension is its greatest torment . . . (p. 66)

While 'apprehension' is primarily intended to mean capture, the
sense of 'understanding' is also present. The soul, imprisoned in
this harsh world, may well be tormented by what it apprehends,
as much as by a physical sense of imprisonment. Certainly the
events of the romance bear this out.

The political situation causes a sensitive Prince such as
Arethusius to ponder how he should behave. If the power of
virtue were self-evident, such a consideration would be un-
necessary, but Arethusius is faced with the paradox of his father's
death. Meleander tells him to follow the example of his
Grandfather, who was able to remain on his throne because of
his ability to dissemble, 'for dissimulation is as necessary in
Princes actions, as the Sword of Justice to be drawn when there
is occasion' (p. 391). Arethusius does not approve of his

Grandfather's methods, but is faced with a political reality which calls constant virtue into question:

sometimes we must dissemble towards people, or to enemies both at home and abroad: I cannot deny it . . . so it be done notwithstanding with that vertue, and magnaminity of soul, befitting a Princes condition. (p. 392)

In the end, Arethusius puts forward a compromise which is almost contradictory: 'I would have a Prince always to prosecute his designs although with secresie, yet without hypocrisie' (ibid.). This conclusion is forced upon him when he tries to place the dictates of morality against the extreme dangers of the world in which he must try to regain his throne.

Arethusius is supported by the image of his father, steadfastly refusing to acknowledge the right of his judges to try him. Yet the events of the romance question Arethusius' assertion of the strength of individual conscience, however noble that assertion may be:

Arethusius replied, that man was a world within him self, being not to be deprived of an inward felicity by any power or tyranny, if he proved not the destroyer thereof by his own passions. (p. 416)

Euarchus did meet his death with a supreme fortitude, which lends some strength to his son's words. The principal characters must all face the questions raised by the central dilemma. Only Creses is able to find peace by converting to the religion of Delphos: an act preceded by considerable doubts as to its political consequences. Yet Creses is still bound up in the uncertainties of politics. Even Parismenus, after he becomes a priest, is forced to enter the devious political world in his attempts to aid Arethusius.

The Princess Cloria has a dramatic structure, revolving around Euarchus' death at the centre of Part Three, and concluding with Arethusius' restoration at the end of Part Five. After Part Three, Cloria is no longer the firm centre of attention, despite the claims of the preface that each part is conscientiously tied to her situation. The power of history may appear to shape the fiction, as it does when Cloria's marriage to Narcissus occurs at the beginning of Part Four, surrounded by ominous reminders of

Euarchus' death (see p. 353). After Arethusius learns of Narcissus' death, a solemn concern for the political situation overrides all other aspects of the romance. Cloria, now a widow, is still a very important character, but our expectation that a romance will end, as even *Argenis* does, with a marriage, is disappointed.[25] The achievement of Arethusius' restoration assumes an even greater importance than before, as all our attention is focused on it.

This is not a chivalric romance, but a political one. Arethusius does not fight his way home; our sense of an inevitable return is reinforced. Arethusius 'hoped the instability of things, would of necessity àt last bring him to his Rights . . .' (p. 445). The confusion and potential anarchy, the uncertainty felt by those involved in such unusual events, lead to a desire for order, a desire to restore the rightful king and so turn the world right-side up again. The emblem of Arethusius' return is glimpsed as early as Part One, in the impresa of a knight at the joust held by Orsames:

In his shield was pictured a King, with a drawn sword in one hand, and a whip in the other, whilest a multitude of common people appeared to beg his mercy; his intention being onely expressed by this Motto: *However I will prevail by love.* (p. 88)

Arethusius' return has a religious as well as a political resonance. The possible symbol of the father's death and the son's 'resurrection' is not exploited directly, although echoes of this are at times present in the reader's mind. Arethusius says 'You Gods . . . how great are your mercies, for not onely defending innocency by your goodness, but rendring Crowns in your justice to the true owners of them' (p. 610). In his triumph, he forgets his earlier query as to why the Gods have not acted immediately; indeed, why did they allow his exile in the first place? History makes this conclusion inevitable, and it is gladly embraced by fiction. Perhaps this retrospective historical knowledge sustains us through the uncertainty pervading the romance elsewhere. The frontispiece reassures us, with its picture of a transcendent

[25] The marriage of Hesperiana and Orontes does provide an opportunity for a wedding pageant towards the end of the romance. However, even this has primarily a political significance, and is seen as a symbol of peace—for example, in the triumphal arch with the theme of 'Beauty/overcoming War, it self becomes most famous' (p. 601).

Charles I, King and martyr, and Cloria wearing the wreath of
victory standing beneath him. The couplet below this picture,
however, asks a very pertinent question, before pointing to the
religious conclusion achieved by Arethusius' return:

> What Sacrifice can Expiate past Crimes
> Are left to Jove; Our King must bless the Times.

IV. Conclusion

The prose romance, with Sidney's sophisticated structure but a
new, plain style, was a more suitable genre to encompass the Civil
War than the heroic poem. Davenant's *Gondibert* and Cowley's
Davideis are ambitious, unfinished, and ultimately, most readers
agree, unsatisfying. Earl Miner sensibly notes that although in
these heroic poems we 'sense intermittent political or historical
pressures', no detailed correspondence between fiction and
history can be found.[26] Where the romances meet the war head
on, the heroic poems hint at it, but finally skirt round it. Cowley's
attempt to write an epic directly on the Civil War was baulked by
royalist defeat at the battle of Newbury in 1643—and probably
also by the recognition that his attempt was unsuccessful as
literature.[27] The incorporation of material from it in *Davideis* is a
retreat from such a confrontation. *The Princess Cloria* would have
provided Christopher Hill with a much more satisfactory
example of the royalist literary response to the Civil War than
Cowley's poem, which he uses in his important study of *Milton
and the English Revolution*.[28] The heroic poem had the elevation but
not the detailed realism which the political romance brought to
the subject of the Civil War.

The idea that the prose romance, as developed into a vehicle
for political allegory by Barclay, was a perfect genre to
incorporate the experience of the Civil War is recognized in the
prefaces of the surviving examples. These romances are able to
combine a concern for the heroic individual with a knowledge of
larger events; as the preface to *Theophania* puts it: 'you will find
Man, and the Passions of Man . . . and (it may be) Traverses of

---

[26] Earl Miner, *The Restoration Mode from Milton to Dryden* (Princeton, 1974), p. 73.
[27] Abraham Cowley, *The Civil War*, ed. Allan Pritchard (Toronto, 1973), p. 4.
[28] London, 1977.

State, set down as in a Mapp or Chart before you' (A3^v). The preface to *The Princess Cloria* notes that 'the Ground work for a *Romance* was excellent . . . since by no other way almost, could the multiplicity of strange Actions of the Times be exprest, that exceeded all belief' (A^v).[29]

---

[29] This is reminiscent of Clarendon's view of the war expressed in his great history; he noted the 'transactions . . . hardly to be paralleled in any other time, or place, for the wonderful turns and passages in it', *History of the Rebellion* (Oxford, 1826), Dedication prefixed to Vol. 3 of First Edition, Vol. 1, p. 43.

Chapter 12

The French Heroic Romance

The young Dorothy Osborne, writing to William Temple in 1653, urgently asks him: 'have you read Cleopatra? I have sixe Tomes on't heer that I can lend you, if you have not, there are some Story's in't you will like I beleeve'.[1] She is referring to the French heroic romance *Cléopâtre*, by Gautier de Coste de la Calprenède, one of a number of romances which were the height of literary fashion in Paris, and which became equally fashionable in England—particularly with Royalists, many of whom acquired a taste for all things French during their enforced exile after the Civil War. The heroic romance form grew out of the *roman d'aventure*, which flourished between 1619 (the date of the first version of Gomberville's *L'Exil de Polexandre*, the most influential adventure romance) and 1640. The *roman d'aventure* is episodic and chivalric, while the heroic romance, which developed between 1640 and 1665, has an epic structure, and is more concerned with the primacy of love and its effects than with external events.[2]

Women played an important part in the creation of this form, both as writers and as members of the literary salons which cultivated the ideal patterns of behaviour exemplified by

[1] *The Letters of Dorothy Osborne*, ed. G. C. Moore Smith (Oxford, 1928), p. 21; further references are to this edition.

[2] The heroic romance has been labelled the '*roman de longue haleine*', '*roman historico-épique*', and '*heroische-galante roman*', see T. P. Haviland, *The Roman de Longue Haleine on English Soil* (Philadelphia, 1931); Maurice Magendie, *Le Roman française au XVIIᶜ siècle de L'Astrée au Grand Cyrus* (Paris, 1932); Wolfgang von Wurzbach, *Geschichte des Französischen Romans* (Heidelberg, 1912); other useful studies on the form and its background are: George Saintsbury, *A History of the French Novel* (London, 1917), Vol. 1, Chap. 8; Antoine Adam, *Histoire de la littérature française au XVIIᶜ siècle* (Paris, 1948), Vol. 1, Chap. 4, Vol. 2, Chap. 3; Gustave Reynier, *Le Roman sentimental avant L'Astrée* (Paris, 1908); Georges Mongrédien, *La Vie littéraire au XVIIᶜ siècle* (Paris, 1947); Claude Aragonnès, *Madeleine de Scudéry: Reine du tendre* (Paris, 1934); Moses Ratner, *Theory and Criticism of the Novel in France from L'Astrée to 1750* (1938, rpt. New York, 1971); Georges Mongrédien, *Madeleine de Scudéry et son salon* (Paris, 1946); Dorothy McDougall, *Madeleine de Scudéry* (London, 1938).

characters in the romances.[3] The reputation of these circles of *précieuses* has had to be rescued from the satire directed at them by contemporaries, notably by Molière in *Les Précieuses ridicules*.[4] The 'feminism' of these romances is much less radical than Mary Wroth's, and the ideal of the *honnête homme* and the elaborate analyses of love-dilemmas can become wearing and superficial. Nevertheless, the increased sophistication in structure, and the emphasis on detailed character analysis, mark an important development in fiction. Madeleine de Scudéry wrote three major romances—*Ibrahim* (1641), *Artamène ou Le Grand Cyrus* (1649–53), *Clélie* (1660–3)—and presided over a salon. Discussions held by her friends were continued and developed in her fiction.[5]

The romances were almost invariably translated into English fairly soon after their appearance in France. The number of translations, as well as the circulation of original versions (Dorothy Osborne read them in French), indicates a large audience in England. Anyone who even glances at one of these romances today will immediately be struck by their length. Scudéry's *Cyrus* is considerably longer than *Clarissa*; the English translation of La Calprenède's *Cassandre* (1642–5, trans. by Sir Charles Cotterell, 1652), an average-sized work, is 1,400 folio pages long. This expansiveness was regarded as an admirable quality by contemporary readers. One of the characters in Madeleine de Scudéry's *Almahide* says to the narrator of an extremely long story, 'the passages which you relate are so pleasant, and the stories so well told, that the longer they are the more delectable are they to them that are capable to discern their Elegancy' (II. 2, p. 125).[6] However, these romances did appear in separate parts, like a novel by Dickens, and during her correspondence with William Temple, Dorothy Osborne sends him her beloved *Cléopâtre* and *Cyrus* one part at a time (she refers to the parts as 'Tomes'). The reader is expected to enter the world of the romance and inhabit it for some time, participating in the

    [3] See Ian Maclean, *Woman Triumphant: Feminism in French Literature 1610–1652* (Oxford, 1977); Dorothy Anne Backer, *Precious Women* (New York, 1974).
    [4] See Domna C. Stanton's stimulating article 'The Fiction of *Préciosité* and the Fear of Women', *Yale French Studies*, 62 (1981), 107–34.
    [5] Bibliographical information is taken from R. C. Williams, *Bibliography of the Seventeenth-Century Novel in France* (New York, 1931), and Ralph W. Baldner, *Bibliography of Seventeenth-Century French Prose Fiction* (New York, 1967).
    [6] References are to *Almahide*, trans. J. Phillips (1677).

characters' discussions and analyses of their emotional dilemmas.
The French romances concentrate on one overriding theme,
succinctly stated by Bishop Huet in his account of the form
published in 1670: 'Romances . . . have Love for their principal
Theme, and meddle not with War or Politicks but by accident.'[7]
The English imitations, as we shall see, 'meddle' quite considerably with war and politics; but before we discuss English
developments, we need an anatomy of the form as it developed in
France.

I. Prose Epic

Writers like Madeleine de Scudéry were very conscious of their
reliance on epic structure: 'I call regular those which are
according to the rules of an Heroick Poem.'[8] In the preface to
Ibrahim the need for narrative unity is stressed: 'all the parts . . .
should make but one body . . . well-ordering is one of the
principal parts of a piece' (A2, A2ᵛ).[9] This narrative method is
consciously linked with that of the classical epic:

the [ancients] have not done like those Painters, who present in one and
the same cloth a Prince in the Cradle, upon the Throne, and in the
Tombe, perplexing, by this so little judicious a confusion, him that
considers their works; but with an incomparable address they begin
their History in the middle, so as to give some suspence to the Reader,
even from the first opening of the Book; and to confine themselves
within reasonable bounds they have made the History (as I likewise
have done after them) not to last above a year, the rest being delivered
by Narration. (A2ᵛ)

Authors took some pains to begin their narrative dramatically.
Scudéry's *Grand Cyrus* is a good example:

The Conflagration of Sinope was so great, that the very skie, the Sea,
the valleys and tops of Mountains though far remote were all
illuminated by its flames . . . (p. 1)[10]

Once the reader's attention is captured, retrospective narration is

---

[7] Pierre Huet, *A Treatise of Romances and their Originals* (1672, first published in French
in 1670), p. 6.
[8] Huet, p. 62.
[9] References are to *Ibrahim*, trans. H. Cogan (1674).
[10] References are to *Artamenes or The Grand Cyrus*, trans. F.G. (1653-5).

used to explain the events leading up to the opening of the romance.

II. History

The heroic romances declare themselves to be historical; as Scudéry says:

I have observed the Manners, Customs, Religions, and Inclinations of People: And to give a more true resemblance to things, I have made the foundations of my work Historical. (*Ibrahim*, A2ᵛ)

During a discussion which occurs in *Clélie* we are told 'the Writer takes pains to study the Age well he makes choice of, to improve all the rarities of it, and to conform to the customs of places he treats of . . .' (IV. 2, p. 201).[11] Ancient Greece and Rome particularly attracted authors, but they could range even further; an exotic locale was preferable, hence the attraction of Turkey and Granada. A whole range of historical figures and situations are depicted, from Horatius at the bridge to Sappho and her poetry. The authors, in accordance with the doctrine of *vraisemblance*, declare that accuracy is important.[12] They may have made an effort to achieve some sense of historical accuracy, but this is hampered by the desire to continue the discussions of the salons in the romances. The characters are seventeenth-century people in exotic dress. Aragonnès notes that *Cyrus* is '*un roman contemporain, déguisé à l'antique*', and Antoine Adam enlarges this analysis:

Enfin le roman héroïque prétend donner aux contemporains l'image de la société française, de la société galante. Car ce mélange d'héroïsme et de galanterie qui définit les Oroondate et les Cyrus, n'est pas du tout, ne prétend pas être une peinture exacte des héros de l'antiquité.[13]

This approach extended to Scudéry's portrayal of members of her own salon in her romances.[14]

The result of this combination of historical colouring and protestations of *vraisemblance* with a detailed depiction of the

---

[11] *Clelia*, trans. G. Havers (1655); references are to this edition unless otherwise noted.
[12] See Ratner, pp. 21–7.
[13] Aragonnès, p. 128; Adam, Vol. 2, p. 127.
[14] McDougall, pp. 109–12; Victor Cousin discovered a key to *Cyrus*, which he published in his *La Société française au* XVIIᵉ *siècle d'après Le Grand Cyrus de Mlle Scudéry* (Paris, 1858), Vol. 1, pp. 333–7.

précieuses and their concerns is not unlike Shakespeare's history plays. The 'Elizabethan Romans' of *Julius Caesar* are similar to the baroque French Romans, or Greeks, or Persians, of the heroic romances. The romance writers did make an effort to 'research' their chosen periods, and to create a sense of the past, but for the reader today this effort is swamped by the overriding concern with the ideas of the salons. The original readers, however, reacted favourably towards what was undeniably an advance in the technique of historical fiction.

III. Analysis

Members of the salons and characters in the romances devoted a large amount of time to the analysis of delicate emotional dilemmas. The paradigm of this process is the section of *Cyrus* which contains the 'Histories of unfortunate lovers' (III. i, pp. 17–82) told to Cyrus. He has to decide which lover is the most unfortunate, the 'absent lover', the 'Lover not loved', the 'Lover in Mourning', or the 'jealous lover'. The reader is implicitly invited to join this inquiry. The process of analysis requires an involvement of a quite sophisticated kind from the reader; the narrative is not so much read as studied.

The initiating action of the heroic romance is the separation of the hero and heroine. A proliferation of secondary stories arises from this situation, and the reader of these extremely long narratives must give him or herself up to the suspension of any narrative *dénouement* while the process of analysis takes place. Each new character relates his or her own history when first introduced into the narrative. Characters provide detailed accounts of their past lives to explain their situation: 'It is requisite I relate the whole Story of my life' is a typical response from a new character (Thrasibulus in *Cyrus*, III. 3, p. 151). These life stories are referred to as histories, but rather than 'whole' stories, they are devoted to accounts of love and its effects. Thrasibulus' 'whole Story' is soon revealed to be 'The History of Thrasibulus and Alcionida' (ibid.).

The heroic romance in this way mirrors the milieu in which it flourished. Reflection, not action, was the lot of the women who ran the salons and who wrote so many of these romances, and of women like Dorothy Osborne who read them. Within the romances, heroic action has a place, but it always leads back to stasis, to an emotional dilemma, and to further analysis. Resolution of the narrative is suspended as action invariably leads not to the rescue of the heroine, but to further abduction, further delays, further subsidiary stories. Heroic action is usually described retrospectively, rather than presented directly.

The narrative structure of the heroic romance involves an accumulation of subsidiary stories which are not resolved when first related by new characters, but are instead woven through the whole work. In this way the reader is invited to consider the situations of a number of characters during the leisurely progress of the narrative, and this process occurs in the gaps between the histories related by each character, rather than only when they are speaking. Scudéry emphasizes that the writer of heroic romances is more interested in character analysis than in action for its own sake:

Certainly there is nothing more important in this kind of composition, than strongly to imprint the Idea, or (to say better) the image of the Heroes in the mind of the Reader, but in such sort, as if they were known to them; for that it is which interesseth him in their adventures, and from thence his delight cometh, now to make them be known perfectly, it is not sufficient to say how many times they have suffered shipwreck, and how many times they have encountered Robbers, but their inclinations must be made to appear by their discourse . . . (*Ibrahim*, A3^v)

Dorothy Osborne's comments provide invaluable evidence about how an intelligent, enthusiastic woman read these works. Analysis is very much to the fore:

I am glad you are an admirer of Telesile as well as I, in my opinion tis a fine Lady, but I know you will pitty Poore Amestris strangly [*sic*] when you have read her Storry. i'le swear I cryed for her when I read it first though shee were but an imaginary person, and sure if any thing of that kind can deserve it her misfortunes may. (p. 85)

It is worth noting that Dorothy Osborne was a sophisticated reader who recognized that her involvement with the characters necessitated a willing suspension of disbelief ('though shee were but an imaginary person'). The stories (that is, histories) of various characters are singled out for special attention:

there is a story of Artemise that I will recomende to you, her disposition I like extreamly, it has a great deal of Gratitude int, and if you meet with one Brittomart pray send mee word how you like him. (p. 24)

you will meet with a story in these part's of Cleopatra that pleased me more then any that ever I read in my life, 'tis of one Delie, pray give mee your opinion of her and her Prince. (p. 31)

Osborne responded with enthusiasm to the dilemmas offered by the romance for the reader's consideration:

there are fower Pritty Story's in it [*Cyrus*] . . . tell me wch you have most compassion for: when you have read what Every one say's for himself, perhaps you will not think it soe Easy to decide wch is the most unhappy as you may think by the Titles theire Storry's bear, only let mee desyre you not to Pitty the Jelous one, for I remember I could doe nothing but Laugh at him, as one that sought his owne vexation . . . L'Amant Absent has (in my opinion) a Mistresse, soe much beyonde any of the rest that to bee in danger of loosing her, is more then to have lost the others . . . if you have mett with the beginning of the story of Amestris & Aglatides, You will finde the rest of it in this part I send you now, and tis to mee one of the Prittiest I have read and the most Naturall. (pp. 81–2)

Osborne's favourite story is praised as being 'the most Naturall'— which shows her acceptance of *vraisemblance* as the main aim of the heroic romance.

John Barclay's self-conscious approach to the political/ allegorical romance, which involves a discussion of the form within *Argenis* itself, is paralleled in *Clélie*, one of Scudéry's romances, which contains discussions between the major charac- ters about the aims of the new romance form. Amilcar prefaces his account of the 'History of Artaxander' with a few remarks about the process of telling such stories:

I am not fit to be my own Historian; But if you desire to have a relation of some such adventure, I have had a hundred friends in my life, who have had many gallant and extraordinarie adventures which I am acquainted with as well as my own; and you need onely but to tell me, what kind of Storie you would have . . . (I. 3, p. 89)

After Amilcar finishes the history, the listeners discuss the individuals in it in the same way that Dorothy Osborne approaches the characters in *Cyrus*:

For my particular (said *Clelia*, seeing *Amilcar* had no more to say) I am far from repenting, for I do think these two beginnings of love worth a whole History. For my part (said the Prince *Sextus*) I am very affectionate unto *Artaxander*, because me thinks he resembles *Amilcar*. Truth is (replied *Aronces*) *Artaxander* is set out in an excellent character: I concur with you (said the merry *Plotina*) but yet me thinks if *Amilcar* had been in *Artaxanders* place, he would either not have *Pasithea* so slightly . . . (I. 3, p. 115)

The characters in the history are then revealed as disguised portraits; for example, Artaxander is really Amilcar himself. This mirrors the nature of the romance, which itself contains portraits of Scudéry's salon members. This Chinese-box effect is the product of the obsessive analysis which was practised in the salons. While the concern for correct behaviour (the interest in the *honnête homme*, for example) did have some social importance, essentially the romances reflect the inward-looking nature of the salons. The self-conscious encapsulation of critical description within the literary work is, despite its technical similarity, not a sophisticated literary game, such as that played by many modern novelists, but simply a reduplication of the discussions held in the salons. Dorothy Osborne's comments indicate that readers who were not members, who had no cognizance of the salons' relationship with the romances, still entered into the salon milieu, into the analytical passion and analysis of passion.

The characters in *Clélie* move on to a discussion of the use of the *récit*, and the need to embroider history. Anacreon observes,

I cannot but believe, but the History you have read is almost all of it invented. Yet it is contrived ingeniously enough, (added he); for me thinks, 'tis not onely handsomer than the truth, but with all more probable. History mentions nothing more of *Hesiode*, than that he dwelt at the Town of *Ascra* . . . (IV. 2, pp. 199–200)

Anacreon himself is the product of just such an ingenious contrivance. The discussion then compares the heroic romance which strives for *vraisemblance*, and thus for the decorum of fictional representation, with earlier romance forms which are full of 'prodigies' (IV. 2, p. 201). The major aim of the new form is verisimilitude: 'when you invent a Fable your purpose is to be believ'd, and the true art of Fiction is handsomly to resemble truth' (ibid.). The final point in the discussion is made by Herminius, who praises the heroic romance's approach to history: he advises the writer to choose a historical period which is

neither too familiar nor too distant, and then flesh out the known
historical facts with humanizing fictional details.

IV. Portraits

The interest in analysing characters and their predicaments
produced a new technique of characterization: the portrait. Each
character is described through a portrait: an analysis of appearance and personality. While the Character form concentrates on
general types, enumerating details to build up a personalized
image of a courtier, or even of an object like a bottle of canary
wine, the portrait tries to build up an image of a particular
individual by concentrating on unique, sometimes even contradictory characteristics. A good example is this portrait of
Corantus, from Scudéry's *Clélie*:

. . . [he] has a noble, but very sweet and civil aspect, though sometimes
his air seem[s] a little cold and careless. He has brown hair, a very
handsome head, somewhat a long visage, a pale complexion, small and
black eyes, but nevertheless his looks are very ingenious, and even his
silence speaks him such, for in discourse, he hears, like one who
admirably well understands that which is spoken to him, and who could
speak more than he does. All his deportments are such as become a man
of his quality, and his mind is perfectly fram'd for converse with the
world; he loves ingenious composures and their Authors; he has a
melancholy aspect, and nevertheless loves all pleasures. His Soul is
naturally passionate, and though the outside of his person and his mind
speak him one of those faithful Lovers which the world so rarely affords,
yet he is always a serious wanton, or if you will, a tolerable inconstant;
for no doubt some are not such. However he maintains confidently that
he is faithful, because he says he never deserted any woman who gave
him not cause of complaint. He is one of those who account it no
infidelity to make little affections occasionally by the by, which arise in
their heart during their greater passions. But this is constantly true,
where he loves, he loves ardently, he minds nothing but his passion, he is
very inclinable to jealousie, he resents the least unpleasing things with a
strange vehemence; and, in fine, is acquainted with the greatest delights
and the extremest rigours of love.   (1678 edn., V. 3, pp. 698–9)

The reader's response to this method of characterization does not
depend upon any knowledge of the *roman à clef* element in these
romances. Dorothy Osborne was evidently unaware of this aspect
of the volumes which she read, but she still treated the portraits as

individuals who invited sustained reflection and discussion. Her correspondence with William Temple constituted, to some extent, a *salon à deux*; a chance to turn the portraits around in order to view them from every angle.

V. Structure

Readers who are now unwilling to study the heroic romance carefully because of the immense length of the form miss encountering a fascinating approach to narrative structure. Despite their size, the heroic romances are constructed with great care. The aim of the author was to achieve a narrative unity:

> The Addresse of him which employs them [the 'several Histories'] should hold them in some sort to this principal action, to the end, that by this ingenious concatenation, all the parts of them should make but one body, and that nothing may be seen in them which is loose and unprofitable.   (*Ibrahim*, Preface, A2)

Thus the proliferating *récits* and subsidiary histories must be part of an overarching pattern, and related to the main history. The epic unity professed by these authors necessitated the extensive use of the *récit* to encompass events outside the restricted narrative time-scheme. The histories do not form unconnected digressions, but are interwoven with each other, like a series of connected sub-plots. Characters familiar to the reader as major actors in one history may reappear as minor actors in another. Settings also recur, and as the reader proceeds the 'world' of the romance becomes quite clearly defined until, by the end, many apparently discrete histories are seen to be part of a larger whole.

This structure may be illustrated by a brief consideration of La Calprenède's *Cassandre*, a much shorter romance than any by Scudéry, and therefore easier to summarize. The main action of *Cassandre* revolves around the abduction of Statira, the widow of Alexander the Great, and of her sister Parisatis by Perdiccas, and the attempts of their lovers, Oroondates and Lysimachus, to rescue them. Virtually all heroic romances have this basic plot: abduction and repeated attempts at rescue. However, the *in medias res* opening of *Cassandre* takes only seven pages to shift into the first retrospective history. The narrative present is a very small proportion of the romance, interposed between the eighteen histories which constitute the greater part of *Cassandre*. To use the terminology of Gérard Genette, whose refinement of concepts associated with narrative structure is particularly useful in a consideration of this complex form, the narrative of the heroic romance is principally composed of 'anachronies'—breaks in narrative time through the use of analepse (flash-back) and prolepse (flash-forward).[15]

The greater part of *Cassandre* is made up of the histories of Oroondates, Lysimachus, Berenice, Roxana, and Arsaces; all of these characters are related to or closely associated with each other. When the histories of *Cassandre* are set out in a table which groups together *récits* which, although they are scattered through the romance, continue the same story, it is clear that there are nine complete histories, expanded to eighteen by interspersing them with each other and with the narrative present (see Table). This elaborate web of interconnecting *récits* is a development of the form used by Sidney in the *New Arcadia*, but the heroic romance has moved away from the focus on a small set of major characters. The multifarious yet connected histories achieve a unity-in-variety, a satisfying baroque structure. They provide varied sub-plots, while still being inextricably bound up with the main action.

The use of the *récit* in this structure has an important effect on the analytical approach to character and action discussed above. The retrospective *récit*, offered by a character about him or herself or about another character, implies that the present may only be explained by a detailed account of the past. The present is a mystery—a fact which is emphasized by the use of the *in medias res* opening. Present events continue as the *récit* is spoken, but the reader is pulled away from the narrative present into a receding set of explanations.

The opening of Scudéry's *Cyrus* usefully illustrates this technique. The capture of Sinope and second abduction of Mandana are described; Cyrus is imprisoned by Mandana's father, and then his friend Chrisantes relates Cyrus' history to his supporters. This history reveals Cyrus' identity and explains his role in the affairs of Persia, but it is interrupted: the narrative returns to Cyrus' present situation in prison, where he is soon told the

---

[15] See Gérard Genette, *Narrative Discourse*, trans. Jane Lewin (Oxford, 1980), Chap. 1.

The Histories in Cassandre

(1)
'The History of Oroondates'
(I. 1, pp. 7–57)

'The Continuation of the History of Oroondates and Statira'
(I. 3, pp. 64–172)

'The History of Statira'
(I. 5, pp. 126–44)

'The History of Cassandra' (i.e. Statira)
(III. 1, pp. 99–199)

(2)
'The History of Lysimachus'
(II. 1, pp. 182–238)

(3)
'The History of Thalestris Queen of the Amazons'
(II. 3, p. 250–II. 4, p. 32)

'Orontes' History'
(II. 4, pp. 15–21)

'The History of Orontes'
(V. 2, pp. 53–60)

(4)
'The History of Berenice'
(II. 5, pp. 49–69)

'The Continuation of the History of Berenice'
(III. 5, pp. 59–69)

'The Continuation of the History of Berenice'
(IV. 6, pp. 62–73)

'The History of Arsaces'
(IV. 2, p. 109–IV. 5, p. 59)

(5)
'The History of Alcione'
(II. 6, pp. 64–90)

(6)
'The History of Roxana'
(III. 2, pp. 127–41)

'The Continuation of the History of Roxana'
(V. 1, pp. 16–29)

(7)
'The History of Hermione'
(III. 4, pp. 3–25)

(8)
'The History of Deidamia'
(IV. 1, pp. 83–107)

(9)
'The History of Barsina'
(V. 3, pp. 68–91)

'History of Aglatidas and Amestris'. The reader is now confronted
with three narrative levels. The two histories (later shown to be
connected) explain different aspects of the present situation. A
continuation of Cyrus' history reaches the events depicted at the
beginning of the romance, but the history of Aglatidas is as yet
unresolved, and meanwhile present events have moved on. The
reader must wait for a hundred pages before Aglatidas' history is
resumed, by which time ten further histories have been started.

The narrative is pulled back towards the past, and the reader
must concentrate in order to keep track of the complex temporal
levels of the proliferating histories. However, connections between the histories become apparent as the romance proceeds,
and this increasing sense of cohesion counteracts the initial
impression of numerous disparate narratives. A diagram is a
useful way of representing these patterns.

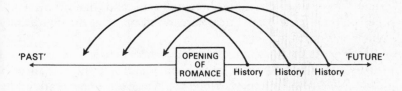

The Structure of the Heroic Romance

Third-person impersonal narration is constantly superseded
by the first-person *récit*. The *récit* turns the past into speech, and
speech overwhelms action. A combat in the narrative present will
immediately lead to speech, to history, to the past—as if action
must be erased by words. This structure forces the reader to desist
from any impatient desire for narrative resolution, and instead to
enter into creative speculation in the manner of Dorothy
Osborne. The narrative moves inwards, rather than forwards,
and the conclusion is never a surprise—not so much because it is a
stock device, but because we feel we are moving in a circle: the
conclusion is not the end of a narrative line, but the moment
when the stasis suggested by the romance's structure is finally
reached.

VI. The Heroic Romance in England: *Parthenissa*

Some elements of the heroic romance form were used in the political/allegorical romances discussed in the preceding chapter. As the French romances became fashionable, more overt imitations were produced; these have a distinctive character, and are not exact replicas of the works being produced across the channel. *Parthenissa*, the most ambitious of these works, reflects the pervasive political concerns of England in the Interregnum, and explores the dilemmas facing an ambitious man during that troubled time.[16] *Parthenissa* also reflects the complexity of its author's personality. Roger Boyle, first Earl of Orrery, is described by his biographer as a 'many-faceted' and 'elusive' character.[17] He served both Parliament and Crown in the Civil War, and was a friend of both Cromwell and Charles II. The fact that, like his brother Robert, he had many interests was characteristic of the century—as were his personal manoeuvres. His main claim to recognition by literary historians has been his initiation of the Restoration heroic drama, and, like his plays, *Parthenissa* reflects his political career and many of the political dilemmas of his age.

Five parts of *Parthenissa* were published between 1651 and 1656, and a sixth part in 1669, which still left the romance incomplete, although the 740 folio pages provide ample material for comments about Boyle's general aims.[18] *Parthenissa* is written in strict observance of the unities outlined by Madeleine de Scudéry. It opens at the oracle of Hierapolis with the arrival of Artabanes, and all the *récits* which make up the romance are related there, or nearby. Three characters are the centre of attention: Callimachus, the 'prince' of the oracle's priests, listens to the histories of Artabanes and his friend Artavasdes. He in turn favours them with his own history. The histories involve the three loves of these heroes, and become the histories of Artabanes and Parthenissa (which also contains a long account of a fourth pair, Perolla and Izadora), Artavasdes and Altazeera, and Callimachus and Statira. Artabanes' and Artavasdes' stories are

---

[16] A less politically conscious heroic romance, *Eliana* (1661), is still considerably harsher in its treatment of passion than any of the French works which it imitates.

[17] Kathleen M. Lynch, *Roger Boyle First Earl of Orrery* (Knoxville, 1965), p. 234.

[18] This is the length of the 1676 edition referred to here; the pagination jumps from p. 404 to p. 484, the last page being numbered 807.

interconnected, structurally and thematically, while Callimachus'
rather different history takes up the last part of this incomplete
romance.

Artabanes, the heir to the throne of Media, was brought up
with Pacorus, son of the King of Parthia, and fell in love with
Parthenissa, the daughter of a Parthian general. He fought with
the Parthians against the Armenians, and so met the valiant
Artavasdes. When we reach this stage of his history, the history of
Artavasdes is introduced—he is an Armenian prince, in love with
Altazeera, the King's daughter. Artabanes' history continues,
and we hear how the Parthian prince Surena wooed Parthenissa,
and how Artabanes received apparent proof of her unfaithful-
ness. He left Parthia in dismay and reached Italy, becoming a
slave. There he led a slave revolt, and was named Spartacus
(allowing Boyle to provide an historical account of his activities).
At this point we hear 'The Story of Izadora and Perolla', which
involves Hannibal's invasion of Italy.

Artabanes/Spartacus learns that Parthenissa is falsely maligned. We then return to Artavasdes' history, to learn how he was
forced to leave Armenia, and so his story mingled with that of
Artabanes. Altazeera, after some resistance, agreed to marry
Pacorus, driving Artavasdes to despair. He eventually gained the
throne of Armenia, and learned that Altazeera had been tricked
into believing that he no longer loved her. But her marriage to
the noble Pacorus could not be broken. Eventually, Artavasdes
agreed to consult the oracle. We are then told how Artabanes
returned to Media and was reconciled with Parthenissa, but she
was carried off by Surena. Artabanes and Surena fought a
number of times (Surena conducting himself nobly), but King
Arsaces, who had also fallen in love with Parthenissa, threatened
her (and executed Surena), whereupon Parthenissa apparently
took poison. The despairing Artabanes eventually reached
Hierapolis to consult the oracle.

Part Five of *Parthenissa* begins with the complicated history of
Callimachus, the son of Nicomedes, King of Bithynia. He was
raised in Athens, unaware of his parentage, and his history
centres around his love for Statira, daughter of Mithridates,
which eventually leads him to fight on Mithridates' side against
Nicomedes when Nicomedes tries to regain his throne. *Parthenissa*
ends when Callimachus has just been betrothed to Statira, only to

have Mithridates turn against him owing to suspicious circumstances surrounding his escape from captivity by Nicomedes.[19]
We also catch a glimpse, near the end of Part Five, of two ladies
who arrive near the temple of Adonis, and who certainly appear
to be Parthenissa and Altazeera. The promise of reconciliation is
held out to us, but Boyle did not proceed to its ultimate
conclusion.[20]

Parthenissa is less concerned with the love and gallantry which
feature in the French romances than it is with political power and
its use. Proliferating histories are avoided, and the narrative
focuses on two clear story-lines: the interwoven histories of
Artabanes and Artavasdes, and the history of Callimachus.
Boyle's political speculation is most evident in a series of debates
which replace the French romance's *questioni d'amore*. For
instance, at one point, Ventidius, the Roman general, tells
Artavasdes how Rome fared after the death of Julius Caesar; and
this leads to a debate on the respective virtues of monarchies and
commonwealths. Ventidius states:

> you that subject your selves to a successive Monarchy, are tyed to your
> Rulers as to your Fate, you must submit to the bad as well as the good;
> whereas we are confin'd to ours but as to our Cloaths, if they are sullied,
> unfit, or worn out, we make our selves new ones. (p. 348)

Artavasdes replies that power must be vested in a single
individual: 'an internal quiet . . . proceeds from a general
submission to one Authority' (ibid.). He goes on to note that the
Romans usually place their trust in this maxim, and cites the
institution of Dictator.

Ventidius argues that 'Power is best plac'd in the

---

[19] I find it difficult to agree with Kathleen Lynch's speculation that 'Perhaps Orrery
found some resemblance between the tragic predicament of Henrietta, Duchess of
Orleans, married to a hateful husband, and the unhappy Statira, betrothed by parental
authority to an unloved prince' (p. 191). One might look to the unhappy marriage of
Altazeera and Pacorus, rather than Statira's betrothal, which she defies at the end of the
romance because, in fact, the ceremony betrothing her to Callimachus has taken place.
The dedication of Part Six to Henrietta does not necessitate such a direct identification—
it was customary to declare that one's 'perfect' heroine was modelled on the noble
dedicatee.

[20] The 'Summary of *Parthenissa*' provided by Charlotte E. Morgan in *The Rise of the
Novel of Manners* (New York, 1911), pp. 138–42, is not completely reliable; Lynch
provides a more accurate, though less detailed, account, pp. 189–92.

Representatives of the People' (p. 352). He then makes an astute observation, which seems to reflect Boyle's own thoughts:

The design of Usurping the Sovereignty, is less like to be undertook, under the Government of a Commonwealth, than under that of a Monarch; for if the intended Usurper have success against the Forces of a King, he finds the People prepar'd to embrace that form of Regiment; but though he have success against the Forces of a Commonwealth, he will find a new difficulty, in constraining the People to submit to Monarchy; in one he is to destroy but the Governor, but in the other, the Governors and Government. (p. 353)

He goes on to explain that even if one establishes the government in one man, the worthiest man should be *chosen*.

Despite Ventidius' persuasions, Artavasdes will not agree to attempt to gain the crown of Armenia, because of his 'unalterable resolution of usurping neither upon my kings, nor my Princesses rights' (p. 356). While Artavasdes has the last word, Boyle does not leave us completely satisfied. This dilemma produces a dialectical argument with no simple solution. Ventidius explains how the soldier is caught in the middle of such a conflict:

Governors under either Regiment [i.e. monarchy or commonwealth], have establish'd . . . principles to destroy the generousest Calling; a calling without which they could do nothing, and for which they seldom do anything; sometimes they make the prosperity of it necessary to the existence of a State, and sometimes the destruction of it as necessary; sometimes they say it hinders, or revenges oppression; and sometimes it invites, and continues it; sometimes they make it a Scaffold, to raise their structure to the Clouds; then use it like a Scaffold, and lay it in the dust. These last words I spake, to evince the most noble, is the most unfortunate profession; it sowes merit, and reaps ingratitude . . . (p. 355)

These, one feels, are the bitter thoughts of the author of *A Treatise of the Art of War* (1677); the servant of Crown and Parliament, monarchy and commonwealth, Charles and Cromwell.

Ventidius' speech contains some sharp, pragmatic statements about power: 'the Sword hath introduced most Governments, since it does maintain all, and since it only can ruine any Government . . .' (p. 354). Artavasdes is caught in the middle of conflicting arguments and interests, a common situation in this romance. Boyle uses an almost dialectical structure, with the

stories of Artabanes and Artavasdes set against the story of
Callimachus. Oppositions balance, the reader finds it difficult to
choose an alternative, and this difficulty is shared by the
characters themselves.

Artabanes and Artavasdes are on opposing sides in battle, yet
they become friends; neither has a real stake in the war. We
cannot seize on a single situation and inflate it into a principle.
Artabanes as Spartacus leads a noble revolt, while Artavasdes
will not attempt to gain the Armenian throne. Circumstances,
rather than absolute principles, dictate right and wrong actions.
And a man who wishes to survive Civil War, Interregnum, and
Restoration must become adept at judging what actions may be
allowed by circumstances.

An early example of Boyle's approach is the story of Perolla
and Izadora, contained within Artabanes' history. Perolla's
father supports Hannibal, while Izadora's father supports the
Romans. Defying his father, Perolla fights against Hannibal, who
manages to capture both Perolla and Izadora's father. Izadora is
left in a position to save one life only:

It reduced me either to imploy my request for my Fathers, and so lose
my friends Life: or if I preserv'd *Perolla*'s, I must lose *Blacius*'s . . . Alas,
how sad a conflict had I betwixt my Duty and my Affection?
(p. 141)

The conflict between love and honour will, of course, become a
favourite motif in the Restoration heroic play. The story of
shifting fortunes and conflict continues, until the two fathers and
their children appear before Spartacus. Both fathers accuse their
children of disloyalty: Perolla's 'best performances are crimes',
while Izadora's father accuses her of 'want of Duty' (p. 234). But
the lovers plead for their fathers' lives, and a reconciliation does
ensue.

Artavasdes and Artabanes face even more complicated dilemmas, of a more political nature. Artavasdes' father, Anexander, is
the husband of King Artabazus' aunt; Artabazus has a son,
Tigranes, and a daughter, Altazeera. Armenia is in constant
political turmoil—we first hear of Artavasdes defeating a plot by
Celindus (married to Artabazus' other aunt) to kill the King and
force Altazeera to marry his son Tuminius. Then Crassolis
intrigues to place Tigranes on the throne. As the King's favourite,

he is able, unsuspected, to raise a successful rebellion. After a period of considerable confusion, Artabazus is safely restored to his throne, but Crassolis cannot be discredited, and so his intriguing continues.

Artabazus is portrayed as a weak king who places his realm in danger through blind trust in a man like Crassolis. (I do not, however, think that this is a depiction of Charles I, in the manner of the political/allegorical romance; *Parthenissa* has a general, rather than a particular, political relevance.) We again encounter the motif of son against father. When Armenia is at war with Parthia, Pacorus, the King of Parthia's son, falls in love with Altazeera. He offers his services to Artabazus, and fights against his father's troops. This gesture also ends in reconciliation.

Artavasdes' dilemma occurs when Altazeera marries Pacorus under the false impression that Artavasdes was unfaithful. Then he has the discussion with Ventidius recounted above. If any one principle does emerge, it is that of personal loyalty. When the Romans order the execution of Pacorus, captured in battle, Artavasdes saves his rival. Artavasdes' political impasse becomes a personal one when he visits Altazeera in disguise and she discovers that she was tricked into believing him to be unfaithful. The triangle is sealed shut by Pacorus' honourable behaviour, which impresses Artavasdes; and after a long debate with Altazeera, Artavasdes agrees to leave.

Artabanes' story contains similar complications. In his absence, Parthenissa is pursued by Surena, and by Arsaces, the King of Media. Artabanes' father Moneses, the heir to the Median throne, was driven out of Media by Merinzor, and the lovers' fortunes shift rapidly as Merinzor leads a civil war against the King. Parthenissa apparently takes poison to prevent Arsaces from resorting to violence in his pursuit of her.

Callimachus' history is darker than the two which take up the first two-thirds of the romance. He is also faced with a dilemma, in the midst of political confusion. At the beginning of his history a tangled and blood-stained genealogy outlines how the heirs to the throne of Bithynia schemed and fought against each other. Callimachus' father, Nicomedes, was a weak king, who aroused the enmity of Mithridates by marrying Princess Fontamyris, and Callimachus was raised in Athens, ignorant of his parentage. (He remains ignorant throughout the romance as it stands, although there are clear signs that he would have discovered the truth if Boyle had completed *Parthenissa*.)

Mithridates is initially portrayed as a ruthless conqueror, and one sympathizes with the desire of the inhabitants of Miletus (where Callimachus was taken when Athens became unsafe) to remain neutral in the senseless and vicious conflict between Mithridates and Rome. Callimachus fell in love with Monyma, but she married Mithridates. Callimachus then aided his unknown father in a battle against Betuitus, but soon afterwards he met Statira, Mithridates' daughter. Through his love for her, Callimachus found himself fighting with Mithridates against Nicomedes.

Mithridates intends to marry Statira to Ascanius, the King of Cyprus. This leads to a long debate between Statira and Callimachus on parental power. Callimachus claims that obedience should be founded only upon 'Reason' (p. 661); that a parent should have the power only to oppose a marriage, but not to arrange one. Statira answers with a rather sophistical argument, which indicates that the issue of the exercise of power *per se* lies behind this debate:

If a child were to be Judg, whether the Parent or himself had the highest reason, or when His Father was acted by the principles of a just paternal power, or by his passion, 'tis as, if not more like, he might err, as his Parent; and what was not consonant to his desires, he might say, proceeded from his Fathers having a less degree of reason than himself, or was occasion'd by his Passion; so that if the inconveniences of allowing the disobeying power to the child, and the undisputed power to the Parent, be equally great in themselves; and that the not having any Rule establish'd between both, is more prejudicial, certainly the giving of the precedency to the Father is but just, since it is most likely that a person who has many years experience more than another, should have a greater quantity of it . . . (p. 662)

The question of when one has grounds to disobey echoes through *Parthenissa*, and no single or simple answer is provided.

Statira's marriage to Ascanius is averted by Nicomedes' assault, and Callimachus' love becomes the centre of attention. Nicomedes gives him his freedom after he has been captured, and Callimachus frees Statira, and rescues Mithridates from near defeat. He is granted his wish to marry Statira, but just after the betrothal, Ascanius, thought to be dead, reappears and demands her hand. Evidently Callimachus' true identity is soon to be revealed, for Mithridates turns against him, owing to the suspicious circumstances surrounding his escape from Nicomedes. But the romance ends before this occurs.

Within *Parthenissa*'s analysis of power and individual action, situations balance each other, leading into the heart of a political crisis. Personal positions also form a series of balances, preventing us from making a comfortable choice. The histories of Artabanes and Artavasdes are intricately connected and balanced (the similarity of the two names is, I am sure, far from accidental). Both men are separated from their loves by guile: Artabanes thinks that Parthenissa is unfaithful; Altazeera thinks that Artavasdes is unfaithful. Artabanes was brought up with Pacorus, who marries Artavasdes' love Altazeera. Both men are involved in a series of civil wars as they pursue their loves. They begin as enemies, but soon become friends. Both are driven to despair: Artabanes through Parthenissa's apparent death, and Artavasdes through Altazeera's marriage. They both meet at Hierapolis to receive enigmatic comfort from the oracle. There they hear Callimachus' story, which is another example of the confusion brought about by love and the abuse of power—son must unwittingly fight father, without Perolla's noble excuse. Neither Mithridates nor the Romans (with the exception of the gallant Ventidius, who refuses to obey the Senate's orders) can gain much sympathy from us.

The characters in *Parthenissa* must also be considered in relation to its themes. Boyle does not use portraits to introduce his characters. Although, as we have seen, Scudéry was able to use the portrait in the depiction of complex, even contradictory characters, Boyle may have avoided it because it does give the reader a firm hold upon the character—a point on which he may focus. Boyle also avoids the creation of convenient opponents for his heroes, and this too colours our response. The gallant rival, a stock romance character, is deftly put to thematic use, as is the weak king.

Artabanes and Artavasdes must both contend with gallant rivals: Surena and Pacorus respectively. We see events through the eyes of Artabanes and Artavasdes; naturally we sympathize with them, as they pursue their loves through a tangled web of war and intrigue. They do not, however, vie with villains, but with noble men, who also demand our sympathy; Mazarus, Artamenes' repentant rival in *Cyrus*, may be one of the sources behind this approach. Artabanes' rival Surena struggles with his conscience as soon as Parthenissa is in his power. He saves Artabanes' life more than once (favours which are, of course, returned), and one is certainly forced to agree that '*Surena* not only knew what belonged to a Gentleman, but practised it . . .' (p. 553). Here we are on more familiar heroic romance ground. Yet Surena is indirectly responsible for placing Parthenissa within Arsaces' reach, and despite all his soul-searching, he does not release her in time to save her. However, he is executed when he tries to oppose Arsaces' cruelty, and thus dies a noble death.

Similarly, Pacorus plays an important part in Artavasdes' history. He is driven by his love for Altazeera to fight against his father. Altazeera eventually marries him, but only because she has been tricked (not by Pacorus) into believing that Artavasdes no longer loves her. When Artavasdes confronts her, and she learns of his innocence, the dilemma is acute. Pacorus proves his virtue by refusing to suspect Altazeera when she is found in the arms of the disguised Artavasdes (they have in fact both fainted, and are quite innocent). Pacorus suffers because she is maligned, not because he suspects her. His true nobility leads Altazeera to ask Artavasdes to leave.

This impasse has led Artavasdes to consult the oracle, which promises relief:

> Despair not Artavasdes, since the time
> Predestin'd for thy sufferings, is but brief;
> Fortune unto thy virtue will resign,
> And perfect joy, succeed to equal Grief. (p. 523)

One does not know how this will occur, but judging by romance precedents, I suspect that Boyle intended to devise a noble death for Pacorus. As matters stand, we have a very effective impasse.

Even Ascanius, Callimachus' rival, dismays Callimachus by his nobility and his offer of friendship. But in Callimachus' harsher history, Ascanius returns to snatch his prospective bride away, and we do not encounter any soul-searching, as we did when Surena played a similar role. Villains are not numerous. Monyma, for example, defeats our expectations entirely. When

Callimachus appears at Mithridates' court, Monyma's love for him returns, but she does not try to thwart his pursuit of Statira—she declares her love, but that is all. The reader's impulse to classify a character at once is often forestalled.

The heroes in *Parthenissa* are exposed to misfortune which occurs when a power vacuum is created by a weak king, who allows a favourite to exercise control, or a foreign power to overrun his country. Artabanes' father Moneses has retired from Media, and later he gives the crown to Artabanes. Artabazus places his trust in traitors: Celindus and then Crassolis. In the background, we hear of Hannibal's advance through Italy and his death; of Julius Caesar's death; of chaos in Rome as Spartacus leads the slaves in revolt. The juxtaposition of periods of tumult made possible by the use of the *récit* enhances the underlying concentration on power and its abuse. In Callimachus' history, Cornelius Cinna and Caius Marius usurp power in Rome, in the face of Mithridates' continuing victories. Boyle chooses his historical period with care, and uses it to enhance his thematic concerns.

A hero faced with a weak king and a gallant rival is deprived of a suitable opponent. Civil wars produce circumstances where divided loyalties are ubiquitous. Intrigue frustrates the hero: Artabanes and Artavasdes are tricked into separation from Parthenissa and Altazeera. Callimachus is also unaware of his identity, and does not know why Nicomedes releases him—an act which arouses Mithridates' suspicions. (We do not know either, but we may guess that Nicomedes has recognized his son.) Political tension in *Parthenissa* is reflected in tense personal situations.

Dorothy Osborne was rather disappointed when she read *Parthenissa*. She admits that 'tis handsome Language', but complains that

all the Story's have too neer a resemblance with those of Other Romances, there is nothing of new or surprenant in them, the Ladys are all soe kinde they make noe sport . . . (p. 143)

She prefers her French romances: 'there is a little harshnesse in most of [*Parthenissa*'s] discourses . . .' (p. 144). *Parthenissa is* a harsh romance—although it is neither as harsh nor as unoriginal as Dorothy Osborne (writing with one eye eagerly on 'a peece of

Cyrus by mee, that I am hugely pleased with', p. 144) believes it
to be. Boyle exploits the possibility of stasis inherent in the heroic
romance—the ability it provides to check time's momentum,
allowing us to contemplate, at carefully chosen moments, the
political and personal dilemmas that are a constant feature of the
narrative.

Near the centre of *Parthenissa*, Artabanes and Artavasdes
finally consult the oracle. This provides us with the longest
passage in the romance which occurs in the 'present' (pp. 517–
24). An elaborate ceremonial procession is described; within the
temple is a series of paintings: the judgement of Paris; Venus' love
for Anchises—in fact, 'all the real or imaginary Loves of that
Bright Goddess' (p. 518); and then Jupiter's pursuit of Io and
Callisto. The contrast between the gentle goddess and the violent
god is emphasized, but so is the plight of those they both pursue.
In further contrast, we see Perseus in pursuit of the three
Gorgons. The tableaux begin to emerge as pictures of love's ill
effects:

the Amours of *Aurora* and *Cephalus*, with the Death of the unchaste and
jealous Procris; and to shew the power of Love indeed, and that the Sea
it self cannot quench its flames, there were also manifested at large, how
the god of that cold Element fell in love with the fair Amphitrite.
(p. 520)

Then Artabanes sees a painting of Psyche, which he thinks
resembles Parthenissa. In this painting is depicted the whole story
of Psyche's tragedy, brought about by her jealous sisters. This
painting style, the simultaneous presentation in one picture of a
whole series of events making up a single story, superimposes
segments of time just as the structure of the heroic romance does.
Artabanes' identification of Psyche with Parthenissa is not
completely alarming, as the painting ends with her 'ascent into
Heaven, to marry her god' (p. 520).

Artavasdes sees a picture of '*Leucothoe*, who as much resembled
the fair Altazeera as *Psiche*'s did *Parthenissa*' (ibid.). It depicts
Phoebus' pursuit of her, and his abandonment of Clitie (a
negative image of the Pacorus/Altazeera/Artavasdes triangle).
We are reminded of the opposition between parents and
children, which is such a feature of *Parthenissa*, when the painting
turns to Orchamus' attempt to bury his daughter alive.

The two heroes interpret these paintings rather literally:

Our two Hero's found not only a resemblance in Beauty, but in
Fortunes, betwixt those two Nymphs, and their two Princesses. For
Artabbanes was confident the gods had taken his *Parthenissa* from the
Earth, but to marry her to one of them in Heaven, as the lovely Psiche
was . . . And *Artavasdes* thought, that what Orchamus had done to his
daughter *Artabazus*, or misfortune had done to *Altazeera*, who he
considered as buried alive in *Pacorus*'s embraces. (pp. 521–2)

Boyle does not actually provide the reader with more information
than Artabanes and Artavasdes; however, our expectations lead
us to oppose their interpretations of the paintings. Setting readers
against characters with whom they normally identify makes this
quiet moment less reassuring than one might expect. A more
hopeful oracle follows the heroes' rather unimaginative
interpretations. The oracle is a necessary balance, as the symbols
in the paintings are rather ambiguous, however they may be
interpreted.

Parthenissa reflects its author's considerable knowledge of war
and politics. Battles are described with a convincing attention to
detail. The situations and characters we expect to find in a heroic
romance are provided for us, but *Parthenissa* moves beyond
conventions in its approach to structure and to theme. Love and
its effects, the overriding concern of the French heroic romance,
does not loom so large. Political power must be dealt with as the
hero pursues his love, and it may lead to his frustration.

We do not know how Boyle planned to continue these themes.
As *Parthenissa* stands, it holds out enticing threads which have not
been fully woven together. It contains a serious analysis of
individuals caught in a world where political power is abused;
where trust is rare, friendship and love doubly precious.
Parthenissa indicates, as do a number of English romances, that
the form of the heroic romance developed in France was not as
restrictive as one might think, nor were English heroic romances
dull copies of the productions of Scudéry and her colleagues. It is
heartening to hear, from Roger Boyle's brother Robert, that
Parthenissa 'had been accorded in London "amongst divers of the
Witts a very favorable Reception" '.[21]

[21] Cited from a manuscript source by Lynch, p. 85.

Chapter 13

Picaresque Fiction

'Give me leave to lead you by the hand into a wilderness where are none but monsters . . .'; a world of cony-catchers, cut-purses, and rufflers.[1] England developed a rich tradition of roguery in literature, from the anonymous 'cursitors' and criminals of the sixteenth-century cony-catching pamplets, through to Meriton Latroon, Richard Head's 'English Rogue', and Defoe's Moll Flanders. English picaresque fiction is an impure mixture of modes, combining many native elements with the European picaresque tradition,[2] and it will be useful to examine these influences individually.

I. Jest-Books

The jest-book is perhaps the most enduring form of popular literature to have appeared in the sixteenth century—collections of jokes and humorous tales still feature prominently on the best-seller lists. Beginning with the highly successful *Hundred Merry Tales* (1525–6), jest-books increased in number and variety, particularly in the early years of the seventeenth century;[3] P. M. Zall notes that 'the making of jest-books became an industry in the seventeenth century, expanding with the development of a larger reading public.'[4] The jest-book has been divided into three

[1] Thomas Dekker, 'Lantern and Candlelight', in *Writings*, ed. E. D. Pendry (London, 1967), p. 177.
[2] F. W. Chandler examines 'English Picaresque Origins' in *The Literature of Roguery* (London, 1907), Vol. 1, Chap. 2; more general and abstract analyses of picaresque have been undertaken by Stuart Miller, *The Picaresque Novel* (Cleveland, 1967), and, at a much more sophisticated level, by Claudio Guillén 'Towards a Definition of the Picaresque' and 'Genre and Countergenre: The Discovery of the Picaresque', in *Literature as System* (Princeton, 1971); the principal European examples are studied by Richard Bjornson, *The Picaresque Hero in European Fiction* (Madison, Wisconsin, 1977).
[3] See F. P. Wilson, 'The English Jestbooks of the Sixteenth and Early Seventeenth Centuries', *HLQ* II (1938–9), 124.
[4] P. M. Zall, ed., *A Nest of Ninnies and Other Jestbooks of the Seventeenth Century* (Lincoln, Nebraska, 1970), p. ix.

categories: 'collections of detached jests', 'jest-biographies', and
'collections of comic short stories'.[5] Critics hunting for antecedents of the novel have placed great emphasis on the second
category, the jest-biography. However, an exploration of
Renaissance fiction itself must approach the influence of the jest-
book cautiously, and avoid an anachronistic view which sees
these writers as in some way anticipating a form which they
would probably have scorned—had they known of its existence.

Most jest-biographies simply attribute jests (many of them
traditional) to a single figure—for example, *Tarleton's Jests*
(1611), which uses Richard Tarleton, the most famous
Elizabethan clown.[6] It is quite misleading to see this as an
attempt to achieve a unity derived from the depiction of a single
character. Tarleton is a convenient peg upon which certain
actions are hung. Jests are attributed to him, or to Will Summers
or some other historical figure, and a few may even have been
performed by these individuals, but the jests themselves remain
isolated, and there is little development from jest to jest. One
example of a jest-biography which rises above this shaky
continuity is *Dobsons Drie Bobbes* (1607), which Wilson calls a
'rogue-novel'.[7] Its most recent editor, E. A. Horsman, is more
cautious, but stresses that it achieves 'a continuity quite unusual
among the "jest-biographies" '.[8] Dobson does become a character, and is not simply a convenient figure to whom jests are
attached. The early sections of *Dobson Drie Bobbes* are particularly
convincing in their depiction of both Dobson's career and the
town of Durham, but this work is an exception, an example
which other writers of jest-biographies did not choose to follow.
Some interesting attempts to achieve a unity of sorts may be seen
in Robert Armin's *Fool Upon Fool* (1600–5); *The Pleasant Conceits of
Old Hobson* (1607); and, perhaps, *The Pinder of Wakefield* (1632).
However, the mainstream of jest-books continued unchanged; or
at least unchanged as regards any move towards unity. In 1660,
for example, we find that *The Tales and Jests of Hugh Peters* is very
similar to an Elizabethan jest-biography, and indeed many of the
jests stem from Elizabethan predecessors.

The enormous amount of borrowing (plagiarism is not quite

[5] Wilson, p. 122.   [6] For further examples, see Wilson's bibliography.
[7] Wilson, p. 142.
[8] *Dobsons Drie Bobbes*, ed. E. A. Horsman (Oxford, 1955), p. xvi.

the right word, as it implies a standard of originality which would
not have occurred to writers of jest-books—and of many other
books of the period) indicates the conservative nature of the jest-
book mode. Stanley Kahrl has shown how sixteenth-century jest-
books were influenced by medieval exempla.[9] Through the long
process of borrowing and reworking, jests appear again and again
over long periods of time.[10] Changes did occur, but in terms of the
mode itself, and its contemporary influence, the important
changes were not those manifested in *Dobsons Drie Bobbes*. Writers
of jest-books did not move towards a greater 'novelistic' unity of
action and depth of characterization. In fact, any development
one might detect indicates a move in the opposite direction,
towards a concision bordering on increased fragmentation.

Zall notes that 'over the century we can see a developing
preference generally for economy at any cost'.[11] Some jest-books
become almost solely concerned with language, rather than with
jests which develop in the direction of tales. A good example is
Robert Chamberlain's *Conceits, Clinches, Flashes and Whimzies*
(1639)—the title alone conveys its interest in 'short-term' quick
jokes, based on language rather than action. Those jest-books
that were still concerned with action often reduced the ex-
traneous details which added some dimension of life to the trick.
Such jests are always unmotivated and, in our eyes, cruel. This is
a very important point if one wishes to understand the nature of
picaresque in seventeenth-century England. The jest-books add
to the sense of unmotivated action in a cruel, fragmented world,
viewed from an ambiguous moral perspective. Only *Dobsons Drie
Bobbes* offers some explanation for the jester's often cruel
activities, but readers were obviously not interested in such
explanation. Jests are merely 'Very prettie and pleasant, to driue
away the tediousnesse of a Winters Euening' (*Pasquil's Jests*,
1609, title-page). This lack of motivation allows them to be
passed on from jest-book to jest-book, from jester to jester, be he
Will Summers, or 'George Peele Gentleman' (*Merrie Conceited
Jests of George Peele Gentleman*, 1607).

When elements of the jest-book pass into other, more complex
forms of fiction, this unmotivated quality, disturbing to us but,

---

[9] Stanley Kahrl, 'The Medieval Origins of the Sixteenth-Century English Jest-
Books', *Studies in the Renaissance*, 13 (1966), 166–83 *passim*.

[10] Ibid., pp. 172–3; on this point see Wilson, pp. 126–7.   [11] Zall, p. xv.

we must remember, 'pleasant' to contemporaries, is also passed on. In Robert Greene's *Black Book's Messenger* (1592), a work close to the cony-catching tradition, one of Greene's sub-headings indicates the influence of the jest-book: 'A merry jest how Ned Browne's wife was cross-bitten in her own art'.[12] The intermingling of forms, so much a feature of seventeenth-century fiction, is present in these late sixteenth-century works to a lesser degree. But *The Black Book's Messenger* leads us from the jest-book to an even more important influence on English picaresque fiction.

II. The Native Rogue Tradition

A. V. Judges' splendid anthology, *The Elizabethan Underworld*, illustrates the development of Elizabethan and Jacobean cony-catching pamphlets.[13] Copland's *Highway to the Spital-House* (1535–6) and Walker's *Manifest Detection of Dice-Play* (1552) may be seen as precursors of a mode of which the most popular embodiment is John Awdeley's *Fraternity of Vagabonds* (1561). Awdeley's work, and Thomas Harman's *Caveat for Common Cursitors* (1566), became standard compendia of tricks, which were repeated throughout the following century. Cony-catching pamphlets, like jest-books, passed incidents down to each other like family heirlooms. Richard Head had no need to return to Harman and Awdeley in his search for rogues' tricks, as their collections had been reused more than once, by Robert Greene, Dekker, and many others.

The cony-catching pamphlets provided, like the jest-books, an enormous reserve of incident, lore, and language which writers of picaresque fiction could use. Chandler calls these works 'The Anatomies of Roguery', indicating their attempt to convey the rogue's life in all its aspects.[14] Two elements predominate: the actual tricks themselves, and the thieves' society—its laws, hierarchy, and special language. Structurally, these works are as episodic as the jest-books, but the close attention to detail builds up a very convincing picture of the world of the rogue.

Frank Aydelotte claims that these works move from reflections of contemporary social conditions in the sixteenth century to

---

[12] In A. V. Judges, *The Elizabethan Underworld* (1930, rpt. London, 1965), p. 262.
[13] Ibid., *passim*.   [14] Chandler, Vol. 1. Chap. 3.

more purely literary exercises in the seventeenth century, as these conditions changed.[15] However, while criminal life may have changed its character somewhat by the Restoration, it did not at all diminish.[16] It is more useful to see the cony-catching pamphlets as feeding into a diverse stream of picaresque fiction, which certainly depended on particular literary conventions, but which still reacted to social conditions (as will be seen in the discussion of criminal biography, below).

The cony-catching pamphlets, like the jest-books, are fragmented; scenes (and Greene in particular does use scenes) shift rapidly. An important aspect of these works, if one is concerned with their influence on picaresque fiction, is the ambivalent moral stance of the author. Greene provides the best example of this: the very title of *A Notable Discovery of Cosnage* (1591) proclaims both that it is 'Written for the general benefit of all Gentlemen . . .', *and* that it contains 'a delightful discourse of the cosnage of Colliers'.[17] The preface piously ends with 'an humble sute to all Iustices, that they will seeke to root out these two roagish Artes, I commit you to the Almighty', while the pamphlet ends with a contrary address: 'Now Gentlemen by your leaue, and heare a merry iest.'[18] This goes well beyond the accepted notion of fiction's end being to delight and teach. The reader is lulled into having his cake and eating it too—he may vicariously enjoy the rogue's tricks, and also believe that he is reading a moral condemnation of the same rogue, while preparing himself to avoid being the gull he delights in reading about. This ambivalence colours the more unified picaresque works also, and in the course of the seventeenth century the initially convincing moral tone of the Spanish picaresque disappears in its English imitations, in part owing to the influence of the anarchic impulses contained in jest-books and cony-catching pamphlets.

At the beginning of the seventeenth century, the mantle of the cony-catching tradition was taken up by Thomas Dekker. *The Bellman of London* (1608) and *English Villainies Discovered by Lantern*

---

[15] Frank Aydelotte, *Elizabethan Rogues and Vagabonds* (1913, rpt. Oxford, 1967) p. 118.

[16] See Maurice Petherick, *Restoration Rogues* (London, 1951), Chap. 1.

[17] Ed. G. B. Harrison (1922–6, rpt. Edinburgh, 1966), p. 15.

[18] Ibid., p. 58.

and Candlelight (1608) each went through eight editions, in thirty-two and forty years respectively.[19] Dekker borrowed freely, but 'if he showed little originality in matter, his treatment of it justified his thefts'.[20] Dekker's attractive style makes his account of rogueries gentler than Greene's. In a preface to one of the later editions of *Lantern and Candlelight*, Dekker cleverly sums up the moral duplicity noted above: 'Read and laugh; read and learn; read and loathe. Laugh at the knavery; learn out the mystery; loathe the base villainy.'[21] This highly comforting separation of responses seems to ask more from the reader than he can possibly give—but it is a wonderful sanction. And readers laughed, learned, and loathed in great numbers during the century, particularly when the cony-catching pamphlets began to influence picaresque fiction.

III. Spanish Picaresque

Lazarillo de Tormes is now accepted as a precursor of the Spanish picaresque tradition, rather than a fully-fledged picaresque novel.[22] It was certainly associated with Alemán's *Guzmán de Alfarache* by seventeenth-century readers, and its popularity coincides with the popularity of Alemán's novel, which is universally regarded as the most important single example of the picaresque in Spain. *Lazarillo* was translated into English in 1576 by David Rowland (the original appeared *c.* 1554). After a second printing in 1596, this translation went through eight editions in the course of the following century, while the English translation of *Guzmán* went through seven—an indication of how eagerly the Spanish picaresque novel was read and assimilated.[23] The Spanish works found, on the whole, worthy translators; James Mabbe, the translator of Alemán, produced a translation

[19] See A. F. Allison, *Thomas Dekker: A Bibliographical Catalogue of the Early Editions* (London, 1972).
[20] Chandler, p. 105; see Aydelotte, pp. 131–3; and, for borrowings in *Lantern and Candlelight*, Pendry, pp. 321–4.
[21] Pendry, p. 183.
[22] See Alexander A. Parker, *Literature and the Delinquent: The Picaresque Novel in Spain and Europe 1599–1753* (Edinburgh, 1967), p. 4. and Donald McGrady, *Mateo Alemán* (New York, 1968), p. 44; although Dale Randall, in *The Golden Tapestry* (Durham, Nth. Carolina, 1963) argues against this view (p. 59).
[23] See Charles C. Mish, *English Prose Fiction 1600 to 1700: A Chronological Checklist* (Charlottesville, 1967).

of considerable merit.[24] If we place *Lazarillo* and *Guzmán* side by side, as seventeenth-century readers evidently did, both the range and continuity of the Spanish picaresque become apparent. *Lazarillo* is concise, economical, and arresting. Lazarillo's adventures begin almost immediately, when he is handed over to his first master, the old blind man. *Guzmán*, on the other hand, is a much larger work, digressive and circumlocutory. Alemán begins by having Guzmán address the reader, and admit that his story is, in fact, a 'Discourse':

Curious reader, The desire which I had to recount my life unto thee, made me make greate haste to ingulfe my selfe therein, without first preparing some things fit to be related, which (serving as an induction and entrance to the matter) had beene very needfull for the better informing of thy understanding: (for beeing essentiall to this Discourse) they would likewise have given thee no small content.[25]

Guzmán's story really only begins in Chapter Three of the novel.

However, one also notices important affinities. Both picaros face a hostile world. *Lazarillo* in particular uses hunger as a virtual leitmotif, and Guzmán too must fight for survival. The world is amoral, and must be dealt with as such: 'Mans life is a warre-fare vpon earth, there is no certainty therein' (*Guzmán*, p. 57). Against this is set the perspective of the reformed, older Guzmán de Alfarache, who is narrating his own story. Lazarillo also has an acute moral sensibility, and commits 'crimes' with great reluctance, particularly at first.[26] This tension between a moral nature and an apparently amoral environment is also present in the third great example of the Spanish picaresque novel, Francisco de Quevedo y Villegas's *Buscón* (1626, trans. 1657). Quevedo adds an extra dimension to this tension through the combination of the picaro's adventures and the author's satirical and penetrating style. This aspect of Spanish picaresque fiction has been interestingly discussed as 'moral ambiguity', although not all critics are in agreement as to the amount of control exercised by Alemán in particular.[27]

[24] For the translations, see Randall's excellent discussion, Chap. 7.
[25] *The Rogue or the Life of Guzman de Alfarache*, trans. James Mabbe (1622), ed. J. Fitzmaurice-Kelly (London, 1924), Vol. 1, p. 37.
[26] See Robert Alter, *Rogue's Progress* (Cambridge, Mass., 1964), Chap. 1.
[27] Christine J. Whitbourne, 'Moral Ambiguity in the Spanish Picaresque Tradition', in *Knaves and Swindlers*, ed. Whitbourne (Hull, 1974), pp. 1–24; on Alemán, see Randall, pp. 178–9.

Alemán and Quevedo depict the breach between reflection and action, morality and pragmatism, as a product of the harsh world in which the picaro must survive. Alemán's Guzmán de Alfarache underlines this dual nature of the picaro's outlook as he presents a retrospective account of his life. The rogue pamphlet held the seeds of such a comprehensive understanding, but English picaresque fiction turned away from the dilemma portrayed in the Spanish works to confront a moral abyss. English readers, however, were very interested in the figure of the picaro, of the rogue—a word made popular by Mabbe, who entitled his translation of Alemán *The Rogue*. Ben Jonson prophesied truly in his dedicatory poem to Mabbe's translation: 'For though Spaine gave him his first ayre and Vogue,/ He would be call'd, henceforth, the English-Rogue' (p. 31). Richard Head took this suggestion literally, and called his account of Meriton Latroon *The English Rogue*. 'Guzman' also became a synonym for rogue; one of the criminal biographies of James Hind was called *The English Gusman* (by George Fidge, 1652). One could be a gusman, and practise gusmanry.[28]

According to Alexander Parker, the 'individual character' plays an important role in *Guzmán* and *Buscón*.[29] This exploration of character was not taken up in England until Defoe drew on the picaresque tradition in his depiction of Moll Flanders. Nevertheless, the early Spanish novels prodded English writers in the direction of more substantial works than the small, fragmented jest-book and rogue pamphlet; but the Spanish novels which followed the three great examples of the picaresque represent, in the eyes of many critics, a considerable decline.[30] Juan de Luna's sequel to *Lazarillo* was often bound with the original work, under the title of *The Pursuit of the Historie of Lazarillo de Tormez* (1622 et seq.), while Castillo Solórzano's *Garduña de Sevilla* was translated as *La Picara* (1665). These works come much closer to the peculiar amalgamation of modes which eventually characterized English picaresque fiction. Moralizing statements are now only half serious—'We men are somewhat akin to laying Hens: for if

---

[28] For example, see *Don Tomazo* (1680), in Spiro Peterson, ed., *The Counterfeit Lady Unveiled and Other Criminal Fiction of Seventeenth Century England* (New York, 1961), p. 203.
[29] Parker, p. 72.
[30] See Peter Dunn, *Castillo Solórzano and the Decline of the Spanish Novel* (Oxford, 1952), *passim*.

we mind to doe any good, we presently proclaime and kackle it abroad . . .' (*The Pursuit*, p. 62)—as the world itself has become more chaotic. Carlos García's *La Desordenada Codicia de los Bienes Ajenos* (1619), translated as *The Sonne of the Rogue* (1638), is as digressive as Alemán, but without any coherent moral perspective. His depiction of various thieves in prison is very close to the atmosphere of a cony-catching pamphlet or rogue anatomy. In this sense, it passes into the protean literary world of picaresque fiction, sharing incidents with the *Histoire des Larrons*, and naturally, like so many other works, contributing its share of incidents to *The English Rogue*.

English readers tended to interpret foreign masterpieces in a rather arbitrary, deflating fashion; for example, *Don Quixote* was read as an entertaining farce, rather than a complex fiction.[31] The interest in Spanish picaresque is reflected in Mabbe's translation of the 'ur-picaresque' *La Celestina*, by Fernando de Rojas (*c.* 1499-1502), which he entitled *The Spanish Bawd* (1631). Grimmelhausen's *Simplicissimus*, the major German example of picaresque fiction, was not translated, while French works, such as Charles Sorel's *Francion* (1623, trans. 1655), were not really influential until the eighteenth century.

IV. Criminal Biography

The criminal biography has been characterized as 'a little known *genre* most frequently mentioned by historians of the novel and students of Daniel Defoe attempting to explain the rise of realism'.[32] Criminal biography began before *The English Rogue*, with three James Hind biographies appearing in the 1650s,[33] but most of these works appeared alongside picaresque fiction from the mid 1660s to the end of the century (and, incidentally, well into the following century).

The criminal biography takes a highwayman, thief, or con-man from real life and presents his story, usually adding a certain amount of fictitious material. On the whole, these works are

---

[31] See Edmund Gayton, *Pleasant Notes Upon Don Quixote* (1654); and Randall, pp. 91–3.

[32] Robert R. Singleton, 'English Criminal Biography 1651–1722', *Harvard Library Bulletin*, 18 (1970), 63 and n. 1; Singleton's valuable bibliography lists thirty-one criminal biographies and autobiographies published before 1700.

[33] *The Pleasant and Delightful History of Captain Hind* (1651); George Fidge, *Hinds Ramble* (1651), and *The English Gusman* (1652).

fictionalized biographies; as with the jest-books and cony-catching pamphlets, material is reused from one work to another. Spiro Peterson indicates how an actual person's activities are transformed into a criminal biography, noting a 'threefold pattern: the crime, the journalistic pamphlets, and the fictionalized criminal biography'.[34] Ernest Bernbaum's detailed account of the 'Mary Carleton Narratives' demonstrates this process at work on the figure who inspired more written accounts than anyone else in the period.[35] The criminal biography helped to stimulate the interest in the individual rogue which enabled picaresque fiction to achieve at least a centre of interest, if not complete structural cohesion.

The native rogue tradition continued to play an important part. Many criminal biographies contain elements of the jest-book and rogue pamphlet, and a considerable number borrow actual incidents from them. When criminal biography was only just emerging this influence was very strong: the biographies of James Hind are shaped to a considerable degree by the jest-book. The title-page of George Fidge's *The English Gusman* states that it contains 'a full Relation of all the severall Robberies, madd Pranks, and handsome Jests done by him' (1652 edn.). During the Interregnum, Hind's character as a Royalist highwayman was emphasized by sympathetic pamphleteers. This jest-book element is still well in evidence in *No Jest Like a True Jest: being a compendious record of the merry life, and mad exploits of Capt. James Hind* (c. 1674). As criminal biographies were produced in greater numbers, some of them left this jest-book influence behind, but it was never completely abandoned; one constantly discovers how enduringly popular the native rogue tradition was. *The Witty Rogue Arraigned* (1656), an account of Richard Hannam, also promises to relate 'the several Robberies, mad Pranks, and handsome Jests by him performed' (this piece of plagiarism demonstrates the appeal of the jest-book element; the work itself, though, does not repeat Hind's escapades). The influence was still at work even after the publication of more independent and developed works such as Francis Kirkman's *The Counterfeit Lady*

Unveiled (1673). *Sadler's Memoirs* (1677) relates 'his most notorious Pranks', and uses tricks from cony-catching pamphlets (see
pp. 5–7, 10–13). Similarly, *The Life of Captain James Whitney*
(1692–3) concentrates on his 'more Comical Rencounters' (p. 2).

One can distinguish between relatively derivative pamphlets
and the more substantial criminal biographies; the latter focus on
a central character, and use fictional additions with some skill to
shape his story. Incident, as in picaresque fiction, predominates
in most of these narratives; a few outstanding examples, however,
turn their attention to the criminal himself. Francis Kirkman's
The Counterfeit Lady Unveiled retells the fascinating story of Mary
Moders, 'alias Mary Stedman', a wonderfully enterprising
woman, whose most startling exploit involved her masquerading
as a German princess. A double confidence trick ensued, as the
John Carleton she eventually married was falsely presented to
her as a nobleman of wealth by his greedy family. Mary and John
Carleton wrote their own accounts of these incidents. Kirkman,
when he came to write his biography after Mary Carleton's death
(she was hanged for thieving in 1673), was able to draw on a
considerable amount of material, and he actually incorporated a
substantial section of her own narrative, *The Case of Madame Mary
Carleton*.[36] The most interesting part of *The Counterfeit Lady
Unveiled* is the account of Mary Carleton narrated by Kirkman: a
penetrating approach to character, which Peterson describes as
an 'effort at psychological realism'.[37]

Kirkman describes her early love of romances as an explanation of her behaviour:

from her frequent and often reading, she believing all to be true, she was
much in love with the actions of those great and renowned heroes, and
supposed herself to be no less than a *heroina*. (p. 15)

Kirkman is not interested in the type of steadily unfolding
biographical narrative perfected by Defoe (see his own comment,
p. 21). Towards the end, character analysis is largely abandoned
in favour of incident, and Kirkman begins to stress his moral
stance: 'Well, let her go for a base, lewd woman, but time will
come that she must repent this unhandsome, ungrateful action'
(p. 59).

[36] See Peterson's notes; page references are to his edition of Kirkman.
[37] Ibid., p. 6.

The tone is more problematic in four other more substantial works: *The Life and Death of Mrs Mary Frith* (1662); Elkanah Settle's two works, *The Life and Death of Major Clancie* (1680), and *The Compleat Memoirs of . . . Will. Morrell* (1694); and *Don Tomazo* (1680). The redoubtable Mrs Mary Frith was nick-named Moll Cutpurse, and she was a well-known figure in the early part of the century.[38] She dressed in male attire and led a sternly independent life, to the delight of her biographer, who exclaims that 'her heroick impudence hath quite undone every *Romance*' (p. 17).[39] A firm royalist like Hind, Moll greeted the King in 1638: 'I put out my Hand and caught Him by His, and grasped it very hard, saying, *Welcome Home* CHARLES! His *Majestie* smiled . . .' (p. 97). The lively style has, by this stage, quite entranced the reader, who sees things from Moll's perspect-ive, and is ready to smile too. This ability to bring isolated scenes to life takes a momentarily solemn turn when, for a wager, Moll rides through town dressed as a man. She is discovered, and a jeering crowd gathers, leading to a passage which shows her tender side, using an accomplished interior monologue:

In my own thoughts I was quite another thing: I was Squiresse to *Dulcinea* of *Tobosso*, the most incomparably beloved Lady of *Don Quixot*, and was sent of a Message to him from my Mistress in the Formalities of *Knight Errantry*, that I might not offend against any *punctilio* thereof which he so strictly required; and also to be the more acceptable to my lovely *Sancho Pancha*, that was trained up by this time in Chivalry, whom I would surprise in this disguise. These quirks and quillets at that instant possest my fancy, but presently I had other representations. Me thought those about the door were the very people that gazed at *Jane Shore* . . . (pp. 77–8)

Elkanah Settle's account of Major Clancie delights in the careful elaboration of detail surrounding a relatively small number of incidents. The narrative passes smoothly from confidence trick to confidence trick. Clancie, we are told, began as a page to a French ambassador, who placed far too much trust in him. Settle explains how the boy was left alone with his master's belongings, and tried on his fine clothes. He then

begins to propose to himself, how happy and fortunate should he be, if

[38] See Singleton, pp. 77–8, and *The Roaring Girl* (1608?).
[39] References to *The Life and Death of Mrs Mary Frith* (1662).

he could order matters so, as to keep all this finery by which he was so altered, that he might but appear to all others, as to himself in the Glass. (p. 5)[40]

This convincing explanation of the confidence-man's impulse towards disguise for its own sake reminds us that all of these developed examples of criminal biography explore impostors: Mary Carleton, William Morrell, Thomas Dangerfield—even Moll Cutpurse dresses as a man, although not in order to trick people. A greater interest in character and motivation coincides with a consideration of identity as protean. The reader identifies with the criminal in the disguise and the confidence trick, although in these works shifting narrative tone may also distance the reader from the central character.

Settle was a dramatist, and his second criminal biography, *The Compleat Memoirs of . . . Will. Morrell* (1694), relishes the creation of dramatic scenes. In the course of his life Morrell marries eighteen unsuspecting women, and his amatory adventures are related with gusto. Settle's vivid, dramatic presentation is best illustrated by an early incident, when Morrell takes up his first disguise in order to gull a farmer, bargaining for his cattle, but announcing that he has no money with him (the use of dialect adds to the scene's impact):

'You know, sir [says Morrell's accomplice], you have laid out all your money already, and what should we handle cattle unless we had cole to buy 'em. I confess they are for your turn above any I have zeen in the whole vair, but that's nothing, the money, master, the money'. 'The money?' replies the countryman. 'Troth, that shall make no difference, nor break squares between us, if you and I can agree, the cattle are at your service, I suppose you are some honest gentleman hereabouts, and the money will do my work next market day. Pray, what may I call your name?' 'My name is Walters', replies our cattle-merchant. 'Walters, master?' answers our countryman. 'What, any relation to his worship the noble Sir William Walters?' 'Aye, friend, a small relation, a brother of his.' 'A brother of Sir William's!' Off goes the countryman's bonnet at the next word, and a long scrape made . . .   (Peterson, p. 304)

Don Tomazo (1680) is a biography of Thomas Dangerfield, who played a part in the Meal-Tub Plot. His political activities, however, are studiously avoided in *Don Tomazo*, which con-

---

[40] References to *The Life and Death of Major Clancie* (1680).

centrates on his early experiences and his life as a counterfeiter.
Don Tomazo is clearly influenced by picaresque fiction, referring
to 'Guzman and Lazarillo de Tormes' in the preface.[41] The story
of Dangerfield is related with an irresistible exuberance, and the
comic tone is maintained throughout much of the narrative. The
detailed account of Tomazo's boyhood describes his flight from
his stern father to Scotland with his friend Jemmy, one of his
father's Scottish servants. Jemmy leads him to expect a lavish
welcome, but his hopes are amusingly dashed when he confronts
Jemmy's family home:

It was a hovel or rather sty, in length about six and thirty foot, not
covered cathedral-like with lead nor yet with glittering copper after the
Swedish manner, but according to the Scotch custom very meanly
thatched with oaten reeds, not such as the Arcadian shepherds piped
withal, but plain downright illiterate straw. (p. 192)

Numerous slyly comic observations underline Tomazo's plight,
such as the description of his 'horse in a cold trance, wondering
what was become of the grass that used to grow in England'
(p. 196).

The language in *Don Tomazo* is at times reminiscent of Nashe,
as is the disconcerting attitude to cruelty in the following passage,
which recounts the fate of Tomazo's confederates, convicted of
'coining':

Both [were] convicted by their confessions and forced to evaporate their
souls in boiling oil, as Philip had done, by an enforced torment in this,
the better to prepare them for the bituminous tarpits of the other world.
(p. 227)

Don Tomazo ends with Dangerfield's imprisonment, but not his
death; because of this, it does not end on the repentant note
typical of the less developed criminal biographies.

Louis Wright suggests that:

The biographies of characters from low life were peculiarly attractive
to substantial citizens because they provided a glimpse of a segment of
life within their own world, peopled by types familiar to them, yet
fascinating because it was forbidden.[42]

---

[41] References to *Don Tomazo*, in Peterson.

[42] Louis B. Wright, *Middle-Class Culture in Elizabethan England* (Chapel Hill, Nth.
Carolina, 1935), pp. 412–13.

One historian of the true rogues who created the background for the fictionalized biographies notes that 'England during the Restoration period was unusually rich in rogues'.[43] But as criminal biography developed, drawing from the very beginning on a native literary tradition and fuelled by the picaresque fiction which grew at the same time, literary precedents and concepts became as important as, if not more important than, the lives of the actual criminals. The introduction to *The Grand Pyrate: Or, The Life and Death of Capt. George Cusack* (1676) states that 'The World hath been long entertained with Accounts of *Highway-men* and *Land-Robbers*, but Piracies and Sea-Robbers [have been] for the most part . . . under the guard . . .' (p. 3). In other words, a literary mode and demand have been created, which are responded to in literary terms.

The most interesting criminal biographies consider the reasons behind the rogue's actions, although the actions themselves are presented in a comic manner. However, the bulk of these works entirely avoid the question of motivation, and simply present individuals who have an inherent propensity to steal or trick people. James Hind's father was a saddler, 'in good Reputation and credit', who sent him to school, but Hind loved listening to stories of robberies and jests.[44] Childhood experiences of this sort may be presented in a very convincing manner, but the reasons behind them are quietly ignored, or implicitly regarded as the sins to which all flesh is heir. This example is from *The German Princess Revived: or The London Jilt* (1684):

having arrived to the Age of Eleven Years, her Father and Mother being one Day Invited a-broad to Dinner, she took the Opportunity, and finding where her Mother had laid up some Money to the value of 30 or 40 s. upon a Shelf in the Kitchen, she took the same, together with the Handkerchief wherein it was tied . . . (pp. 1–2)

The use of circumstantial detail to build up a convincing narrative reached a considerable level of achievement towards the end of the century, and this aspect of the criminal biography prompts rather unsettling questions concerning the relationship between truth and the mere appearance of truth. A fascinating illustration is provided by two different accounts of the murder of one Dr Clinch. *The Last Words of a Dying Penitent* (1692) was

[43] Petherick, p. 1.   [44] *The English Gusman*, p. 1.

supposedly written by Henry Harrison, who was found guilty of the murder. He provides an extremely detailed, circumstantial account of various shady dealings surrounding a poor widow, all implicating a man named Robert Rowe. Rowe replied with *Mr Harrison Proved the Murtherer* (1692), an equally circumstantial account, but one which of course reaches quite opposite conclusions. One may assume that, as Harrison was found guilty, his narrative cannot be trusted. But the narratives themselves are equally convincing; one (and perhaps both?) is a fictionalized work, drawing on the techniques perfected by the criminal biography.

This rather unsettling dilemma may have been part of the motivation for *The Memoires of Monsieur Du Vall* (1670), by Walter Pope. *The Memoires* could be described as an anti-criminal biography: a very clever parody, which mocks the form itself, while using it to satirize the exaggerated regard for all things French manifested by, Pope maintains, the ladies of the day. Pope concentrates on the absurd regard the ladies have for Du Vall, simply because he pretends to be French. Pope also gently ridicules the typical criminal biography's claim to present new, ingenious tricks:

This is the place where I should set down several of his Exploits, but I omit them, both as being well known, and because I cannot find in them more ingenuity than was practiz'd before by *Hind* and *Hannum*, and several other *meer English* Thieves.[45]

Pope follows the convention by providing his criminal's epitaph; this again cleverly satirizes his two main targets:

> Here lies Du Vall: Reader, if Male thou art,
> Look to thy purse; if Female, to thy heart. (p. 211)

The criminal biography continued to maintain a moral ambiguity similar to (and perhaps derived from) that found in the cony-catching pamphlets. A few of these biographies have no pretensions to instruct, and in this are closely allied to the works of picaresque fiction which developed alongside them. Almost all the others, however, provide the same dual satisfaction discussed above in reference to the cony-catching pamphlets: identification

[45] References to Charles C. Mish, ed., *Restoration Prose Fiction 1660–1700: A Representative Anthology* (Lincoln, Nebraska, 1970), p. 206.

and superiority; vicarious crime *and* complacent sermonizing. In this sense, all these works avoid the more frightening, but also more challenging abyss confronted by those picaresque works which recognize the full implications of society's challenge to the rogue, and the rogue's challenge to society.

V. Imaginary Voyages and Travel Literature

Travel and travel literature were both extremely popular throughout the seventeenth century. An exuberant genre like the picaresque was naturally influenced by the expanding world pictured in travel narratives. Picaresque fiction is episodic, and focuses on a wandering character, or group of characters, while travel narratives encapsulate the movement and energy which may be created by the picaresque. Douglas Bush notes that, in the early part of the century, 'the spirit of travel and maritime discovery continued to affect every kind of imaginative and reflective literature'.[46] James Sutherland indicates that this importance did not diminish after the Restoration, when one still finds that 'various accounts of unknown lands and their inhabitants made a considerable impact on the contemporary imagination'.[47]

The travel narratives did not simply supply an image; their influence on the picaresque was more direct. The picaresque narrative generates an urgent momentum, sometimes to an alarming extent. This momentum must be maintained, and actual travel incidents are often used for this purpose. The characters are always travellers, and this movement remains a feature of the picaresque in the works of Defoe and Smollett. Even a criminal biography influenced by the picaresque, such as *Don Tomazo*, utilizes this technique. Dangerfield travels to Scotland at a very early age, when he runs away from home, and is soon moving through Europe evading the law. Picaresque fiction also caters for readers' insatiable interest in detailed descriptions of new countries: fashions, manners, flora and fauna,

---

[46] Douglas Bush, *English Literature in the Earlier Seventeenth Century*, rev. edn. (Oxford, 1962), p. 190.

[47] James Sutherland, *English Literature of the Late Seventeenth Century* (Oxford, 1969), p. 295.

and so on. *The English Rogue* is enlivened by descriptions of old and new countries.

In the imaginary voyage tale one sees another case of mutual influence. The imaginary voyage is also a genre which draws on a variety of sources. Philip Gove, while making a number of minute discriminations, notes 'an affiliation between such apparently different types as the utopia and the picaresque, both forms of the adventure romance, and both occasionally coinciding with the imaginary voyage'.[48] The picaresque, significantly, does not take over the imaginary voyage's utopian concerns; once again movement, and also satire, rather than idealism, are the staple elements of picaresque fiction at this time. However, sustained satire such as that found in Joseph Hall's *Mundus Alter et Idem* (1605, trans. 1609), or even topical religious satire seen in Louis Fontaines' *Jansenia* (trans. 1672), is absent from picaresque fiction. The picaresque does possess a satirical impulse, as will be seen below, but it is fragmented, not carefully maintained in the manner of Hall's Menippean satire.[49]

One of the most remarkable imaginary voyages written during the century bears a close affinity to the picaresque: Bishop Godwin's *The Man in the Moon* (1638). In this famous work, Domingo Gonsales is carried to the moon by a trained group of swans. Despite this uncertain means of transport, Godwin includes a considerable amount of knowledgeable astronomical speculation. Gonsales meets the inhabitants of the moon, and this enables Godwin to move into an elaborate, utopian description of a world where people 'doe hate all manner of vice, and doe live in such love, peace and amitie, as it seemeth to bee another Paradise' (p. 39).[50] First, however, Godwin economically outlines the rather picaresque adventures of Gonsales, 'youngest of 17 Children', who fends for himself in France and the Indies. Godwin includes a description of the 'blessed *Isle* of S. *Hellens*' (p. 7), and Gonsales' voyage to the moon only begins after he is shipwrecked on the '*Island* of *Tenerik* [*sic*]' (p. 13). The narrative detail, beginning with Gonsales' travels in recognized, though

---

[48] Philip Babcock Gove, *The Imaginary Voyage in Prose Fiction* (New York, 1941), p. 164; Gove's main concern is with the eighteenth century.

[49] For a detailed consideration of *Mundus Alter et Idem*, see Richard A. McCabe, *Joseph Hall: A Study in Satire and Meditation* (Oxford, 1982), pp. 73–92.

[50] References to *The Man in the Moon*, ed. G. McColley (Northampton, Mass., 1937–8).

220   13. PICARESQUE FICTION

exotic, areas, makes his eventual description of the moon-journey extremely convincing. No picaresque work attempts to travel quite so far!

Henry Neville is content to remain on this earth, in two tantalizingly brief pamphlets, which carry some of Defoe's narrative techniques in embryo. *The Isle of Pines* (1668) presents the narrative of George Pine, who relates how he was shipwrecked on an island with four women. The island afforded food and shelter, and Pine lived without shame with the women, reaching the age of 80, at which time he was able to count 1,789 descendants! Neville presents numerous small, convincing details in this narration, but at certain points one suspects that one is reading a parody of a travel narrative. On the other hand, Neville may have had a serious purpose in creating a place which might 'prove a Paradise' (p. 231).[51] Pine's attitude to sexuality must have surprised many readers:

Thus we lived for sixteen years. Till perceiving my eldest boy to mind the ordinary work of nature, by seeing what we did, I gave him a mate, and so I did to all the rest, as fast as they grew up, and were capable. (p. 234)

This may be satire, or philosophical speculation. The bland, convincing narrative surface is difficult to penetrate, although I suspect that Neville has his tongue in his cheek when he has Pine (rather too obsessed with fecundity?) conclude 'the general name of the whole [i.e. all his descendants] the ENGLISH PINES; whom God bless with the dew of heaven, and the fat of the earth. Amen!' (p. 235).

A New and Further Discovery of the Isle of Pines (1668) has no suggestion of satirical purpose, but contains an even greater attention to detail. It is the narrative of 'Cornelius Van Sloetten', who 'discovered' Pine's descendants and Pine's narrative, and it too anticipates Defoe's facility for the convincing use of circumstantial detail:

April the 26*th* 1667. We set sail from *Amsterdam*, intending for the *East-Indies*; our ship had to name the place from whence we came, the *Amsterdam*, burthen 350 Tun. and having a fair gale of Wind, on the 27 of *May* following we had a sight of the high Peak of *Tenariffe*.[52]

[51] References to *Shorter Novels: Seventeenth Century*, ed. Philip Henderson (1930, rpt. London, 1967).

[52] Henry Neville, *A New and Further Discovery of the Isle of Pines* ... (1668), p. 2.

VI. Picaresque Fiction: *The English Rogue*

The picaresque novels which grew out of these diverse sources
flourished from the appearance of *The English Rogue* in 1665 until
the end of the century. *The English Rogue* itself was an outstanding
success; there were at least eight complete editions from 1671 to
1700. It is a long, sprawling work (or perhaps series of works),
and it is difficult to deal with in itself. Critics have managed to
indicate the extent of the complicated borrowing from various
works in which Head and Kirkman indulged.[53] But *The English
Rogue* also presents bibliographical problems, and it is not at all
surprising that among the small number of scholars who mention
it, only one, Strickland Gibson in his bibliography of Francis
Kirkman, has been able to present an entirely accurate picture of
its publishing history.[54]

Part One of *The English Rogue*, written by Richard Head, was
first published, without a licence, in 1665. Three editions
followed in 1666; the first licensed edition in 1667.[55] William
Winstanley says of Head that

he betook him to his Pen; and wrote the first part of the *English Rogue*:
which being too much smutty, would not be Licensed, so that he was
fain to refine it, and then it passed stamp.[56]

This is reflected in the entry in the Stationers' Register:

Master Richard Head. January 5 1666. Entred . . . under the hands of
Master Roger L'Estrange and Master Richard Royston warden a copie
or book intituled The English Rogue corrected and amended with
additions vj^d.[57]

While these expurgations were apparently carried out by Head,
a significant number of additions began to appear in later
editions (1668, 1671), and these may well have been the work of
Kirkman, as Head refused to write the second part of the work, a

[53] See esp. Chandler, Vol. 1, pp. 211–21; also C. W. R. D. Moseley, 'Richard Head's
"The English Rogue": A Modern Mandeville', *YES* 1 (1971), 102–7; and Allen H.
Lanner, 'Richard Head's Theophrastan Characters', *N & Q* 215 (1970), 259.
[54] Strickland Gibson, *A Bibliography of Francis Kirkman* (Oxford, 1947).
[55] Not in 1665 as claimed by Michael Shinagel, ed., *The English Rogue* (Boston, 1961),
p. i.
[56] William Winstanley, *The Lives of the Most Famous English Poets* (1687), p. 208.
[57] Gibson, p. 121.

task undertaken by Kirkman himself (see preface to Part Two, 1668).[58]

A complete critical edition would be necessary if all these changes were to be traced through successive editions. The changes themselves, however, may be summarized. Head removed approximately twenty passages of erotic description, often of only a sentence or two, but on a few occasions a whole poem was excised or substantially altered. The additions made by Kirkman are much more extensive, ranging from the rephrasing of a sentence to the insertion of complete chapters. The edition of 1665 contains fifty chapters, while the 1680 edition contains seventy-six. Kirkman, or perhaps Head in the course of his expurgations, corrected a large number of grammatical errors found in the 1665 edition: the printer was to blame for only a small proportion of these.

Despite the fact that a considerable proportion of *The English Rogue* is unoriginal, the result is not simply a patch-work quilt made up of poorly stitched source material. The reader who is familiar with the material discussed in the preceding sections of this chapter recognizes incidents and situations, but they are smoothly integrated into the narrative. Much of this material would no doubt have been forgotten by the general public, or perhaps readers enjoyed this new suit cut from old cloth for its own sake. Certainly Head and Kirkman achieved a popular success. *The English Rogue* was altered, reduced to the size of a pamphlet, renamed, but kept reappearing—in 1671, 1680, 1693, 1697, 1701, 1719, 1723, 1741, and 1759.[59]

Any general analysis of *The English Rogue* is made difficult by its length and its apparently disorganized nature. The task becomes much easier when Part One is viewed as a relatively self-contained narrative. This approach does not depend on the question of authorship; Part One is the relatively unified story of Meriton Latroon, while Parts Two, Three, and Four are much

---

[58] I have considered the expurgations and the reasons for them at greater length in 'Alterations to *The English Rogue*', *The Library*, Sixth Series, 4 (1982), 49–56.

[59] See Gibson, p. 125; for convenient access, my basic text, to which page numbers in parentheses refer unless otherwise noted, is the 1875 (although this date does not always appear) reprint of the 1680 edition of all four parts (no place of publication is indicated— one may assume it to be London). While it reprints the title-page of the first edition (1665), it is not a reprint of that edition. I have checked quotations from it against the original editions of all four parts (Part I, 1665; II, 1668; III and IV, 1671).

more digressive, with Meriton making only an occasional appearance.[60]

Richard Head presents the story of Meriton Latroon, a 'Witty Extravagant' who relates his own narrative from his birth in Ireland, through his adventures and tricks in various places, to his final marriage in 'Bantam' to an Indian. The story, even with Kirkman's later additions, is brisk and full of vivid incidents. Head does not linger, but moves from trick to trick, place to place, as rapidly as Meriton himself. Perhaps the later interpolations are necessary to prevent the reader from becoming rather dizzy. The narrative quite naturally gathers its material from a multitude of sources as it proceeds: Head includes 'cant-dictionaries' and descriptions of confidence tricks from the cony-catching pamphlets; situations from Spanish picaresque novels and English criminal biographies; exotic descriptions from travel books when Meriton leaves England. To the sources discussed earlier in this chapter, Head even adds Characters, two at least stolen from earlier works.[61]

By keeping our attention focused on Meriton, Head draws

[60] Kirkman, in the preface to the reader of Part Two, tells us how Head refused to write a second part (A4-A4ᵛ). The preface to Part Three is signed by Head and Kirkman, and states that 'we have equally club'd in its composition' (iii, 1671, A2ᵛ). Head, however, dissociated himself from all except Part One in the preface to *Proteus Redivivus* (1675):

According to the promise made in my Postscript to the first part of the English Rogue, I purposed to have finisht that Book in a Second Part, travelling him through all the gentiler parts of Europe, Topographically describing all places of eminency, with an account of what Tricks and Rogueries he committed where ever he came, but the Cudgels were snatcht out of my hands before I had fairly laid him down, I intending to have had but one more bout at the same Weapons, and so have compleated the Rogue, but seeing the Continuator hath allready added three Parts to the former, and never (as far as I can see) will make an end of pestering the World with more Volumes, and large Editions, I diverted my intention into this Subject. (A4-A4ᵛ)

Moseley does not accept this disclaimer (op. cit., p. 101). Certainly Parts Three and Four differ from Part Two—they do have a firmer structure, and a much more vivid narrative style. It seems strange, however, that Head so firmly dissociated himself from such a popular enterprise, emphasizing this on the title-pages of both *Proteus Redivivus* and *The Miss Display'd* (1675), both by 'the Author of the First Part of The English Rogue'. A falling out between Head and Kirkman is no reason for Head to claim the authorship of the perhaps slightly notorious Part One, but not of the equally popular Parts Three and Four. This question of authorship is unlikely to be clarified any further, and does not interfere with my analysis: one can clearly separate Part One from the continuations, regardless of their author(s).

[61] See Lanner, *passim.*

these elements together. While Head claims that he 'skimm'd not off the Cream of other mens Wits, nor Cropt the flowers in others gardens to garnish my own *Plots;* neither have I larded my Lean Fancy with the Fat of others *Ingenious Labours*' (preface, pp. vii-viii), a more accurate picture is presented in his disingenuous disclaimer:

some may say, That this is but actum agere, a Collection out of *Guzman*, *Buscon*, or some others that have writ upon this subject; *Crambem bis coctam apponere*, and that I have onely *squeez'd* their Juice, (adding some Ingredients of mine own) and afterwards *distill'd* it in the *Lymbeck* of my own Head. (p. vii)

Perhaps the most important thing added by Head is his own point of view; at times witty, at times crudely obscene, but always challenging. His part of *The English Rogue* stalks the unsuspecting reader, who allows his sympathy to be secured, only to find that his idealizing view is destroyed mercilessly. This process is at work even in the later parts of the work, but Head presents it in an acute form.

Meriton is not a developing character. He moves in and out of focus disconcertingly, at times simply a voice recounting incidents, at times a convincing creation who enlists our interest. The opening few chapters present Meriton at his most human, as he describes his family background ('After a long and strict Inquisition after my Fathers Pedegree, I could not find any of his Ancestors bearing a *Coat*: surely length of time had *worn* it out', I. 1), and his childhood. Head presents some wonderfully realized incidents which animate this introductory view of Meriton: his battle with one of his father's turkeys, which 'could not endure the sight of a Red Coat, which I usually wore' (p. 16); his advancement at school through his ability 'to bribe some of the upper Form to make my Exercises' (p. 20), and his humiliation when his true ignorance is discovered; his first 'Ramble' away from home, when 'The first dinner I made was on Blackberries and Nuts, esteemed by me very delicious fare at first' (p. 33), although soon 'I began to loath my afore-named *Manna*, Blackberries, Nuts, Crabs, Bullies &c., and longed to taste of the Flesh-pots again' (p. 34).

The energy and appeal of the writing continues when Meriton meets a group of gypsies, but as the narrative proceeds, the initial view of Meriton is modified. When he becomes an apprentice, he seduces a maid, and when she becomes pregnant, 'I bethought my self how to be rid both of Cow and Calf' (p. 103). Head has made Meriton quite convincing up until now, so this callousness distresses the reader. Meriton does indeed trick the maid onto a ship sailing for Virginia, although this incident is somewhat softened in Part Three, when Meriton and the maid are reunited—the chilling personal amorality of Part One is not consistently carried over to the sequels.

This disarming incident immediately follows the attractive and well-known 'Character of a Bottle of Canary'—even if this Character is not original, we do attribute it to Meriton. Soon the narrative carries us with it again, especially when Head exploits the erotic potential of Meriton's disguise as a girl. All four parts of *The English Rogue* continue to state their moral purpose: 'herein you may see Vice pourtrayed in her own proper shape' (I. iv). Head, however, exploits the moral ambivalence attached to the picaresque in England; he himself refers to: 'my Satyrical [and] Cynical Humour' (I.vi). While other authors were quite probably unconscious of the contradictions involved in their 'moral' approach to the depiction of roguery, Head actually manipulates this ambiguity.

When Meriton begins to roam around the country, tricking people, seducing women, stealing goods and, occasionally, hearts, he often leaves behind mocking poems addressed to his victims: 'Madam, I'm gone, no wonder, for you know,/Lovers encounters are but touch and go' (p. 106). Meriton's energy and Head's witty style combine to engage the reader, clouding the incidents themselves. Head is careful to avoid making Meriton a murderer; he is callous, but not totally destructive. When we summon up our energy to condemn him, Head's 'Satyrical' humour snaps into focus: 'And damn all Brothels too to Hell; but stay/What house is not a Brothel-house I pray?' (p. 382). When we may feel exasperated, simply by the accumulation of tricks (and just in case we are becoming bored with all this wickedness), Meriton is caught, condemned to death, and turns penitent (p. 385). He delivers a long, impressive sermon after his conversion, but then is reprieved and transported. Exciting adventures in strange lands follow, the energy is generated once more, and Meriton's irrepressible rogueries return. A frontispiece which appears with many editions captures the essence of this process. It is a portrait of Head (the verses underneath begin 'The Globe's thy Studye . . .'), who presents an impressive, dignified figure— one might imagine him writing a sermon. However, stepping out of a strange landscape at the level of his head (he was fond of the pun) is an impish satyr, crowning him with a laurel wreath.

The satyr is perhaps most apparent in Head's occasional use of a style reminiscent of Nashe at his most exuberant. The hunger that helps to give *Lazarillo* its balanced moral perspective is here—perhaps under the influence of Quevedo as well as Nashe—turned into an appropriate subject for comic, stylistic manipulation:

In those places I learned to take Tobacco, which was the chiefest part of my food; living in a manner by Smoak, as the Camelion by Air. I fed so lightly, that I durst not stir abroad in a high wind; neither durst I fight, lest one single stroak should have hazarded my dissolution; continued drinking had so washed me, that my body was transparent, you might have seen within me (without dissection) the motion of the heart; you could have observed but little as to my liver, it long since had lost its use in the conveyance of the blood, for my stomack had nothing therein contained to supply it; like an Inns-a-Court-Kitchen out of Term-time. In short, I appeared like a walking *Skeleton*. (p. 150)

This style is also used to describe grotesque characters, descend-ants of the tapster in *The Unfortunate Traveller* (see pp. 121–2).

Head lures us into an anarchic world which mocks the values and morality of the reader. Meriton's amoral viewpoint is expressed with an energetic humour; and his adventures speed the reader towards a nihilistic chasm. Meriton himself constantly averts his course, however, and recognizes the abyss before him. Head avoids making Meriton an unregenerate character—a number of moralizing comments are already in the first edition, and these are increased by Kirkman's additions. Meriton's actions belie his moral comments, but he is, at various times, quite conscious of this fact. The reader, however much less of a rogue than Meriton, also does not live up to the moral maxims he doubtless formulates, and is forced to recognize this fact at these points in the narrative.

Part One, taken on its own, has a similar framework to *Moll Flanders*: the (relatively) repentant Meriton, married to his

Indian wife and quite prosperous, relates his misdeeds and comfortably reflects, 'let my Life be to the Reader, as a friend Fal'n in a pit, that gives warning to another to avoid the danger' (p. 465). The reader remains uneasy, and there are times when the narrative underlines this unease. The 1665 edition, with its erotic passages, emphasizes Meriton's Casanova-like qualities, but Head's depiction of sexuality also contains something of the despair to be found in Rochester's later poems (although Head is usually flippant, rather than bitter). There are a number of references to impotence, including the poem beginning 'What Prodigy is this? or what Portent/Is threatned to me by this dry Event?' (1665 edn., p. 98). Head's erotic passages are not just crude and sensational, but also emphasize the emptiness following satiety, the sense of nihilism which Meriton does, at times, recognize as the consequence of his amoral outlook. The furious energy and the enumeration of incidents which carry the reader along are countered by this lack of fulfilment: 'I was so fierce at first, I soon was spent:/Storms and high winds are never permanent' (1665 edn., p. 70). The expurgated editions retain a considerable portion of the erotic element, and the accompanying brief despair:

Some two months we spent in all manner of self-pleasing delights, till at last I began to be tyred with her too frequent invitations; the more I endeavoured to satisfie her, the further I was from it. (p. 358, see also p. 290)

As a picaresque protagonist, Meriton seems to have complete freedom of action, but this is only an apparent freedom; he has freed himself from internalizing society's constraints, but his actions are still circumscribed by those constraints—he is imprisoned more than once. As a rogue, Meriton is engaged in outwitting society, and the lure of the rogue, for the presumably innocent reader, is a vicarious involvement in this cunning freedom. Just as society's moral stance is ambivalent, mirrored in the reader's combined feeling of admiration and condemnation, so the rogue creates an uncertain position for himself. The trickster is often tricked, as when Meriton falls in love with and marries an apparently innocent girl who is in fact already pregnant and, as a wife, quite a match for him (Chap. 21). Even the cynical unity which they eventually achieve (Meriton as

pimp and his wife as prostitute) does not last for long. Meriton
always finds himself alone; either he runs from others, or they run
from him. We often meet groups of criminals, highwaymen,
gypsies—but Meriton himself never stays with a group of
'associates' for very long:

I resolved to have no more to do with them, but would snip securely by
my self, knowing, that in any secret design, if many are concerned, their
business cannot be long kept private. (pp. 171–2)

The rogue's freedom depends on his solitude. Other people are
a threat, for once he has stepped beyond the constraints of
society's rules he can have no faith in other people, who might
well follow his lead. It is ironic that the bands of thieves,
described with such zest, form a rigidly hierarchical society
themselves, with their own rules, as well as their own language.
Much may be made of their loyalty, but a rogue like Meriton
does not rely on this idealistic view of honour among thieves. So
he escapes again from a society and a set of rules, but this means
the rejection of human contact.

Meriton's liaisons, his marriages, his friendships, do not last.
He turns people into objects (a maid who carries his child into a
cow and her calf) in order to distance himself from them. The
reader's enjoyment of Meriton's tricks places him in a similar
position, for he too regards other characters as butts for jokes,
rather than as victims. Because Meriton always moves on, we do
not see the suffering he causes. Even when his victims reappear in
the sequels, they have long since recovered from his initial
villainies (although the affection which he generates in young
ladies may linger).

Meriton's solitude is part of his protean nature. He changes his
identity, donning disguises to aid him in his confidence tricks.
These disguises allow him to escape, but escaping from any
involvement with other people does not only have beneficial
consequences. By seeking an identity outside society, not simply
beyond its rules but beyond human contact *per se*, Meriton draws
near to an anarchic situation. The materialistic viewpoint of the
rogue, and of the picaresque work he inhabits, prevents the
search for an identity beyond that offered by society from taking
on the more positive nature seen in the spiritual autobiographies

which were developing at this time.[62] Despite occasional moralistic reflections, Meriton does not search his own soul for an
identity; he slips from one disguise to another in a world of
surfaces—life consists of tricks and deceptions, not just the
rogue's life, but also the lives of those he tricks.

In one of his more convincing reflections, Meriton says:

Nothing jars the Worlds harmony more, than men that break their
ranks; and nothing renders Man more contemned and hated, than he
whose actions onely tend to irregularity. One turbulent spirit will even
dissentiate the calmest Kingdom: so did my past unruly and disorderly
life ruine my self, as well as many families. (p. 463)

Creating a conclusion for a picaresque novel is always a difficult
task, with this nihilism staring the rogue (and the reader) in the
face. Head approaches but then rejects the solution of the
criminal biography: repentance and death. He chooses the
unsettling solution which Defoe adopted: repentance, prosperity,
and a joyous recounting of past crimes which seem to conflict
with moral commentary. In the case of Meriton, a sequel is
promised, and does seem inevitable. The success of Head's
creation ensured that such a sequel would be provided, if not by
Head himself, then by the enterprising Francis Kirkman.

Writing the second part alone, Kirkman abandoned Meriton as a
narrative centre, and when Head joined him to write the third
and fourth parts (if he in fact did so), the unity of Part One, its
focus on Meriton, was never resumed. We enter a world which
structurally reflects Meriton's personal chaos: Part Two is
digressive and increasingly fragmented, and although the narrative is somewhat pulled together by reintroducing characters from
Part One, who indulge in a series of *récits*, incidents are not drawn
together as they were by Meriton's narrating voice. Parts Three
and Four achieve a somewhat tighter structure, but one still
dominated by Kirkman's attitude: 'This relation is full of variety'
(preface, Part Two, b3).

Meriton, after a brief recapitulation of his adventures in Part
One, and a rather superfluous discussion of the Indian religions,
meets a group of rogues from England. Two of them are women

[62] See Paul Delaney, *British Autobiography in the Seventeenth Century* (London, 1969),
Chaps. 5 and 6, where this is evident in the autobiographies of Presbyterians and
Sectarians.

in disguise: Mary, one of the girls he left pregnant at a boarding school when he was disguised as a woman, and Dorothy, the farmer's daughter he seduced and abandoned (I. 315). Before they relate their adventures, one of their companions relates his own story, which takes up the bulk of the volume (II. 49–288).

This rogue's actions are not the central feature of his account; instead, he presents us with a panorama of trades, and the dishonest dealings associated with them. Incidents are jumbled together to illustrate how only one fact is constant in a chaotic world: dishonesty. The accusing finger now points back at the reader; Meriton as scapegoat is replaced by surgeons, cooks, nurses, shoemakers, locksmiths, tailors, bakers, innkeepers, lawyers, scriveners, booksellers—all of them following the motto: 'who steales not, knows not how to live in this world' (II. 51). The rogue is now a figure who protects himself by trickery. He is indeed more attractive than those who profess to lead an upright life while they actually dodge the law. Kirkman says in the preface that he will give 'an account of the greatest *Knaveries* which I know' (a5ᵛ), and so scriveners and booksellers receive a great deal of attention—Kirkman's autobiographical work, *The Unlucky Citizen* (1673), indicates how he himself entered these two professions.

When one enters this world one either cheats or becomes the cheater's victim: 'I find that saying to be verified which I had often heard, That the World consisted but of two sorts, *Knaves* and *Fools*, and that the one lived by out-witting and Cheating the other' (II. 185). Restoration society was certainly full of rogues and dishonest practices, but the picaresque creates a world of extremes, where trickery is ubiquitous.[63]

The narrative increasingly turns to the presentation of a series of vignettes, especially when the two women, Mary and Dorothy, tell their stories. Mary's fairly brief narrative does initially enlist our sympathies, as Meriton's did. She has placed herself in the service of a bawd, and slowly but inevitably descended from superior courtesan to common prostitute. Her view of life is, naturally, coloured by this: she is not remorseful, but her sense of pleasure as being transitory mirrors Meriton's experience:

Although I was well enough pleased with my nights lodging, and so was

---

[63] See Petherick, *passim*.

my bedfellow: yet, as the longest day, so will the longest night have an end; and no pleasure is lasting, neither would ours continue . . . (II. 357)

Dorothy's story is much longer (II. 366–III. 203), but much more fragmented. It does not present her life coherently; rather, it is constantly interrupted by the report of other people's experiences. She breaks off a number of times, aware of this disunity, but Meriton and Mary urge her to continue: 'I pray be as full and free in your recital as you can, for we cannot think any thing to be tedious that is so pleasant' (III. 98). Meriton's world is chaotic, but he has a firm grip on his past adventures. With the narratives he now listens to, we reach the reflection of this disorder in the lives of the narrators and in the stories themselves. This is accentuated when Dorothy's story is interrupted (with her consent) by interpolated stories from Meriton and Mary (III. 204); and she breaks off while present events take over (Mary is murdered and Dorothy herself barely recovers from poison administered by Meriton's Indian wife), not completing her story until Part Four (pp. 24–89).

A move towards cohesion is made when Meriton is reunited with Jane, the girl he sent to Virginia when she became pregnant (III. 293). However, the narrative itself continues to be disjointed, as anecdote replaces history. The captain of the ship which the characters all join tells his (very digressive) story, and then Jane tells the story of a man she once knew, a story which is appropriately left unfinished at the end of the fourth part.

The reader should not expect narrative unity, but rather follow the listeners within the work, who delight in the 'large Catalogue of all sorts of notorious Rogueries' (Part III, preface, A2). The vignettes themselves become more vivid as these jagged narratives proceed; any sense of a central, developing character blurs, but isolated incidents come sharply into focus. An example is the following vivid traveller's 'tall-tale':

Whilst we anchored at the Island of St. *Helena* there happened a sad Accident; whilst we were recreating and refreshing our selves in the Island, one of our men (that brought us ashore in the Skiff) being an excellent Swimmer, stript himself, and over the side of the Boat he went, he had not been long in the water before such as stood on the shore to see him swim, perceived a *Shark* to make towards him; who cryed out, A

Shark, a *Shark*, hasten to the Boat; which he did with incredible speed, and had laid his hands on her side as the *Shark* snapt at his Leg, and having it in his mouth turned on his back, and twisted it off from the knee. The fellow protested to me that when this was done, he felt no pain anywhere but under his Arm-pits; the fellow was drest and perfectly cur'd; afterwards this very *Shark* was taken by one of our men, fishing for him with a great piece of Raw-Beef, and when his belly was ripp'd open, the Leg was found whole therein. (IV. 1–2)

Such set-pieces are quite frequent; they are to be enjoyed as isolated creations, seldom linked to any developing situation.

The moral ambiguities and structural anarchy of *The English Rogue* may now be considered in relation to its most important theme: the contradictions inherent in the world of commerce. This theme is explored, in different ways, in all four parts. In Part Two, we receive the apprentice's view of his master's tricks, and the masters, as noted above, are a cross-section of all major trades. The chapter-titles alone show what impression we receive of these trades: 'He is bound Prentice to a Taylor, the Knavery of that trade' (II. 110); 'He serveth a Plaisterer, sheweth some cheats in that Trade' (II. 118).

The tricks of the masters are mirrored by the tricks of their apprentices. Commerce opens up innumerable opportunities for cheating, and each trade provides unique possibilities. These growing occupations are shown in the worst possible light. The self-interest necessary to achieve success shades easily into outright dishonesty—that, at least, is the view of *The English Rogue*, and many other native picaresque works. Two interesting passages develop this theme, both concerning groups of apprentices who join together to exploit their masters. The apprentices do not indulge in individual tricks, as the rogue figure does; their robberies are organized into a commercial system. In the first case, they have a warehouse, where they exchange goods stolen from their masters:

I was much amazed to see such variety of Wares lie upon a long Table, as Silks, Stuffs, Cloth, Linnen and Woolen, Stockings, Ribbands, Muffs, Hoods, Scarfs, and the like. (I. 81)

Their activities are a continuation of the business world: 'They told me my Credit was good, which is the Soul of Commerce'

(I. 82). The distinction between legitimate business and their activities is unclear, because their masters also practise deception.

In Part Two, Kirkman discusses the deceptions indulged in by book-sellers, and then describes a similar association of book-sellers' apprentices, who band together in order to earn extra money (pp. 218–22). This mocking picture of trade leads to an acute reflection: 'now I meditated on nothing more than how I might get money enough, for that was the only thing that made crooked things straight; and if a man have enough of that, he may defie all men' (p. 222). The world of the rogue and the world of the tradesman suddenly become mirror images instead of opposing principles. Similarly, the pattern of society is both mocked and reflected by the hierarchy, rules, and language of rogues. A clear line cannot be drawn between the upright, honest world of the reader and the amusing but amoral world of the rogue.

Sections which carry this challenge to society, and to the 'respectable' trading sector in particular, are contrasted with more humorous depictions of roguery. Two passages deserve close attention. Dorothy's story is diverted when she begins to describe the inn where she once stayed. The whole inn is run by rogues:

knowing of one anothers tricks, they out-vyed one another, striving and contending which should exceed in Roguery, and so sly and cunningly they carried it, that 'twas difficult to discover them, especially when they all joined together to cheat or abuse any body; but when they fell out among themselves, they made excellent sport in acting the revenges they took upon one another. (III. 88–9)

The accounts of trickery begin to enlist the reader's sympathy, especially when the tricks are directed against those who deserve to be tricked. One example, which also illustrates the convincing use of dialogue, is the description of Christmas 'in time of [the] rebellion' (III. 102). The 'Cook-maid' decides to trick the puritans, who attempt to enforce their restrictions against traditional Christmas cheer. The officers appear

to see and examine our Kitching, where they found not the Jack a going, yet they found a good fire, and the pot a boyling: 'How now,' said Master Church warden, 'How dare you break the Lawes, by dressing victuals on this day? What have you in the Pot?' Quoth the Maid, 'Nothing but plumb porridg.' 'How,' said the Church-warden, 'Superstitious Porridg? this is a very great offence, and deserves as great punishment, to do thus in contempt of the Laws; I will see your Master fined for this, and severely punished.' 'Well,' replied she, 'but I pray, Master Church-warden, be not so angry, but be pacified; which I know you will be, when you see further what is in the Pot, and with what the porridge are [sic] made; and lest you should mistake I will shew you;' whereupon she went to the Pot and took out a large pair of Rams-horns, and said, 'Look you, Master Church-warden, this is the meat; how like you it? I hope so well, that you will tast of the broath your self without scruple of conscience?' (p. 103; I have replaced italics with inverted commas.)

The inn becomes a symbol of mirth, particularly at the times when cruel tricks are superseded by eating contests (p. 109), and the innkeeper's dishonesty is made more attractive than the zeal of those who condemn all mirth.

But the darker side of this freedom asserts itself once again, for the wife of the innkeeper is a wicked woman, who murders people (something the rogues we identify with never do), and the innkeeper himself eventually helps her to murder a gentleman 'for his money' (IV. 26). The quest for wealth undermines the rogue's freedom, and ties him to the society from which he tries to escape. The 'morality' of *The English Rogue* is not found in the unconvincing sermons and moralizing comments of the characters, but in these telling incidents, where the worlds of commerce and the rogue come together.

In Part Four, Jane offers the story of 'a jolly old Blade', which is unfortunately left unfinished. The story deals mainly with the 'Blade's' son, but his own story is particularly interesting. He begins as a brewer's clerk, cheats his master, and so takes control of the business, eventually marrying the brewer's widow. The ex-clerk grows wealthier, and when his wife dies, he 'resolved to be wary in his second choice, and to have both pleasure and profit' (IV. 253). The cajoling but ambiguous phrase 'pleasure and profit' is so closely associated with the rogue literature discussed here that we may anticipate the conclusion which follows. He cautiously chooses a country wife of 'four and twenty', but his expectations of a quiet and frugal life (he is now 60, and has become something of a miser) are dashed when his wife realizes that she is married to 'the chiefest man in the Parish' (p. 254).

She immediately begins to compare her house with her neighbours' houses, deciding that it needs to be refurbished. Suddenly, everything is seen in purely materialistic terms, as the wife's acquisitive instinct grows. When she becomes pregnant, she sees the event solely in terms of the items which must now be acquired:

And next, all her business was in making provision against the Bantling should come to Town; there must be new Blankets, Beds, Rowlers, Pilches, Clouts, Shirts, Head-bands, Biggins, and a world of such kind of little Utensils provided; and the Cradle and Groaning-Chair must also be bought and made ready . . . (IV. 256)

The husband provides all these:

But all of them was nothing considerable to her next demand, and that was a Cup-boards-head of Plate; some there was in the house, *viz.* a beer-bowl, a Beaker, a Salt, and a dozen of Apostle Spoons: but these must be changed, and others provided; *viz.* one large Tanckard, two smaller of an equal size, one Plate, one Sugar-dish, two or three Porringers, two Caudle-Cups, two dozen of Spoons, a couple of Candlesticks, one pair of Snuffers; and such a large Inventory of this kind of Ware she did reckon up, that it troubled her Husband, and almost broke his heart to think how to satisfie the ambitious humour of his Wife . . . (p. 257)

The reader is almost as overwhelmed as the husband by this enumeration. Such is the 'respectable' station the husband has entered by cheating his master. His wife goes on to bear a son, while his attempted parsimony increases, so he turns to petty thefts, taking a 'Hawking-bag' to official assemblies and stealing food (p. 264), and even utensils, and stealing bricks from a building site.

As the son grows up, his mother spoils him, supplying him with money, to his father's distress. He turns out to be a complete profligate, but he remains within the world created by his father, and he has none of the attractive qualities of Meriton. Instead of childish tricks which may amuse the reader, he quickly learns to manipulate his indulgent mother, and even his father; he even pretends to commit suicide to elicit their remorse (and, of course, more funds). He continues on this path after his father's death. His exploits as a young man are numerous, and follow the course one might expect after such a beginning. Part Four ends before his story is completed, but the direction it will take is plain.[64]

During one of the times when Meriton is close to starvation, he sets his wits to work. Entering an ordinary, he sits down by two men who are eating 'powdred Beef and Turnips' (I. 155):

I slipt my hands through a hole, in the form of an heart, which was in the partition that divided us, and laying hold on the Turnips, I spake aloud, You hoggs, are ye at the Roots? (ibid.)

Claiming to be 'in a merry humour today', he joins them, and when they become angry exclaims 'I value your anger no more than the drinking this Pot, which I swallowed at two gulps, and so bid them farewel' (p. 156). The convincing dialogue, Meriton's need, the relatively harmless trick, all enlist the reader's interest and sympathy. (The trick itself, as one might expect, is a very old one.) But we still see how, even in jest, Meriton sees people as objects or as animals: the diners are 'hoggs', just as the pregnant maid is a cow (notice, for example, his description of his wife's lover as 'her Stallion', p. 200). The fact that the hole is 'in the form of an heart' is doubtless a fortuitous detail, but one cannot help remarking the apt gesture by the rogue who, even at his most attractive, banishes sentiment.

Chapter Sixteen begins with a paean to crime:

I began to think that the Art of stealing might be reckoned amongst the liberal Sciences; for though it may be called an *Handicraft*, yet it cannot be looked on as *Mechanick*. This is the *Art*, the right Practice whereof is the true *Philosopher's stone*, the *Elixer* of life; with which many turn *Poyson* into *Medicine*, coarse cloath into cloath of Gold, hunger into fulness and satiety, convert rags into Sattins, and all this done by a quick wit, and slight of hand. (I. 166)

This virtually follows the incident discussed above, and the reader's indignation is quelled by the evident truth of Meriton's assertion. Meriton enters a house:

resolving if I met any to beg an Almes of them, having before

---

[64] In 1689 an edition appeared subtitled 'In Five Parts. The Fourth Edition, with large Additions, further compleating the whole History of his Life' (Gosport, Printed by J. Phillpot near the Blue Bell, in Middle-street). In fact, this is only 200 pages long, and it rearranges material from the complete early editions, adding a few incidents to provide an end for the narrative. Neither Head nor Kirkman could be responsible for any abridgement at this late stage.

premeditated what I had to say, *viz.* that I was a poor distressed young
Gentleman, my Father, Mother, nay, all my Relations I knew, being
dead, and that not knowing what to do, was forced (under the Covert of
the night) to beseech the assistance of charitable minded persons.
(p. 166)

This is a deception, but it is also true—Meriton *is* without friends,
and without support. He steals a 'good Camlet-cloak'; afterwards

thinking of what dangerous consequence this might prove, I resolved to
walk more confidently, and not let my eyes discover any thing of fear, by
reason of guilt. This loose garment had so of a sudden Metamorphosed
those thoughts I had of my self but a little before, my eye being
continually on my Cloak, I could not conceit my self less then the best of
the young Templers, that walk the streets to show themselves. (p. 167)

His guilt stems from self-preservation, but the cloak itself is
extremely important. Meriton cannot search his soul for an
identity; he relies on externals, but he does this because the world
puts such value on them.
    During an earlier period of extreme want, when Meriton
'appeared like a walking Skeleton' (p. 150), similar attention was
focused on his threadbare cloak, a 'thin transparent garment'
stripped ('all but the cape') from him by servants at an inn when
he could not pay (p. 152). Meriton's identity seems embodied in
this cloak: 'I loved my Cloak so well, as that it grieved me much
to be compelled to part with it' (p. 153). Although stripped of
almost everything, his resilient energy is displayed in a burlesque
poem which he addresses to the cloak, and which increasingly
questions any self-sufficiency beyond display:

> Nay when I had thee, scarcely did I know
> Sometimes whether I had thee on or no.
> Thou wert so thin, and light . . . (p. 154)

With his new, substantial cloak, Meriton is able to enter a
'Gaming Ordinary' (p. 167) where, despite his lack of funds, he
decides to 'resolutely take up the Box, and I threw a Main, which
was 7: a great deal of money was presently set me . . .' (ibid.).
Here his cloak is indeed his identity, and it allows him to take his
money and leave: 'I thanked my propitious Stars and the
Gentlemen, who had rather lose their money than suspect any

that hath the garb of one well Extracted' (p. 168). We are then
told of the fall from grace of ordinaries:

Questionless Ordinaries were first impartially founded, inderdicting all
play but which was upon the Square; but since, by the connivance of the
Box-keepers, when the Table grows thin, and few at it, let the stranger
beware. (ibid.)

We are warned of a number of tricks practised upon the innocent,
but Meriton indicates how impudence and dishonesty (after all,
he threw the dice without any funds to pay for a loss) are
successful weapons to use against such cheats. It is implied that
Meriton uses the weapons already wielded by others, with
greater zest, wit, and, of course, success.

Then he proceeds to an inn, where the landlord 'was very loath
to entertain me, his lodger having served him a scurvy trick
the night before' (p. 168). No, Meriton does not play another
trick:

I shewed myself that night very exceeding noble, concealing my success
at play, that he might conclude the greatness of my expence proceeded
from the nobleness of my nature, having a good estate to back it. (p. 169)

His assumed character of wealth and nobility contrasts strongly
with the dissolute nature of the truly rich and 'noble' characters
in *The English Rogue*. But Meriton is only making another gesture;
the narrative must move on as quickly as possible, leaving behind
a series of impersonations, jests, victims, repentances, and oases
such as this one.

VII. The Influence of the Picaresque

The English Rogue spawned many imitations as the popularity of
picaresque fiction increased during the late seventeenth and
early eighteenth centuries. An international bevy of rogues
appeared (all, however, produced by English writers): *The French
Rogue* (1672); *The Dutch Rogue* (1683); *The Irish Rogue* (1690); *The
Scotch Rogue* (1706). The step from these works to Defoe's *Captain
Singleton* (1720) and *Moll Flanders* (1722) is a question of
development, rather than a dramatic emergence of a new form.
Richard Bjornson notes that *The English Rogue*, with its 'profound
disjunction between its overt condemnation of illicit behaviour

and the morality implied in the narrative', points towards Defoe's novels.[65]

It is difficult to determine exactly which section of the reading public responded to these works. Continuations of early cony-catching pamphlets fall into the class of cheap chapbooks, available for the bottom rung of the reading public, but a work such as *The English Rogue* is too large and too expensive to be placed in a similar category. Book prices for this period averaged slightly less than one penny per sheet, which puts *The English Rogue* beyond the reach of anyone who had less than a few shillings to spend on a book.[66] E. H. Miller's comment on the Elizabethan period still applies: large books 'sold for shillings, and people earning £10 annually could not afford such prices'.[67] Important support for this view of *The English Rogue* is supplied by the chapbook versions which appeared. Chapbooks of chivalric romances were very short, and were the cheapest form of prose fiction produced during the period. In 1679 *The Life and Death of the English Rogue* appeared: a thirty-two page chapbook. In 1688 an even shorter (22 page) version appeared, printed in the black-letter type favoured by chapbook versions of romances. Priced at a few pence, these would have been within the reach of the very poorest readers, while the considerably more expensive, complete editions of *The English Rogue* would have been available only to more prosperous members of the commercial and trading classes—or perhaps their apprentices, if they acquired as large an illicit income as Head and Kirkman indicate in their novel.

The picaresque taps a vein of anarchy which is both exhilarating in its buoyant energy, and disturbing in its questioning of thematic and formal stability. This anarchy of form, seen in the episodic structure of picaresque narrative, stems from the protagonist. The English picaro does not always have as much

[65] Bjornson, *The Picaresque Hero*, p. 164; unfortunately, Bjornson's brief discussion of *The English Rogue* is not completely reliable, and for some reason he refers to the authors as George Head and Richard Kirkman (p. 161 and index).
[66] See Frances R. Johnson, 'Notes on English Retail Book-Prices, 1550–1640', *The Library*, Fifth Series, 2 (1950), 90; her comment on this earlier period, that 'Popular fiction apparently sold at approximately the standard rate' (p. 92), still applies after the Restoration.
[67] E. H. Miller, *The Professional Writer in Elizabethan England* (Cambridge, Mass., 1959), p. 41.

freedom as the reader believes him to have, and at times this imaginary freedom appears as an indictment of society's own rules, which are evaded by apparently respectable citizens in their own self-interest. This is Hobbes's world: the 'warre of every man against every man'.[68] The world of romance is neo-Platonic, not simply owing to the fashionable neo-Platonism of Henrietta Maria and Stuart court masques, but because the symbolism of heroic romance mirrors the order evoked by neo-Platonism. In the romance, harmony is achieved through balance; the purity of ideal forms is conveyed through refined love, and the stability of marriage and monarchical rule. The picaresque, on the other hand, turns to Hobbes's crushing dictum: 'I put for a generall inclination of all mankind, a perpetuall and restlesse desire of Power after power that ceaseth onely in Death.'[69]

The English Rogue reflects tensions generated by the changing role of commerce, and the new relationships between individuals in a city like London. It appeared only a few years after the Interregnum ended, and it embraces some of the comic and satiric implications of 'the world turned upside down'—a literary motif which became very real during the Civil War.[70] The eclectic nature of English picaresque and rogue literature may account for its long, vigorous life, which makes it a barometer of social, as well as literary, change.

---

[68] Thomas Hobbes, *Leviathan*, ed. C. D. Macpherson (Harmondsworth, 1974), p. 188.
[69] Ibid., p. 161.
[70] For a discussion of this concept, see Ian Donaldson, *The World Upside-Down: Comedy from Jonson to Fielding* (Oxford, 1974), esp. pp. 21–3.

Chapter 14

John Bunyan

While the influence of earlier prose fiction on Bunyan should not be over-emphasized, various traditions and impulses in seventeenth-century fiction provide a context for *The Pilgrim's Progress*, *Mr. Badman* and *The Holy War*. The elaborate source-hunting indulged in by earlier critics of *The Pilgrim's Progress* is summarized by James Wharey, who concludes that all that may be found are some analogues for the allegory, and a traditional use of the pilgrimage as a symbolic vehicle.[1] One such analogue may be used to illuminate some of the unique features of *The Pilgrim's Progress*, which has a place in the didactic tradition, the meditation tradition, and the emblem tradition, and which also draws on romance and allegory.[2]

I. *The Parable of the Pilgrim*

Simon Patrick published his *Parable of the Pilgrim* in 1665. It has never been a strong contender as a source for Bunyan's allegory, except for its tantalizing title. Wharey justifiably notes that it has 'almost no incidents . . . and . . . the amount of allegorical matter is very slight'.[3] Patrick's book begins with Theophilus feeling 'a thought stir in his soul, remembring him of a place called *Jerusalem*, which he had totally forgot in all his travels . . .' (p. 3).[4] He quickly meets a guide, a 'Director', who tells him how to make his pilgrimage to Jerusalem. But the bulk of the book contains an analysis of the journey's implications, rather than a

[1] James Blanton Wharey, *A Study of the Sources of Bunyan's Allegories* (Baltimore, 1904), p. 136.
[2] See U. Milo Kaufmann, *The Pilgrim's Progress and Traditions in Puritan Meditation* (New Haven, 1966); Roger Sharrock, 'Bunyan and the English Emblem Writers', *RES* 21 (1945), 105–16.
[3] Wharey, p. 97; Roger Sharrock, in *John Bunyan: The Pilgrim's Progress* (London, 1966), calls it 'prosy and unimaginative' (p. 15).
[4] References are to Simon Patrick, *The Parable of the Pilgrim* (1665).

description of the journey itself. The director produces ex-
hortations, sermons, and didactic essays; for example,
'Chap. IX, A More particular Discourse of Resolution; and
of the manner how to form such an one as will be sound and
firm' (p. 39).

Patrick only mentions his allegorical characters; unlike
Bunyan, he does not really allow them to appear, to exist as
concrete beings. The director introduces the pilgrim to 'two
Companions, Humility and Charity' (p. 58), but the reader
meets only a description of the abstract quality instead of the
character ('Of Divine Charity', Chap. 12). Even when
Theophilus' actual journey begins more than half-way through
the book, the narrative is still overwhelmed by Patrick's didactic,
expository impulse. Christian actually meets Apollyon and the˙
Giant Despair; Theophilus is merely *told* 'of the many enemies he
was to expect, that would assault his Resolution . . .' (p. 168).
He does not even reach Jerusalem at the end of the book!

Bunyan's defensive verse-preface to his allegory must be seen
in the context of the overt didacticism found in works like *The
Parable of the Pilgrim*. Patrick preaches, he tells the reader what to
believe; Bunyan's allegory, although it *'contains/Nothing but sound
and honest Gospel-strains'*, *'seems a Novelty'* (p. 145).[5] When Bunyan
asks *'May I not write in such a stile as this?'* (p. 140), we may recall
the direct method of Patrick, which stood as the obvious norm for
such a work. In his preface, Bunyan produces an elaborate series
of metaphors in defence of his method, all of them arguing that
his didactic purpose is disguised, not absent; his allegory is an
angel to catch a fish, a *'Pipe, and Whistle'* to tempt birds (p. 141).

Bunyan vividly imagines further objections: 'they want solid-
ness: *Speak man thy mind*:/They drown'd the weak; Metaphors
make us blind' (p. 141). The modern reader may tire of Bunyan's
protests, but they were not unjustified. The continuation written
by T.S. which appeared in 1682 as *The Second Part of the Pilgrim's
Progress* has a much plainer didactic purpose, and sacrifices
Bunyan's 'snares' for Patrick's plain speech. *Mr. Badman*, which
Bunyan originally saw as a sequel to his allegory (*'it came into my
mind to write, as then, of him that was going to Heaven, so now, of the Life*

---

[5] References are to John Bunyan, *Grace Abounding and The Pilgrim's Progress*, ed. Roger
Sharrock (London, 1966).

and Death of the Ungodly . . .')[6], uses a dialogue form, in which the didactic tradition is much more apparent. We have already seen the importance of the didactic impulse in the fiction of the time, in romances as well as religious allegories, and recent critical discussions of *The Pilgrim's Progress* have argued about the degree to which Bunyan's didactic intent is balanced by his imaginative freedom.

II. *The Pilgrim's Progress*

The conclusion of Bunyan's verse-preface is in fact a celebration of the power of the imagination, and the appeal of the fable:

> *Wouldest thou loose thy self, and catch no Harm?*
> *And find thy selfe again without a charm?*
> *Would'st read thy self, and read thou know'st not what*
> *And yet know whether thou art blest or not,*
> *By reading the same lines? O then come hither,*
> *And lay my Book, thy Head and Heart together.* (p. 145)

While Bunyan's use of material from the romance tradition cannot be detached from his didactic purpose, it still contains some of the appeal of 'pure' narrative for its own sake. In drawing on popular romance, Bunyan was risking censure for being frivolous: 'But some love not the method of your first,/Romance they count it, throw't away as dust' (p. 277). (This is a relatively early example of the use of the word 'romance' in a pejorative sense.)[7] The popular romances, however, fed Bunyan's imagination in his youth: 'Give me a ballad, a news-book, George on horseback, or Bevis of Southampton.'[8] We have seen how the chivalric romance moved down through the ranks of the reading public in the seventeenth century; Bunyan was influenced by a tradition in its decline, although his transformation of it reveals some of its strengths. He probably read redactions of *Bevis* and *The Seven Champions of Christendom* (in which St George appears); they would have been in a similar price-bracket to a ballad or a news-book.

---

[6] John Bunyan, *The Life and Death of Mr. Badman and The Holy War*, ed. John Brown (Cambridge, 1905), p. 3.

[7] *OED*, sect. 6.

[8] Quoted in Henri Talon, *John Bunyan: The Man and His Works* (London, 1951), p. 2, n. 8.

One can relate some of the incidents in *The Pilgrim's Progress* quite directly to chivalric romance motifs, and in some cases even to specific romances.[9] In the combat with Apollyon and the encounter with Giant Despair, the allegory is cast in the terms of a chivalric romance, and Christian's quest has some of the elements of a romance hero's quest. The allegorical landscape, which changes symbolically without being very convincing geographically, is also a feature of romance. Christian is really only seen as a chivalric character in his combat with Apollyon; generally he is more pilgrim than knight. But in the second part, Mr Great-heart is given a larger chivalric role to play. As the protector of Christiana's party, and many other pilgrims, he resembles the figure of the knight, whose task is to aid people in distress. Great-heart combats Giant Grim, Giant Maul, Giant Slaygood, a monster, and Christian's old enemy Giant Despair.

Spenser had already demonstrated the effectiveness of an allegorical use of chivalric romance conventions.[10] Bunyan's genius led to an eclecticism, which mingled romance castles and Bedfordshire sloughs to form a symbolic setting. Bunyan took from the debased chivalric romance one of its most enduring features—the knight on a quest, combating evil and rescuing the innocent. But Bunyan's characters, his Christian and his Great-heart, are much more convincing than Sir Bevis and St George: when they draw their swords, the reader is instantly involved. The fact that the chivalric element is used sparingly further increases its appeal; we do not read about one combat after another.

The chivalric element in *The Pilgrim's Progress* is not large; it is just one of a series of balanced elements present in the allegory, elements which have led to some critical controversy in recent years. U. Milo Kaufmann has traced the influence of the Puritan meditation on *The Pilgrim's Progress*. He begins by separating three elements out of the narrative: myth (in Kaufmann's terms, this refers to the events of the narrative), allegory, and the 'literal-didactic'.[11] He then discusses how Puritan hermeneutics colours

[9] See the comparison between Christian's combat with Apollyon, and St George's with the dragon in *The Seven Champions of Christendom*, pointed out in *The Pilgrim's Progress*, ed. Wharey, rev. Sharrock (Oxford, 1960), p. 322.

[10] See Harold Golder, 'Bunyan and Spenser', *PMLA* 45 (1930), 216–37.

[11] Kaufmann, p. 7.

the events found in the allegory: 'Behind every event is discerned the Word . . .'.[12] Kaufmann suggests that 'An earmark of his [Bunyan's] narrative procedure is the arresting of the forward thrust of the action while experience is reviewed not for the entertainment but for the edification of the listener'.[13]

Stanley Fish carries Kaufmann's suggestion even further, arguing that *The Pilgrim's Progress* is 'antiprogressive'.[14] Fish sees progress in the allegory as illusory; events must not be taken at face value: 'Perceiving correctly in spiritual terms means ignoring what is plainly there . . .'.[15] Fish's account usefully emphasizes the 'subtext' of Bunyan's allegory, and brings out the importance of its spiritual teaching, its rejection of any equation of appearance with truth; however, it does ignore 'what is plainly there' for the ordinary reader. John Knott Jr. counters Fish's position, stressing Christian's journey as a sequence reaching a definite climax, in his article, 'Bunyan's Gospel Day: A Reading of *The Pilgrim's Progress*'.[16] Most recently, A. Richard Dutton has taken up a position almost diametrically opposed to that of Fish. He sees less organization in the allegory than Fish and Knott, claiming that it was written specifically for Bunyan's Bedford congregation, not for the world at large.[17] Dutton sees Christian's journey as an inevitable progress stemming from his assurance of election.[18] Dutton ignores the narrative surface almost as much as Fish, for Christian may be assured of election in symbolic terms when his burden falls from his back, but his doubts, and his tribulations, are only beginning. The reader shares Christian's uncertainty throughout the allegory. Suspense is no more lost than it is when we read a Victorian novel knowing that the hero and heroine will ultimately marry.

In their eagerness to defend rather extreme positions, critics have ignored the more obvious aspects of the narrative. The reader of *The Pilgrim's Progress* is a sojourner too, even if he is not a member of Bunyan's congregation. He travels with Christian, and Bunyan's skill in depicting characters ensures that the reader

[12] Ibid., p. 112.   [13] Ibid., p. 23.
[14] Stanley Fish, *Self-Consuming Artifacts* (Berkeley, 1972), p. 229.
[15] Ibid., p. 245.
[16] *ELR* 3 (1973), 443-61.
[17] A. Richard Dutton, ' "Interesting but tough". . . Reading *The Pilgrim's Progress*', *SEL* 18 (1978), 445.
[18] Ibid., p. 447.

is involved in Christian's trials and joys. The allegory contains a series of balanced oppositions, and critics have disturbed this balance by seizing on only one side of each opposition—the side which supports their interpretation. The element of stasis amplified by Fish is present, and so is the element of progress stressed by Dutton. The narrative constantly moves from action to reflection and back to action (a very different movement from Fish's concept of action 'dissolving' into puzzled speculation).

When Christian loses his burden the reader does not relax at this assurance of election, for Christian immediately encounters the Hill Difficulty, falls asleep, and loses his roll. From the action of this episode we move to the static catechizing which takes place at the House Beautiful. In the second part, the catechizing becomes much more obtrusive; it even includes a literal catechism of Christiana's children. But in the first part, the narrative oscillates between the emblems, discussions, and didacticism of the House Beautiful, and the excitement of the battle with Apollyon. This is not to suggest that the House Beautiful sequence has no narrative content whatsoever, but it is a quiet moment, containing a great deal of homiletic material.

This opposition is also apparent if one considers the effect of the marginal glosses on the narrative. Bunyan uses three types of gloss: a pure description of the narrative such as 'Apollyon *in a rage falls upon* Christian' (p. 186); an interpretation of an event, such as 'Christian *wounded in his understanding, faith and conversation*' (when we are only told in the narrative that Christian is wounded 'in his *head*, his *hand* and *foot*', p. 187); and, by far the most numerous, the citation of biblical references. One can see an increasing tension with the narrative momentum here: the descriptive glosses summarize narrative events; the interpretative glosses pull the reader up and reinforce the didactic point of the allegory; the biblical citations, if the reader follows them up (as Bunyan's contemporaries certainly did), drag against the narrative. The didactic, the expository, the interpretative, balance the narrative surface, the 'action'. The reader soon learns that no event in *The Pilgrim's Progress* is contingent; a purpose rules all action.

Bunyan's eclecticism is responsible for bringing so many disparate elements together. The reader rarely cavils at this, but it is difficult for the critic to determine the exact thread which holds these contraries in a balance. One obvious answer is Bunyan's prose style, that 'clear stream of current English', as Southey described it.[19] Roger Sharrock has pointed out that 'there is little in this prose of the influence of the English Bible . . .';[20] it is a more 'earthy' language:

And moreover, at this Fair there is at all times to be seen Juglings, Cheats, Games, Plays, Fools, Apes, Knaves, and Rogues, and that of all sorts. (p. 211)

The narrative of *The Pilgrim's Progress* itself is filtered to the reader through a mediator: the dreamer. Once again Bunyan creates a balance. The famous opening sentence places the narrator, the dreamer, in the foreground:

As I walk'd through the wilderness of this world, I lighted on a certain place, where was a Denn; And I laid me down in that place to sleep: And as I slept I dreamed a Dream. I dreamed, and behold *I saw a Man clothed with Raggs standing in a certain place, with his face from his own House, a Book in his hand, and a great burden upon his Back.* (p. 146)

The dreamer remains obtrusive for a short time, partly through the almost formulaic phrase 'So I saw in my Dream' (pp. 147, 149, 150, 151). He questions Help directly, but then he gradually fades from the action; while we are still aware that we view the narrative through his eyes (most dramatically in the famous incident where the dreamer wakes and then dreams again, thought to be a reference to Bunyan's release from his first term of imprisonment), it is Christian who becomes the centre of attention. However, at the conclusion of the first part we return to the dream framework: 'So I awoke, and behold it was a Dream' (p. 271). The device is more perfunctory in the second part, which has a more casual framework: 'Shall it be my Lot to go that way again, I may give those that desire it, an Account of what I here am silent about; mean time I bid my Reader *Adieu*' (p. 399).

Stanley Fish notes how the conclusion of the first part makes us aware of the narrator as 'not our guide, but our fellow'.[21] The dreamer views the narrative, rather than controls it. Perception, both literally and in the sense of understanding, is an important

---

[19] *The Pilgrim's Progress: A Casebook*, ed. Roger Sharrock (London, 1976), p. 57.
[20] *John Bunyan: The Pilgrim's Progress*, p. 60.   [21] Fish, p. 263.

element in the allegory. Fish notes that 'there is in *The Pilgrim's Progress* an inverse relationship between visibility and reliability . . .'.[22] In the context of the balance of opposites in the allegory, it is important to note Bunyan's creation of landscape and actions which, almost in anticipation of Bishop Berkeley's philosophy, only exist when perceived. The allegorical landscape, like many a romance landscape, has a symbolic rather than a geographic cohesion; houses, hills, sloughs, appear in order to make an allegorical point. Only Bunyan's language convinces the reader that the slough is real:

Now I saw in my Dream, that just as they had ended this talk, they drew near to a very *Miry Slow* that was in the midst of the Plain, and they being heedless, did both fall suddenly into the bogg. The name of the Slow was *Dispond*. Here therefore they wallowed for a time, being grieviously bedaubed with the dirt; And *Christian*, because of the burden that was on his back, began to sink in the Mire. (p. 150)

The slough is not a vivid physical creation; rather, Bunyan brings to life the feeling of being caught in it.

These features of the landscape only exist when viewed directly; they often have to be pointed out to the characters: '*Do you see yonder high hill*' (p. 154); 'Look before thee; dost thou see this narrow way?' (p. 161). The dreamer is also watching the narrative, and at times the reader gains the impression that he is peering into the scene: 'I looked then after *Christian*, to see him go up the Hill . . .' (p. 173). This is the dreamer's usual position, although he is occasionally able to enter the narrative world and find out more directly the significance of what he sees: 'Then I stepped to him that pluckt him out . . .' (p. 151).

The allegory is poised between direct explication, and the dream narrative which involves the reader and demands his concentration. Although Faithful, in a very different context, says '*I see that Saying, and Doing are two things* . . .' (p. 203), the allegory does not separate the two. In *The Pilgrim's Progress* action is didactic, just as the expository is encompassed in dialogue between the characters:

This kind of discourse I did not expect [Talkative says], nor am I disposed to give an answer to such questions, because. I count not my

self bound thereto, unless you take upon you to be a *Catechizer* . . .
(p. 207)

'Wouldst thou see Truth within a Fable?': Bunyan is preacher
and poet. We do *The Pilgrim's Progress* an injustice by reading it
only as didactic, or only as fable; only as a progress, or only as a
stasis; only as realistic, or only as allegorical. All these oppositions
combine to form Bunyan's masterpiece.

III. *Mr. Badman*

In 1680, two years after the publication of *The Pilgrim's Progress*,
Bunyan published a sequel:

As I was considering with my self, what I had written concerning the Progress *of
the* Pilgrim *from this World to Glory: and how it had been acceptable to many in
this Nation: It came again into my mind to write, as then, of him that was going to
Heaven, so now, of the Life and Death of the Ungodly, and of their travel from this
world to* Hell. *The which in this I have done, and have put it, as thou seest, under
the Name and Title of Mr.* Badman . . . (p. 3)[23]

Mr. Badman suffers from an unmerited neglect, despite occasional
asides from critics who mention its interest without examining it
in any detail. The depiction of Mr Badman, a character related
to the picaresque tradition, has forced historians of the novel to
acknowledge Bunyan's achievement, but they are not satisfied
with *Mr. Badman* as a whole, although it is seldom accorded
sufficient space for a careful appraisal.[24]

Mr. Badman suffers even more than *The Pilgrim's Progress* if it is
read as a novel in embryo: apparently a failed attempt at a
coherent work. Such preconceptions lead to disparaging remarks, such as 'Bunyan was hampered by the dialogue framework . . . '.[25] Even Henri Talon, sympathetic critic of Bunyan as
he is, feels that 'the book is drawn out by . . . lengthy digressions . . .'.[26] Maurice Hussey, in the most valuable commentary available on *Mr. Badman*, makes it quite clear that we

[23] References to *The Life and Death of Mr. Badman and The Holy War*, ed. John Brown
(Cambridge, 1905).
[24] See Arnold Kettle, *An Introduction to the English Novel* (London, 1969), Vol. 1, p. 40;
Walter Allen, *The English Novel* (London, 1954), p. 31.
[25] Lynn Veach Sadler, *John Bunyan* (Boston, 1979), pp. 68–9.
[26] Talon, p. 235.

cannot avoid Bunyan's moral purpose: 'Bunyan fits in at the last moment [of the 'religious book'], forming the novel from the guide to godliness, the last great medieval figure.'[27] Even here, the use of the word 'novel', with its implication of a structural form unknown to Bunyan, may lead us to censure *Mr. Badman* for failing to achieve a unity alien to Bunyan's purpose.

Charles Baird sympathetically examines Bunyan's use of the dialogue form, pointing out how Wiseman and Attentive 'generate continued interest and become distinct, lively participants in a drama'.[28] It is possible to explore the immediate attractions of *Mr. Badman* while still respecting Bunyan's didactic purpose, which was to present the reader with a salutary example:

Here therefore, courteous Reader, I present thee with the Life and Death of Mr. Badman *indeed: Yea, I do trace him in his Life, from his Childhood to his Death; that thou mayest, as in a Glass,* behold with thine own eyes, the steps that take hold of Hell; and also discern, while thou art reading of Mr. Badmans Death, whether thou thy self art treading in his path thereto. (pp. 3–4)

This is not an idle undertaking; author and reader must endure the taint of the example from whom they draw their moral lesson:

I know 'tis ill pudling in the Cockatrices *den, and that they run hazards that hunt the* Wild-Boar. *The man also that writeth Mr.* Badmans *life, had need to be fenced with a* Coat *of* Mail . . . (p. 7)

As we have seen, this is the traditional formula used to introduce English picaresque novels, criminal biographies, and cony-catching pamphlets. The writer states that he is presenting the reader with a warning. Robert Greene, throughout his series of cony-catching pamphlets written in the 1590s, issues directions such as:

By reading this little treatise ensuing, you shall see to what marvellous subtle policies these deceivers have attained, and how daily they practise strange drifts for their purpose. I say no more, but, if all these

[27] Maurice Hussey, 'John Bunyan and the Books of God's Judgements: A Study of *The Life and Death of Mr. Badman*', *English*, 7 (1948–9), 167.
[28] Charles W. Baird, *John Bunyan: A Study in Narrative Technique* (New York, 1977), p. 77; see pp. 77–80.

forewarnings may be so regarded, to the benefit of the well-minded, and
just control of these careless wretches, it is all I desire . . . [29]

Greene claims a social purpose and a moral duty:

This, Gentlemen, have I searched out for your commodities, that I
might lay open to the world the villainy of these cozening caterpillars,
who are not only abhorred of men, but hated of God, living idly to
themselves and odiously to the world.[30]

This moral stance was continued by the criminal biographies of
the following century. Francis Kirkman introduces his *Counterfeit
Lady Unveiled* (1677) with the pious ejaculation:

And she may very well serve as a looking glass wherein we may see the
vices of this age epitomized. And to the end that we may see her vices
and thereby amend our own wicked lives is the intent of Your Friend,
F.K.[31]

The tradition is in turn taken up by the picaresque novel.
Richard Head introduces the first part of *The English Rogue*
(1665) in a now very familiar fashion:

This good use I hope the Reader will make with me of these follies, that
are so generally and too frequently committed every where, by
declining the commission of them (if not for the love of virtue, yet to
avoid the dismal effect of the most dangerous consequences that
continually accompany them). ('The Epistle to the Reader')

It is therefore scarcely surprising to find this formula used by
Defoe:

*Every wicked Reader will here be encouraged to a Change, and it will appear that
the best and only good End of a wicked mispent Life is Repentance . . .*[32]

In the more familiar *Moll Flanders*, Defoe reproduces the cony-
catching pamphlet platitudes exactly:

ALL the exploits of this Lady of Fame, in her Depredations upon
Mankind stand as so many warnings to honest people to beware of

---

[29] Robert Greene, *The Third and Last Part of Cony-Catching* (1592), in Gamini Salgado,
ed., *Cony-Catchers and Bawdy Baskets* (Harmondsworth, 1972), p. 234.
[30] *The Second Part of Cony-Catching* (1591), in Salgado, p. 198.
[31] In Spiro Peterson, ed., *The Counterfeit Lady Unveiled* (New York, 1961), p. 11; see also
Don Tomazo (1680), in Peterson, p. 186.
[32] Daniel Defoe, *Colonel Jack*, ed. Samuel Holt Monk (Oxford, 1970), p. 2.

them, intimating to them by what Methods innocent People are drawn in, plunder'd and robb'd, and by Consequence how to avoid them.[33]

This traditional didactic formula, however, is contradicted by the attractive presentation of the rogue. The moral stance is ambivalent; the didactic purpose is often only a very thin disguise. In the midst of this tradition, from Greene to Defoe, *Mr. Badman* is unique, for Bunyan alone adheres to his didactic purpose, and carries out the promise of his preface. The examples I have mentioned help to explain why Bunyan cast his account of Mr Badman in the form of a dialogue. The didactic commentary of Wiseman and Attentive forestalls the dangerous allure of a first-person account of a rogue's career, or the vicarious involvement of a half-sympathetic third-person account. *Mr. Badman* stands as a unique example of a successful presentation of the purported didacticism underlying rogue literature.

Readers today may misunderstand Bunyan when he states '*I have also put it into the form of a Dialogue, that I might with more ease to my self, and pleasure to the Reader, perform the work*' (p. 3). He does not refer to the events of Mr Badman's history, but to the didactic commentary surrounding it, which is given a fictional context by the dialogue form. We should not criticize the dialogue framework for its interference with the narration of Mr Badman's life, but praise it for its effective conveyance of Bunyan's moral stance. We can reach a clearer understanding of *Mr. Badman*'s structure if we see it as a careful balance between the overtly homiletic commentary, and the illustrative incident. The work can, for this purpose, be divided into reflection by Wiseman and Attentive; the depiction of Mr Badman's life; and isolated illustrative vignettes (such as the story of 'one W.S. a man of a very wicked life', p. 86). For the first two-thirds of *Mr. Badman*, the commentary of Wiseman and Attentive occupies almost exactly the same amount of space as the story of Mr Badman and other illustrative stories combined.[34] In the final third, the commentary occupies twice as much space as Mr Badman's history. Bunyan produces his unexpected account of Mr Badman's quiet death, but the increasing emphasis on

[33] Daniel Defoe, *Moll Flanders*, ed. G. A. Starr (Oxford, 1971), p. 4.
[34] Based on a page count of Brown's edition: 19 pages to Badman, 7 to illustrative stories, and 24 to commentary.

didactic comment ensures that Mr Badman himself does not occupy the centre of the stage.

What exactly is Bunyan's didactic purpose? He presents the reader with a negative example, depicting a path we should shun: '*My endeavour is to stop an hellish Course of Life, and to save a soul from death . . .*' (pp. 7–8). But the target is general, as well as personal; the faults outlined are widespread:

The Butt *therefore, that at this time I shoot at, is wide: and 'twill be as impossible for this Book to go into several Families, and not to arrest some, as for the Kings Messenger to rush into an house full of Traitors, and find none but honest men there.* (p. 4)

Bunyan is writing social criticism at a time when, in his eyes, the Restoration world was blatantly corrupt: '*England shakes and totters already, by reason of the burden that Mr. Badman and his Friends have wickedly laid upon it . . .*' (p. 4). The sense of urgency is almost overpowering; Bunyan is impelled to save English society from what he sees as imminent destruction:

wickedness like a flood is like to drown our English world: it begins already to be above the tops of mountains; it has almost swallowed up all; our Youth, our Middle age, Old age, and all, are almost carried away of this flood. O Debauchery, Debauchery, what hast thou done in England! Thou hast corrupted our Young men, and hast made our Old men beasts; thou hast deflowered our Virgins, and hast made Matrons Bawds. (p. 9)

Bunyan was, naturally, distressed at the moral laxity which he saw around him (in implicit contrast to the Interregnum). However, he also had a more constructive purpose. Mr Badman has various moral faults, but Bunyan also focuses on his commercial deceit. Bunyan is actively engaged with the problem of how a man may deal with the world of commerce without jeopardizing his religious beliefs. This is not the place to enter into a debate over Puritanism and the rise of Capitalism; suffice it to say that *Mr. Badman* does offer a practical morality, carefully supported by biblical citation. This is most evident in the discussion following the account of Badman's 'Breaking' (p. 93)—that is, falsely declaring himself bankrupt, and paying his creditors five shillings in the pound.

This event leads not just to a criticism of Mr Badman's actions, and moral reflection, but also to a series of directions about practical business morality. First Attentive prompts Wiseman to explain how the Bible condemns such practices, but he also wishes to know '*What would you have a man do that is in his Creditors debt . . .*' (p. 96). Wiseman's advice is stern and idealistic, but not impossible:

If none of these two will satisfie them, let him proffer them his Body, to be at their dispose, to wit, either to abide imprisonment [at] their pleasure, or to be at their service, till by labour and travel he hath made them such amends as they in reason think fit, (only reserving something for the succour of his poor and distressed Family out of his labour, which in Reason and Conscience, and Nature, he is bound also to take care of:) . . . (p. 101)

This advice is suddenly turned into much more specific criticism by Attentive:

But suppose now, that Mr. Badman *was here, could he not object as to what you have said, saying, Go and teach your Brethren, that are Professors, this lesson, for they, as I am, are guilty of Breaking* . . . (p. 102)

Wiseman sees such men as exceptions ('Professors, such perhaps there may be, and who, upon earth can help it? Jades there be of all colours', pp. 102–3), but the accusation is still there: 'a Professor should not owe any man any thing, *but love*' (p. 104). We might here recall the point made about *The Pilgrim's Progress* by Richard Dutton: Bunyan was writing specifically for his Bedford congregation.[35] (I think that Dutton's observation is, in fact, much more relevant to *Mr. Badman* than to *The Pilgrim's Progress.*)

While fully conversant with contemporary fraudulence and trickery, Bunyan is able to align it with Biblical examples and injunctions:

If his customers were in his Books (as it should goe hard but he would have them there; at least, if he thought he could make any advantage of them,) then, then would he be sure to impose upon them his worst, even very bad Commodity, yet set down for it the price that the best was sold at: like those that sold the Refuse Wheat, or the worst of the wheat; making the Sheckle great, yet hoisting up the price: This was Mr. *Badmans* way . . . (p. 114)

[35] Dutton, p. 445.

Bunyan can see how the individual suffers in an age of commercial enterprise:

> your *Hucksters*, that buy up the poor mans Victuals by whole-sale, and sell it to him again for unreasonable gains, by retale, and as we call it, by piece meal; they are got into a way, after a stingeing rate, to play their game upon such by Extortion: I mean such who buy up Butter, Cheese, Eggs, Bacon, &c. by whole sale, and sell it again (as they call it) by penny worths, two penny worths, a half penny worth, or the like, to the poor, all the week after the market is past. (p. 116)

Of course *Mr. Badman* ends with advice which is moral, rather than commercial: a disquisition following Badman's deceptively quiet death. Bunyan's didacticism may have a pragmatic edge at times, but its subtle awareness of the world may not always be noticed by the reader today. Badman's quiet death indicates that wickedness is not always able to be perceived; that the bad man might not reveal his soul to the world. Wiseman points out that such a death offers no chance of repentance, and so is in fact a punishment. But to the observer it is disturbing: 'He cannot gather that sin is a dreadful and bitter thing, by the child-like death of Mr. *Badman*' (p. 177).

We are also made aware of the fact that sin is not always punished on earth, despite the fact that *Mr. Badman* contains cautionary tales of exemplary punishments:

> But as for Judgement upon them in this life, it doth not always come, no not upon those that are worthy thereof. *They that tempt God are delivered, and they that work wickedness are set up*: But they are reserved to the day of wrath, and then for their wickedness, God will repay them to their faces. (p. 73)

Bunyan's didacticism is distinctive and intelligent; if we ignore this side of *Mr. Badman*, or see it as interfering with the 'story' of Badman, we pass over one of its strengths, just as we distort its purpose.

The above discussion should not minimize the importance of Mr Badman as a character, or the appeal of the various stories and events in the work. While Badman's death is surrounded by didactic commentary, it is also prepared for in the course of the narrative; it is a carefully contrived climax. Wiseman, at a very early stage, says that 'the Manner of his death was so correspond-

ing with his life' (p. 19). We do not, therefore, expect the quiet
death of Badman, which is turned into an even more salutary
exemplum than a violent death. Prompted by this comment of
Wiseman's, Attentive, throughout the narrative, betrays some
impatience to hear about the death, to reach the climax of the
story: '*Well, Sir, now I have heard enough of Mr.* Badmans
naughtiness, pray now proceed to his Death' (p. 126). Charles Baird
emphasizes the interplay between 'Attentive's fluctuating
avidity and discontent and Wiseman's bland refusals . . .'.[36]

Mr Badman is an entirely static character as far as his morals
are concerned: he was 'Master-sinner from a Childe' (p. 20).
Once again, Bunyan's portrait may be allied to the English rogue
tradition, most particularly to the criminal biography.
Motivation is not an issue in this genre; the rogue is, almost
inevitably, born a rogue (unlike the Spanish *picaro*, who is driven
to fend for himself by force of circumstances). Similarly, Bunyan
does not offer any motivation for Mr Badman's crimes—but he
does have an explanation, which is presented by Wiseman:
'There were several sins that he was given to, when but a little one,
that manifested him to be notoriously infected with Or[i]ginal
corruption; for I dare say he learned none of them of his Father
or Mother' (p. 20). Attentive underlines the doctrine which,
however alien to the modern reader, was a most convincing
explanation of Badman's behaviour:

*This was a bad Beginning indeed, and did demonstrate that he was, as you say,
polluted, very much polluted with Original Corruption. For to speak my mind
freely, I do confess, that it is mine opinion, that Children come polluted with sin
into the World, and that oft-times the sins of their youth, especially while they are
very young, are rather by vertue of Indwelling sin, than by examples that are set
before them by others.* (p. 20)

Two elements of *Mr. Badman* which critics have singled out
cannot be ignored here: Bunyan's style, and certain scenes
depicting Badman's character. Both aspects of *Mr. Badman*
enable Bunyan to capture the reader's involvement, as he
presents his *exemplum. Mr. Badman* is a dialogue, and Bunyan
takes great care to use an appropriate style, which evokes speech
patterns. The didactic commentary, with its citation of Biblical
references and its point-by-point exemplification of rules for

---

[36] Baird, p. 78.

conduct, is enlivened by the interplay between Wiseman and Attentive. It is conversational, humanized: 'I will answer you as well as I can. And first to the first of your questions' (p. 96).

The story of Mr Badman, and the shorter cautionary tales, are cast in an even more flexible style, which creates the impression of a story being told quite spontaneously, with suitable asides and ejaculations:

I will tell you of another. About four miles from St. *Neots*, there was a Gentleman had a man, and he would needs be an Informer, and a lusty young man he was. Well, an Informer he was, and did much distress some people, and had perfected his Informations so effectually against some, that there was nothing further to do, but for the Constables to make distress on the people, that he might have the Money or Goods; and as I heard, he hastened them much to do it. Now while he was in the heat of his work, as he stood one day by the Fire-side, he had (it should seem) a mind to a Sop in the Pan, (for the Spit was then at the fire,) so he went to make him one; but behold, a Dog (some say his own Dog) took distaste at something, and bit his Master by the Leg; the which bite, notwithstanding all the means that was used to cure him, turned (as was said) to a Gangrene; however, that wound was his death, and that a dreadful one too: for my Relator said, that he lay in such a condition by this bite, (as the beginning) till his flesh rotted from off him before he went out of the world. (p. 87)

The presence of the speaker is emphasized through the use of 'Well', 'Now', and the fourth long, circumlocutory sentence; and the story's authenticity is enhanced by reference to a number of oral sources ('some say his own Dog').

We have already seen how Mr Badman is a static character, bad from birth for no concrete reason. His attitude alters briefly only twice, when his fear of death leads him to a very temporary repentance. The scene of his first repentance is an excellent example of Bunyan's ability to add a third dimension to a character principally intended to be a negative example:

In this fit of sickness, his Thoughts were quite altered about his wife; I say his Thoughts, so far as could be judged by his words and carriages to her. For now she was his *good* wife, his *godly* wife, his *honest* wife, his *duck*, his *dear*, and all. Now he told her, that she had the best of it, she having a good Life to stand by her, while his debaucheries and ungodly Life did always stare him in the face. Now he told her, the counsel that she often gave him, was *good*; though he was so *bad* as not to take it. (p. 144)

Similar attention was devoted to the account of Badman's pursuit of his first wife. Badman carefully plans his conquest of the orphaned, religious girl:

Well, when he was come, and had given her a civil Complement, to let her understand why he was come, then he began and told her, That he had found in his heart a great deal of love to her Person; and that, of all the Damosels in the world he had pitched upon her, if she thought fit, to make her his beloved wife. The reasons, as he told her, why he had pitched upon her were, her Religious and personal Excellencies; and therefore intreated her to take his condition into her tender and loving consideration. As for the world, quoth he, I have a very good trade, and can maintain my self and Family well, while my wife sits still on her seat; I have got thus, and thus much already, and feel money come in every day, but that is not the thing I aim at, 'tis an honest and godly Wife. Then he would present her with a good Book or two, pretending how much good he had got by them himself. He would also be often speaking well of godly Ministers, especially of those that he perceived she liked, and loved most. (p. 72)

We are then shown Badman's rapid resumption of his true character after the marriage has taken place:

Now she scarce durst go to an honest Neighbours house, or have a good Book in her hand; specially when he had his companions in his house, or had got a little drink in his head . . . If she did ask him (as sometimes she would) to let her go out to a Sermon, he would in a currish manner reply, *Keep at home, keep at home, and look to your business, we cannot live by hearing of Sermons.* (p. 76)

However arresting this side of *Mr. Badman* may be, we must keep it in perspective by resisting the temptation to dismiss Bunyan's moral purpose, and concentrate on his style or his depiction of character. No division is possible: Mr Badman is a character created for a didactic purpose. The homiletic commentary of Wiseman and Attentive enfolds Badman's story, and Bunyan's art is seen in his skilful, beguiling use of the English rogue tradition to create a true guide to good conduct through the depiction of a negative example.

IV. *The Holy War*

Most scholars express dissatisfaction with *The Holy War*, perhaps Bunyan's most ambitious work (he wrote nothing else during its composition, from 1680 to 1682). Macaulay believed that 'the *Holy War* . . . if the *Pilgrim's Progress* did not exist would be the best allegory that ever was written', but in this century scholars have been much less admiring.[37] With the exception of E. M. W. Tillyard, who awards *The Holy War* high praise as 'England's Puritan epic', Bunyan's most massive allegory has been seen as a 'magnificent failure'.[38]

Bunyan insists, once again, that his new allegory is 'truthful':

> *Let no man then count me a Fable-maker,*
> *Nor make my name or credit a partaker*
> *Of their derision: what is here in view,*
> *Of mine own knowledg, I daresay is true.* (p. 2)[39]

The insistent 'I' in the verse-preface has led critics to read the allegory as, in part, relating to Bunyan's own conversion from sin.[40] But *The Holy War* has a much larger scope; the allegory encompasses the fall of man, his redemption, and his subsequent backsliding, with reference to contemporary political and religious events.

The Holy War describes how the town of Mansoul, initially subject to King Shaddai, was conquered by Diabolus. It is regained by Shaddai's army which is led, eventually, by his son Emanuel. The town is forgiven and restored to its rightful ruler, but despite the trial of several leading Diabolonians, a number still lurk in the town. The town's loyalty is undermined by 'Mr. *Carnal Security*' (p. 150), and Emanuel withdraws. Diabolus, seizing his opportunity, attacks again, aided by troops of Doubters. Mansoul comes to its senses and tries vainly to resist. Emanuel is petitioned frequently and finally relents, beating back Diabolus and repulsing a second attack by the Bloodmen. He makes a final speech to the town, looking forward to the time when Mansoul will be rebuilt '*into mine own Country, even into the Kingdom of my Father*' (p. 247), and warning the town to 'hold fast till I come' (p. 250).

[37] Quoted in Sadler, p. 81.

[38] E. M. W. Tillyard, *The English Epic and Its Background* (London, 1968), p. 406; Roger Sharrock, *John Bunyan* (London, 1968), p. 136; the new scholarly edition by Roger Sharrock and James Forrest may stimulate a renewal of interest.

[39] All references to John Bunyan, *The Holy War*, ed. Roger Sharrock and James F. Forrest (Oxford, 1980).

[40] Sharrock, *John Bunyan*, p. 120.

John Brown writes that 'judged by the standard of epic
completeness, and by the power of laying hold of the simple
instincts of the heart, *The Holy War* is greatly inferior' to *The
Pilgrim's Progress*.[41] However, the scope of the later allegory has
recently led some scholars, notably E. M. W. Tillyard, to view it
as a type of epic; its theme takes in those of *Paradise Lost* and
Paradise Regained combined, as well as contemporary religious
events. On the other hand, the label 'epic' does not always imply
praise: ' . . . it attempts to be "epic-like", as if Bunyan's increasing fame caused him unconsciously to strive for an ornate and
"literary" style.'[42] Bunyan was certainly conscious of his literary
success when he came to write *The Holy War*, as can be seen
from the concluding verse 'ADVERTISEMENT to the READER', which
reiterates his authenticity as the author of *The Pilgrim's Progress*,
and goes on to state:

> Also for *This*, thine eye is now upon,
> The matter in this manner came from none
> But the same heart, and head, fingers and pen,
> As did the other. (p. 251)

Tillyard's view of *The Holy War* as an epic depends largely on
his sense of its grand scope and 'ampler rhetoric'.[43] However, he
admits that there is a 'serious deficiency' in the allegory's
structure: 'it is repetitive.'[44] A major cause of the reader's
dissatisfaction is the sense that the second half of *The Holy War* is a
'replay' of the first half: Mansoul is once again besieged by
Diabolus and rescued by Emanuel. This sense of repetition stems
from an emphasis on the action at the expense of the allegory.
The same war is not fought twice: the *meaning* of the second battle
for Mansoul is quite different. Once again, we cannot ignore
Bunyan's allegory, and concentrate entirely on the surface of his
narrative. Tillyard has a very broad definition of epic, and while
The Holy War is indeed grand in scope, and may well depict epic
battles, it is not epic in structure. The prose epic, written by the
French heroic romancers, had obvious epic characteristics,
including epic structure. Bunyan had their model available, but
his interest lay in extending the matter of his allegory. We should

---

[41] John Brown, *John Bunyan: His Life, Times and Work*, revised F. M. Harrison
(London, 1928), p. 310.

[42] Sadler, p. 85.   [43] Tillyard, p. 403.   [44] Ibid., p. 402.

not be misled by the fact that the theme of *The Holy War* overlaps *Paradise Lost* into a belief that Bunyan wrote what was primarily an epic.

Bunyan orders us, as he did in *The Pilgrim's Progress*, to be always alert as we read *The Holy War*: we must interpret, unveil the allegory:

> *Nor do thou go to work without my Key,*
> *(In mysteries men soon do lose their way)*
> *And also turn it right if thou wouldst know*
> *My riddle, and wouldst with my heifer plow.*
> *It lies there in the* window, *fare thee well,*   The
> *My next may be* to ring thy Passing-Bell. (p. 5)   Margent

But the interpretation of this, his most ambitious allegory, is a difficult task. Objections to the structure of *The Holy War* (or the lack of a structure) usually arise from confusion about the levels of allegory in the work. One may have to conclude that Bunyan loaded his allegorical rift with too much ore, but his over-all control is always apparent.

There are three major levels of allegory in *The Holy War*.[45] The first is a religious allegory, depicting the fall of man and his redemption; the second presents contemporary events, such as the Civil War and Charles II's administrative reforms; the third may be seen as a depiction of the conversion of an individual soul. These three levels interact: they are three levels of interpretation, not three separate streams of incident.

Mansoul begins in a state of innocence, easy prey to the temptations of Diabolus:

the people of *Mansoul* now, are every one simple and innocent; all honest and true: nor do they as yet know what it is to be assaulted with Fraud, Guile, and Hypocrisy. (p. 13)

Bunyan creates a less individual version of the Fall: not Adam and Eve, but Mansoul, with all its inhabitants, is tempted. We miss Milton's individualized Adam and Eve, but gain a strong sense of the general fall of man. Taking the traditional allegorical image of the soul as a fortress, Bunyan peoples it with the same symbolic characters as those found in *The Pilgrim's Progress*: Lord

---

[45] See the introduction to *The Holy War*, p. xxvi.

Willbewill, Ill-pause, Lord Innocent, Mr Conscience, *et al.*[46] The cast of characters is much larger; the individual is shattered into symbolic fragments, each representing a single human quality. When the town falls through the weakness of its inhabitants, the Mayor, Lord Understanding, is replaced by Lord Willbewill (in Bunyan's gloss, 'The *Will* takes place under *Diabolus*', p. 22); the Recorder, Mr Conscience, is also removed.

Initially, the forces of King Shaddai are led by Boanerges in an attempt to win back Mansoul. Bunyan then depicts the soul's receptivity to persuasion (Boanerges has been parlying at Eargate): 'The Understanding and Conscience begin to receive conviction, and they set the soul in a hubbub' (p. 58, margin). When Emanuel joins the army, he 'took with him at the Commandment of his Father, forty four Battering Rams, and twelve slings, to whirle stones withal' (p. 69), which Bunyan carefully glosses as 'The holy Bible containing 66 [*sic*] Books'. This is a good example of the difficulty encountered by a reading of the allegory which tries to find a logical movement forward in time. At this stage of the allegory, Christ's redemption is placed against the Fall, but Christ's story is not related, the Passion is a *past* event, because the Bible is used as a weapon against the recalcitrant soul. Redemption follows the Fall, but only in a general sense. This difficulty (which of course only arises from a reading which demands a detailed correspondence between the allegory and a single interpretation) is compounded by Mansoul's backsliding. On the religious level of the allegory this may well, from Bunyan's point of view, represent the decline of the Church prior to Emanuel's second victory (the Reformation). But this is far from clear-cut, and when we turn to the contemporary references further complexities are apparent.

The Holy War contains a host of details relating to the Civil War and the Restoration. Scholars have often noted that the battles in Bunyan's allegory are staged as seventeenth-century battles; similarly, political issues of the period are present in *The Holy War*. However, Bunyan does not recount the tumultuous events of the mid-seventeenth century in strict chronological order. It is tempting to see Diabolus's first attack upon Mansoul as Charles I's 'ungodly' rule; Emanuel's triumph as Cromwell's (he

[46] See Sharrock, pp. 118–19.

has 'new modelled' Mansoul, p. 85); Diabolus's second ascendancy as Charles II's Restoration; and Emanuel's final victory as a Millenarian promise. However, this neat scheme is not possible within the terms of the allegory, for the detailed references to the Restoration occur during Diabolus's first success, in other words, before the Civil War.

John Brown has pointed out that 'Diabolus new modelling the corporation changing mayor, recorder, aldermen, and burgesses at pleasure, was simply doing the same thing the King and Lord Ailesbury were doing at Bedford about the time *The Holy War* was written.'[47] The detail in this section extends to a depiction of Roger L'Estrange as 'one Mr. *Filth*', whose productions are glossed as 'Odious Atheistical Pamphlets and filthy Ballads & Romances full of baldry' (p. 31). But this detail occurs during Diabolus's first conquest of Mansoul; if we insist on looking for a chronological account of contemporary events, we find that Charles II's actions occur before Cromwell's success.

Neither the religious nor the political levels of allegory, therefore, provide a chronological plot: they form discrete sequences of events. The reader can put them in order, but the plot that Bunyan gave *The Holy War* is a psychological one. The third level of allegory is the most important structurally: the soul's temptation, its rejection of temptation, its backsliding, and its final acceptance of the promise of redemption.

After Emanuel wins his second victory over Diabolus, a number of Doubters are put on trial. The purge is not complete, however:

some few more of the subtilest of the *Diabolonian* tribe, did yet remain in *Mansoul*, to the time that *Mansoul* left off to dwell any longer in the Kingdom of *Universe*. (p. 244)

Emanuel makes a long speech to the inhabitants of Mansoul, reminding them that ''*Twas I that put life into thee*, O Mansoul . . .' (p. 246). An end to their troubles is at hand:

For yet a little while, O my Mansoul, *even after a few more times are gone over thy head, I will (but be not thou troubled at what I say) take down this famous Town of* Mansoul, *stick and stone, to the ground. And will carry the stones thereof, and*

---

[47] Brown, p. 311; and see the introduction to *The Holy War*, pp. xx–xxv.

the timber thereof, and the walls thereof, and the dust thereof, and the inhabitants thereof, into mine own Country, even into the Kingdom of my Father; and will there set it up in such strength and glory, as it never did see in the Kingdom where now it is placed. (p. 247)

The Millenium, it seems, is not far off:

First, *I charge thee that thou dost hereafter keep more white and clean the liveries which I gave thee before my last withdrawing from thee. Do it, I say, for this will be thy wisdom. They are in themselves fine linnen, but thou must keep them white and clean. This will be your wisdom, your honour, and will be greatly for my glory. When your Garments are white, the world will count you mine.* (p. 248)

(See *Revelation*, 3:4–5; 7:13–14.) But the end of *The Holy War* does not really strike a Fifth Monarchist note. The redeemed soul awaits apocalypse, but Emanuel offers instruction, advice about behaviour until that time (*'Nor must thou think always to live by sense, thou must live upon my Word'*, p. 250).

The Holy War is a much more complex, sophisticated work than *The Pilgrim's Progress*, but for that very reason, perhaps, it has much less popular appeal. It does not grip the imagination as frequently, although it satisfies the intellect. This is not to say that it is devoid of narrative interest. The characters are vignettes, rather than full-length portraits, but no less vivid for that— particularly Willbewill, the mayor who changes sides. The battles are expertly described. One might mention here Bunyan's use of the romance convention of describing knights and their impresae, a device—traditionally with symbolic implications— which he uses for both sides in the struggle (pp. 36–7, 68, 186, 229). Without the driving structure of the pilgrimage, Bunyan is unable to produce the narrative momentum necessary to balance the static nature of his allegory: the action of *The Holy War* has struck many readers as repetitive, leading nowhere. But the allegory itself does progress, and the patience necessary to disentangle it is rewarded.

Chapter 15

Reactions to Romance

'This age hath more abounded with Romances then any other', observed Edmund Gayton in 1654.[1] However, the romance form interacted with other forms of fiction. At times it was mocked (or at least its faults were); and different types of romance were published to satisfy the demands of a heterogeneous reading public.

I. Popular Chivalric Romance

The assimilation of the chivalric romance by a new reading public at the end of the sixteenth century has already been discussed (see above, Chap. 8, Sec. I). This movement of the chivalric romance down through the levels of the reading public continued into the seventeenth century, by which time three main areas of popular romance are discernible: the medieval romance, such as *Huon of Bourdeaux* (printed by Wynkyn de Worde *c.* 1534) and *Valentine and Orson* (printed by de Worde *c.* 1518);[2] the Spanish and Portuguese romances, such as *Amadis*; and the native English imitations by writers like Forde and Johnson.

By the beginning of the seventeenth century sophisticated romances, following the lead of the *Arcadia*, were printed in newly fashionable roman type (which travelled from Italy to England at the end of the sixteenth century via the Netherlands, where English printers bought their type), while the popular chivalric romances continued to be printed in black-letter gothic type throughout the century. The use of this unfashionable type-face is indicative of the conservative nature of the form and its readers, who are characterized by Charles Mish as 'the middle-class

---

[1] Edmund Gayton, *Pleasant Notes Upon Don Quixote* (1654), p. 270.
[2] See Margaret Schlauch, *Antecedents of the English Novel 1400–1600* (Warsaw/London, 1963), pp. 51–64.

reading public, which . . . continued to consume stories not only
old-fashioned in content but old-fashioned in appearance'.[3]
While Professor Mish notes this as an example of the seventeenth-
century division into 'two reading publics, the upper-class and
the middle-class', his assertion that 'The lower class can hardly be
said to constitute a segment of the reading public' is contradicted
by the emergence of chapbook abridgements of chivalric romances.[4] Margaret Spufford's recent study of seventeenth-
century chapbooks and their readership indicates a wide range of
cheap reading matter aimed at the newly literate.[5] Starting from
the premiss of a considerable increase in literacy (a thesis
supported by recent demographic research), Spufford provides a
detailed account of the chapbook market and publishing system.
Her chapbook sample is based on Samuel Pepys's collection,
which reflects the range of material available in the 1680s. The
chapbooks range from conduct manuals to religious works, from
ballads to redactions of romances. However, the study excludes
books more than 72 pages in length (priced over sixpence).[6]

By confining her attention only to the very lowest level of the
reading public, Spufford neglects the complexity of the position
of the prose fiction of the period. We have already seen how even
stories from the *Arcadia* existed as chapbooks; and *The English
Rogue*, which in its complete version was intended for a more
literate audience than that analysed by Spufford, also appeared
in chapbook form. Emanuel Forde's chivalric romances began,
in the late 1590s, as relatively substantial books: *Montelyon* is 186
pages in length, and *Parismus*, with the addition of its sequel
Parismenos, is 248 pages long. While the popularity of these books
continued in the seventeenth century, chapbook redactions
existed alongside them. Any one chivalric romance might exist in
a variety of versions.[7] Both the larger versions and the chapbooks
were printed in black-letter, and were read by a less sophisticated

[3] Charles C. Mish, 'Black Letter as a Social Discriminant in the Seventeenth Century',
PMLA 68 (1953), 629.
[4] Ibid., p. 627.
[5] Margaret Spufford, *Small Books and Pleasant Histories: Popular Fiction and Its Readership
in Seventeenth-Century England* (London, 1981); see also the useful dissertation by John
Gaunt, 'A Study of English Popular Fiction 1660–1700' (University of Maryland,
unpublished Ph. D. thesis, 1972), which Spufford does not cite.
[6] Spufford, p. 131.
[7] See Gaunt, pp. 51–69.

public than the newly fashionable, more expensive heroic romances, printed in roman type.

Thanks to Spufford's careful study of the chapbook market, we have evidence of a great variety of interests catered for by books priced between 2½d. and 6d. in 1664, when the average agricultural and building wage was 12d. per day.[8] It is very difficult to draw clear distinctions between these readers and the readers of the larger chivalric romances, which cost a few shillings. In 1673 Lawrence Price's abridgement of *Valentine and Orson* appeared, based on the 1637 redaction. This has aptly been described as 'an abridgement of an abridgement of a translation of an abbreviated version'.[9] However, it did not *replace* the longer versions; Pepys owned a 1674 edition priced at 1s. 6d., while Price's 18-page version probably cost 2d.[10]

The various modes of fiction did not have fixed barriers between them, and numerous complementary influences were at work between different types of fiction written for different audiences. Chapbook fiction might include medieval chivalric romance, Elizabethan chivalric romance, Deloney's 'mercantile' fiction, the picaresque, and even small sections of the *Arcadia*. Sometimes chapbook versions were changed quite dramatically to suit a different audience, such as the chapbook *Guy of Warwick*, which leaves out Guy's genealogy and concentrates on his achievement of social success through his martial prowess.[11] But often the chapbooks were like *Reader's Digest* versions of novels, shortened and simplified modifications of their originals. The chivalric romance was passed on to each new group of readers in the seventeenth century. In 1575 Captain Cox, a Coventry mason, owned (among other books) 'King Arthurz book, Huon of Burdeus, The foour suns of Aymon, Beuys of Hampton, The squyre of lo degree, The Knight of courtesy . . .'.[12] When redactions of these books were made in the seventeenth century they were available for readers much poorer than the relatively prosperous Cox; furthermore they were available throughout the

[8] Spufford, p. 48.
[9] Gaunt, p. 61.
[10] Spufford, p. 256, lists the longer chivalric romances collected by Pepys, with their prices.
[11] Ibid., pp. 225–7.
[12] Louis B. Wright, *Middle Class Culture in Elizabethan England* (1935, rpt. London, 1964), p. 84.

length and breadth of the kingdom, owing to the extensive distribution system examined at length by Spufford.[13]

Wealthy and not so wealthy readers enjoyed chivalric romances for a considerable length of time. Redactions of Deloney's fiction indicate that his stories of mercantile success appealed not just to the already successful, but also to the poor and aspiring. Chivalric romance and picaresque fiction may have shared the same audience, judging by the example of Francis Kirkman, whose association with *The English Rogue* has been outlined in a previous chapter. In 1671 Kirkman published his translation of *Don Bellianis of Greece*, and for the 1673 edition he wrote his own second and third parts. Apart from his not entirely reputable career as scrivener turned bookseller, which he describes in the partly autobiographical *Unlucky Citizen* (1673), Kirkman was a voracious reader of chivalric romances, which he discusses in the preface to *Don Bellianis*: 'I my self have been so great a Lover of Books of this Nature, that I have long since read them all.'[14]

The preface is a roll-call of these books, with ardent recommendations that the reader should peruse them, preferably in the order indicated by Kirkman. We begin with what we may see as an inadvertent admission of the true level of these romances— although Kirkman himself is only stressing their immense imaginative appeal when he mentions *The Seven Wise Masters of Rome*, and states that in Ireland

next to the *Horn-Book*, and Knowledge of Letters, Children are in general put to Read in this; and I know that only by this Book several have learned to Read well, so great is the pleasure that Young and Old take in the Reading thereof. (Preface, unpaginated)

Kirkman goes on to produce a catholic list of works: *Fortunatus* (1676); Emanuel Forde's *Parismus, Parismenos, Montelyon Knight of the Oracle*, and *Ornatus and Artesia*; *Valentine and Orson*; *The Seven Champions of Christendome*; *Fragosa* (1618); *Bevis of Southampton*; *Tom of Lincoln* (by Richard Johnson, first edition 1599?); and numerous others. He laments the passing of these writings, for he claims that they

are now grown so scarce that you can hardly purchase them, and yet

---

[13] See Spufford, Chap. 5.
[14] See also *The Unlucky Citizen* (1673), pp. 10–13.

they are not worth the Printing agen, being now out of use and esteem by an other sort of Historyes, which are called *Romances*, some whereof are written originally in *English*, as namely, that Incomparable Book of its time called, *The Countess of Pembrokes Arcadia, Gods Revenge against Murther* [which is scarcely a romance, and is perhaps cited because its great popularity makes it part of the competition against chivalric 'histories'], *Bentevolio* and *Vrania* [Nathaniel Ingelo's religious allegory] . . . (Preface)

Kirkman certainly exaggerates when he claims that these works are out of print. The very year of his translation saw editions of *Montelyon, Parismus, Valentine and Orson*, and (a year earlier) *The Seven Champions of Christendome*. The wily Kirkman is never beyond touting his own wares as unique. Yet he is astute enough to document the fashionable romance, which at one level of readership has eclipsed the older history. It is important to note that all these works mention 'history' in their titles (for example, *The Famous History of Montelyon Knight of the Oracle*). They do not, despite our classification, consider themselves to be romances. The word 'history' in a title would alert a contemporary reader to the contents; it is, along with the use of black-letter type, indicative of a conservative approach.

Kirkman's own second and third parts to *Don Bellianis* are obviously the work of an avid reader of popular chivalric romances; all the familiar motifs are present. A chapter-heading will indicate some of these stock devices:

How *Don Bellianis* went with the Damsel of the Princess *Matarosa*, to relieve her out of the hands of the Gyant *Altifer* and his Company: And how he and his Company overcame the Gyant and his two Brethren and Company, and Released the Princess and her brother *Baltasino*: And how she knew him to be the *Knight of the Golden Image*, and how she and her Brother left him, to depart towards *Babylon*. (Part ii, Chap. 13)

Emanuel Forde, in the preface to *Parismus*, warns us that in these works we should 'Expect not the high Stile of a Refined Wit, but the plain Description of Valiant Knights' (1696 edition, preface). They are designed to amaze and delight the reader through their sheer exuberance—although Anthony Munday, in the dedication of the second part of *Palmerin of England*, sees a great value in this form of pleasure. He cites the story of Quintus Curtius, who recovered from an illness by reading the history of Alexander the Great:

By this example may be gathered . . . how necessary it is (oftentimes) to read Histories, which in the judgement of the wise, are esteemed as healthfull to the minde, as Phisick is accounted wholesome for the body; yea, oftentimes more, for that the sudden inward conceit of delight (wherewith Histories are plentifully inriched) may sooner break and qualify the extremity of a painful disease, than the long and laboursome applying of Phisical Receipts. (1664 edn., Part ii, A2ᵛ)

Only a little of the charm of medieval romance remains— enough, however, to satisfy a large number of extremely eager readers. *Don Flores of Greece*, a further part of the *Amadis* series, was first translated in 1664: 'Finding by experience what good acceptation Histories of this nature have found' (A2).

Whether in the form of long romances or chapbooks, these works fed a strong desire to fantasize on the part of the reader:

But when I came to Knight Errantry [Kirkman says], and reading *Montelion Knight of the Oracle*, and *Ornatus and Artesia*, and the Famous *Parismus*; I was contented beyond measure, and (believing all I read to be true) wished my self Squire to one of these Knights . . .[15]

At a time when sophisticated romance incorporated actual historical events and political situations, the popular chivalric romance portrayed a world increasingly distant from that of its readers—although those same readers did see some of the pressures of their society reflected in picaresque fiction. Thus we cannot see popular fiction in the period simply as either escapist entertainment, or as a reflection of social change and aspirations; different forms of fiction responded to different needs within the same audience.

II. Anti-Romance

The anti-romance is best considered as a form of parody; it mimics and mocks the conventions of romance. (The definition used here relates only to the works under discussion, which have certain unique features; it is not intended to be of general application.) Although it is not specifically described, anti-

[15] Ibid., p. 11.

romance enters John Jump's four-fold division of burlesque
under the heading of parody.[16] But the prose anti-romance
requires its own subdivisions, which will emerge in the course of
an examination of French and English examples. Fielding helps
to clarify the situation if we place *Shamela* and *Joseph Andrews* side
by side, the former appearing as parody, the latter as in part
parodic, but growing beyond simple antipathy to Richardson.
Anti-romance too may be divided into the more purely burlesque
or parodic (for example, Chaucer's 'Tale of Sir Thopas', or
Robert Anton's *Moriomachia*, discussed below), and the more
complex treatment of romance, where parody grows into a
developed work of fiction, which increasingly refers inwards to
itself, rather than outwards to its object of parody—the greatest
example of this being *Don Quixote*. Fielding himself makes a
similar division, calling the two categories burlesque and comic,
in the preface of *Joseph Andrews*:

no two Species of Writing can differ more widely than the Comic and
the Burlesque: for as the latter is ever the Exhibition of what is
monstrous and unnatural, and where our Delight, if we examine it,
arises from the surprising Absurdity, as in appropriating the Manners of
the highest to the lowest, or *è converso*; so in the former, we should ever
confine ourselves strictly to Nature from the just Imitation of which will
flow all the Pleasure we can this way convey to a sensible Reader.[17]

I will appropriate this division into burlesque and comedy for the
purposes of exploring anti-romance.

The most interesting, and yet most easily overlooked, feature
of anti-romance is its long life, and its benign association with
romance. Romance and anti-romance are interdependent: one
cannot see anti-romance as an attempt to destroy or refute
romance. In this sense, Fielding's destruction of Richardson in
Shamela is not paralleled in anti-romance of the seventeenth
century. It may be helpful, however, to look back to Chaucer's
'Tale of Sir Thopas', seen by George Kitchin as the beginning of
'the true art of parody'.[18] Chaucer's control, at the beginning of a
genre, is impressive. 'Sir Thopas' hits at form and content,

[16] John Jump, *Burlesque* (London, 1972), p. 2; burlesque is subdivided into travesty,
hudibrastic burlesque, parody, and the mock-poem.
[17] Henry Fielding, *Joseph Andrews*, ed. Martin Battestin (Oxford, 1967), p. 4.
[18] George Kitchin, *A Survey of Burlesque and Parody in English* (Edinburgh, 1931), p. 8.

mocking conventions of character, situation, description, and even rhyme-pattern. But 'Sir Thopas' is not vituperative; it is high-spirited, but genial. Thopas himself, who absurdly falls 'in love-longynge,/Al whan he herde the thrustel synge',[19] shares, at such a moment, some of the endearing qualities of Don Quixote (who similarly falls in love through the prompting of convention, rather than in reality). More important than this is the fact that Chaucer's knowledge and love of the romances he gently mocks made the anti-romance possible. This is pointed out by F. N. Robinson:

Doubts have been expressed from time to time as to the presence or extent of literary satire in the tale, especially on the ground that Chaucer admired the romances and wrote excellent ones himself. But this would not have prevented him from recognizing or burlesquing their many absurdities.[20]

I would put the point even more strongly: it is quite wrong to see romance and anti-romance as in some way mutually exclusive. Just as today, the reader who appreciates Henry James may still enjoy Max Beerbohm's famous parody of him. Indeed, a lover of James will appreciate the parody even more than someone who dislikes, and therefore has not assimilated, James's style and conventions. The writer and the reader of anti-romance are often united in their affection for the romance. The Canterbury Tales, after all, contains 'The Knight's Tale' as well as the 'The Tale of Sir Thopas'. One may see an interesting tension, perhaps even a mutual questioning, but not an exclusive choice which has to be made by the reader. The anti-romance is always self-conscious; it revels in its close knowledge of the romances it mimics:

> Men speken of romances of prys
> Of Horn child and of Ypotys
> Of Beves and of sir Gy
> Of sir Lybeux and Pleyndamour,—
> But sir Thopas he bereth the flour
> Of roial chivalry![21]

A metamorphosis takes place, rather than a mockery.

[19] Chaucer, Works, ed. F. N. Robinson, 2nd edn. (Oxford, 1974), p. 165.
[20] Ibid., pp. 736–7.   [21] Ibid., p. 166, ll. 897–902.

The most impressive example of the anti-romance impulse in Renaissance prose fiction is, of course, *Don Quixote*. Cervantes, like Chaucer, overturns any easy opposition between romance and anti-romance. E. C. Riley explains this by stating that 'to some extent the *Quixote* is parody, but it is unusual in containing the object of the parody within itself, as a vital ingredient.'[22] But once again, this does not take us far enough, for Cervantes allows the romance, in the person of Don Quixote, to reply to anti-romance criticism. This becomes quite explicit in the great debate between Quixote and the Canon about romances.[23] This is indeed a debate, and not a simple condemnation of romance. Even the Canon is unable to spurn the romance completely:

> notwithstanding all the evill he had spoken of such bookes, yet did he find one good in them, to wit, the subject they offered a good wit to worke upon, and shew it selfe in them; for they displayed a large and open plaine, thorow which the Pen might runne without let or incumbrances . . . (I. iv. 20, p. 241)

Yet Don Quixote's defence is even more interesting, and emphasizes the anti-romancer's love for the object of his satire. It is a defence of the heart, rather than the head; when arguments cease, the Don simply displays the romance's spell:

> reade them but once, and you shall see what delight you shall receive thereby: if not, tell me what greater pleasure can there be, then to behold (as one would say) even here and before our eyes, a great lake of pitch boiling hot, and many Serpents, Snakes, Lizarts, and other kinds of cruel and dreadfull beasts swimming a thwart it, and in every part of it, and that there issues out of the lake a most lamentable voyce, saying 'O thou Knight . . .'. (I. iv.23, p. 260)

As the brief tale continues, it weaves a spell which quietens the listeners, even as it smiles at romance conventions. The Don himself is both a figure of fun and of affection. His final defence encapsulates the absurdity *and* the reality of his imitation of romance:

> I dare affirme of my self, that since I am become a Knight Errant, I am valiant, curteous, liberall, well mannered, generous, gentle, bold, mild,

---

[22] E. C. Riley, *Cervantes' Theory of the Novel* (1962, rpt. Oxford, 1968), p. 36.
[23] See Thomas Shelton's translation, ed. James Fitzmaurice-Kelly (1896), Part I, Bk. 4, Chaps. 20–3; references are to this edition.

patient, an indurer of labours, imprisonments, and inchauntments . . .
(I. iv.23, p. 263)

This is unanswerable. Cervantes presents us with the most
developed example of the symbiotic relationship between romance and anti-romance, indicating that the anti-romance
impulse does not necessarily set the head against the heart, the
real against the ideal, but may instead embody the necessary
balance between the two.

Cervantes' great example was not fully absorbed in England
until Fielding wrote *Joseph Andrews* 'in Imitation of The *Manner*
of Cervantes' (title-page, 1742). During the seventeenth century,
anti-romance in England followed a more parochial but still
important path. It may be summarized, returning to my initial
division of anti-romance, as a tendency towards burlesque rather
than comedy. However, the French anti-romances were also
avidly translated and read, and they provide an example of the
comic which ultimately inspired Fielding.

The best-known English parallel to *Don Quixote* is not a work of
prose fiction, but a play: Francis Beaumont's *The Knight of the
Burning Pestle* (c. 1607). A consideration of burlesque drama is
beyond the scope of this chapter, but *The Knight of the Burning
Pestle* indicates how seventeenth-century fiction came to differ
from Cervantes' comic approach to anti-romance. Beaumont
burlesques the popular romances, but presents no Don Quixote
to defend them—only the Citizen, his wife, and Rafe, who are
themselves simply objects of satire. Andrew Gurr notes that
'Beaumont . . . was aiming less directly at the romances than
Cervantes.'[24] It is true that the anti-romance in England easily
turns to social satire, yet it also maintains an exuberant but
mocking attitude of burlesque.

One of the earliest prose anti-romances in this vein is Robert
Anton's *Moriomachia* (1613). Printed in black-letter in imitation
of its targets, *Moriomachia* mocks the popular chivalric romances.
Anton describes the slapstick adventures of 'Sir Tom Pheander,
the Mayden Knight, or Fayry Champion, otherwise, The Knight
of the Sun, otherwise, The Knight of the Burning Pestle' (B3ᵛ)—
Beaumont's burlesque has already become a precedent. Anton
mocks the chivalric romance's attachment to magic, and the

²⁴ Andrew Gurr, ed., *The Knight of the Burning Pestle* (Edinburgh, 1968), p. 3.

hero's mysterious parentage (Pheander is actually a bull, metamorphosed into a man by the Fairy Queen). His astute burlesque of chivalric furniture (his 'Coate-armour was of singular proofe, checkered Motley, Vert and Argent, party Pale, ribd with rowes of Gules and Or from the very Gorget to the skirts', B4), and of the joust (satirized by Pheander's combat with Sir Archmoriander), recalls the vigorous precedent set by Nashe in *The Unfortunate Traveller*. Anton also breaks off to indulge in a long, static piece of social satire (D3ᵛ-E2) during an eclipse supposedly caused by the Knight of the Moon lying on top of the Knight of the Sun—a hit at naïve allegorizing. *Moriomachia* exemplifies the English taste for burlesque with a touch of social satire. *The Knight of the Sea* (1600) is perhaps less sure because it is an attack 'on so many fronts'; it is, if anything, even more strongly burlesque than *Moriomachia*.[25] The English anti-romances were directed at the chivalric romances, which were no longer fashionable.

In France, the anti-romance quickly turned to the newly fashionable pastoral romance, as exemplified by Honoré d'Urfé's *L'Astrée* (1607–21). Charles Sorel's *Le Berger Extravagant* appeared in 1627. It is much closer to Cervantes' work than any English production during the century; close enough to be called an imitation. Sorel depicts the adventures of Lewis who, like Don Quixote, tries to live in conformity with the romances he reads and begins by changing his name, in his case to the more pastoral 'Lysis'. As the Don becomes a knight, so Lysis becomes a shepherd, in imitation of the characters in *L'Astrée*. The French anti-romances take over some of Cervantes' ambivalent attitude to the object of satire, although this is not consistently maintained: in *Le Berger Extravagant*, Lysis' extravagances enchant Anselme and his friends, who actually create an elaborate, though false, world which will shape itself to fit Lysis' fantasy, just as the Duke and Duchess humour Don Quixote in the second part of Cervantes' work. In both cases, what begins as a joke becomes an increasing absorption into the world of the 'madman'; the imagination shapes reality, as the romance vision overcomes pragmatic opposition. Thus Anselme's companions

---

[25] John J. O'Connor, *Amadis de Gaule and Its Influence on Elizabethan Literature* (New Brunswick, N.J., 1970), p. 217, and see the discussion on pp. 217-20.

eventually relate Lysis' visions as truths, when they meet his guardian:

All the way-long *Philiris* and his Companions entertained Adrian and his wife with the wonders of *Lysis* his life, and his strange adventures. They knew not whether they should take all for true misfortunes, or for fictions; and that which troubled them most was, to see the serious fashions of those from whom they had those fine relations.[26]

Sorel's anti-romance was not translated until 1653. *The Extravagant Shepherd*, as the translation was entitled, introduces the term 'Anti-Romance' in its sub-title. In a preface which examines the work book by book, the translator, John Davies, states that

it is the most serious *Satyre* and gravest Work that ever came into the world, and of no small importance: For if in *Religion* we value so much Books that combat and overcome *Errour*, I see not why it should be a less acceptable action in *Morality*, to endeavour the eradication of *Folly*.[27]

The work is not as solemn as Davies makes out, but French anti-romance is certainly comic—in Fielding's sense—rather than burlesque, in the manner of the native English tradition. From the 1650s onwards, anti-romance increased in importance in England, and both modes, comic and burlesque, contributed to the development of fiction.

Ronald Paulson associates satire with realism in anti-romances:

the early novel was created in an age when moral justification was still necessary and the description of everyday life for its own sake was considered frivolous; therefore the 'real' had to be attacked in order to be presented.[28]

This is applicable to French anti-romance, rather than English, for the social satire found in English anti-romance is associated with fantasy and burlesque, rather than with realism. In Paul Scarron, as Paulson points out, the balance established by Cervantes is maintained; he combines 'romance and anti-romance and so suggest[s] a larger, more generous grasp of

[26] Charles Sorel, *The Extravagant Shepherd*, trans. John Davies (1654), Bk. 12, p. 25.
[27] Ibid., d5.
[28] Ronald Paulson, *Satire and the Novel in Eighteenth-Century England* (New Haven, 1967), p. 18.

reality'.[29] Scarron's *Roman Comique* (1651) enters the mainstream of English fiction through Fielding's work, but was extremely popular during the Restoration, and its influence was already in evidence then.

The native anti-romance continued to burlesque chivalric romance, and indulge in social satire. *Don Samuel Crispe* (1660) and *The Knight Adventurer Or, The Infamous and Abominable History of that Terrible Troublesome and Vain-glorious Knight Sir Firedrake* (1661) differ very little from *Moriomachia*, despite the passage of half a century. Redactions of the popular chivalric romances were, as we have seen, more popular than ever, providing convenient targets. But the more recent developments in romance, outlined in earlier chapters, stimulated French anti-romances which were also translated at this time: Perdou de Subligny's *The Mock-Clelia* (1678), and Furetière's *Le Roman Bourgeois*, translated as *Scarron's City Romance* (1671). Furetière writes what is almost an anti-romance by implication, rather than a direct mockery of romance:

I will honestly and plainly tell you some little Tales or Gallantries happened amongst Persons that are neither Hero's nor Heroines, that neither defeat Armies nor subdue Kingdoms, but being honest People of an ordinary condition, fairly Jogge on the High-way. (p. 2)

Similarly, *The Mock-Clelia* is only sporadically concerned with Juliette who, like Lysis and the Don, has had her head turned, this time by Madeleine de Scudéry's productions (as Arabella will similarly be affected in Charlotte Lennox's *Female Quixote* of 1752). Instead, it concentrates on the very down-to-earth love affairs of various French nobles.

While *Don Samuel Crispe* contains only the fairly mild social satire found in *Moriomachia*, other contemporary anti-romances concentrate on political satire. *Don Juan Lamberto* has already been mentioned in connection with the political/allegorical romance. The imaginative exaggeration made possible by burlesque anti-romance finds its target in current political issues, and the potential of such works for propaganda re-emerges in works like *The Pagan Prince* (1690), one of a number of very scurrilous burlesques aimed at James II.

[29] Ibid., p. 35.

These prose works contain much heat, but little light. However, it was the development of the English burlesque anti-romance in the direction of satire that paved the way for Samuel Butler's great achievement in *Hudibras* (1663, 1664, 1678). John Wilders notes the influence of Cervantes, but Butler draws more on the burlesque than on the comic tradition of anti-romance.[30] As in *Don Juan Lamberto*, the anti-romance is the vehicle for satire, and of course *Hudibras*'s targets are much larger and more general. We begin with a social comment—'When *civil* Fury first grew high,/And men fell out they knew not why' (I.i.1–2)— while more purely anti-romance passages are presented as asides. But Butler's wit, and his own verbal energy, increase the power of his casual blows at romance conventions.

Hudibras exemplifies the importance of exuberant humour in the anti-romance, a humour evident in all the English works. One couplet in particular encapsulates the burlesque juxta-position of an idealizing form and the concrete world which, at least initially, opposes any idealization: 'And though Knights Errant, as some think,/Of old did neither eat nor drink' (I.i.325–6). The anti-romance opposes the heart with the head or, more specifically, the mind with the body. In this sense it is related to the picaresque, which emphasizes the physical world hostile to idealism by making virtual motifs of violence and ordure.

The deflation of idealism is well illustrated by Samuel Holland's *Don Zara Del Fogo* (1656), a substantial and very popular anti-romance (it had another edition in the same year under the title *Wit and Fancy in A Maze*, then reappeared in 1660 as *Romancio-Mastrix: Or, A Romance on Romances*). Holland sees the current profusion of romances as a symptom of the frightening growth of all literature: 'In this Scribling Age, when the *Writing Evill* (a disease that will in time destroy us) is become epi-demicall . . .' (Dedication).[31] While Holland may begin with the idea of curing the disease, he soon loses himself in the exhilaration of invention, for *Don Zara* is much longer than the redactions of chivalric romances which are its targets.

Holland's work illustrates one further important aspect of the English anti-romances. The overt target often recedes, as the

---

[30] Samuel Butler, *Hudibras*, ed. John Wilders (Oxford, 1967), p. xxxiii; references are to this edition.

[31] References to *Don Zara Del Fogo* (1656).

exuberant burlesque gathers momentum. Holland exaggerates romance style, and uses what Jump defines as travesty (the treatment of a subject 'in an aggressively familiar style')[32] in order to mock conventional personification:

It was now that mungrell hour when the black brow'd night, and grey ey'd morning strove for superiority, when the mirror of Martial spirits *Don Zara del Fogo* sweeping the somniferous God from off his ample front with that Broom of Heaven his face-pounding fist . . . (p. 1)

The tension between mock high style and low subject is increased when the crudely physical becomes even more obtrusive:

At every close where the Knight either wounded the Gyant, or rescued the Lady, in token of the ardency he bare to such illustrious Acts, he gave liberty to his nayles to bring blood from either buttock, for such was the ranckness of his courage, that not onely his soul, but his skin had a perpetuall itching after honourable Attempts, augmented by a herd of small Cattel, which some Authors will have to be the Geniusses of deceased Worthies, all waiting upon this man of men, which I confess I cannot credit since it was *Soto*'s custome (in order to his Masters special command) every morning to kill some of them. (pp. 3–4)

But Holland is not content to confine his energy; his burlesque extends beyond romance conventions. *Don Zara* contains a series of burlesque glosses, mocking the historical 'scholarship' which had become so pervasive. For example, the gloss on Soto's 'Ashen plant' reads: 'This kind of weapon the old Romans termed a pile; the Arabians that border upon Italy a Iavelin; The Brittains a half-pike. See Scaliger de usu clubibus, I 6 p. 10000' (p. 6). Indeed, Holland's work becomes increasingly akin to Rabelais's wild satire. Don Zara's adventures become more and more absurd, and Holland mocks the pastoral, Edenic landscape: 'here Potatoes & ripe Grapes offered themselves to his lips, there Pomgranates and luscious Dates contended which first should salute his goodly-siz'd grinders' (p. 35).

When Don Zara meets the witch Lamia, who takes him to the underworld, Holland is able to parody epic conventions, depicting most unclassical punishments ('*Nero* cobbling of shooes', p. 98); and describing a quarrel between the Greek and Trojan heroes, followed by one between the English poets, who argue

---

[32] Jump, p. 2.

about the merits of Chaucer, Jonson, Spenser, Shakespeare, and
Fletcher (pp. 101–2). Holland then turns his attention to
travellers' tales, which he mocks with a description of 'No-Land'.
Finally, he concentrates on the masque (many seventeenth-
century romances contain elaborate descriptions of masques),
taking ten pages to describe the masque of 'Venus and Adonis'
(pp. 153–64), 'A splendid, pompeous, & delightful show,/ (Some
say) by Johnson, Jones, or Inigo' (p. 151). This story turns into
another travesty, with the boar depicted as being infatuated with
Adonis:

Here the Boar endeavouring to express love to Adonis, wounds his
tender skin with his Tusk, which kills him.
ADONIS— O I'm slain,
              This bawdy Boar hath wrought my bane. (p. 161)

Holland's imagination is inexhaustible; indeed an amalgam of
'Wit and Fancy'. We conclude with Don Zara mounted on a
winged hog, which carries him to Africa. The freedom made
possible by the anti-romance form is exploited to the full.
    The anti-romance may be seen as an attempt to bring the ideal
and the pragmatic as close together as possible. It does not
destroy romance: it creates an ironic tension between romance
motifs and their potential absurdity. In England in particular,
the anti-romance is energetic and exuberant, rather than cold
and rational. It is possible to indicate how anti-romance points
towards the Restoration novel by briefly considering an unusual
'translation' of Voiture's *Histoire d'Alcidalis et de Zélide* (1658).
This was translated in 1671 by T.D. as *Zelinda*, and mistakenly
attributed on the title-page to 'the French of Monsieur de
Scudery'. Voiture's work is half-way between romance and
nouvelle, but he left it unfinished. T.D. offers a fairly accurate
translation of Voiture's own work,[33] but then concludes the
story, developing the narrator into an ironic, sophisticated voice,
similar to that found in Congreve's *Incognita* and other
Restoration novels. Romance incidents are allowed to occur, but
they are distanced by the narrator's tone:

The next day was solemniz'd with more than usual Sports, when

---

[33] It may be compared with *The History of Alcidalis and Zelide*, a faithful translation
which leaves the work in its unfinished state, found in *A Collection of Select Discourses Out of
the most Eminent Wits of France and Italy* (1678), pp. 141–93.

Alcidalis, swelled with joyful hopes, performed such extravagant Deeds of Agility and Strength, as I dare not particularize, lest the incredulous Reader should distrust the truth of all the rest. (p. 85)

The anti-romance may, as Paulson noted of Scarron's work, contain rather than refute the romance. So here the narrator offers a serious description of the reunion of Alcidalis and Zelinda (p. 120), but his ironic, light tone detaches himself and the reader from the story:

. . . (here is a large Field for the Author to expatiate on the vicissitude of humane things; but the Gentle Reader would think him very in-humane, nay in my Conscience accessory to their Murthers, if he suffered, three of the most Illustrious Persons in the World, to lye neglected on the ground, and dye for want of careful attendance, while he was shewing his common-place Wit, therefore he hastens to their relief, with resolution to save them all if he can) . . . (p. 117)'

This passage also contains the self-consciousness found else-where in anti-romance; the conventions may be used with full awareness, while the reader's attention is drawn to them as conventions. *Don Quixote*, of course, is one of the greatest examples of self-conscious fiction. It explores the paradoxes of the writer, the work, and the audience, testing the conventions which allow prose fiction to create a world. *Don Quixote* is written at the interface of the imagination and reality, and at that interface, no easy distinction between the two is possible. This becomes most apparent in the second part, where the supposed authority of Cid Hamet Benengeli is made much of, and the spurious second part is freely discussed by the characters, while Don Quixote and Sancho meet people who have read about them in the first part of the book which they inhabit. No other anti-romance approaches such subtlety, but as one can see in *Zelinda*, all anti-romance does tend to be self-conscious.

In England, this self-consciousness is usually playful, in keeping with the attraction of the burlesque. The mock title-page of *The Knight Adventurer* proclaims 'This being the 25th Edition; and never twice before Printed' (1663). *The Adventures of Covent Garden* (1699), written 'In Imitation of Scarron's City Romance', contains a blank dedication page headed 'To all my Ingenious Acquaintance at *Will's Coffee-House*'. The author explains 'My Dedication looks very Blank upon the Matter, and 'tis no

Wonder, since I expect no Present for it' (A4). The work mocks itself, and the spirit of deflation and irony is always in the air.

The English tradition of burlesque anti-romance continued even after Fielding turned to the more serious comedy of the French anti-romance. The focus of Charlotte Lennox's *Female Quixote* (1752) moves from Arabella's adventures towards a certain amount of social satire after she enters society. Margaret Dalziel notes that 'Mrs Lennox's purpose, unlike that of Cervantes, is wholly comic.'[34] It is interesting to look back at the development of anti-romance in the seventeenth century from this perspective. While the French anti-romance turns towards realism ('Nothing but what is natural and probable will go down with us'),[35] in England exuberant burlesque turns further away from verisimilitude than the romance itself. Verisimilitude is an experiment conducted within the confines of the heroic romance, while the anti-romance moves towards the power of the imagination, illustrated by mocking exaggeration. The combination of romance and anti-romance, rather than any crude attack on romance, contributes to the familiarity and ironic tone of the Restoration novel.

III. 'Impure' Romance

In the countryside of Tempe, Pandion (disguised as Danpion to facilitate his attempt to regain his kingdom, which has been usurped by Hiarbas) and his companion Periander, wandering lost through the verdant forest, suddenly see 'a young Wench rubbing of an old Beldame, and pulling her by the Nose, striving to fetch life in her' (p. 151).[36] The reader pauses suspiciously here, wondering if he has mistakenly turned to another work, for this is John Crowne's *Pandion and Amphigenia* (1665), a serious romance narrated in an overwhelmingly ornate style ('By this time Sols resplendent Rays had exhaled the Crystall drops of dew, that hang like liquid Pearls on the Grass tops, and rarified them into an Aerial substance . . .', p. 18). For numerous exquisite pages, characters have acted as Cleodora does at the opening of Crowne's romance, when she 'arose, and dispossessed

---

[34] Charlotte Lennox, *The Female Quixote*, ed. Margaret Dalziel (Oxford, 1970), p. xiv.

[35] Paul Scarron, *Scarrons Comical Romance* (1676), pp. 227–8.

[36] References to John Crowne, *Pandion and Amphigenia* (1665).

her downy Bed of those perfections, which that Night had been a treasure of' (p. 1). Swords have claimed the lives of knights, but the reader has scarcely thought of the heroic actors in *Pandion and Amphigenia*, even the more villainous ones, as possessing noses, let alone having them pulled.

But this is Crowne's romance still, and our quotation only the introduction to further startling incidents. Danpion and Periander, desperate for shelter, enter the cottage of an 'ill-favoured crooked-backt, ruffianly Rustick' (p. 152). The 'old Beldame' appears again and her daughter stumbles over her as they enter the cottage; she

> tumbled her Grandam with her heels over her head, in the manner of a Christmas gambole, and threw her bum with such a force upon the door sill, that even beat the wind out of her body (I mean backwards) and made her haunches like a couple of wrinkled bladders that had been smoked seven years in a chimney corner, rebound with the violence of the fall, insomuch that they had been beaten flat and disfigured had they not been well stiffned with age. (p. 154)

During the night, such fabliau incidents continue: the cat upsets 'a great close-stool-pan' (pp. 156–7); the family engage in an undignified fight at breakfast; and so on. Understandably, Danpion and Periander move to the rather more respectable dwelling of the shepherd Thyrsis. But there they are pursued by his two daughters, Phyllis and Arethusa, and are forced to engage in an undignified combat with the girls' jealous rustic sweethearts. Yet when they are finally led out of the wood by Battus (p. 173), they return to Crowne's rarefied romance world. As the scene changes, so the style resumes its previous elevation as if no alteration had occurred: 'It was when the black brow'd night triumphing over the day, sate shaking her dewy locks in her Ebony throne . . .' (p. 175)—only a few pages earlier, Danpion and Periander had sat down at breakfast to observe a 'bundle of Kitchin-stuff' (p. 163).

Pandion and Amphigenia is not a unique curiosity, an aberrant case of a young author lapsing from decorum. A number of romances either contain fabliau or picaresque incidents, or in other ways combine the preciosity which romance had attained by the mid-seventeenth century with a completely different, low style. These include the following works of the 1650s and 1660s:

Samuel Sheppard's *Amandus and Sophronia* (1650), Thomas
Bayly's *Herba Parietis* (1650), John Dauncey's *The English Lovers*
(1662), and Crowne's *Pandion and Amphigenia* (1665). This
development may be viewed from two perspectives: as part of a
constant presence of low incidents or plots in romance, and also
as part of the development of anti-romance impulses that led to
the Restoration novel.

Sidney, in the *Defence of Poetry*, mounts a famous attack on
plays which 'be neither right tragedies, nor right comedies'.[37]
While he might well retort that the *Arcadia* is not a play, and if
regarded as one is not a tragedy, we may nevertheless be tempted
to call it a 'mongrel tragi-comedy', and in it Sidney very
delicately but deliberately contrives to 'match hornpipes and
funerals'.[38] Even amidst the greater dignity of the revised *New
Arcadia*, with the ironic first-person authorial comment of the *Old
Arcadia* removed, we still have the low characters Dametas,
Mopsa, and Miso to provide comic relief, and Sidney also added
the comic joust between Dametas and Clinias in the captivity
episode. Of course Sidney treats these low characters with
decorum too—one is in no danger of finding a close-stool referred
to in the *Arcadia*—but he does, in his greatly respected romance,
indicate that one may make use of low characters and comic
incidents.

Elizabethan fiction provides one example of a mixture of
romance and picaresque which comes closer to the impure
romance of the mid-seventeenth century than Sidney's restrained
comic relief. This is Henry Chettle's *Piers Plainnes Seven Years
Prenticeship* (1591; discussed above, Chap. 7, Sec. II). Chettle's
story begins as a pastoral, but Piers's first-person account
introduces two further levels. His own story is related in a style
akin to Nashe's, and bears some resemblance to Jack Wilton's
story in *The Unfortunate Traveller*; but Piers alternates between
this personal story, and the fortunes of Hylenus, ruler of Thrace,
his children, and Aeliana, the Queen of Crete. This is a romance
tale; the characters speak in a heightened rhetoric, while Aeliana
speaks pure euphuism. Chettle creates three interpenetrating

[37] *Miscellaneous Prose of Sir Philip Sidney*, ed. K. Duncan-Jones and J. Van Dorsten
(Oxford, 1973), p. 114.
[38] Ibid., pp. 114, 115.

realms: the pastoral frame, Piers's picaresque adventures, and the royal family's romance.

Chettle's juxtaposition of opposite worlds is far removed from the anti-romance impulses of *The Unfortunate Traveller*. Piers's story does not mock Aeliana's speeches. The contrast is a development to a more extreme state of the comic sub-plot used by Sidney. Decorum is maintained in the *Arcadia* because Dametas, Miso, and Mopsa are secondary characters in every sense, but Piers is the principal character in Chettle's work. It is as if Dametas were to relate, in an appropriate style, the adventures of Pyrocles and Musidorus.

These precedents were largely ignored by the romances of the early seventeenth century, which were intent on attaining a suitably 'high' level of style, and which scorned even Sidney's use of low characters. But towards the middle of the century, this combination of romance with its opposite began to attract writers again. In 1640 Richard Brathwait published a romance which signals its combination in the title-page: *The Two Lancashire Lovers: Or the Excellent History of Philocles and Doriclea*. Romance motifs predominate, but Brathwait's story is rooted in an English economic reality. Doriclea is the daughter of a prosperous gentleman, who opposes her attachment to her tutor Philocles, and tries to persuade her to marry the old but wealthy Mardanes. Romance elements tend to predominate as the work gathers momentum, and moves towards Philocles' discovery of his inheritance, his disguised sister's attachment to his best friend, and his happy marriage to Doriclea. But Brathwait, particularly in the early part of the work, introduces familiar speech and comic characters. One of Doriclea's suitors, the naïve rustic Camillus, courts her in these words: 'Yaw, Iantlewoman, with the saffron snude, you shall know that I am Master Camillus, my Mothers anely white boy' (p. 18). Not particularly startling, perhaps, but one must try to re-create the impact that the use of such language in a romance must have had after some forty-five years of increasing refinement.

Brathwait has perhaps the slight taint of hack-writer clinging to him, and fashionable readers may have ignored a romance with 'Lancashire' in its title. But ten years later, more respectable writers also began to move away from a completely unsullied romance world. Samuel Sheppard was Ben Jonson's amanuensis.

He would have been particularly respectable in the Interregnum romance world, being a royalist who suffered imprisonment for his loyalty.[39] His romance, *The Loves of Amandus and Sophronia* (1650), is similar to Crowne's in its sudden juxtaposition of romance and picaresque or fabliau. Sheppard does at least warn the reader what is coming:

Now for that the Reader will have enough of dolorous discourse, ere the History be brought to a period; it will not be amisse, if I recite one pleasant passage, that happened to the two Colonels, Venantius, and Palladius. (p. 33)

Then we are plunged into the vulgar world of picaresque violence, and fabliau jests, in which once again ordure figures prominently. From a scene in a brothel, we move straight to a ceremonious masque presented to Amandus. The critic must once again reconsider any easy generalizations about the complete independence of romance and picaresque in the seventeenth century.

It is strange that such an assumption has been made about fiction, when the combination of elements in the drama presents a counter-example. English drama 'thrust in the clown by the head and shoulders to play a part in majestical matters'.[40] The analogy is perhaps not so much with the role of the fool in *King Lear* as with the integration of romance and satire in *As You Like It*, which is not quite the same thing as the juxtaposition of romance and anti-romance in *Don Quixote*. A mutual questioning occurs as we absorb the alternating commentary of Touchstone, Jacques, Rosalind, and Orlando, the result of 'balancing one convention against another'.[41] Richard Levin also explores 'the relationship between a very romantic or heroic main action and a subplot that apparently mocks these lofty sentiments in a debased or cynical version of the same experience'.[42] This relationship strengthens pastoral romance by refusing to shield it from criticism, by allowing it to recognize its limitations, but also to

---

[39] See *DNB* entry under Samuel Sheppard.

[40] Sidney, p. 114.

[41] Eugene Waith, *The Pattern of Tragicomedy in Beaumont and Fletcher* (New Haven, 1952), p. 82.

[42] Richard Levin, 'The Unity of Elizabethan Multiple-Plot Drama', *ELH* 34 (1967), 435.

criticize, through its idealism, the limitations of its attackers. One
remembers that the *Arcadia* too presents a far from simple, or
merely prettified, pastoral world: 'et in Arcadia ego' is part of
Sidney's theme.

In the middle of the century, barriers between modes of fiction
were particularly flexible. Crowne and Sheppard produced their
juxtapositions of romance and fabliau/picaresque at a time
when the French heroic romance was at its most popular in
England. The French romances also attained a certain self-
conscious recognition of anti-romance impulses. Hylas in
D'Urfé's *L'Astrée* mocks the over-refinement of love in romance,
and Scudéry follows D'Urfé's lead in *Clélie*. One must recognize
the possibility of balance as discussed in the context of anti-
romance: the seventeenth-century reader did not feel obliged to
exclude either impulse. The thematic potential of such a balance
has been explored most suggestively by William Empson, in
reference to the double-plot of drama. Even on the most
elementary level, the comic interlude 'relieves boredom and the
strain of belief in the serious part, but this need not imply
criticism of it';[43] in the use of the double-plot, apparent opposites
may interact. Some of his ideas are taken up in an extended
discussion of 'multiple plots' by Richard Levin, who sees the low
sub-plot as a 'foil', which may, far from being destructive of
romance idealism, be 'added to bring out the superior qualities of
the "centerpiece" characters'.[44] This is certainly the case in the
Arcadia, where Dametas and Mopsa may well be seen as comic
foils for Musidorus and Pamela. It is also relevant to the masque,
which under Jonson's careful direction balances the anti-masque
and masque worlds: 'The antimasque world was a world of
particularity and mutability—of accidents; the masque world
was one of ideal abstractions and eternal verities'.[45] The masque
is particularly close to the prose romance world (many romances
throughout the century include detailed descriptions of masques). While the anti-masque began as a foil, to be conquered by
the idealized and allegorical world of the masque, it grew in

[43] William Empson, *Some Versions of Pastoral* (1935, rpt. Harmondsworth, 1966), p. 29; and
see Chap. 2, *passim*.
[44] Richard Levin, *The Multiple-Plot in English Renaissance Drama* (Chicago, 1971),
p. 111; and see Chap. 4, *passim*.
[45] Stephen Orgel, *The Jonsonian Masque* (Cambridge, Mass., 1965), p. 73.

importance, partly owing to King James's enthusiasm for its inherent comedy.[46]

One may still think that the shock of the low incidents in the romances of Crowne and Sheppard is not dispelled when the high style is resumed; that the contrast between the precious and the vulgarly physical is so extreme that the aftertaste of the anti-masque is still present. Yet this is only because the juxtaposition is one of incident, rather than character. Don Quixote and Sancho Panza are opposites, but as characters they may coexist, and even influence each other . In the simpler world of these romances, one must see the contrast in more static, symbolic terms, but some of the thematic relevance detected by Empson may be present even here. Although a romance like *Amandus and Sophronia* apparently banishes the body, it all turns on passion and desire—Rhoxenor lusts after Sophronia. Even in the more restrained *Pandion and Amphigenia*, love is physical as well as spiritual (Pandion's passion is aroused when he first sees Amphigenia bathing naked). While the hero may be nobly restrained, the heroine is inevitably pursued by lustful villains. The most refined romance balances precariously on the edge of a fiery pit of emotional fervour; the sudden introduction of a brothel scene, or a knockabout fabliau jest, recognizes this.

This does not, one should again stress, imply the rejection of the romance idealization—an opposition, not a norm, is juxtaposed with it. The picaresque world is another extreme, an anti-idealization, and its constant reversion to violence and ordure is equally a symbolic overstatement of a possibility. The world is neither as cynical as it is depicted in picaresque, nor as innocent as it is depicted in romance.

Crowne and Sheppard are, nevertheless, not very satisfying from an artistic point of view. Some other less vivid examples of this trend are more successful as narratives. The attempt to confront romance with its opposite is most successful when the two modes are integrated, rather than simply juxtaposed. Thomas Bayly's *Herba Parietis* (1650) separates the two worlds; the romance characters do not stray into a fabliau world as they do in *Pandion and Amphigenia*. Bayly uses a separated story, a true sub-plot: 'The fantasticall Wooing, Humoursome Wedding, and

[46] Ibid., p. 76,

Platonick love that was between Corderius and Fortunata'
(pp. 72–90).[47]

In 1662 Thomas Heywood's *The Fair Maid of the West* (Part I,
late 1590s?; Part II, 1630?) was turned into a novel entitled *The
English Lovers* by John Dauncey. It is a reasonably faithful
adaptation; Dauncey uses the *récit* structure of the heroic
romance, and Heywood's play takes on the character of a
picaresque romance. [48] Two worlds are integrated, as Captain
Goodlake, 'borne nigh unto the famous City of Sarum in the
County of *Sommerset*' (p. 8), joins Sir Walter Raleigh's fleet, while
his friend Spencer courts Bess Bridges, 'a *Tanners* Daughter of
Somersetshire' (p. 35). Dauncey moves back and forth between
these two worlds. He may include fabliau incidents at Bess's
tavern, as she remains loyal to the absent Spencer (ii. 47–54), or
the high romance 'Tragick-History' (p. 45) of 'The Loves of
Schiarra and Florelia' (ii. 13). The combination already exists in
Heywood, but the fact that Dauncey adapted Heywood's play at
this time indicates the influence of a growing interaction between
romance and picaresque techniques in fiction.

These examples are symptomatic of a general disappearance of
barriers between modes of fiction at this time. The political/
allegorical romances of this period, although their form derives
from the French heroic romance, also display this juxtaposition.
An example is Richard Brathwait's *Panthalia* (1659), with its long
inset-story 'The Pleasant Passages of *Panthalia*, the Pretty Pedlar'
(pp. 146–224), set in the midst of a romance treatment of the
Civil War. To avoid any implication that this is simply a *penchant*
of Brathwait's, one can also cite the example of Sir George
Mackenzie's *Aretina* (1660), with its introduction of jests and
picaresque incidents in a style reminiscent of Nashe.

This is not simply a case of picaresque or realistic impulses
moving into romance, for romance in turn influenced other
narrative forms as may be seen from a number of autobiographies
of the period. Sir Kenelm Digby turns himself and Venetia
Stanley into Theagenes and Stelliana in the romance auto-

[47] References to Thomas Bayly, *Herba Parietis*, 1650 (facsimile, Brummell Press, 1969).
[48] See Brownell Salomon, ed., *Thomas Heywood's 'The Fair Maid of The West' Part One* (Salzburg, 1975), p. 36.

biography he wrote around 1628.[49] Digby was writing private
memoirs which were not intended for publication, and they were
in fact not published until the nineteenth century: 'If these loose
papers should have the fortune to fall into any man's hands, to the
which they were never designed. . . .'[50] Thus his autobiography
demonstrates the acceptance of romance conventions as a means
of structuring one's life story. The two impulses—to describe
one's adventures accurately, and to cast them as romance—
combine in the author, even if the result is a little incongruous.
Another example is Lord Herbert of Cherbury's autobiography
(written *c*. 1643–4), with its self-portrait of an amusing (to us)
figure, who throws out challenges in a manner at times close to
that of Don Quixote, yet this is combined with serious diplomatic
activity.

Charles Croke's *Fortune's Uncertainty* (1667) is an even clearer
case of the balance of romance and picaresque impinging upon
autobiography. Croke depicts himself as Rodolphus, and describes his unruly days at school and Oxford, his activities in the
Civil War, and as a bond-slave in Virginia (the last probably
fictitious), ending with an appropriate touch of romance when he
meets the woman 'born to be his'.[51] By relating his history in the
third person under a romance disguise, Croke turns a rather
disreputable life into a felicitous tale.

We have been viewing the balance between romance and
picaresque from the perspective of the romance; but the same
interaction of forms affects the picaresque. If in the romance the
juxtaposition tempers idealism, but also strengthens it by
allowing it to absorb criticism, similarly in the picaresque such a
juxtaposition questions picaresque's anti-idealism, and tempers
its cynicism. *The English Rogue* moves towards a reconciliation of
its characters when Meriton meets the woman he has abandoned, and is forgiven by her; Head and Kirkman allow room
for love in the midst of their very physical world. This is seen to a
much greater extent in *The Scotch Rogue* (1706), where romance
elements play a considerable part in shaping the narrative.

---

[49] See Kenelm Digby, *Loose Fantasies* (not his title), ed. V. Gabrieli (Rome, 1968),
p. xxviii.

[50] Ibid., p. 171.

[51] See Isobel M. Westcott, ed., *Fortune's Uncertainty or Youth's Unconstancy* (Oxford,
1959), pp. viii–ix; quotation from p. 66.

Certainly the moral ambiguity in English picaresque distinguishes it from romance, but romance motifs are present from the middle of the century onwards.

Authors are often coy about their experiments. Crowne actually proclaims that 'My endeavours have been rather to delineate humours and affections, than to affect humorous delineations' (A5^v). When Pandion encounters a woman having her nose pulled, when romance and picaresque confront each other, mind and body are juxtaposed. Each form recognizes itself as a strategy, a symbolic exaggeration; when they confront each other both forms are enriched. Don Quixote and Sancho Panza see, for a time, through each other's eyes.

Chapter 16

Two Voyagers: Margaret Cavendish and John Dunton

I. Utopias and Imaginary Voyages

A. L. Morton has written that 'At no time is there such a wealth of Utopian speculation in England as in the seventeenth century.'[1] Spurred on by the political speculation which precipitated and proceeded from the Civil War, writers such as James Harrington produced utopias which strove to create a new political order in England. These are of more interest to the political historian than to the literary critic; utopias which partake more of fantasy than of hard-headed political speculation contain a much greater narrative interest. Thus we are not here concerned with the great works of speculation produced by notable writers of utopias such as Bacon, Campanella, Comenius, or Harrington.

The imaginary voyage, by its very nature, gives fantasy a freer reign than the utopia, but it often includes a utopian society when the voyage's destination is reached, as we see, for example, in Bishop Godwin's *Man in the Moone* (1639). Sven Liljegren's research has pointed to the influence, in turn, of travel narrative on the utopia, while the 'true' voyages also fed the narrative techniques of fiction.[2] In the two idiosyncratic works under discussion here, Margaret Cavendish's *Blazing World* and John Dunton's *Voyage Round the World*, there are a number of elements taken from utopian fiction and imaginary voyages. While both works are extremely eclectic, they have in common a large component of narrative self-consciousness. John Dunton expresses this chiefly in his style, which bears some similarity to that of Sterne in *Tristram Shandy*, while Margaret Cavendish expresses

---

[1] A. L. Morton, *The English Utopia* (London, 1952), p. 60.
[2] Sven B. Liljegren, *Studies in the Origin and Early Tradition of English Utopian Fiction* (Uppsala, 1961), Chap. 2.

it through her depiction of herself and her husband in an unusual
utopia-cum-imaginary voyage.

II. The 'Blazing World' of Margaret Cavendish

The image of Margaret Cavendish as an oddity, a picturesque
eccentric, has been indelibly fixed by Samuel Pepys, who took
considerable pains to seek her out during her visit to London in
1667. Pepys was not alone in his interest, 'for all the town-talk is
nowadays of her extravagancies', and on one encounter Pepys's
prying eyes were blocked by '100 boys and girls running looking
upon her'.[3] Margaret Cavendish, Duchess of Newcastle, was
notorious as an authoress—a rare phenomenon in the seventeenth century, although it is worth remembering that a number
of women did turn to prose fiction in the period under
consideration. 'The whole story of this Lady is a romance', Pepys
wrote, 'and all she doth is romantic.'[4]

Despite the efforts of Douglas Grant in his elegant biography,
Margaret the First, readers still regard Cavendish as an eccentric
oddity; not, of course, without some justification, but with an
unfortunate tendency to refuse her work any merit at all.[5]
Margaret Cavendish tried her hand at virtually every genre
available: poetry, short-story, letter, biography, autobiography,
essay, drama, natural history, and imaginary voyage. She took
herself most seriously as a natural philosopher, although her
interest was purely speculative, rather than experimental.
Considering her visit to the Royal Society during the London
visit described by Pepys and the experiments she saw there (such
as the reduction of 'a piece of roasted mutton into pure blood'),
this preference of speculation to experiment seems both logical
and intelligent.[6]

Cavendish's intellectual and literary aspirations led to contemporaries labelling her as mad and, as Sandra Gilbert and
Susan Gubar observe, 'finally the contradictions between her
attitude toward her gender and her sense of her own vocation

---

[3] Samuel Pepys, *Diary*, ed. Robert Latham and William Matthews, Vol. 8 (Berkeley
and Los Angeles, 1974), 26 April 1667; 10 May 1667.

[4] Ibid., 11 April 1667.

[5] Douglas Grant, *Margaret the First* (London, 1957).

[6] Pepys, *Diary*, 30 May 1667.

seem really to have made her in some sense "mad" '.[7] In the midst of a tremendous interest in scientific speculation and experiment, Cavendish was not content merely to write a romance, as Mary Wroth had done, but insisted on participating in a male intellectual preserve. While her husband offered her moral support, in the world at large she was either mocked, or indulged because of her social position. Excluded from the male centres of scientific speculation, from participation in the new Royal Society, she created a utopia in which she could depict her own scientific society, and in which women were not barred from the pursuit of knowledge. *The Description of a New World, Called the Blazing World* first appeared in 1666 at the conclusion of Cavendish's *Observations Upon Experimental Philosophy*. Her own natural philosophy is an important part of *The Blazing World*. She moved from an atomic theory of nature to a notion of the interaction between motion and the three divisions of nature: rational matter, sensitive matter, and inanimate matter.[8] The work to which *The Blazing World* is appended is a critique of Robert Hooke's *Micrographia* (1665), and it belittles the use of the microscope, while emphasizing Cavendish's own view of self-moving matter, which is best perceived by the naked eye.

The Blazing World is presented as a light dessert to follow the heavy meal of natural philosophy:

If you wonder, that I join a work of Fancy to my serious Philosophical contemplations; think not that it is out of a disparagement to Philosophy; or out of an opinion, as if this noble study were but a Fiction of the Mind . . . (sig. b)[9]

Having assured us that she does not wish in any way to place her philosophy in a frivolous context, Cavendish states that her purpose was:

to divert my studious thoughts, which I employed in the Contemplation thereof, and to delight the Reader with variety, which is always pleasing. But lest my Fancy should stray too much, I chose such a Fiction as would be agreeable to the subject I treated of in the former parts; It is a Description of a New World, *not such as* Lucian's *or the* French-man's *World in the Moon; but a World of my own*

---

[7] Sandra Gilbert and Susan Gubar, *The Madwoman in the Attic* (New Haven and London, 1979), p. 63.

[8] See Grant, pp. 196–8.

[9] References are to Margaret Cavendish, *A Description of a New World Called the Blazing World* (1666).

Creating, which I call the Blazing-World: *The first part whereof is* Romancical, *the second* Philosophical, *and the third is meerly* Fancy . . . (b^v—b2)

Despite this defence, the work has been derided by the few scholars who have read it. The most scathing dismissal occurs in Frank and Fritzie Manuel's comprehensive study *Utopian Thought in the Western World*, where *The Blazing World* is briefly mentioned as a 'personal daydream' which 'Border[s] on schizophrenia'.[10] The normally sympathetic Grant states that 'few other works of science fiction can equal the confused ridiculous fantasy of the Blazing World.'[11]

Not *all* works of fiction deserve to be rescued from oblivion, and *The Blazing World* may irritate students of serious utopias. But as a product of a powerful imagination it invites the attention of those interested in narrative. Henry Perry remarks that 'the exuberant imagination and absolute naturalness behind this lack of form produce a charm which many more perfect works of art are entirely without.'[12] '*I have made a World of my* own', Cavendish writes in her preface, '*for which no body, I hope, will blame me, since it is in everyones power to do the like*' (b2). Her imaginary voyage bears the same relation to her natural philosophy as Bishop Godwin's *Man in the Moone* bears to John Wilkins's *Discovery of A World in the Moone* (1638). Wilkins carefully speculates 'That 'tis probable there may be inhabitants in this other World, but of what kinde they are is uncertaine', while Godwin writes 'a work of Fancy'.[13]

The Blazing World is not a voyage to the moon, but a sojourn in a parallel world, which adjoins our own at the North Pole. The swift establishment of verisimilitude at the beginning of the tale, so essential for stories of this kind, is impressive, as Cavendish describes how a young Lady, 'often using to gather shells upon the shore' (p. 2), is carried away by a merchant who has fallen in love with her. Their ship is carried by a storm to the North Pole, where the extreme cold kills all but the lady, who is carried into another world.

[10] Frank and Fritzie Manuel, *Utopian Thought in the Western World* (Cambridge, Mass., 1979), p. 7.
[11] Grant, p. 208.
[12] Henry Ten Eyck Perry, *The First Duchess of Newcastle and her Husband as Figures in Literary History* (1918, rpt. New York, 1968), p. 258.
[13] John Wilkins, *The Discovery of a World in the Moone* (1638), p. 187.

The lady soon becomes the Empress of this new world, and rules over a fascinating range of inhabitants: bear-men, bird-men, worm-men, fly-men, ant-men, ape-men, parrot-men—all with talents suited to their particular physiology. Cavendish is not really interested in the utopian possibilities of this new world, only devoting a few pages to its orderly, monarchical government, few laws, and single religion (p. 16). In fact, the new Empress does not consider this situation to be at all ideal, because women are excluded from worship. She institutes a conversion 'to her own Religion, and to that end she resolved to build Churches, and make also up a Congregation of Women, whereof she intended to be the head her self . . .' (p. 60). Religion may be the Empress's chief concern, but natural philosophy was Margaret Cavendish's great love, and it makes its appearance when the Empress assembles her 'Virtuoso's' and questions them at inordinate length about their many fields of expertise; they report to her like so many members of her own Royal Society:

The Bear-men were to be her Experimental Philosophers, the Bird-men her Astronomers, the Fly- Worm- and Fish-men her Natural Philosophers, the Ape-men her Chymists, the Satyrs her Galenick Physicians, the Fox-men her Politicians, the Spider- and Lice-men her Mathematicians, the Jackdaw- Magpie- and Parrot-men her Orators and Logicians, the Gyants her Architects, &c. (pp. 15–16)

Cavendish's own views are confirmed by the assembled company, and the Empress is able to act upon them in a manner which would no doubt have made Robert Hooke, for one, tremble and hide his telescope:

the Empress began to grow angry at their Telescopes, that they could give no better Intelligence; for, said she, now I do plainly perceive, that your Glasses are false Informers, and instead of discovering the Truth, delude your senses; Wherefore I Command you to break them . . . (p. 27)

The society depicted in *The Blazing World* is scarcely perfect before or after the Empress's attempted reforms. Criticism is double-edged, for the Empress visits our world, and 'wonder'd that for all there were so many several Nations, Governments, Laws, Religions, Opinions, &c. they should all yet so generally agree in being Ambitious, Proud, self-conceited, Vain, Prodigal, Deceitful, Envious, Malicious, Unjust, Revengeful, Irreligious,

Factious &c.' (p. 104). She does, however, express great admiration for the King and Queen of England. Her own blazing world has suffered from her meddling, and she realizes that 'the world is not so quiet as it was at first, I am much troubled at it; especially there are such continual contentions and divisions between the *Worm- Bear-* and *Fly-* men, the *Ape*-men, the *Satyrs*, the *Spider*-men, and all others of such sorts, that I fear theyll break out into an open Rebellion, and cause a great disorder and ruine of the Government . . .' (p. 121). The societies of virtuosi are dissolved to restore peace and harmony, and the main point of this side of the work seems to be a critique of formal and experimental approaches to natural philosophy.

The Empress then decides to write her own 'caballa' (philosophical system), and requires the aid of a secretary. After rejecting numerous ancient and modern worthies (including Plato), she settles on 'the *Duchess* of *Newcastle*, which although she is not one of the most learned, eloquent, witty and ingenious, yet is she a plain and rational Writer, for the principle of her Writings, is Sense and Reason . . .' (p. 89). With this remark begins the introduction of the person of the author into her own work of fiction; a technique which is not unprecedented in the period (we have seen how Barclay appears, albeit disguised, in his *Argenis*), but which is here a most prominent aspect of the imaginary voyage.

The Duchess persuades the Empress to abandon her project, but the two become fast friends, and the Duchess (strictly speaking, her 'soul', which travels from our world to the Blazing World) visits frequently: 'their meeting did produce such an intimate friendship between them, that they became Platonick Lovers, although they were both Females' (p. 93). The Empress reassures the Duchess that her title is the highest under the King's, while the Duchess announces her desire to be an empress of a world herself.

The spirits who advise the Empress warn against any attempt to conquer another world; as an alternative, they point out that 'every humane Creature can create an Immaterial World fully inhabited by immaterial Creatures, and populous of immaterial subjects, such as we are, and all this within the compass of the head or scull; nay, not only so, but he may create a World of what fashion and Government he will, and give the Creatures thereof such motions, figures, forms, colours, perceptions &c. as he pleases . . .' (pp. 96–7). The Duchess is much taken with this suggestion, and vows to 'reject and despise all the worlds without me, and create a world of my own' (p. 98). This apparent literary reflection soon turns to another exploration of natural philosophy, as the Duchess rejects the theories of Thales, Pythagoras, Plato, Epicurus, Aristotle, Descartes, and Hobbes in favour of a world based on her own theory of 'rational self-moving Matter' (p. 101).

The Duchess and Empress then visit our world. After a view of the King and Queen, as noted above, they move on to 'those parts of the Kingdom where the Duke of *Newcastle* was' (p. 108). This provides an opportunity for Margaret Cavendish to praise her husband unreservedly, and point to the severe losses which he incurred through the Civil War. The Duke's lament that fortune has always been his enemy leads to a fantastic trial of Fortune before the Duchess leaves the Blazing World.

The short second part of *The Blazing World* relates how the Empress aids her native country, which is 'embroiled in a great War' (p. 1). This reference to England's difficulties during the Dutch Wars is not particularly specific—which is not surprising in view of what happens when the Empress comes to aid the land of her birth. Cavendish's fantasy may just possibly persuade us to suspend disbelief when it is set in another world, but we cavil at reports of fire-stones, fish-men, and gold ships aiding the English fleet. This cavilling occurs only because a certain amount of verisimilitude is achieved in the first part; the second must be read as pure fantasy.

The Duchess herself is again prominent, and Cavendish shows herself to be aware of the criticism to which her singular behaviour has made her liable (and perhaps also shrewdly aware of the hypocrisy of those who indulged her because of her social position): 'If you were not a great Lady, replied the Empress, you would never pass in the World for a wise Lady; for the World would say your singularities are Vanities' (II. 26). She also defends her plays, which have been criticised because they 'are not done by the Rules of Art' (II. 29); the defence leads to the Empress's offer to build her a theatre.

The Blazing World is a most unusual blend of imaginary voyage, utopia, and autobiography. In the preface, Cavendish explains how she '*chose such a Fiction as would be agreeable to the Subject I treated of in the* former parts' (b^v—b2), and so endeavoured to blend her scientific and imaginative impulses:

though I cannot be Henry *the Fifth, or* Charles *the Second, yet I endeavour to be* Margaret *the* First; *and although I have neither power, time nor occasion to conquer the world as* Alexander *and* Caesar *did; yet rather then not to be Mistress of one, since Fortune and Fates would give me none, I have made a World of my own* . . . (b2)

III. *A Voyage Round the World*

The semi-autobiographical hero of John Dunton's *Voyage Round the World* never actually leaves England, although a trip to New England (and even further afield) was promised for a future volume which never appeared. Dunton was an eccentric but important figure in the murky world of the Grub-Street booksellers, and only recently has his role as an author been taken seriously.[14] One must be wary of treating Dunton with too much solemnity, but his erratic (and large) output of pamphlets and broadsheets, religious tracts and journals, original and plagiarized, contains much of interest. *A Voyage Round the World* was published in 1691, and has its origins in an unsuccessful periodical of 1689, *A Ramble Round the World*.[15] *A Voyage* has been noted, albeit disparagingly, for its resemblance in style to *Tristram Shandy*.[16] A direct influence on Sterne is a distinct possibility, and the popularity of *Tristram Shandy* led to a reprint of *A Voyage Round the World* in 1762 under the new title *The Life, Travels, and Adventures of Christopher Wagstaff, Gentleman, Grandfather to Tristram Shandy*.[17]

Recent criticism of *A Voyage Round the World*, although more sympathetic, has contrasted it unfavourably with Dunton's autobiography, *The Life and Errors of John Dunton*, which appeared in 1705. J. Paul Hunter's article, 'The Insistent I', is a stimulating exploration of Dunton's style, concerned mainly with the *Life and Errors*.[18] Hunter hints that 'One could easily make a

[14] See the excellent biography by Stephen Parks, *John Dunton and the English Book Trade* (New York, 1976).

[15] Ibid., p. 49.

[16] Wayne C. Booth, *The Rhetoric of Fiction* (1961, rpt. Chicago, 1975), p. 237.

[17] Parks, pp. 50–1.

[18] J. Paul Hunter, 'The Insistent I', *Novel*, 13 (1979), 19–37.

case for *A Voyage Round the World* as an autobiographical novel or as an anti-novel', but feels that it 'does not, unfortunately, sustain the energy that sometimes enlivens individual sentences and paragraphs'.[19]

We are, today, liable to be attracted by any notion of an 'anti-novel', and perhaps our search for anti-realism in early fiction is in as much danger of being anachronistic as an earlier search for realism. I would certainly wish to emphasize the experimental nature of *A Voyage*, but Dunton's book is explicable in terms of contemporary methods of writing fiction. The plagiarism in the book, previously unrecognized, also points to its links with other modes of fiction.

The title-page of *A Voyage* promises a pot-pourri for the interested reader: 'The whole work intermixt with ESSAYS, HISTORICAL, MORAL, and DIVINE; and all other kinds of Learning'. No less than ten prefatory poems and also a prose introduction precede the actual narrative. In his narrative, Dunton plays games with the reader: we encounter the story of a 'Rambler', sometimes named Don Kainophilus, sometimes John Evander (or Vander), and the narrative switches back and forth between the first and third person. Hints as to the identity of the protagonist are thrown out to the reader, denied, reiterated— although numerous clues point to John Dunton. This is a game of false-identity, and in the second chapter of the second volume, Dunton teases the reader who has recognized him:

I *Kainophilus*, the very and real Author of these *Rambles*, now take upon me to Answer for my own *Honour*, and the Satisfaction of the World, and prove notwithstanding all the fruitless Allegations to the contrary, and some seeming appearances, that neither *John-a-nokes*, nor *Jack-a-styles*, nor *Will-wi-the-wisp*, nor any other Person yet named or suspected are the *real Authors* of this Book, or the *real Evander*, but that I, and only I am he; and who I am, is yet, and ever shall be a *Secret* as long as I please, since the World neither does, nor for all its *fleering* perhaps ever shall or can know me. (II. 22–3)[20]

'A poetical Explanation of the Frontispiece' provides a verse summary of *A Voyage*, and is quoted during the first two-thirds of the work, before Dunton abandons this rough structure. It

[19] Ibid., pp. 27, 28.
[20] References are to *A Voyage Round the World* (1691).

indicates that *A Voyage* has an autobiographical framework, and will describe Evander's rambling life from his boyhood to his adult travels. We do indeed learn a good deal about Evander's rambles, but Dunton's narrative is no more direct, no more uninterrupted, than Tristram Shandy's account of his life. From the very beginning, the narrator buttonholes the reader:

D'Ye laugh Mr. Reader? why e'ne much good may't do ye; I know what you are going to say, as well as if I were in the *Belly* of ye: but don't think I'll humour ye so much as to name your *Objections*, for I intend to answer 'em without ever troubling the World with knowing what they are. (p. 1)

Dunton's style relies on surprising the reader, on undermining his expectations, and most particularly on taking him into the narrator's confidence—but only up to a certain point, before some information is withheld, or a digression ensues:

My *Name* is (or shall be) KAINOPHILUS, my *Birth place of Abode and Fortunes*,—you aren't like to know, unless you read this Book and almost a *dozen* more, for 'tis impossible to comprize such *great things* in a little compass, and tho' the world has heard of *Homer in a Nutshell*, yet no Man alive ever saw *Tostatus on a Silver penny*. But in short, if ever *Fernand Mendez, Pinto*, had strange luck, who actually *Rambled* over 999 Kingdoms, 50 Empires, 66 Commonwealths, was 100 *times Cast away*, 40 times Stript, 50 times Whipt, 21 times sold for a Slave, 50 times Condemn'd to Death, and a 1000 *times Killed*, Murthered, and stark *cold and dead*—in the Imagination I say of his Enemies; I say again, if he deserved Recommendation and Admiration, making the world *stare agen* with his *Super-gorgonick wonders*, if Modesty would give me leave, I could say— much more, do I so. Who have— . . . (p. 2)

This style may be seen as, in part, a development of the intrusive Restoration narrative voice, the voice of Motteux or Oldys. Of course this is not unique to the Restoration, and indeed a very important predecessor is named more than once in *A Voyage* ('in this I have the honour to imitate the Great *Montaigne*', III. 4), but the use of an intrusive narrator became widespread in the 1680s and 1690s.

Style and subject are complementary, for Dunton's narrative focuses on a Rambler, 'a thing wholly consisting of Extreams' (see 'the Impartial Character of a Rambler', pp. 9–20). '*My Life is a continued Ramble, from my Cradle to my Grave*' (p. 25), and one should not be surprised if the writer rambles as he tells his story: 'The Text containing the very cream, flower, heart and marrow of my *Rambles*—my Explanations and Comments whereon shall be the stuffing of this Book . . .'(p. 26).

It was quite probably Dunton who gave Sterne the idea of beginning a narrative prior to the birth of the hero: 'Chap. I. *Of my Rambles before I came into my Mothers Belly, and while I was there*' (p. 27). *A Voyage* has only one character—Evander—and the circumlocutions of the narrative, unlike those in *Tristram Shandy*, are unrelieved by any portrait of an Uncle Toby. Evander's rambles are extremely solipsistic, and rambling is the narrator's leitmotif, for restlessness is seen as the essence of existence: 'All matter is in motion, and therefore perpetually chang'd and alter'd . . .' (p. 27).

We are promised a full account of Evander's rambles, but in fact hear only of his childhood, apprenticeship in London, and a few small sojourns in England. Digression so overwhelms the narrative that three volumes provide only one third of Evander's life. In a way, Dunton's autobiography, *The Life and Errors*, is a sequel to *A Voyage Round the World*—even though the former is strictly autobiographical, while *A Voyage* is only loosely based on autobiographical details. The consequent imaginative freedom, and the comedy it makes possible, characterize the earlier work.

Although Evander's story is a spiral rather than a straight line, the reader is presented with a series of vivid vignettes, revealing events which have had a particular impact on the narrator. Often these are the basis of the stylistic somersaults which give the book its characteristic tone. Evander's childhood, while the subject of amused and amusing circumlocutions and digressions, is convincing in many details:

I came *peeping into the World agen*, as brisk as a little *Minew* leaps up at a Fly in a *Summers Evening*; and soon fall [*sic*] a tugging at my Nurses brown Breasts, *as hard as the Country fellows do the Bell-ropes on a Holyday* . . . I began to *burnish apace*, and thrive amain,—and had enough to let out as well as to keep there,—*painting Maps in my Clouts almost every hour, of all those Worlds I should afterwards Ramble over.* (pp. 38, 39)

With such details, we can reconstruct a realistic picture of a free spirit, a man with a great wanderlust. Evander was a very dutiful apprentice, with a kind master, but he was unable to sit still in London. Dunton could have written a more conventional narrative, but *A Voyage Round the World*, despite its numerous touches of realism, is not a straightforward autobiographical account. Like Swift's *Tale of a Tub*, its form swallows up its content; its subject is its own creation; its attention is focused inward upon itself, as it 'rambles' into existence.

Anyone familiar with *Tristram Shandy* will recognize the slightly mock-naïve air as the narrator explores and explains the problems he has in writing his story:

From henceforward Reader, don't expect I shou'd give *every distinct Ramble* a distinct Chapter, for truly I can't afford it any longer; for the Chapters being heavy things, and the Rambles brisk *little airy Creatures*, the last run away so fast, and *scamper* about at such a mad rate, that the first, do what they can, can't keep pace with 'em, being besides a great many, one still *begetting another*, and running all *different ways* from one another. (p. 46)

The humour present throughout the work is enhanced by a number of poems presented to the reader as serious reflections on various events, while in fact they have a distinctly mock-heroic air. A good example is a brief poem commemorating Evander's close escape, as a child, from choking to death on 'a *bearded Ear* of Grass or Corn' (p. 64):

> Anacreon *dy'd, O hone, O hone!*
> *By the blunt Dart of a Grape-stone,*
> Adrian *our Country-man the Pope,*
> *Was Choakt with Fly—sad! not with Rope:*
> *Stranger than both* Evander's *Fate,*
> *By bearded Wheat sent to Deaths Gate* . . . (pp. 64–5)

This hyperbole turns Evander's life into a comic display designed to surprise the reader at every turn, just as Dunton's style is based on surprise:

Thus do I love to elevate and surprize, and *sprinkle* now and then some of that same in my writings which is so *remarkable* in my self—that people should miss what they expected and find what they never lookt for—tho' both still very excellent . . . (p. 108)

A Voyage Round the World does not lack sentiment, provided by Evander's affectionate depiction of his father, and (with humorous overtones) his frequent apostrophes to his beloved Iris.

Evander's wise father provided his rambling son with some moral stability, and tried to keep some sense of reality before him. As one might now expect from the structure of *A Voyage*, the death of Evander's father is described twice; the details provided are legion, from the exact date ('Nov. 4 1676', p. 129), to the exact cause ('the incurable putrefaction of some Morbid *Juices* in the Renal Concavities', p. 121). In the third volume, we are presented with '*An Exact Copy of my Father's* Dying Councel' (p. 59); a sensible bourgeois series of maxims concerning 'Soul', 'Body', and 'Estate'. Although Evander's love for his father is convincingly portrayed (this is one of the more obvious auto-biographical sections in the book: Dunton's own father's death was identical in every detail to Evander's),[21] the humorous exaggeration, ubiquitous in the book, will not be suppressed, and surfaces in a macabre image of Evander, his father, and Iris, all 'bedded' in the same grave:

> And there let him lye till I come to him—and how sweetly shou'd he and I and Iris lye there together in one anothers Arms—Lye further Father; you have got all the Bed to your self, and thrust us out upon the very Bedsted, but tho' you had possession first, yet two to one's odds.—However I'll be a dutiful Son dead and living, and rather lye upon the Boards than hurt your Ribs, which by this time may be a little tender. (I. 119–20)

Iris also is a figure from Dunton's life: his first wife Elizabeth Annesley, referred to as Iris throughout the *Life and Errors*.[22] Iris hovers over *A Voyage* as Evander's touchstone, epitome of all that is admirable: 'my *most excellent Master*, the very best of *Men*, as *Iris* of Women . . .' (II. 34). Iris does not play an active part in *A Voyage* as it stands; she is only referred to in passing by Evander, and accordingly is very like a presiding Muse. Some constancy, if not complete coherence, is added to the work by her presence.

While the style of Dunton's narrative becomes less flamboyant in the last volume, the subject matter continues on its wayward course, as Evander pursues any topic which interests him: '*I love a Digression*, I must confess with all my Heart, because 'tis so like a *Ramble* . . .' (I. 142). At the beginning of the second volume, Dunton provides, in his opening chapter, '*The Explanation of the* First Book *of these* Rambles, *and the Design of the* whole' (p. 1). The book's formless nature, and its surprise tactics, are readily admitted: 'They can neither find beginning nor ending, head nor tail, nor can't for their Lives tell what the Author would be at, what he drives at or intends in *part* or *whole*' (p. 2). Evander is quite unashamed, and continues to play peepo with the reader: 'Perhaps I had never any mind you should know what I mean, nor what to make on't' (p. 4).

Dunton is able to turn a question on its head by taking it literally:

That ever any Man in his Senses (but all are not *Evanders*) should question the Usefulness of this Design, and the past or following Volumes! That in the first place 'twas highly *useful to Me*, which none need doubt I think the *Principal Verb*, I can assure 'em by my own Experience, t'has Turn'd a penny these hard times . . . (II. 6)

The 'true' purpose of authorship—and of course no man but a blockhead ever wrote for anything but money—far from being hidden behind a moralistic screen, is waved like a flag.

Following this, the 'highlights' of the preceding volume are enumerated: 'Chap. 5 pag. 60 has an equally pleasant and profitable Discourse of *School-Masters* . . .' (II. 12). The exhausted reader is forced to yield. The idiosyncratic style provides a sure test of authorship:

So great a Glory do I esteem it to be the *Author* of these *Works*, that I cannot without great injury to my self and Justice, endure that any shou'd own 'em who have nothing to do with 'em, like the fellow at *Rome*, who pretended to *Virgil's* Verses. But I need take no other way to confute these *Plagiaries* than *Virgil* himself did, requiring the Tally to his *Vis non vobis*.—Let any Man write on at the rate this is already written, and I'll grant he is the *Author* of this Book, that before, and all the rest to the end of the *Chapter*.—No, there is such a sort of a *whim in the style*, something so like my self, so Incomprehensible (not because 'tis Nonsense) that whoever throws but half an Eye on that and me together, will swear 'twas spit out of the mo[u]th of *Kainophilus*.—This by the bye. (II. 19)

So in another paradox, another circular argument, the author's identity is secured by the fact that only he could have written the pages before us.

The style does begin to lose some of its liveliness in the second volume, but the pursuit of digressions is undiminished. Dunton's attitude is quite didactic, not to say moralistic, when the dutiful

Evander is given a long sermon to preach against atheists and debauched apprentices. Evander is a model apprentice himself, except for his 'rambling', and he appreciates his considerate master.

The reader is still teased with the possible revelation of Evander's true identity:

And now I am about Godly Books, commend me to *Dunton's Blessed Martyrs*, which I remember, among other things, I had once upon my *Note*.

I shall never forget that *Remarkable Person*, tho I were to live as long as his *Raven*—I had the *Honor* that time to see and discourse with him; and I confess the World is in the right, and he's *something* like that *Evander* which makes such a splutter in't—but I'm still of the same mind I was before—they can never prove I *am he*—(II. 69)

We do not find Evander as a traveller until the third volume—and then he only goes as far as Buckinghamshire. Dunton's own rambles to America are treated in his *Life and Errors*.

Evander's intense interest in himself does admittedly pall in time, and it is perhaps to the work's advantage that only three volumes were completed. It is not that Evander's life is uninteresting, simply that Dunton achieves very little of Sterne's psychological penetration, while his games with narrative structure fall short of the metaphysical speculation of *Tristram Shandy*. Evander admits to being a fool, before making the mock-naïve confession: 'It may be now some will admire that I fall so foul on my *own Intellectuals*. Why *Reader* know, that I do it in hopes that the novelty of the Humour will sell my Book' (III. 32). Evander's ramble to Buckinghamshire is actually much less interesting than the earlier part of his narrative.

'Fish, flesh or fowl?', one might enquire of Dunton's creation. This account has stressed an element which, though certainly not unique, is arresting, and sympathetic to the modern reader: the narrative's self-consciousness. 'Alas, *Reader*, Writing is as natural to me as Eating', Evander writes (III. 21), and he explores the process of writing in full view of the reader. However, *A Voyage Round the World* can be linked to a number of popular modes of fiction prevalent during the seventeenth century. It is one of a number of eclectic works which mix modes, but the diversity in Dunton's narrative is quite extreme. The imaginary voyage is present more in promise than in performance, perhaps, but the narrative is presented as a 'voyage', and Dunton mentions some famous predecessors in the genre, including Mandeville and Coryat. Evander does not leave England in the work as it stands, but clearly he is already a traveller.

The dialogue form is used on a few occasions, particularly in the third volume (pp. 13–15; 58–9); not at any great length, but the dialogue between Evander and his father in particular adds a realistic touch. Similarly, we are presented with a selection of 'My own Mother's Letters (which she sent to her several Relations) given me by my Father at our last parting' (III. 62–8).

The autobiographical form, and even the obtrusive narrator, are present in the picaresque novel and criminal biography. We have also seen how the exuberant language of Nashe was carried on, if in a diminished state, by Richard Head. It is, therefore, no surprise to find that Dunton, resorting to plagiarism in the third volume of his narrative, turns to these allied modes of fiction. He admits that some of his material is borrowed: 'Tis true, I cannot deny but in this Book there are many things that may perhaps one day have bin made known to me by other Writers; but if they have, I have utterly forgot by whom' (III. 24).

The first of these borrowings is a passage taken from *The English Rogue*, describing Evander's rejection of the rough fare which has sustained him on his ramble.[23] The second is a passage from *Don Tomazo* describing a broken-down hovel.[24] While not significant in themselves, these passages help to identify the nature of Dunton's narrative. One can see plagiarism as an acknowledgement of association with the works pillaged, and this confirms a strong picaresque element in *A Voyage Round the World*. This does not detract from its undeniable originality, but simply emphasizes its eclectic nature. Dunton and Cavendish both conducted lively and idiosyncratic experiments with narrative.

---

[23] Richard Head, *The English Rogue* (1665), p. 34; cf. Dunton, Vol. 3, p. 56.
[24] *Don Tomazo* (1680), in *The Counterfeit Lady Unveiled and Other Criminal Fiction of Seventeenth Century England*, ed. Spiro Peterson (New York, 1961), p. 192; cf. Dunton, Vol. 3, p. 366.

Chapter 17

The Restoration Novel

I. Introduction

Some time after the Restoration there were important changes in the nature of prose fiction. These changes are not a product of the 1660s—a period, as we have seen, during which the anti-romance, the picaresque novel, and the last of the long heroic romances, all jostled for attention.[1] The large influx of translations from the French, which critics have seen as exerting an important influence on these changes, reached their peak during the 1680s.[2] But the translations cannot be held entirely responsible for a form which also draws on the native tradition, especially on the English approach to drama.

The most important movement during the period from around 1670 to the end of the century was the replacement of the long romance by the short novella, a change reflected in the use of the word 'novel' on numerous title-pages. This change culminated in Congreve's famous distinction in the preface to *Incognita* (1692) between romances and novels, which 'are of a more familiar nature' (p. 32).[3] But we have seen how fiction does not follow a clear and single line of development, and writers of Restoration novels had at their disposal a number of different types of French *nouvelles*. The works of Aphra Behn, Congreve, and other Restoration novelists draw on a variety of influences, and must also be seen in the context of a variety of translations.

In France, the work of Mme de la Fayette stands as the highest achievement in the new *nouvelle* form. Both La Fayette's work, and the general movement from the romance to the *nouvelle* in

---

[1] See Benjamin Boyce, 'The Effect of the Restoration on Prose Fiction', *Tennessee Studies in Literature*, 6 (1961), 77–82.

[2] See ibid., and Charles C. Mish, 'English Short Fiction in the Seventeenth Century', *Studies in Short Fiction*, 6 (1969), 279.

[3] A. Norman Jeffares, ed., *Incognita and The Way of the World* (London, 1966); references to *Incognita* are to this edition.

France, have been carefully studied.[4] Most critics note the
general change of narrative structure ('Le roman héroique était
un *poème*; le roman nouveau est une *histoire*'),[5] or the important
interest in 'greater psychological insight and analysis of inner
feelings',[6] which leads Dorothy Dallas to speak of 'Le roman
psychologique'.[7] *La Princesse de Montpensier* (1662), La Fayette's
first but extremely powerful essay in the new mode, was
translated in 1666.[8] Her masterpiece, *La Princesse de Clèves*,
appeared over a decade later, in 1678 (it was translated in the
following year). By that date, both in France and in England, the
nouvelle was well established in all its various forms.

Over a hundred of these works were available in translation in
England. The peak period is the 1680s, forming the background
for the best English novels, which were written in the late 1680s
or very early 1690s. It is possible to see a number of forms taken
by the *nouvelle*, all of them popular in England, judging by the
number of translations.[9] The two forms most frequently translated were the *nouvelle historique* and *nouvelle galante*. The *nouvelle
historique* is best known today in the example of *La Princesse de
Clèves*, although this novel has been classified in other terms.[10]
The setting for the narrative is always a comparatively recent
period of history, unlike that of the heroic romance, whose
authors tended to choose distant and more or less exotic periods.
The central interest, however, is love; the *nouvelle historique*
explores the psychology of love, seen either in wholly invented
personages who move in the historical setting, or in historical
characters. La Fayette is most interested in character and
psychological analysis. César Saint-Réal's accomplished and
influential *Dom Carlos* (1672, translated as *Don Carlos* in 1674)
pays more attention to historical events. Marie-Catherine
Desjardins produced three important works in this mode: *Le*

---

[4] See especially Dorothy Dallas, *Le Roman Français de 1660 à 1680* (Paris, 1932); Henri
Coulet, *Le Roman jusqu'à la Révolution* (Paris, 1967); Frédéric Deloffre, *La Nouvelle en France
à l'Age classique* (Paris, 1967); on La Fayette see Stirling Haig, *Madame de la Fayette* (New
York, 1975), and the appended bibliography.

[5] Coulet, p. 210.   [6] Mish, p. 279.   [7] Dallas, p. 80.

[8] The text may be found in Charles C. Mish, ed., *Restoration Prose Fiction 1660-1700*
(Lincoln, Nebraska, 1970), pp. 1-33.

[9] See the discussion by Mish, 'English Short Fiction', pp. 279-96.

[10] See Barbara Woshinsky, *La Princesse de Clèves: The Tension of Elegance* (The Hague,
1973), *passim*.

Journal amoureux (1668, translated as *Loves Journal*, 1671); *Les Annales galantes* (1670, translated as *The Loves of Sundry Philosophers*, 1673); and *Les Désordres de l'amour* (1675, translated as *The Disorders of Love*, 1677).[11]

The *nouvelle galante* uses the same technique in a more or less contemporary setting. The emphasis is still on analysis, and at times the distinction between a *nouvelle* set in the very recent past and one set in the present is hard to maintain. Indeed, some critics do not distinguish between the two at all: Coulet speaks of the *nouvelle 'historique et galante'*.[12] But in a work like Gabriel de Brémond's *The Pilgrim: A Pleasant Piece of Gallantry* (translated by Peter Bellon in 1680) there is a concentration on intrigue and love affairs in a contemporary setting, and much less interest in characters' psychology than that shown by La Fayette. Peter Bellon, the translator, wrote a second part to *The Pilgrim* which was published in 1681, and reveals the influence of the Spanish novella. It increases the importance of the plot, of action, which is already more important in Brémond's work than in a *nouvelle* by La Fayette or Desjardins.

During this period, the Turks and their customs attracted the attention of Europe, and the exotic and erotic possibilities of the seraglio were of paramount interest for writers. The oriental tale continues the analysis of love and psychology in the setting of the seraglio; Juan de Préchac and Mlle La Roche Guilhem wrote a number of novels in this mode. This setting may be used for a tragic story of some power: for example, *Ottoman Gallantries* (1687), with its historical basis in the life of the Bassa of Buda, or Sebastien Grenadine's *Homais Queen of Tunis* (1681). An exotic setting does not necessarily preclude psychological analysis or the creation of moving events.

In the *nouvelle*, one sees a movement deriving from developments already present in the heroic romance: the interest in *vraisemblance*, the attempt to justify the accuracy of the historical setting, the use of the portrait to analyse characters, and the increasing interest in the self-contained *histoire* and *récit*. The movement towards some of the features of the *nouvelle* may be seen in Scudéry's *Clélie*. Writers became conscious of the change, but it

---

[11] See Bruce A. Morrissette, *The Life and Works of Marie-Catherine Desjardins* (Saint Louis, 1947), pp. 82–116.

[12] Coulet, p. 263.

was not seen as a complete repudiation of romance, especially in England.

Further developments in French fiction produced the vogue of the secret history and scandal chronicle, where attention moves from the fictional intrigues of the past to purportedly true intrigues of the present. Here the appeal of the *roman à clef*, present in the romances, joins with the new technique of depicting amorous affairs. Again, numerous translations were made of works such as Louis du Bail's *The Famous Chinois* (1669), and later in the century, of much more scandalous creations such as *The Cabinet Open'd* (1690). Interest led to large, pseudo-historical compilations like Claude Vanel's *The Royal Mistresses of France* (1695). In England, political allegory is again evident in novels such as *The Fugitive Statesman* (1683), or *The Pagan Prince* (1690). But the French interest in amorous affairs appears in an imitative work such as *The Amours of the Sultana of Barbary* (1689), which treats of Charles II and the Duchess of Portsmouth. The works of Mrs Manley carry this mode into the eighteenth century.

The partly or wholly fictitious memoirs, which are really novels in an autobiographical form, offer a more artistic expression of this interest in 'true histories'. Desjardins' early *Memoirs of the Life and Rare Adventures of Henrietta Silvia Moliere* (1672) has been classified as a 'pseudo-autobiographical novel'.[13] Gatien Courtilz de Sandras wrote a number of excellent examples, including *The French Spy* (1700), which often brings Defoe to mind.

The French *nouvelle*, in all its forms, was extremely popular and influential in England, but English fiction written during this period reflects other influences too. The Spanish novella had been available to English writers for quite some time (Cervantes' *Exemplary Novels* were translated in 1640), but it became most influential during this period. Several collections of Spanish novellas were translated, including *The Spanish Decameron* (1686) and *Quevedo's Novels* (1671—in fact, a version of Salas Barbadillo's *Don Diego de Noche*); Paul Scarron's important, individual translations of Cervantes' *Exemplary Novels* from Spanish to French were re-translated into English by John

---

13 See Morrissette, Chap. 7.

Davies in 1665, and appeared in various forms after that. Congreve's *Incognita* is the most notable example of the novella's influence, and it will be discussed below. More direct imitations were also produced, a good example being Philip Ayres's *The Revengeful Mistress* (1696). In the Spanish novella, great emphasis is placed on action and intrigue; the plot is always brisk, in contrast to the psychological analysis which slows down the French *nouvelle*.

Just as English anti-romance is more knockabout than the French, so English writers were attracted to the fast pace of the novella plot. The Restoration novel combines the analysis and the concern with love of the *nouvelle* with the brisk plot of the novella; as we shall see, the relative importance of the two elements may vary greatly.

The English Restoration novel may thus be defined as a mode which draws on various sources; it is not just an imitation of any one, or even all, of the forms of French *nouvelle*. It can best be defined through particular examples. The work of Aphra Behn, who tried her hand at novels which between them reflect every influence present during the period, is particularly useful as an aid to defining the Restoration novel.

II. Aphra Behn

This young fellow lay in Bed reading one of Mrs. *Behn's* Novels; for he had been instructed by a Friend, that he would find no more effectual Method of recommending himself to the Ladies than the improving of his Understanding, and filling his Mind with good Literature.[14]

Henry Fielding's heavily ironic comment is a relatively mild example of the abuse which Aphra Behn sustained not only during her career as a writer, but also, after her death, as a 'shocking' example of a woman who wrote in the bold and bawdy Restoration style. Her example was followed by the growing number of women who wrote fiction in the early eighteenth century—still disreputable writers such as Maria Manley or Eliza Heywood, who nevertheless paved the way for Fanny

[14] Henry Fielding, *Tom Jones*, ed. Martin Battestin and Fredson Bowers (Oxford, 1975), Vol. 2, p. 530.

Burney and Jane Austen.[15] As well as an extremely large output
of plays, poetry, and translations, Behn wrote thirteen novels
which encompass the whole range of influences operating on
Restoration fiction.

The recent appearance of two major biographies may herald a
more serious interest in Aphra Behn, although her works have
received much less attention than her life.[16] Behn was always
responsive to popular trends, and she was a novelist of some skill.
Criticism of her fiction has been hampered by bibliographical
inaccuracies, in part stemming from Montague Summers's
edition of her works, which is not very reliable. F. M. Link has
largely corrected the chronology presented by George Woodcock
in his early study, but Behn's novels need to be given definite
publication dates, as well as conjectural dates of composition.[17]
Only four works were published during Behn's lifetime: *Love
Letters Between a Noble-Man and his Sister* (Part I, 1683; Part II,
1685; Part III, *The Amours of Philander and Silvia*, 1687); *Oroonoko:
Or, The Royal Slave* (1688); *The Fair Jilt* (1688); and *The Fatal
Beauty of Agnes de Castro* (1688—sometimes attributed to Behn,
but actually a translation from J. B. de Brillac). After her death
appeared *The History of the Nun: Or, The Fair Vow-Breaker* (1689)
and *The Lucky Mistake* (1689); and following the first collection of
her novels in 1696, increasing interest led to more posthumous
publications: *The Adventure of the Black Lady*; *The Court of the King
of Bantam*; *The Nun: Or, Perjur'd Beauty*; *The Unfortunate Happy
Lady*; *The Unfortunate Bride: Or, The Blind Lady a Beauty*; *The
Wandering Beauty*; *The Unhappy Mistake: Or, The Impious Vow
Punish'd* (all 1698); and *The Dumb Virgin: Or, The Force of
Imagination* (1700).

Internal references date some of these works around 1684
(*Bantam, Unfortunate Happy Lady*, possibly *Unhappy Mistake*). But

[15] Virginia Woolf singled out Aphra Behn as the precursor of later professional women
writers, the first proof for women that 'money could be made by writing', in *A Room of
One's Own* (1929, rpt. London, 1979), p. 62; for the writers who followed Behn, see John
Richetti, *Popular Fiction Before Richardson: Narrative Patterns 1700-1739* (Oxford, 1969),
Chaps. 4-6, and Robert Day, 'Muses in the Mud: The Female Wits Anthropologically
Considered', *Women's Studies*, 7, No. 3 (1980), 61-74.
[16] Maureen Duffy, *The Passionate Shepherdess: Aphra Behn 1640-89* (London, 1977);
Angeline Goreau, *Reconstructing Aphra: A Social Biography of Aphra Behn* (Oxford, 1980).
[17] George Woodcock, *The Incomparable Aphra* (London, 1948), pp. 241-2; Frederick M.
Link, *Aphra Behn* (New York, 1968), Chap. 8.

whatever Behn's own artistic development might have been, the full range of her work is an excellent illustration of the various approaches to the novel form taken by Restoration writers. Many critics, even Link whose discussion is by far the most accomplished, try to divide the novels into 'romance' and 'realism', or even to distinguish these two elements in individual works.[18] These terms are far too general to be of use. One may see certain techniques associated with realism in some of the novels: the use of contemporary settings, natural dialogue, characters of a lower social level than royalty or nobility. These characteristics are certainly to be found in a number of Restoration novels. But Behn is working within a series of conventions which do not distinguish between romance and realism in this way. *Oroonoko* treats its protagonist as a character in a heroic romance, while it is also singled out for its 'realism' in the use of setting and a reliable narrator. Behn is aware of the popularity of both the elevated hero of romance, and the detailed description of setting, and so puts both devices to good use.

Love Letters, her first novel to be published, is an excellent example of the diverse strands woven into her work. The first part (1683) is an extremely accomplished epistolary novel, perhaps the earliest example in English.[19] The use of the letter form to depict an emotional conflict began with the enormously popular *Lettres portugaises* (1669, translated in 1678).[20] Behn continues the use of the letter to depict every possible range of emotion (as Richardson was to do), but, following the usual English trend, adds a greater interest to the narrative through a plot which develops as the letters proceed. This novel does not merely draw on the mode of the novel in letters, it also reflects interest in secret history, for it is based on the true scandal surrounding Lord Grey, who ran away with his wife's sister Henrietta Berkeley.[21]

The influence of the *nouvelle historique* and scandal chronicle becomes more evident in the second and third parts of the novel

---

[18] See Link, p. 139; Rowland Hill, 'Aphra Behn's Use of Setting', *MLQ* 7 (1946), 189; Arlin G. Meyer, 'Romance and Realism in the Novels of Aphra Behn and Previous Prose Fiction' (unpublished Ph.D. dissertation, Ohio University, 1967).

[19] See Robert A. Day, *Told in Letters: Epistolatory Fiction Before Richardson* (Ann Arbor, 1966), pp. 159–64.

[20] See ibid., pp. 33–8; the translation may be found in *The Novel in Letters*, ed. Natascha Wurzbach (London, 1969), pp. 3–21.

[21] See Day, p. 160; the text of the first part is in Wurzbach, pp. 201–82.

(1685, 1687), especially in Part Three, which depicts Grey's involvement in the Rye House Plot, and Monmouth's rebellion. In Part Two, letters are no longer the principal vehicle of narration. The plot grows increasingly tortuous (Robert Day calls it 'labyrinthine'),[22] necessitating the use of third-person narration. At the same time, a series of intrigues develop, reminiscent of the Spanish novella, and Silvia's character becomes quite complex as she egoistically manipulates her lovers. Behn holds our interest in Silvia throughout, although the three parts utilize such different techniques as almost to be separate novels.

Charles Mish points to Behn's great ability to write tragic scenes of considerable power.[23] Behind this achievement one can see La Fayette's interest in character, and the tragic fate which pursues her characters; and also the darker strain of the novella, where the characters are engulfed by a tangled intrigue plot. As well as her translation of *Agnes de Castro*, four of Behn's novels are tragic novellas: *The Fair Jilt*; *The History of the Nun*; *The Nun: Or, Perjur'd Beauty*; and *The Dumb Virgin*. These novels all have foreign settings and strong plots. The story may verge on the sensational, as in *The Dumb Virgin*, a tale of 'innocent' incest with a bloody finale. But in *The Fair Jilt* and *The History of the Nun*, the characters of Miranda and Isabella are vividly portrayed, with the intention of involving the reader in their tragedies. The 'Amorous but extremely Inconstant' (pp. 13–14) Miranda manages to survive the threatened punishment which she brings upon herself through her passionate, headstrong, and at times vindictive actions.[24] Isabella's story is, perhaps, a moral tale—so the opening sentence proclaims it to be: 'Of all the Sins, incident to Human Nature, there is none, of which Heaven has took so particular, visible, and frequent Notice, and Revenge, as on that of *Violated Vows*, which never go unpunished . . . ' (pp. 1–2).[25]

Sensational scenes are exploited; for example, the abortive beheading of Prince Tarquin in *The Fair Jilt*, or Isabella's murder of Henault (the husband who had been missing for five years, during which time she had married Villeroys) in *The*

[22] Day, p. 161.   [23] Mish, 'English Short Fiction', p. 300.
[24] References to *The Fair Jilt* (1688).
[25] References to *The History of the Nun: Or, The Fair Vow-Breaker* (1689).

History of the Nun.[26] Behn's attention to detail gives these scenes their power, and her realization of these women's emotions gives them a psychological interest which justifies their violence. But she is also capable of ending *The Fair Jilt* on a very understated note. After describing the retirement of Miranda and Tarquin to Holland, she simply concludes, 'Since I began this Relation, I heard that Prince *Tarquin* dy'd about three quarters of a Year ago' (p. 120).

A number of the novels are set in contemporary England, and have been duly praised in a helpful article by Rowland Hill for their use of 'realistic locale'.[27] In them we see another influence at work on the Restoration novel: the drama. Restoration comedy was established by 1665, although scholars now stress the continuity with Caroline and earlier comedy.[28] Behn herself wrote numerous plays before turning to fiction, and one should note that two other Restoration novels singled out here were also written by dramatists: Alexander Oldys's *Female Gallant* and William Congreve's *Incognita*. Novels like *The Court of the King of Bantam* and *The Unfortunate Happy Lady* recall the world of Restoration comedy: fops, witty dialogue, and a brisk plot culminating in a successfully manœuvred marriage. Congreve's claim in the preface to *Incognita* must be taken as a pardonable exaggeration: 'I resolved . . . to imitate Dramatick Writing, namely, in the Design, Contexture, and Result of the Plot. I have not observed it before in a Novel' (p. 33). Mrs Behn anticipates him.

The drama as a social institution during the Restoration also appears in these novels. *The Unfortunate Happy Lady* concerns Philadelphia, whose profligate brother Sir William Wilding, despite his income of £4,000 per annum, places her in a brothel in order to encompass her estate. She is rescued by Gracelove, who recognizes her quality only after some attempts at familiarity. He leads her out of the brothel, telling the bawd that he is taking her to a play:

What is play'd to Night? (ask'd the old one) *The Cheats*, Mother, *the*

[26] Maureeen Duffy indicates that *The Fair Jilt* is based, in part, on a true incident (op. cit., pp. 72–3); but a comparison of the account of the beheading in *The London Gazette* as cited by Duffy, and *The Fair Jilt*, reveals Behn's extreme elaboration of the incident.

[27] Hill, p. 189.

[28] See Robert D. Hume, *The Development of English Drama in the Late Seventeenth Century* (Oxford, 1976), pp. 233–8.

cheats (answer'd *Gracelove*.) Ha (said *Beldam* laughing) a very pretty Comedy, indeed! Ay, if well play'd return'd he. (p. 41)[29]

The Court of the King of Bantam has the spirit of Ben Jonson behind it, especially in the character of Mr Wou'd be King, an 'Originall' who has been persuaded at an early age that his name predicts his destiny. In a gay romp, Sir Philip Friendly plays on Wou'd be's humour, in order to provide money for his niece's marriage to Valentine Goodland, and at the same time provide for his ex-mistress Lucy. The novel portrays the amoral sexual world of the Restoration, while following Restoration comedy in providing a romantic ending for the lovers Philibella and Valentine. Beneath the wit and boisterous action, however, echoes the opening sentence: 'This *Money*, certainly is a most Devilish thing!' (1698 edn., p. 1). Behn acknowledges, as do a number of playwrights, the rather harsh bargains being struck beneath the witty banter. Love must have a solid base—one consisting of hard cash, in fact.

Behn's fiction at times tends towards a compressed short-story form, such as in *The Adventure of the Black Lady* (1698), an account of a single incident culminating in a trick played upon 'the Vermin of the Parish (I mean, the Overseers of the Poor, who eat the Bread from 'em)'.[30] On the other hand, she also returns to the tragic novella form in, for example, *The Unfortunate Bride*. Although Link calls *The Wandering Beauty* a 'fairy tale', Hill emphasizes its depiction of the English countryside—another indication that Behn herself does not distinguish, as we now do, between techniques of romance and realism, but instead uses whatever is appropriate at a particular moment in a story.[31] *The Unhappy Mistake*, unaccountably neglected by many critics, contains an excellent characterization of Sir Henry Hardiman, who estranges his son; he is a Squire Western who softens very early on. Link points to this novel's fine use of dialogue:

Beauty and Virtue, Sir, (return'd young *Hardyman*) with the Addition of good humour and Education, is a Dowry that may merit a Crown. *Notion! Stuff! All Stuff* (cry'd the old Knight) *Money is Beauty, Virtue, Good Humour, Education, Reputation, and High Birth.* (pp. 41–2)[32]

---

[29] References to *The Unfortunate Happy Lady* (1698).
[30] Aphra Behn, *All The Histories and Novels* (1705), p. 499.
[31] Link, p. 147; Hill, pp. 193–5.
[32] References to *The Unhappy Mistake* (1698), in *Histories, Novels and Translations* (1700).

Of all Behn's novels, *Oroonoko* has perhaps received a rather undue amount of attention. An enormous amount of energy has been expended on deciding how it relates to Behn's own experiences in Surinam—energy which has cast some light on Behn's biography, but very little on *Oroonoko*.[33] Frederick Link is almost alone in directing attention to the novel's 'structural unity'.[34] A recent study by George Guffey suggests that the novel has a political dimension;[35] while his argument does question any over-idealization of Behn's attitudes to slavery and the 'noble savage', it overstates the case for the novel as a piece of Tory propaganda. It may be that Behn's rosy picture of Surinam is connected with the Dutch 'threat' to England in the shape of William of Orange. Guffey sees Behn's account as linking the loss of Surinam to the Dutch in 1667 with England's potential 'loss' in 1688,[36] but I cannot imagine Behn wishing to connect Oroonoko with King James, for however noble he is, and even if his slave name of Caesar is later echoed by Behn in a reference to James, he is the leader of a revolt. Such an association would recall Monmouth rather more easily than James.

Guffey succeeds in imposing only a thin political colouring on to *Oroonoko*. It remains a *nouvelle galante*, with Oroonoko himself recalling a heroic-romance prince. Behn's strength is in the convincing detail of the Surinam setting (whether based on her own experience, the copying of published accounts, or a distortion of them), and the use of an intrusive first-person narrator, who gains the reader's confidence. It is through the narrator that we feel close enough to Oroonoko to be moved by his cruel fate, to feel both sympathy and the thrill of horror when he kills his wife Imoinda, in order to save her from being

[33] See Ernest Bernbaum, 'Mrs Behn's Biography a Fiction', *PMLA* 28 (1913), 432–53; J. A. Ramsaran, '"Oroonoko": A Study of the Factual Elements', *N&Q* 205 (1960), 142–5; Wylie Sypher, 'A Note on the Realism of Mrs Behn's *Oroonoko*', *MLQ* 3 (1942), 401–5; Ruthe Sheefey, 'Some Evidence for a New Source of Aphra Behn's *Oroonoko*', *SP* 59 (1962), 52–63; H. G. Platt, 'Astrea and Celadon: An Untouched Portrait of Aphra Behn', *PMLA* 49 (1934), 544–59; H. A. Hargreaves, 'New Evidence of the Realism of Mrs Behn's *Oroonoko*', *Bulletin of the New York Public Library*, 74 (1970), 437–44; W. J. Cameron, *New Light on Aphra Behn* (Auckland, 1961); Duffy, pp. 32–41, 265–70; Goreau, pp. 55–66.
[34] Link, p. 140.
[35] 'Aphra Behn's Oroonoko: Occasion and Accomplishment', *Two English Novelists*, by G. Guffey and A. Wright (Los Angeles, 1975), 3–41.
[36] Ibid., p. 34.

punished by Byam, and when he is cruelly mutilated and himself killed.

Behn's works reflect the full spectrum of fictional techniques available to the Restoration novelist. Even the *History of the Life and Memoirs of Mrs Behn*, attached to the 1696 and (in a greatly expanded form) 1698 collections of her fiction, once believed to be by Charles Gildon, now appears to be a miscellaneous compilation, containing a great deal of material from her own pen.[37] This memoir contains pages which also draw on the Spanish novella (see pp. 8–13), and the comic mode noted above (see pp. 29–38).[38] Perhaps the one factor which holds many of these works together is Behn's quest for verisimilitude, derived from the *nouvelle*:

> notwithstanding you may find very surprising things in this Story, I can assure you that whatever is contain'd in it is certainly true; and that I have written nothing but what I have found in the Memoirs which were sent to me out of Denmark . . .[39]

Numerous historical novels echo this asseveration—although one occasionally finds an accurate assessment, as in the refreshing preface to *The Prince of Conde*:

> Though in this little piece there are many Historical Circumstances which may make it seem true, yet my design is not so much to delude, as to divert my Reader, and prevent the Error into which he would fall, should he give too much faith to every particular in it.[40]

Mrs Behn makes many ingenious statements about the authenticity of her stories:

> I was my self an Eye-Witness, to a great part of what you will find here set down; and what I cou'd not be Witness of, I receiv'd from the Mouth of the chief Actor in this History . . .[41]

Her contemporaries did not necessarily swallow these devices whole, but were moved by her stories' truth to life, or so we may deduce from the prefaces to some of her posthumous

---

[37] See the excellent discussion by Robert A. Day, 'Aphra Behn's First Biography', *Studies in Bibliography*, 22 (1969), 227–40.

[38] References to *The History of the Life and Memoirs of Mrs Behn*, 'Written by one of the Fair Sex', in *All the Histories and Novels* (1705).

[39] Rousseau de la Valette, *The Life of Count Ulfield* (1695), p. vii.

[40] Edmé Boursault, *The Prince of Conde* (1675), A3ᵛ–A4.

[41] *Oroonoko: Or, The Royal Slave* (1688), p. 2.

publications, written by Samuel Briscoe. What Briscoe praises is
not truth in a strict sense, but verisimilitude:

in none of her Performances has she shew'd so great a Mastery as in her
Novels, where Nature always prevails; and if they are not true, they are
so like it, that they do the business every jot as well.[42]

Behn impressed Briscoe with the truth to nature expressed
through her art:

Others have sought after extraordinary and scarce possible Adventures,
she happily consulted Nature, which will always prevail; so that I may
call her the *Otway* of this kind of writing.[43]

But what is most attractive to the modern reader is her use of
the first-person narrator.[44] Behn's narrators do not distance the
reader from the action, as does the ironic narrator in a number of
Restoration novels influenced by Scarron and the anti-romance
tradition. The dispute over the truth behind *Oroonoko* arises from
this technique: whatever Behn's own position, the narrator of
Oroonoko easily convinces us of her reliability.[45] This particular
narrator seems to speak with Behn's own voice; she is a
playwright who celebrated Captain Martin (a character in
Oroonoko) 'in a Character of my New *Comedy*, by his own Name'.[46]

Behn's narrators usually speak from a feminine point of view,
and may comment satirically on the situation of women: 'Our
words and thoughts can ne'er agree.'[47] Like Defoe, Behn
provides her narrators with circumstantial accounts of how they
came upon the stories they tell:

I was not above Twelve Years old, as near as I can remember, when a
Lady of my Acquaintance, who was particularly concerned in many of
the Passages, very pleasantly Entertained me with the Relation of the
Young Lady *Arabella*'s Adventures.[48]

[42] Preface to *The Unfortunate Bride* (1698), p. 2.
[43] Preface to *The Wandering Beauty* (1698), pp. 1–2.
[44] See the discussion by Helga Drougge, *The Significance of Congreve's 'Incognita'*
(Uppsala, 1976), pp. 23–5, although she overstates its occurrence elsewhere in
seventeenth-century fiction.
[45] Maureen Duffy's biography, although it contains interesting new information, is
marred by a naïve reading of the novels as biographical evidence, see pp. 121–2.
[46] *Oroonoko*, p. 210. George 'Marteen' is the protagonist in *The Younger Brother*,
published posthumously.
[47] *The Unfortunate Bride*, p. 7.
[48] *The Wandering Beauty*, p. 3.

When used in novels like *The Fair Jilt* and *Oroonoko*, the narrator who gains the reader's confidence provides an effective bridge between us and an exotic or tragic story. At times though, however skilful the device, the story is too perfunctory and sensational for us to become involved. *The Dumb Virgin* would provide any novelist with an excellent lesson in the creation of a reliable narrator: she is a close friend of Maria and Belvedeera, and attended with them the ball at which their tragedy began when Cosmo, their missing brother, unknowingly fell in love with Maria. The narrator has heard part of the story from Cosmo, who was brought up in England under the name of Dangerfield: 'he call'd himself *Dangerfield*, which was a name that so pleas'd me, that since satisfied it was a counterfeit, I us'd it in a Comedy of mine.'[49] But despite all this effort, the bloody conclusion to this particular novel leaves the reader cold.

Just as Mary Wroth overturns many romance conventions by writing specifically from a female point of view, Behn infuses Restoration conventions, which were dominated by aggressive masculine attitudes, with a different set of values. Her novels are, as Angeline Goreau notes, 'dominated by female protagonists'.[50] However, to say that Behn's 'single dominant theme in plays, novels, and poetry is human sexuality—its powers and problems', is to turn a common Restoration obsession into a supposed reflection of Behn's situation as a woman.[51] It is in her articulate and passionate female characters that Behn's own position as a woman in the masculine world of letters (following her career in the equally masculine world of espionage) makes itself felt.

III. Two Approaches to the Restoration Novel

Two particular approaches to fiction which have been traced in Behn's novels are even more apparent elsewhere: dramatic comedies were produced along the lines of *The Court of the King of Bantam*, while on the other hand, some tentative essays in a more serious form appeared.

---

[49] *The Dumb Virgin*, in *Histories, Novels and Translations* (1700), p. 76. Dangerfield does not appear in any extant play by Mrs Behn.

[50] Goreau, p. 285.

[51] Judith Gardiner, 'Aphra Behn: Sexuality and Self-Respect', *Women's Studies*, 7, Nos. 1–2 (1980), 68.

i. Alexander Oldys and Restoration Comedy

Alexander Oldys wrote two novels: *The Fair Extravagant* (1682) and *The Female Gallant* (1692).[52] Although *The Female Gallant* was published in 1692, its reference to King James indicates that it was written between 1685 and 1688. In these works, the influence of Restoration comedy is clear: each contains much brisk, realistic dialogue, a contemporary setting, and a certain amount of satire, held together by a tight plot. Naturally, this comparison would be complicated by any detailed account of Restoration comic drama. In his recent book, Robert Hume divides the comic drama into no fewer than eight types, and still stresses the plays as 'kaleidoscopically variable'.[53] But he also notes its 'formulaic' quality, and its reliance on 'stock characters and situations'.[54] Anyone reading these novels will recognize the world of Etherege and Wycherley (which is not to say that we are given the major dramatists' sophisticated view of this world).

The Fair Extravagant has received some attention in Charles Mish's article on short fiction,[55] so *The Female Gallant* will be used here to illustrate Oldys's approach to Restoration comedy. In this novel we are introduced to Philandra, an amorous, beautiful, and deceitful young lady, who is courted by Sir Blunder Slouch, a wealthy '*Norwich* Factor' (p. 7), and two gallant gentlemen, Bellamant and Worthygrace.[56] In courting her, Worthygrace in particular shows his honesty. Although he and Bellamant admire each other, they duel for her hand. When each fancies he has killed the other, the plot speeds up: they go into hiding, and Philandra is informed of their deaths. Bellamant disguises himself as his twin sister Arabella, while Worthygrace, taking refuge in Paris, sends his sister Henrietta, disguised as their brother Horatio, to see Philandra. Worthygrace falls in love with the real Arabella in Paris; Philandra, on being told by Henrietta of her disguise, persuades her to marry the false Arabella as a joke. She in turn dresses as a man to 'seduce' Arabella—whereupon

---

[52] *The Female Gallant* should not be confused with *The London Jilt: Or, The Politick Whore* (1683). Owing to *The Female Gallant*'s alternative title which heads the first page, *The London Jilt: Or, The Female Cuckold*, this misidentification occurs in the Wing *Short Title Catalogue*, and Mish's *Checklist*. It is corrected by Roger Thompson, '*The London Jilt*', *Harvard Library Bulletin*, 23 (1975), 293.

[53] Hume, p. 128; see pp. 63–148.   [54] Ibid., pp. 128, 71.

[55] 'English Short Fiction', pp. 298–9.

[56] References to Alexander Oldys, *The Female Gallant* (1692).

Bellamant reveals himself, and reverses the seduction. When the disguises, after a suitable amount of titillation, are all shed, Bellamant marries Henrietta in earnest and Worthygrace marries Arabella; while the scheming Philandra, her reputation still intact (for Bellamant cleverly pretends to have been disguised as Arabella in Paris all the time, and therefore Philandra is thought to have innocently shared Arabella's bed) marries Sir Blunder.

Here is an intrigue plot worthy of the most elaborate novella; or, if we keep the drama in mind, reminiscent of Sir Samuel Tuke's popular *Adventures of Five Hours* (1663).[57] But within the plot, Oldys presents a considerable amount of witty dialogue, acute characterization, and at times sharp satire. The story is attractively presented through an ironic narrator, not nearly as subtle as the narrator of *Incognita* (who will be discussed below), but still amusing and personal:

Her Unmarried Names (I won't say her *Maiden Names*, though she was his Chambermaid) were *Winny Wagtail*, of the Great and Notorious Family of the *Wagtails* in *Castle-street*, near *Long Acre*, not far from the Square, where, at present, I have an Apartment. (p. 2)

This quotation also demonstrates the use of comic names within real locations. The narrator's wit may be crude at times, but he moves the story along briskly.

Oldys is at his best when he allows characters to reveal themselves through conversation. His use of dialogue is what most recalls the drama. The characters meet in the Mall at St James's Park, in a scene reminiscent of many a Restoration comedy (one might think of the scene at St James's in *The Man of Mode*). Stopwell rushes up to greet Philandra:

My most Honour'd Lady! (cry'd he out loud) and my Divine Mistress Philandra! How happy am I to see your Ladyship so well recover'd in your Health and Beauty, as to adorn this Walk with what it so long has wanted in your absence?—Madam (interrupted Worthygrace) Mr. Stopwell wrongs the Court-Ladies; some of which are really Great Beauties, who frequently do bless this Park. But, pardon me, Madam I beseech you, if I think *you* have done 'em the greater injury, in appearing so much to their disadvantage——'Sdeath!—what Spark's this? (crys *Bellamant* to himself; with a jealous frown and an angry blush) but straight recalling himself (said he to *Worthygrace* aloud) Sir,

the Lady is out o'danger of being Flatter'd; and you may go on at the
same rate, if you please. (p. 45)

Oldys can also produce some sharp satire, not just the general
ridicule directed at old rich dupes like Sir Blunder. He suddenly
reveals a mature stance on the controversy over Catholicism
during James's troubled reign. Bellamant is a Catholic, which
arouses the ire of Philandra's father, although her mother cannot
understand, why that should be a problem:

How, Madam, (cry'd *Slouch* rudely) Why he's a Papish! Ay, he's a
Papish, my Lady! (echo'd the old dry Trunk) What of that? (said the
young Lady of about Forty) Is not King *James* our Sovereign a Papist?
No, no, my Lady (reply'd Threescore and Twelve) he is a Roman
Catholick. That's the same Thing (said she.) You'll pardon me, my
Lady (returned *Gripely*) for every Subject who is that way given, though
he were a Duke, is a Papish; and the King and Queen only are Roman
Catholicks. (p. 16)

Oldys turns his satire on hypocrisy: people who cannot repress
their anti-Papist feelings, but who do not want to sound
treasonous, and so construct an ingenious but blatant double-
standard. Oldys is not being polemical; Bellamant is not nearly as
admirable as Worthygrace, so this is not pure praise of
Catholicism either. Once again, the quotation indicates Oldys's
command of dialogue.

Unfortunately, mature satire appears only intermittently,
although Oldys almost succeeds in turning his attack on
hypocrisy into a consistent theme. Philandra owes some of her
scheming nature to her mother's example. When news arrives of
Worthygrace's and Bellamant's deaths, mother and daughter try
to outdo each other in creating a scene, and Philandra's mother
acts so well that she dies in earnest: 'she had so strain'd her self in
acting her part, that there was not a joynt about her, that did not
most sensibly suffer in this elaborate Scene' (p. 98).

The bewildering array of disguises in the novel enhances the
sense of the characters as actors.[58] Worthygrace is the single
exception; he only appears as himself. The arch-impostor is
Philandra, a true character study who would be worthy of Aphra
Behn's talents. Clever and calculating from a very early age—'At

[58] Norman Holland has a suggestive discussion of disguise in Restoration comedy in
The First Modern Comedies (Cambridge, Mass., 1959), pp. 45–63.

Twelve Years of Age, the Beautiful and Zealous *Philandra* could tell who was the Fairest, who the Strongest, and who the Wisest Man, which I hope she has not yet forgot' (p. 3)—she convinces everyone of her worth until the very end. She tries to play her two suitors off against each other, and almost succeeds. Her energy is not unattractive—and after all, she is the pivot on which the plot turns, as indicated by her final words with Bellamant:

Are not you a False man? (said she) Ay, Madam (reply'd he) but that is because you are a True Woman.—And let me remind you, that you have had the pleasure *to make a Whore of me, and a Cuckold of my Wife.* (p. 155)

ii. Clitie: *Tragicomedy in the Restoration Novel*

Apart from Congreve, who avoided the choice by creating a different kind of balance, one novelist attempted to take a middle road between Behn's tragic novellas and Oldys's broad comedy. In 1688 Richard Blackbourn's *Clitie* appeared, soon after 'The Author's untimely death' (A3), according to the dedication written by Nahum Tate.[59] Blackbourn evidently wrote three other novels, now known only from an entry in the *Term Catalogues*: 'Three Novels in one, viz. The Constant Lovers, The Fruits of Jealousie, and Wit in a Woman. Together with *Sempronia* or The Unfortunate Mother. By R. Blackbourn, Gent.'[60]

Clitie has a tragicomic plot. Clitie, 'esteem'd one of the greatest Ladies of the Kingdom' (p. 1), is courted by Darbelle and Amasis;[61] Darbelle, the worthier man, has a smaller estate. The two rivals duel, and Darbelle kills Amasis. He has time to learn that Clitie loves him, and they exchange professions of faith before he flees to Florence. For six months all is well; although the King will not pardon Darbelle, he and Clitie correspond frequently. But then Prince Lysidor falls in love with Clitie, and wins the support of her treacherous confidante Mariana. After a struggle with his conscience, he eventually enters into Mariana's scheme to convince Clitie that Darbelle is unfaithful. First Mariana withholds his letters; then she pretends to send her

---

[59] I do not think that Blackbourn can be identified as Richard Blackburne, the doctor who wrote the Latin life of Thomas Hobbes; see *DNB*, Blackburne, Richard.
[60] *Term Catalogues*, ed. E. Arber (London, 1905), II.223.
[61] References to Richard Blackbourn, *Clitie* (1688).

brother after Darbelle, and has him report that Darbelle is
married. When Clitie, her faith shattered, admits she has at least
some feeling for Lysidor, he and Mariana convince everyone that
Darbelle is dead.

Clitie finally agrees to marry Lysidor. Ignorant of the reason
for her silence, Darbelle returns secretly to Paris and learns what
has occurred. He confronts Clitie, and the truth is gradually
revealed. Lysidor, when Mariana (still unsuspected by Clitie)
tells him of Darbelle's return, attempts to kill him, but dies in the
attempt, and Mariana's brother, wounded in the same encounter, confesses the whole scheme. Mariana also confesses and
takes poison. Clitie's father persuades the King to pardon
Darbelle, and we anticipate their marriage.

This plot is reminiscent of the structure of La Fayette's novels,
particularly in the first two parts; the third part is not so
successful, and sacrifices the delicacy of the earlier parts to
melodrama, both in speech and action. Perhaps Blackbourn lost
his nerve, or perhaps he did not even write the final part, which is
headed 'The third and last Part, being an Addition to the two
first Parts' (p. 153). Blackbourn does not use a London setting,
and *Clitie* contains no comic wit in the manner of Oldys. His
plain, elegant style is at times close to Congreve's, although the
novel is not presented through a detached narrator.

As the title indicates, Clitie herself is the centre of attention.
Initially, nothing seems to stand in her way. She has an
understanding father who, although he prefers Amasis' suit,
would never force her to marry against her inclinations. She is
faithful to Darbelle, but is also susceptible to Lysidor, through
her great sympathy for all those around her:

Clitie, (whose Heart was not made of Adamant) was capable enough of
the tender Impression of Love, and cou'd no longer defend it self from
pitying this unfortunate, whom she had made so miserable. (p. 47)

She marries Lysidor partly out of this sympathy, partly in a
desperate attempt to erase the memory of Darbelle:

she had never taken this Resolution, but thereby to free her self wholly
from *Darbelle*, who she cou'd never banish from her Thought, how
unconstant soever she believ'd him. (p. 105)

In this attempt, Clitie almost succeeds: 'Never did two Lovers
seem more contented, they were swallow'd up in Delights, and

felt a reciprocal kindness; they gave mutual Caresses even in publick . . . ' (p. 107). Blackbourn has been carefully building towards Darbelle's return. Its dramatic potential is exploited to the full in two excellent scenes. Darbelle, on learning of Clitie's marriage, dresses as a ghost in order to attend a masquerade, and there he confronts her:

He took a Seat near to *Clitie*'s, and for a long time he fix'd his Eyes on her, without speaking a word, which she soon took notice of. But since Masquerades were design'd only for Adventures, she imagin'd this some Frolick that some Friend of hers had undertaken, and that she shou'd know the meaning of it the next day. (p. 124)

After a tense conversation, Darbelle, still unknown to her, arranges to meet her again 'at the Theatre in the Second Box' (p. 140).

At this second meeting Darbelle's friend La Rock confronts Clitie, and prepares for the coming revelation on a very mundane note, heightening our suspense:

Madame (says he) I believe you will think the time long (if you are not endued with a great deal of Patience) before you hear the Musick, or have any Diversion, which never begins so early. (p. 142)

The 'diversion' of meeting Darbelle face to face leaves Clitie in a state of confusion and panic:

She enter'd into a deep musing, so that she seem'd immoveable; she lean'd against one of the sides of the Theatre, ruminating of a thousand things one after another, and knew not what she shou'd believe. (p. 146)

When the crowds begin to press into the theatre, she departs in great agitation. The theatre is a most appropriate setting for this scene, and is vividly presented. The crowds scare Clitie because Lysidor will be present—a potential spectator of the play of passion in which she has just acted.

The third part of the novel unfortunately turns from concise, dramatic scenes to rather inflated speeches, which do not convince us of the characters' emotions nearly so well. But Blackbourn (or whoever else wrote the final part) does retain his delicacy at the very end. We are not presented with the triumphant wedding of Clitie and Darbelle, merely with their happy reunion under the King's blessing. We assume that the wedding will follow, but after the preceding near-tragedy, it is fitting that the wedding should occur off-stage.

Clitie is perhaps the closest English novel to *La Princesse de Montpensier* and *La Princesse de Clèves* written at this time. Unfortunately the Restoration novel split into an appealing but too often superficial comedy, and an attempt at a serious style which frequently slips into fustian effects. *Clitie* is, like some of Behn's novels, saved by its convincing approach to characterization, and its use of dramatic scenes. One might hope that a writer of Congreve's talent would have seized on this division and closed it, but he chose a different alternative.

IV. *Incognita*: the Elegant Balance

When Congreve wrote *Incognita*, he decided to 'imitate Dramatick Writing . . . in the Design, Contexture and Result of the Plot' (p. 33). We have already seen that he was not as original in this as he claimed to be. Even more important is the fact that he chose to ignore a good many of the new techniques of the Restoration novel discussed above. While he shares (and surpasses) Oldys's use of a witty, self-conscious narrator, he does not set his novel in the milieu of the Restoration comedy. Instead, he uses the novella plot, with its surprising turns and contrivances— its attention to action—in a novella setting: a rather stock Italy.[62] Nor is he interested in the tragedy attempted by Behn, or even the tragicomedy of *Clitie*.

Congreve was attracted by the poise a man of true wit might achieve through the use of a witty, detached, but indulgent narrator, who recounts a cleverly contrived story. It is the 'Unity of Contrivance' which Congreve wishes the reader to recognize and admire—so he tells us in the preface. The precedents for this approach have recently been pointed out by Helga Drougge;[63] the translations (virtually adaptations) of Spanish novellas by Scarron were popular examples, and Congreve owned two editions of *Le Roman Comique* (1655 and 1695).[64] Scarron's

---

[62] Even if he did base some of his descriptions on a travel book; see E. S. de Beer, 'Congreve's *Incognita*: The Source of Its Setting', *RES* 8 (1932), 74–6.

[63] Drougge, pp. 36–40.

[64] John C. Hodges, *The Library of William Congreve* (New York, 1955), items 569, 570. Scarron's novels were frequently translated: see J. E. Tucker, 'The Earliest English Translations of Scarron's Nouvelles', *Revue de littérature comparée*, 24 (1950), 557–63.

'novels' play a prominent part in *The Old Batchelour* (1693, first draft 1689?), when Bellmour carries a copy instead of a prayer-book during his masquerade as Spintext. Fondlewife discovers the deception, significantly lighting upon 'The Innocent Adultery' when he opens the book (IV. iv. 107). Scarron presents the Spanish novellas through the voice of a narrator who is less subtle than Congreve's, but who does comment ironically on the story:

A Gentleman of *Granada*, whose true name I shall forbear to discover, and on whom I will bestow that of *Don Pedro* of *Casteel*, *Aragon*, and *Toledo*, or what you please, since that a glorious name in a *Romance* costs no more than another, (which is haply the reason that the *Spaniards*, not content with their own, ever give themselves of the most illustrious . . .[65]

The use of the ironic, detached narrator occurs in various other novels of this period.[66] Charles Mish aptly describes this narrative technique as 'more sophisticated than any other of its period',[67] and two brief, well-written examples, Joseph Kepple's *The Maiden-Head Lost by Moonlight* (1672) and Walter Charleton's *The Cimmerian Matron* (1668), may be examined in Mish's anthology of Restoration fiction.[68] These stories are both, like the novels of Scarron, based on translations (in this case, both from Erycius Puteanus). Using a witty narrator to add spice to an otherwise cliché-ridden story is relatively easy; and such a narrator's comments may mock the devices used by a novelist like Aphra Behn to achieve verisimilitude.[69] This broad type of parody is evident in the style of René Le Pays's *The Drudge* (1673):

A Cousin of *Zelotide*'s, we called her *Cleonice* in the beginning of this History, was to marry one of her sisters (but truly, Sir, I could never learn what they called her, though I used all possible means to find it out) to a very near kinsman of *Cephisa*'s (but faith, I cannot tell who he was neither). (p. 74)

Such parody may, however, in skilful hands become a device which brings the reader closer to the story. Mish notes the tiny

[65] *Scarrons Novels*, translated by John Davies (1665), p. 1.
[66] See Drougge, pp. 15–20.
[67] Mish, introduction to *Restoration Prose Fiction*, p. x.
[68] Ibid., pp. 163–84; 143–61.   [69] See Drougge, pp. 28–36.

'novels' written by Peter Motteux for *The Gentleman's Journal*
(1692–4), where 'We seem to be listening to an urbane, slightly
cynical, and knowing gentleman telling a story to equally urbane
listeners.'[70]

It is instructive to remember the much earlier use of a
sophisticated narrator commenting on a love story in Gascoigne's
The Adventures of Master F.J. (see above, Chap. 3). Of course
Gascoigne's work was not reprinted in the seventeenth century,
but readers had access to at least half of Sidney's *Old Arcadia*, in
the composite version available throughout the century. Sidney's
narrator is never as consistently ironic as a Restoration narrator,
but he is often digressive, and may at times display a detached
humour. However, this humour is not so apparent if one does not
read the complete *Old Arcadia*, where the narrator is most
obtrusive in the first three books.

While Congreve has many precedents for his use of an ironic
narrator, he also has a number of choices to make. Detachment
and parody, or the intimacy of, for example, John Dunton's
rambler-narrator in *A Voyage Round the World*, which appeared a
year before *Incognita*?[71] *Incognita* is neither cynical and completely
detached, nor is it overly confidential and formless in the manner
of Dunton. Critics attempting to define Congreve's tone have
tended to make a firm choice, while *Incognita* is in fact located
somewhere between the relatively straight-faced narrative described by Aubrey Williams and I. M. Westcott, and the
bewilderingly parodic narrative described by Helga Drougge.[72]
While allowing for much more authorial detachment than
Westcott does, the following analysis begins from her premiss that
'The effect [of the narrative] is a union of moral seriousness and
delicate raillery.'[73]

Incognita is a very tightly-plotted novella—a popular form, as
the editions of Scarron and other collections indicate.[74] Aphra

---

[70] 'English Short Fiction', p. 298.
[71] Dunton constantly describes himself as a 'Rambler', see the full title of *A Voyage
Round the World*.
[72] Aubrey Williams, 'Congreve's *Incognita* and the Contrivances of Providence' in
M. Mack, ed., *Imagined Worlds* (London, 1968), 3–18; I. M. Westcott, 'The Role of the
Narrator in Congreve's *Incognita*', *Trivium*, 11 (1976), 40–8; Drougge, pp. 74–89.
[73] Westcott, p. 42.
[74] Among other collections available were *Choice Novels and Amorous Tales* (1652), and
The Spanish Decameron (1686).

Behn's *The Lucky Mistake* (1689) is a good example, in which she avoids, for a change, the darker tragic story. In *The Lucky Mistake*, as in *Incognita*, two couples pass through a series of obstacles before they are able to marry happily and according to their choice: 'all thought themselves happy in this double Union.'[75] *Incognita* presents just such a story, told in a manner that allows us to enjoy its twists and turns, while the narrator also entertains us with comments which recognize just how conventional many of the events are. This is not to say that Congreve asks us to see his story as a complete parody.[76] We should heed his prefatory remarks:

The design of the Novel is obvious, after the first meeting of Aurelian and Hippolito with Incognita and Leonora, and the difficulty is in bringing it to pass, maugre all apparent obstacles, within the compass of two days. (p. 33)

We know, when we go to see a Restoration comedy, that, for example, Mirabel and Millamant will ultimately marry—the question is, how will the expected end be achieved?

The careful coincidences, the 'design' and 'contrivances' of the plot, have been discussed at length by Aubrey Williams.[77] But to see these as the work of Providence, 'justifications of the ways of God to Man', is to take an over-symbolic and heavy-handed approach, especially as this argument could be applied to any such tightly constructed dramatic plot.[78] Any carefully-plotted novel lures the reader on, anxious to see how the clever manipulation can be kept up, how the puzzle will be solved, the pattern clarified. At the same time, the narrator of *Incognita* also holds us back—at least until the very end. If we share the narrator's sophistication, we may smile at our own impatience:

Now the Reader I suppose to be upon Thorns at this and the like impertinent Digressions, but let him alone and he'll come to himself; at which time I think fit to acquaint him, that when I digress, I am at that time writing to please my self, when I continue the Thread of the Story, I write to please him; supposing him a reasonable Man, I conclude him satisfied to allow me this liberty, and so I proceed. (p. 39)

---

[75] *The Lucky Mistake* (1689), in *All the Histories and Novels* (1705), p. 399.
[76] See Drougge's over-ingenious explanation, pp. 62–73.
[77] Williams, *passim*.
[78] Ibid., p. 17.

By addressing the 'Reader' in the third person, the narrator allows us to take up his sophisticated position: we are invited to 'let him alone', that is, to let the more naive reader alone. With this preparation, the reader who cavils at a later date will receive short shrift:

> I could find in my Heart to beg the Reader's Pardon for this Digression, if I thought he would be sensible of the Civility; for I promise him, I do not intend to do it again throughout the Story, though I make never so many, and though he take them never so ill. (p. 62)

However, the narrator is not completely impervious to the allure of the plot (and so we may assume that the reader too is expected to share his balance of detachment and concern). When the plot is 'wound up' with the arrival of Don Mario, his daughter Leonora, and her lover Hippolito at Aurelian's lodgings, where Aurelian will discover that Incognita is none other than his destined bride Juliana, the style becomes much less poised than before. The two penultimate paragraphs contain a number of long and quite breathless sentences (one of 144 words, p. 84). The action is very rapid (perhaps a parallel to the speeded-up action of the last act of *The Way of the World*) and, most significantly, the narrator's comments are absent. Having ensured that we are not too involved, the narrator allows us to enjoy the excitement of the denouement.

The poise of the narrator is most important in relation to sentiment, and to our attitude towards the characters and their situation. Congreve is not writing an anti-romance; he is not consistently parodying the conventions of love. On the other hand, he recognizes how conventional they are. The vision is that of an older, wiser man, regarding the antics of young lovers with wry indulgence. Some of their actions are amusing, but they are also touching. The poise is there from the opening paragraph describing Aurelian's relationship with his father:

> Aurelian was the only Son to a Principal Gentleman of Florence. The Indulgence of his Father prompted, and his Wealth enabled him, to bestow a generous Education upon him, whom, he now began to look upon as the Type of himself; an Impression he had made in the Gayety and Vigour of his Youth, before the Rust of Age had debilitated and obscur'd the Splendour of the Original: He was sensible, That he ought not to be sparing in the Adornment of him, if he had a Resolution to

beautifie his own Memory. Indeed Don Fabio (for so was the Old
Gentleman call'd) has been observ'd to have fix'd his Eyes upon
Aurelian, when much Company has been at Table, and have wept
through Earnestness of Intention, if nothing hapened to divert the
Object; whether it were for regret, at the Recollection of his former self,
or for the Joy he conceiv'd in being, as it were, reviv'd in the Person of
his Son, I never took upon me to enquire, but suppos'd it might be
sometimes one, and sometimes both together. (p. 35)

This is an urbane view: a paradigm of the narrator's, and the
responsive reader's, over-all position. Don Fabio's emotions are a
mixture of egoism and genuine involvement, while the humorous
'Rust of Age' holds him away from us, in a faintly amusing pose.

Aurelian and Hippolito are more sympathetic than the older
generation, but they have the foibles of youth. They are
attractive, but we must not take them too seriously—a point
made by our wry introduction to Aurelian: 'Aurelian, at the Age
of Eighteen Years, wanted nothing (but a Beard) that the most
accomplished Cavalier in Florence could pretend to' (p. 35).
The two friends exist in a sophisticated narrative. The Florentine
'love of Musick' may have been taken from a travel book,[79] but
this detail turns to mockery of the conventional serenade:

Here you should have an affected Vallet, who Mimick'd the Behaviour
of his Master, leaning carelessly against the Window, with his Head on
one side, in a languishing Posture, whining, in a low, mournful Voice,
some dismal Complaint . . . (p. 38)

Incognita is a novel conscious that it relies on novella conventions,
and able to smile at them. If Aurelian and Hippolito posture in
this way, they are gently mocked. So Hippolito gives rise to a
smile when he is prevented from 'Rhyming' when he sees
Leonora, thereby saving us from 'a small desert of Numbers to
have pick'd and Criticiz'd upon' (p. 78).

Aurelian's first meeting with Incognita at a grand Masque
establishes our interest in him, as well as our amusement. It is
here that Congreve's style becomes vital. He already displays the
light touch, the flexible elegance, which is a feature of his
comedies. James Sutherland aptly describes this as 'a cooler and
more consciously sophisticated affectation in the manner.'[80] We

[79] De Beer, pp. 65–6.
[80] James Sutherland, *English Literature of the Late Seventeenth Century* (Oxford, 1969),
p. 146.

find it, although at a less mature stage, in the conversation between Aurelian and Incognita, which is a most delicate exchange of compliments. They discuss the relationship between dress and character, Incognita astutely noting:

there is your brisk fool as well as your brisk man of sense, and so of the melancholick. I confess 'tis possible a fool may reveal himself by his Dress . . . but a decency of Habit (which is all that Men of best sense pretend to) may be acquired by custom and example . . . (pp. 41–2)

Aurelian shows a ready, endearing wit: ' "Look ye there" (says he), pointing to a Lady who stood playing with the Tassels of her Girdle, "I dare answer for that Lady, though she be very well dress'd, 'tis more than she knows" ' (p. 42). Aurelian's compliments almost go too far: 'Aurelian had a little over-strain'd himself in that Complement, and I am of Opinion would have been puzzl'd to have brought himself off readily' (p. 43). The facility of Congreve's style has lent this conversation a charm which moves the reader in Aurelian's favour.

From this point on, we share the narrator's mixture of amusement and affection. He will not become enamoured, as Aurelian has:

I should by right now describe her Dress, which was extreamly agreeable and rich, but 'tis possible I might err in some material Pin or other, in the sticking of which may be the whole grace of the Drapery depended. (pp. 43–4)

However, the truth of Aurelian's love is also emphasized:

our Friend Aurelian had by this time danced himself into a Net which he neither could, nor which is worse desired to untangle.
His soul was charm'd to the movement of her Body . . . (p. 49)

This is a love affair which begins with a deception. The careful plot turns on such deceptions: Aurelian and Hippolito pretend to be each other after Hippolito has donned Lorenzo's costume to attend the Masque; Juliana maintains her disguise as Incognita. But a sense of the plot as a game predominates—at the end 'it was the Subject of a great deal of Mirth to hear Juliana relate the several Contrivances which she had to avoid Aurelian for the sake of Hippolito' (p. 86). 'The design of the Novel is obvious' (p. 33); so the basic emotional situation is serious: 'Aurelian, who was *really* in Love' (p. 51, my emphasis). Upon this serious base, the game is played, the narrator's wit displayed.

When Aurelian is allowed to see Incognita's face:

Aurelian (from whom I had every tittle of her Description) fancy'd he saw a little Nest of Cupids break from the Tresses of her Hair, and every one officiously betake himself to his task. Some fann'd with their downy Wings, her glowing Cheeks; while others brush'd the balmy Dew from off her Face, leaving alone a heavenly Moisture blubbing on her Lips, on which they drank and revell'd for their pains; Nay, so particular were their allotments in her service, that Aurelian was very positive a young Cupid who was but just Pen-feather'd, employ'd his naked Quills to pick her Teeth. And a thousand other things his transport represented to him, which none but Lovers who have experience of such Visions will believe. (p. 52)[81]

The smiling asseveration of fact leads to Aurelian's vision. It does have a certain charm, but the narrator's voice, still smiling, intrudes: 'fancy'd', 'blubbing', the cupid picking her teeth. This is Aurelian's 'transport', from which he 'awaked' (p. 52)—it is neither rejected nor embraced by the narrator, but simply put in context. It is important for us to believe in Aurelian's love, but also to see its youthful, amusing extravagance. For this extravagance leads to the contrivances of the plot, by impelling all the lovers to keep up their several disguises.

The same attitude prevails when the two friends discuss the state of being in love, after Hippolito almost kills Aurelian by mistake in the dark. Hippolito

passionately taking Aurelian by the Hand, cry'd, Ah! my Friend, Love is indeed blind, when it would not suffer me to see you—There arose another Sigh; a Sympathy seiz'd Aurelian immediately: (For, by the Way, Sighing is as catching among Lovers, as yawning among the Vulgar.) Beside hearing the Name of Love, made him fetch such a Sigh, that Hippolito's were but Fly-blows in Comparison . . . (pp. 55–6)

When Hippolito pens a perfect, elegant love-letter to Leonora, Leonora's doubts about falling in love with a man intended for Juliana (Hippolito is, of course, pretending to be Aurelian) are

---

[81] This passage is examined as a serious comment by Westcott, pp. 43–4; Irène Simon compares it with descriptions of Lyly's Campaspe and Pope's Belinda in her 'Early Theories of Prose Fiction: Congreve and Fielding', in Mack, *Imagined Worlds*, p. 22.

quickly overcome, leading to a series of speculations by the narrator:

I could never get any Body to give me a satisfactory reason, for her suddain and dextrous Change of Opinion just at that stop, which made me conclude she could not help it. (pp. 60–1)

Possible dissatisfaction with the convention by which Leonora's heart is conquered is adroitly turned aside by a piece of witty comment which, for once, does border on cynicism:

I would not have the Reader now be impertinent, and look upon this to be force, or a whim of the Author's, that a Woman should proceed so far in her Approbation of a Man whom she never saw, that it is impossible, therefore ridiculous to suppose it. Let me tell such a Critick, that he knows nothing of the Sex, if he does not know that a Woman may be taken with the Character and Description of a Man, when general and extraordinary, that she may be prepossess'd with an agreeable Idea of his Person and Conversation; and though she cannot imagine his real Features, or manner of Wit, yet she has a general Notion of what is call'd a fine Gentleman, and is prepar'd to like such a one who does not disagree with that Character. (p. 61)

This is virtually the only example of such cynicism (closer to the tone of Motteux). If the modern reader regrets that Congreve did not follow the example of the vivid Restoration setting seen in the work of Behn and Oldys, he must also recognize that the sophisticated tone of *Incognita* depends upon the tension between the novella form and the narrator's voice.

Incognita's design produces the effect of watching a play. The theatre is perhaps the best vehicle for this balance between involvement and detachment—Congreve wrote no more novels. There are times when a delicate touch by the narrator pulls the reader back into the story, at least as much as it raises an eyebrow at the actors. For example, at the end of the scene with Leonora, 'several Ladies of her acquaintance came to accompany her to the place design'd for the Tilting, where we will leave them drinking Chocolate till 'tis time for them to go' (p. 62). Here we have a sudden, though still humorous, glimpse of an ongoing reality. On the other hand, after a passionate speech from Aurelian, the narrator 'places' him with a much more broadly humorous image: Aurelian 'stood mute and insensible like an

Alarum Clock, that had spent all its force in one violent Emotion' (p. 68).

As noted above, the narrator does withdraw from the last hurried pages, as the denouement takes over. But the final paragraph leaves us with another recognition of the pleasing artifice which has been so aware of its own construction:

they all thought it proper to attend upon the Great Duke that Morning at the Palace, and to acquaint him with the Novelty of what had pass'd; while, by the way, the two Young Couple entertained the Company with the Relation of several Particulars of their Three Days Adventures. (p. 86)

We are pleased by the neat plot, but also by the happiness of 'Our Two Cavalier-Lovers' (p. 67). The balance has not yet attained the maturity of Congreve's major plays, with their serious purpose, aptly described by Maximillian Novak: 'Congreve's vision is his suggestion of the possibility of genuine love and a good marriage between a few convincingly sensitive and witty couples in a world of fools and knaves.'[82] *Incognita* balances the sophisticated man's detachment with the appeal of a naïve but true love; the appeal of a pattern with the knowledge of its artificiality. At one point, Hippolito is characterized as having 'a Heart full of Love, and a Head full of Stratagem' (p. 48); this is a most appropriate description of *Incognita* itself.

---

[82] Maximillian Novak, 'Love, Scandal, and the Moral Milieu of Congreve's Comedies', in *Congreve Considered*, ed. H. T. Swedenberg (Los Angeles, 1971), p. 43.

Chapter 18

Conclusion

I. Fiction After 1700

In the preface to her scandal chronicle *The Secret History of Queen Zarah* (1705), Mrs Manley looks back at the changes in fiction outlined in the previous chapter, and concludes that 'The Little Histories of this kind have taken [the] Place of Romances.'[1] But the romance tradition died hard, even if it became unfashionable. In 1715 Jane Barker published *Exilius: Or, The Banished Roman: A New Romance*, and provided a spirited defence of the romance form (on moral grounds) in her preface. However, it was Mrs Manley who captured the attention of early eighteenth-century readers, particularly with her *New Atalantis* (1709): 'all London read it when it first appeared.'[2]

Mrs Manley's successful scandal chronicles draw on the Restoration form discussed in the previous chapter. However, a significant change in the nature of prose fiction did occur in the early eighteenth century. John Richetti has undertaken an analysis of the fiction written between 1700 and 1739, tracing social and 'mythological' patterns, particularly the motif of the 'persecuted maiden' and a 'secular-religious antithesis.'[3] He sums up this period as exhibiting an 'accommodation of fiction to popular taste.'[4] The reading public at this time rejected the sophisticated fiction of the previous century—both the Restoration novel and the now old-fashioned heroic romance—in favour of much simpler forms. Richetti notes that

the 'shift' begins as an attempt to serve the needs of an expanding literate public possessed of severely limited capacities, a public which required the plain style and simple event because ornate style, intricate

---

[1] Sig. A2.
[2] John J. Richetti, *Popular Fiction Before Richardson* (Oxford, 1969), p. 122 and see Chap. 4.
[3] Ibid., pp. 264 and 263.   [4] Ibid., p. 179.

plot, and psychological complication were beyond its comprehension and appreciation.[5]

The reading public for popular fiction had, as we have seen, been growing during the previous century, but a sophisticated readership for fiction also flourished, providing a market for Sidney, the heroic romance, the political/allegorical romance, and the Restoration novel. One might generalize and say that the aristocratic audience was lost in the early eighteenth century, a disappearance best symbolized by Mrs Stanley's 'modernization' of the *Arcadia* in the same year as the penultimate edition of the *Arcadia* in the eighteenth century (see above Chap. 10, Sec. III). The novels of Defoe, Richardson, Fielding, and Sterne still have their roots in earlier forms of fiction, but the general mass of fiction from 1700 to 1739 is written for an audience with simple tastes, and sophisticated readers rejected it altogether, as Mrs Manley's work was deplored by Pope and Swift.[6]

The novels of Defoe, Richardson, and Fielding are all so different that the three authors appear to be producing works which virtually belong to separate genres. These 'early novelists' are working within three distinct traditions of prose fiction. Defoe's novels have, in recent years, been associated with the development of the spiritual autobiography.[7] We have seen how a long picaresque tradition is also relevant to Defoe's fiction, and may even help to explain some aspects of his work which have been the centre of critical debate, such as the moral ambiguity of his depiction of rogues.

The work of Richardson represents the most dramatically 'new' development in fiction in the eighteenth century, although even his work has been placed by Robert Day in the context of previous epistolary fiction.[8] Ian Watt has carefully examined Richardson's depiction of the minutiae of private life, the trivial details of an individual existence, which tell us more about the day-to-day lives of his characters than any previous work of fiction.[9] This was to have important consequences for the future

---

[5] Ibid., p. 127.   [6] Ibid., p. 122.

[7] See G. A. Starr, *Defoe and Spiritual Autobiography* (Princeton, 1965).

[8] Robert A. Day, *Told in Letters: Epistolary Fiction Before Richardson* (Ann Arbor, 1966).

[9] Ian Watt, *The Rise of the Novel* (London, 1957), Chap. 6; Lennard J. Davis's recent book, *Factual Fictions* (New York, 1983), searches for the origins of the novel not in the fiction which preceded it, but in what he terms the 'news/novel' discourse. Davis's work

development of the novel. Yet even Richardson's new fiction acknowledges some debt to the past, seen notably in *Pamela*, which uses (ironically) the name of one of Sidney's princesses, and which seems to have been influenced by a Restoration novel entitled *Vertue Rewarded*.[10]

Fielding's work stands in a very interesting relationship to earlier fiction. Arthur Cooke has traced Fielding's theory of fiction back to the heroic romance.[11] Fielding's notion of the epic derives from the heroic romance, although we have seen that epic structure in romance may be traced back further still. Henry Knight Miller has placed *Tom Jones* in the romance tradition, but the links which he points out are not always convincing, because his view of romance makes no distinction between very disparate modes, viewing such dissimilar works as *Amadis*, the *Arcadia*, and *Euphues* as if they all belonged to the same form.[12] The outmoded chivalric romance has little in common with Fielding's fiction. Although he is concerned with *Joseph Andrews* rather than *Tom Jones*, Homer Goldberg's discussion of the influence of Cervantes and Scarron, as well as Le Sage and Marivaux, on Fielding offers a more useful explanation for what seems to be new about Fielding's fiction, for what distinguishes it from the romance form which provided a theory for the comic epic.[13] Fielding may be said to have combined heroic romance

---

appeared while this book was going through the press, and I cannot do justice to his complex argument in this brief note. The traditions of fiction outlined here, largely ignored by Davis, implicitly question his argument, as they do that of Ian Watt, but Davis's use of a methodology derived from the work of Michel Foucault gives his explanation of the novel's 'appearance' a much more sophisticated basis than that of Watt. This methodology leads Davis to a careful examination of ballads, newspapers and even legal argument to determine a change in the perception of fact/fiction, news/novel. The influence of Foucault can also be seen in a recent book on Nashe by Jonathan Crewe, *Unredeemed Rhetoric* (Baltimore, 1982), although the section on *The Unfortunate Traveller* is disappointing (pp. 67–87). It seems likely that the application of Foucault's ideas to Renaissance prose fiction (and Renaissance literature in general) will be a matter of considerable interest and controversy in the next few years—see also Robert Weimann, 'Appropriation and Modern History in Renaissance Prose Narrative', *New Literary History* 14 (1983), 459–95.

[10] See my '*Vertue Rewarded* and *Pamela*', *N&Q*, New Series, 26 (1979), 554–6.
[11] Arthur L. Cooke, 'Henry Fielding and the Writers of Heroic Romances', *PMLA* 62 (1947), 984–94, *passim*.
[12] Henry Knight Miller, *Henry Fielding's Tom Jones and the Romance Tradition* (University of Victoria, British Columbia, 1976).
[13] Homer Goldberg, *The Art of Joseph Andrews* (Chicago, 1969), pp. 27–72.

theory with anti-romance practice (as exemplified in Scarron and Cervantes).

The 'simplification or vulgarization' of the romance at the beginning of the eighteenth century, analysed by John Richetti, was accompanied by a general rejection by the Augustans of the earlier romance forms.[14] Later in the century interest in earlier romance forms revived, spurred on by the antiquarian interests of Percy, Beattie and Warton.[15] Clara Reeve's *The Progress of Romance* (1785) was an attempt to clarify the confusion which had set in as far as romance was concerned: 'No writings are more different than the ancient *Romance*, and modern *Novel*, yet they are frequently confounded together, and mistaken for each other.'[16] Clara Reeve herself translated John Barclay's *Argenis*, and this somewhat abridged translation was published in 1772 as *The Phoenix*. The influence which this rediscovery of romance had on the gothic novel—Reeve was also the author of *The Champion of Virtue* or *The Old English Baron* (1777)—is a suggestive topic which would justify further investigation.[17] The rediscovery of romance fired the enthusiasm of the Romantic poets. Southey admired the older, chivalric romances, and translated *Amadis*, as well as editing Munday's translation of *Palmerin*: 'you know my great attachment to the old romances'.[18] And Coleridge, having borrowed Southey's copy of *Argenis*, wrote:

It absolutely distresses me when I reflect that this great work, admired as it has been by great men of all ages, and lately, I hear, by the poet Cowper, should be only not unknown [*sic*] to general readers.[19]

However, the Victorian novel drove early fiction from the marketplace, and even from the attention of scholars. Despite the appearance of an appreciative, if insubstantial, book like J. J. Jusserand's *The English Novel in the Time of Shakespeare* (1890), this

---

[14] Richetti, p. 172.

[15] See Arthur Johnston, *Enchanted Ground: The Study of Medieval Romance in the Eighteenth Century* (London, 1964).

[16] Clara Reeve, *The Progress of Romance* (1785) (Facsimile Text Society, New York, 1930), Vol. 1, p. 7.

[17] See Gillian Beer, *The Romance* (London, 1970), pp. 55–8.

[18] *New Letters of Robert Southey*, ed. Kenneth Curry (New York, 1965), Vol. 1, p. 147, letter to C. W. Williams Wynn, 1797.

[19] 'Notes on Barclay's Argenis', *Remains*, ed. Henry N. Coleridge (London, 1836), Vol. 1, p. 256.

neglect continued into the present century. Interest in Elizabethan fiction increased only a decade or two ago, and the seventeenth century has remained largely hidden from sight.

II. Early Theories of Prose Fiction

Despite its strength as a literary form flexible enough to cater for a very wide range of readers, prose fiction sparked off very little critical debate or theorizing during the 150 years discussed in this book. Detailed comments on particular works are rare—we can draw on only a few examples, such as scattered comments on the *Arcadia*, or Dorothy Osborne's comments on heroic romances. On the whole, fiction was accorded silent appreciation—a situation true of other genres as well.

Most of the comments made by the Elizabethans about fiction are to be found in prefaces to individual works. Some echo Sidney's notion that the purpose of poetry (which of course may include prose fiction in Sidney's definition) is to 'teach and delight'.[20] However, a surprising number of authors state that their main aim is simply 'delight', both authors of popular works, such as Emanuel Forde who announces in the preface to *Parismenos* (1599) 'My intent was to please' (A4), and authors of courtly works, such as Lyly who states in the preface to *Euphues and His England*, 'I would you woulde read bookes that have more shewe of pleasure, then ground of profit.'[21]

The majority of remarks made in prefaces and elsewhere concern style, but they are generally asides—professions of a 'low' style, or of a 'simple' style, often contradicted by the actual work. For sophisticated writers, there was much of interest on the question of style in the rhetorical handbooks. George Puttenham, in *The Arte of English Poesie*, states that 'Stile is a constant and continual phrase or tenour of speaking and writing';[22] it is not merely decoration, it 'should delight and allure as well the mynde as the eare of the hearers'.[23] Puttenham devotes a lengthy chapter to the concept of decorum, following classical rhetorical

[20] *Miscellaneous Prose of Sir Philip Sidney*, ed. Katherine Duncan-Jones and Jan Van Dorsten (Oxford, 1973), p. 80.
[21] *Complete Works of John Lyly*, ed. R. W. Bond (Oxford, 1967), Vol. 2, pp. 9–10.
[22] George Puttenham, *The Arte of English Poesie*, ed. B. Hathaway (Ohio, 1970), p. 160.
[23] Ibid., p. 149.

precepts, such as the need to fit the three basic styles, 'high, meane, and base', to their appropriate subjects: 'to have the Stile decent and comely it behooueth the maker or Poet to follow the nature of his subiect.'[24] It is this notion of decorum that lies behind the major Elizabethan debates over style. Euphuism provoked a number of statements about appropriate stylistic devices, which mostly centred on Lyly's extensive use of exempla from natural history. Puttenham warns against the excessive use of antithesis, parison, and tautologia (alliteration),[25] and the imitations spawned by Lyly's style are deplored by Campion: 'that absurd following of the letter amongst our English so much of late affected, but now hist out of Paules Churchyard'.[26]   Sidney's   Astrophil   notes   the   'daintie wits . . . [who] with strange similies enrich each line,/Of herbes or beastes, which *Inde* or *Afrike* hold'.[27] But Lyly did have his supporters, particularly in the years immediately following the appearance of *Euphues*; William Webbe, for example, praised him in *A Discourse of English Poetrie*:

Master Iohn Lilly hath deserued moste high commendations, as he which hath stept one steppe further therein than any either before or since he first began the wyttie discourse of his Euphues . . . let the learned examine and make tryall there of thorough all the partes of Rethoricke, in fitte phrases, in pithy sentences, in gallant tropes, in flowering speeche, in plain sence.[28]

The argument between Nashe and Harvey is mostly concerned with decorum, with a fitting style, free from 'ink-horn' terms. Throughout this possibly trumped-up contest, Nashe asserted the individuality of his style:

Is my stile like Greene, or my ieasts like Tarltons? Do I talke of any counterfeit birds, or hearbs, or stones . . . the vaine which I haue (be it a median vaine, or a madde man) is of my owne begetting, and cals no man father in England but my selfe, neyther Euphues nor Tarlton, nor Greene.[29]

---

[24] Ibid., p. 161.   [25] Ibid., pp. 219–20, 222–3, 261.
[26] 'Observations in the Art of English Poesie', in Gregory G. Smith, ed., *Elizabethan Critical Essays* (Oxford, 1959), Vol. 2, p. 330.
[27] *The Poems of Sir Philip Sidney*, ed. W. A. Ringler (Oxford, 1962), p. 166.
[28] Smith, Vol. 1, p. 256.
[29] 'Strange Newes', *The Works of Thomas Nashe*, ed. R. B. McKerrow, revised F. P. Wilson (Oxford, 1958), Vol. 1, p. 319.

This assertion was made at a time when admiration for Sidney,
expressed on numerous occasions by Harvey, was edging euphuism over into the category of a once fashionable but now
outmoded style. As Harvey wrote, 'The finest wittes preferre the
loosest period in M. Ascham, or Sir Philip Sidney, before the
tricksiest page in Euphues.'[30]

Prose fiction was viewed as a forum for stylistic excellence.
Abraham Fraunce and John Hoskyns both used the *Arcadia* as a
source for rhetorical treatises, and comments on the *Arcadia*'s
excellent style continued to be made well into the seventeenth
century. The only substantial comments relevant to fiction at this
time are directly related to the *Arcadia*; they appear in Sidney's
Defence of Poetry and John Hoskyns's *Directions for Speech and Style*.
Sidney's *Defence* outlines a didactic role for poetry, and specifically includes works of prose fiction in the definition of poetry:
'there have been many most excellent poets that never versi-
fied.'[31] Poetry may teach by providing an image of an exemplary
individual, and Sidney includes Theagenes from Heliodorus'
Aethiopica amongst his examples.[32] Heliodorus is also praised for
'his sugared invention of that picture of love in Theagenes and
Chariclea'.[33] Prose fiction may be 'an absolute heroical poem', as
the *Arcadia* was.[34] It is worth noting here that the *Arcadia* does not
include any completely exemplary characters apart from
Euarchus. Pyrocles and Musidorus are not Cyruses—they have
their faults, and Sidney's practice, when it came to characterization, was more subtle than his theory.

Poetry presents a 'speaking picture'; it is able to teach because
it is able to move the reader, it 'doth not only show the way, but
giveth so sweet a prospect into the way, as will entice any man to
enter into it'.[35] Its power stems from its ability to create a vivid
picture for the reader, to communicate what Forrest Robinson
calls 'mental images'.[36] A work of fiction like the *Arcadia* is
particularly suited to this purpose, containing as it does vivid
characters, moving stories ('tales of Hercules, Achilles, Cyrus,

[30] *Pierces Supererogation* (1593), S2.
[31] *Miscellaneous Prose*, p. 81.
[32] Ibid., p. 79.   [33] Ibid., p. 81.   [34] Ibid.
[35] Ibid., pp. 86 and 92.
[36] See Forrest G. Robinson, *The Shape of Things Known* (Cambridge, Mass., 1972),
p. 136 and *passim*.

Aeneas'),[37] and maxims rooted in action, not harsh philosophy or inflexible history.

Sidney justifies his own practice in the *Arcadia* when he defends the mingling of 'matters heroical and pastoral'.[38] The comments made by admirers of the *Arcadia* often take up hints from the *Defence*. Francis Meres writes 'As Xenophon . . . and a Heliodorus . . . so Sir Philip Sidney writ his immortal poem, The Countesse of Pembrooke's Arcadia in Prose.'[39] During the seventeenth century the *Arcadia* continued to be a touchstone for those who wrote about prose fiction; John Hoskyns was particularly interested in Sidney's approach to character. Sir William Alexander, who wrote a bridging passage to smooth the gap between the *Old* and *New Arcadia*, comments on the romance in his *Anacrisis, Or A Censure of Some Poets Ancient and Modern* (*c.* 1634); he echoes Sidney's notion that 'a Poem might be delivered in Prose', and goes on to express his admiration for Heliodorus, particularly for his 'Invention and Variety of Accidents'.[40] The *Arcadia* is seen by Alexander as a repository of ideal types, 'his chief Persons being Eminent for some singular Virtue, and yet all Virtues being united in every one of them', which contradicts Greville's interpretation of the characters as flawed, and seems more an echo of Sidney's ideal expressed in the *Defence* than an accurate assessment of the characters in the *Arcadia*.[41] Alexander also praises *L'Astrée*, noting that it has a *roman à clef* element, and linking it to Barclay's *Argenis*, 'though the Last in this Kind, yet no way inferior to the First'.[42]

We have seen how Madeleine de Scudéry included an analysis of the heroic romance in *Clélie*. French theoretical interest in the heroic romance was quite extensive, the two notable examples being the preface to *Ibrahim* (1641), and Bishop Huet's treatise, which was translated twice in England, in 1672 and 1715. However, in England interest centred on the heroic play, which was strongly influenced by the heroic romance, particularly in the use it made of plots taken from stories in the French

[37] *Miscellaneous Prose*, p. 92.
[38] Ibid., p. 94.
[39] 'Palladis Tamia', Smith, Vol. 2, pp. 315–16.
[40] J. E. Spingarn, ed., *Critical Essays of the Seventeenth Century* (Bloomington and London, 1968), Vol. 1, p. 186.
[41] Ibid., p. 187.   [42] Ibid., p. 188.

romances.[43] Dryden made some disparaging references to the heroic romances, castigating in particular their exemplary heroes who 'neither eat, nor drink, nor sleep, for love',[44] but despite his personal preference for the Homeric hero ('[I] am more in love with Achilles and Rinaldo than with Cyrus and Oroondates'),[45] he admits the use which he has made of them.

Only in the late eighteenth century do we find an overview of earlier fiction in Clara Reeve's *Progress of Romance*. On the whole, the writers and readers of sixteenth- and seventeenth-century fiction were content with a very small amount of criticism and theorizing.

III. Writing Literary History

When a distinguished scholar like René Wellek announces 'The Fall of Literary History', the general intentions behind the present study may warrant some consideration.[46] In implicit opposition to Wellek's pronouncement, the journal *New Literary History* has, over the past dozen or so years, been the showcase for a proliferation of approaches to the subject (despite certain indications in early issues that a 'crisis' had been reached).[47] Literary studies today may resemble a battleground where competing theories and anti-theories fight for supremacy. Spirited defences of traditional approaches to literary history have been made elsewhere, and these concluding pages are not intended to take a side in any battle, but rather to consider some of the implicit theoretical assumptions which have shaped this book.[48]

Tracing the course taken by fiction during the 150 years considered in this study is a much more compelling scholarly enterprise today than it may have been for an earlier generation less interested in conventions alien to the norms of the realist

[43] See Robert Hume, *The Development of English Drama in the Late Seventeenth Century* (Oxford, 1976), p. 243.
[44] 'Of Dramatic Poesy', in George Watson, ed., *Of Dramatic Poesy and Other Critical Essays* (London, 1962), Vol. 1, p. 42.
[45] 'Of Heroic Plays', ibid., p. 165.
[46] René Wellek, *The Attack on Literature and Other Essays* (Brighton, 1982), pp. 64–77.
[47] Istvan Soter, 'The Dilemma of Literary Science', *New Literary History*, 2 (1970), 86.
[48] See, for example, Howard Erskine-Hill, 'Scholarship as Humanism', *Essays in Criticism*, 29 (1979), 33–52.

novel. An overview of such a large area of literature is not simply a case of the indefatigable in pursuit of the unreadable. A little-known area needs the services of a cartographer before critics, theorists, students, and readers in general can claim it for their various uses.

Ordering a wide range of works involves decisions, many of which relate to two theoretical questions: the use of generic classification, and the causes of literary change. The heuristic value of the concept of genre has been recognized by writers as diverse as E. D. Hirsch, who sees generic categories as 'arbitrary', and Northrop Frye, who implies that his classifications are rooted in human nature.[49] Alastair Fowler's extensive study begins by emphasizing the universality of genre, and its flexibility: 'the character of genres is that they change.'[50] Recently, an article by Jacques Derrida has characteristically seized on the contradiction inherent in genre as a labelling process which is seen as being in the text, but which is also placed on the text:

a text cannot belong to no genre, it cannot be without or less a genre. Every text participates in one or several genres, there is no genreless text: there is always a genre and genres, yet such participation never amounts to belonging. And not because of an abundant overflowing or a free, anarchic and unclassifiable productivity, but because of the *trait* of participation itself, because of the effect of the code and of the generic mark. Making genre its mark, a text demarcates itself. If remarks of belonging belong without belonging, participate without belonging, then genre designations cannot be simply part of the corpus.[51]

Derrida's argument is succinctly stated by Jonathan Culler: 'Though it always participates in genre, a text belongs to no genre, because the frame or trait that marks its belonging does not itself belong'.[52]

The slippery yet indispensable idea of genre affects the choice of subject, as well as the ordering process. This book may have, as one of its aims, the recovery of various genres and subgenres which were important to their authors, original readers, and imitators, but have since been neglected through the vicissitudes

[49] E. D. Hirsch, *Validity in Interpretation* (New Haven and London, 1974), p. 111, and Chap. 3, *passim*; Northrop Frye, *Anatomy of Criticism* (1957, rpt. Princeton, 1973), *passim*.
[50] Alastair Fowler, *Kinds of Literature* (Oxford, 1982), p. 18.
[51] Jacques Derrida, 'The Law of Genre', *Glyph*, 7 (1980), 212.
[52] Jonathan Culler, *On Deconstruction* (London, 1983), p. 196.

of changing literary taste. However, this act of historical recovery may sit uneasily with the initial demarcation of 'prose fiction', a generic label imposed from a modern perspective, and one which would not have occurred to (or appealed to) the creators of the disparate works thus grouped together. This initial act is an example of genre as a heuristic device, a means of opening up an area for investigation.

On the other hand, the minute generic subdivisions used in the course of this study relate to the rediscovery of much more subtle discriminations than blanket terms like 'romance' permit. If 'romance' is used as a monolithic label we lose the sense of the complexity of literary change, which may be recaptured by attending to the difference between, say, Sidney's type of romance and Percy Herbert's. Rosalie Colie has emphasized the Renaissance interest in generic interaction: 'literary invention . . . in the Renaissance was largely generic'.[53] We have seen how prose fiction often involved a jostling together of different genres; both at the fashionable level, where, for example, Sidney mingled heroic and pastoral (and other) elements, and at the popular level, where chapbooks mingled old chivalric romance with tales of apprentices' triumphs, or where Deloney turned to the jest-book and even to euphuism in his mercantile fiction. Renaissance fiction was pre-eminently a series of mixed forms.[54]

Close attention to the fiction of this period also reveals an almost bewildering rate of change in the approach to narrative. The connection between genre and literary change was forcefully expressed by the Russian formalists, whose view that literature is engaged in a process of defamiliarization, of 'making strange' (*ostranenie*), led to a theory of evolution through the line of the 'grandfather' (recovering a genre neglected by the preceding generation) or of the 'uncle' (incorporating 'sub-literary' genres).[55] Literary evolution is seen as 'the dialectical change of forms', whereby genres grow familiar, and thus seek some new input in order to regain the power to 'make strange'.[56] The

[53] Rosalie Colie, *The Resources of Kind* (Berkeley and Los Angeles, 1973), p. 17.
[54] On *genera mista* see ibid., Chap. 3.
[55] Victor Erlich, *Russian Formalism: History-Doctrine* (The Hague, 1955), p. 227, see pp. 215–27.
[56] Boris Eichenbaum, 'The Theory of the "Formal Method"', *Russian Formalist Criticism*, trans. Lemon and Reis (Lincoln, Nebraska, 1965), p. 136.

identification of genres (especially of the 'important' genres, for the formalists have an implicit value-system, which seeks out innovation) relies on the idea of 'genre-markers', which are the '*dominant* devices, i.e. those which subordinate all the other devices needed to make up an artistic whole'.[57]

The relevance of this concept of literary change to an analysis of early fiction is readily apparent. We have constantly seen the interaction of high and low genres—although the hierarchy of high borrowing from low must be countered by recognizing the frequency of the reverse process. The chapbooks are an example of the 'grandfather' genre (chivalric romance) returning, although the process of 'making strange' is not so relevant to this accommodation of an old form to popular taste.

Suggestive as this model of the relationship between genre and literary change may be, it seals literature into the role of a knight on a chess-board, moving in an ever-surprising pattern, but without any concrete motivation. The *direction* of literary change is not explained, and the most convincing critical analyses of the Russian formalists have focused on the gap in their model, which can only be filled by an explanation of why literary change moves in one direction rather than another. Fredric Jameson sees the model as essentially synchronic: 'where all history is understood as the operation of a single mechanism, it is transformed back into synchrony, and time itself becomes a kind of a-historical, relatively mechanical repetition.'[58]

Literature cannot be a completely hermetic system, and the direction of literary change may well depend on the interaction of generic mixture and revitalization with forces such as changes in readership, social conditions in general, and the physical production and distribution of books. During the present account of early fiction we have frequently been forced to turn to such questions. Cheap printing techniques are a prerequisite for the chapbook, which interacts as a form with growing literacy. A new reading public has new tastes, produces new writers. Political change, such as the Civil War, impels writers to incorporate their changed status into a new romance form.

[57] Boris Tomashevsky, 'Literary Genres', trans. L. M. O'Toole, *Russian Poetics in Translation*, 5 (1978), 52.

[58] Fredric Jameson, *The Prison-House of Language* (Princeton, 1972), p. 96; for a related analysis, see Tony Bennett, *Formalism and Marxism* (London, 1979), Chaps. 2–4.

Changes in education produce new readers and writers—notably the case with women in the course of the seventeenth and eighteenth centuries. If this extra-literary dimension is added to the cauldron of generic interaction, it is possible to gain a clearer sense of at least some aspects of literary change.

The theorist and the critic may both look right past (or through) a body of texts unreclaimed by the historian. This has been a 'critical' history, not in the sense that it has been evaluative, but rather because it has engaged in an analysis of individual (and often representative) works, as well as in general ordering, description, and explanation. In the preface to his translation of Charles Sorel's *Extravagant Shepherd* (1654), Sir John Davies remarks that ' 'Tis the sad fate of things, that are not understood, to lose much of their grace . . .' (b2). Literary history seeks to understand; then perhaps the grace will follow.

Bibliography

The bibliography lists all known extant works of fiction published between 1558 and 1700, including translations. Elizabethan fiction is arranged in alphabetical order. Seventeenth-century fiction, which is much more an unknown quantity, has been arranged in a series of generic categories to facilitate future investigation, and to supplement the use of a limited number of representative examples in my text. Each item of the bibliography includes a short title; a reference to the unrevised Pollard and Redgrave *Short Title Catalogue* (given as a number) or the unrevised Wing *Short Title Catalogue* (given as a letter followed by a number); the original of a translation where definitely known; and, for all seventeenth-century items, the pagination of the work if it is not available in a modern edition. Reliable modern editions are cited when available. Place of publication is London throughout, unless otherwise noted. The following abbreviations have been used for anthologies:

Mish, *Short Fiction* = Charles C. Mish, ed., *Short Fiction of the Seventeenth Century* (New York, 1963).

Mish, *Restoration* = Charles C. Mish, ed., *Restoration Prose Fiction 1660 to 1700* (Lincoln, Nebraska, 1970).

Peterson = Spiro Peterson, ed., *The Counterfeit Lady Unveiled and Other Criminal Fiction of Seventeenth Century England* (New York, 1961).

I. Elizabethan Fiction

ACHILLES TATIUS, *Clitophon and Leucippe*, trans. William Burton (1597), 90 (3rd century AD), ed. S. Gaselee and H. Brett-Smith (Oxford, 1923).

Amadis de Gaule, trans. Anthony Munday (1590–92/5), 541–2 (French *Amadis*, trans. Herberay des Essarts *et al.*, 1540–8 et seq.).

ANEAU, Barthelmi, *The Cock* (1590), 633.

APULEIUS, *The Golden Ass*, trans. William Aldington (1566), 718 (2nd century AD).

AVERELL, William, *A Dyall for Dainty Darlings* (1584), 978.

BALDWIN, William, *A Mervelous historye intituled beware the cat* (1570), 1244, ed. W. P. Holden (1963).

BEARD, Thomas, *The Theatre of Gods Judgements* (1577), 1659–61.

C., H., *The forrest of fancy* (1579), 4271.

C., W., *The Adventures of Lady Egeria* (1585?), not in STC.

CARTIGNY, Jean de, *The Wandering Knight*, trans. William Goodyear (1581), 4700 (*Le Voyage du chevalier errant*, 1557), ed. Dorothy Evans (Seattle, 1951).

CHETTLE, Henry, *Kind-Harts Dreame* (1593), 5123, ed. G. B. Harrison (1923).

—— ——, *Piers Plainness* (1595), 5124, in James Winny, ed., *The Descent of Euphues* (Cambridge, 1957).

The Cobler of Caunterburie (1590), 4579, in Mish, *Short Fiction*.

COPLEY, Anthony, *Wits Fits and Fancies* (1596), 5739.

A Courtlie Controuersie of Cupids Cautels, by Henry Wotton? (1578), 5647.

DELONEY, Thomas, *The Gentle Craft* (1598?), 6555–6, in Merritt E. Lawlis, ed., *The Novels of Thomas Deloney* (Bloomington, 1961).

—— ——, *The Pleasant Historie of John Winchcomb* [*Jack of Newbury*] (1597), 6559, in Lawlis.

—— ——, *Thomas of Reading* (1599?), 6569, in Lawlis.

DICKENSON, John, *Arisbas* (1594), 6817.

—— ——, *Greene in Conceipt* (1598), 6819.

FENTON, Geoffrey, *Certaine Tragicall discourses* (1567), 10791 (trans. from Belleforest's and Boiastuau's versions of Bandello), ed. R. L. Douglas (1898).

FORDE, Emanuel, *The Most Famous Historie of Montelyon* (c. 1599), 11167.

—— ——, *The Most Pleasaunt Historie of Ornatus and Artesia* (1595), 11169, in P. Henderson, ed., *Shorter Novels: Seventeenth Century* (1930).

—— ——, *Parismus* (1598), *Parismenos* (1599), usually bound together, 11171.

FRAUNCE, Abraham, *The third part of the Countesse of Pembrokes Yuychurch* (1592), 11341.

G., R., *The Famous Historie of Albions Queene* (1600), 11502.

GASCOIGNE, George, *The Adventures of Master F.J.* (1573/1575), 11635/6, 1st version in C. T. Prouty, ed., *A. Hundreth Sundry Flowers* (Columbia Missouri, 1942), 2nd version in J. W. Cunliffe, ed., *Posies, Complete Works*, Vol. I (Cambridge, 1907–10).

GOSSON, Stephen, *The Ephemerides of Phialo* (1579), 12093.

GRANGE, John, *The Golden Aphroditis* (1577), 12174, ed. H. E. Rollins (New York, 1939).

GREENE, Robert, *Arbasto* (1584), 12217, in A. B. Grosart, ed., *Life and Complete Works* (1881–6)—Grosart's edition is not wholly reliable, but is still the standard edition of Greene's works.

—— ——, *The Blacke Bookes Messenger* (1592), 12223, in Grosart.

GREENE ROBERT, *Ciceronis Amor* (1589), 12224, ed. E. H. Miller (Gainseville, 1954), ed. Charles Larson (Salzburg, 1974).
—— ——, *Euphues His Censure to Philautus* (1587), 12239, in Grosart.
—— ——, *Greenes Farewel to Folly* (1591), 12241, in Grosart.
—— ——, *Greenes Groats-Worth of Wit* (1592), 12245, ed. G. B. Harrison (1923).
—— ——, *Greenes Mourning Garment* (1590), 12251, in Grosart.
—— ——, *Greenes Never Too Late* (1590), 12253, in Grosart.
—— ——, *Greenes Orpharion* (1599), 12260, in Grosart.
—— ——, *Gwydonius: the card of Fancy* (1584), 12262, in Grosart.
—— ——, *Mamillia* (1583/4), 12269/70, in Grosart.
—— ——, *Menaphon* (1589), 12272, ed. G. B. Harrison (1927).
—— ——, *Morando* (1584/7), 12276, in Grosart.
—— ——, *The Myrrour of Modestie* (1584), 12279, in Grosart.
—— ——, *Pandosto. The Triumph of Time* (1588), 12285, in James Winny, ed., *The Descent of Euphues* (Cambridge, 1957), in Geoffrey Bullough, ed., *Narrative and Dramatic Sources of Shakespeare*, Vol. 8 (London, 1975).
—— ——, *Penelopes Web* (1587), 12293, in Grosart.
—— ——, *Perimedes the Black-Smith* (1588), 12295, in Grosart.
—— ——, *Philomela* (1592), 12296, in Grosart.
—— ——, *Planetomachia* (1585), 12299, in Grosart, missing tale in D. Bratchell, ed., *Robert Greene's Planetomachia* (Trowbridge, 1979).
—— ——, *The Spanish Masquerado* (1589), 12309, in Grosart.
H.C., *see* C., H.
HELIODORUS, *An Aethiopian History*, trans. Thomas Underdowne (1569), 13041 (3rd century AD), ed. G. Saintsbury (1924).
JOHNSON, Richard (?), *The History of Tom Thumbe* (1590s?), 14056, ed. C. F. Buhler (Evanston, 1965).
JOHNSON, Richard, *The Most Famous History of the Seauen Champions of Christendome* (1596/7), 14677/8, ed. R. Kennedy (Portland Oregon, 1967).
—— ——, *The Most Pleasant History of Tom a Lincolne* (1599/1607), 14684, ed. Richard Hirsch (Columbia, South Carolina, 1978).
KITTOWE, Robert, *Loves load-starre* (1600), 15026.
Lazarillo de Tormes (1568-9), trans. David Rowland, 15336, (Spanish, 1554), ed. J. E. V. Crofts (Oxford, 1924).
LODGE, Thomas, *An Alarum Against Usurers* (1584), 16653, in Edmund Gosse, ed., *Complete Works of Thomas Lodge* (Glasgow, 1883).
—— ——, *Euphues Shadow* (1592), 16656, in Gosse.
—— ——, *The Life and Death of William Longbeard* (1593), 16659, in Gosse.

LODGE, Thomas, *A Margarite of America* (1596), 16660, ed. G. B. Harrison (1927).

—— ——, *Robert Second Duke of Normandy* (1591), 16657, in Gosse.

—— ——, *Rosalynde* (1590), 16664, in Geoffrey Bullough, ed., *Narrative and Dramatic Sources of Shakespeare*, Vol. 2 (1958).

LONGUS, *Daphnis and Chloe*, trans. Angel Day (1587), 6400 (3rd century AD).

LYLY, John, *Euphues The Anatomy of Wit* (1578), 17051, ed. M. W. Croll and H. Clemens (1916).

—— ——, *Euphues and his England* (1580), 17068, in R. W. Bond, ed., *The Complete Works of John Lyly* (1902).

MAISONNEUVE, Étienne de [Gallarx], *Gerileon of England*, trans. M. Jennynges (1578), 17203 (*Gerileon d'Angleterre*, 1572).

MELBANCKE, Brian, *Philotimus* (1582), 17800.5.

MIDDLETON, Christopher, *Chinon of England* (1597), 17866, ed. W. E. Mead (EETS, 1925).

MIDDLETON, Christopher (?), *The First Part of the Nature of A Woman* (1596), 17126.5.

MONTEMAYOR, Jorge de, *Diana*, trans. Bartholomew Young (1598), 18044 (*La Diana*, 1559), ed. J. M. Kennedy (Oxford, 1969).

MUNDAY, Anthony, trans., *Palladine of England* (1588), 5541, (Claude Colet, *L'histoire palladienne*, 1555).

—— ——, trans., *Palmendos* (1589), 18064 (François de Vernassal, *Histoire de Primaleon de Grèce*, 1550).

—— ——, trans., *Palmerin of England* (1596/1602/1616), 19161–5 (Jacques Vincent, *Palmerin d'Angleterre*, 1553).

—— ——, trans., *Palmerin d'Oliva* (1588/97), 19157–8 (Jean Maugin, *L'histoire de Palmerin d'Olive*, 1553).

—— ——, trans., *Primaleon of Greece* (1595/96/1619), 20366–7 (de Vernassal, op. cit.).

—— ——, *Zelauto* (1580), 18283, ed. J. Stillinger (Carbondale, 1969).

NASHE, Thomas, *Pierce Penilesse* (1592), 18371, in R. B. McKerrow, ed., *The Works of Thomas Nashe*, rev. F. P. Wilson (Oxford, 1958).

—— ——, *The Unfortunate Traveller* (1594), 18380, in McKerrow.

NAVARRE, Marguerite de, *The Queene of Navarres Tales* (1597), 17323 (*Heptameron*, 1558–9).

PAINTER, William, *The Palace of Pleasure* (1566/75, 2nd Tome 1567), 19121–4, (Classical sources, Boccaccio, Bandello, etc.), ed. Joseph Jacobs (1890), ed. H. Miles (1929).

PARRY, Robert, *Moderatus* (1595), 19337.

PÉRIERS, Jean Bonaventure de, *The Mirrour of Mirth*, trans. J.D. (1583), 6784.5 (*Nouvelles récréations et joyoux devis*, 1558).

PETTIE, George, *A petite palace of Pettie his Pleasure* (1576), 19819 (Ovid, Livy, Tacitus, Hyginus, a Saint's Life), ed. Herbert Hartman (New York, 1938).

Phillipes Venus, by Jo. M. (1591), 17143.

Prince Don Bellianis, trans. L. A. (1598), 1804 (Oratio Rinaldi, *Don Belianis*, 1586).

R. G., *see* G., R.

RICH, Barnaby, *The Adventures of Brusanus Prince of Hungaria* (1592), 20977.

—— ——, *Rich his farewell to militarie profession* (1581/94), 20966 (Heliodorus, Ovid, Painter, Pettie, Cinthio, Belleforest, Straparola), ed. T. M. Cranfill (Austin, 1959).

—— ——, *A Right excellent and pleasaunt dialogue between Mercury and an English souldier* (1574), 20998.

—— ——, *The straunge and wonderfull adventures of Don Simonides* (1581, 2nd Tome 1584), 21002–2a.

ROBARTS, Henry, *A Defiance to Fortune* (1590), 21078.

—— ——, *Haigh for Devonshire* (1600), 21081.

—— ——, *Honours Conquest* (1598), 21082.

—— ——, *Pheander the Mayden Knight* (1595), 21086.

SAKER, Austin, *Narbonus* (1580), 21593.

SHARPHAM, E. (?), *The discoverie of the Knights of the poste* (1597), 21489.

SIDNEY, Philip, *New Arcadia* (1590), 22539, in *Works*, ed. Albert Feuillerat (Cambridge, 1912–26).

—— ——, *Old Arcadia* (1578–80?), ed. Jean Robertson (Oxford, 1973).

Tarltons News Out of Purgatorie (1590), 23685.

TILNEY, Edmund, *The Flower of Friendship* (1568), 24076.

TURBERVILLE, George, trans., *Tragical Tales* (1576), 24330 (Boccaccio and Bandello).

TURNER, Richard, *The Garland of a Greene Wit* (1595), 24345.

W. C., *see* C., W.

WARNER, William, *Pan His Syrinx* (1584/97), 25086, ed. W. A. Bacon (Evanston, 1950).

WHETSTONE, George, *An Heptameron of Civill Discourses* (1582), 25337.

—— ——, *The rocke of regard* (1576), 25348.

II. Seventeenth-Century Fiction

1. Sidneian Romance

BIONDI, Giovanni Francesco, *Coralbo A New Romance* (1655), B2935, 143pp. (*Il Coralbo*, 1635).

BIONDI, Giovanni Francesco, *Donzella Desterrada or the banish'd Virgin* (1635), 3074, 230pp. (*La Donzella Desterrada*, 1627).

—— ——, *Eromena or Love and Revenge* (1632), 3075, 195pp. (*L'Eromena*, 1624).

Clidamas, by J. S. (1639), 21501, 152pp.

Eliana A New Romance: formed by an English hand (1661), E499, 289pp.

Evagoras, a romance, by L. L. (1677), L40, 181pp.

GAINSFORD, Thomas, *The History of Trebizond* (1616), 11521, 360pp.

HIND, John, *The Most Excellent History of Lysimachus and Varrona* (1604), 13510, 95pp.

—— ——, *Eliosto Libidinoso* (1606), 13509, 95pp.

MARKHAM, Gervase, *The English Arcadia* (I 1607, II 1613), 17351–2, I 143pp., II 120pp.

REYNOLDS, John, *The Flower of Fidelitie* (1650), R1304, 187pp.

WEAMYS, Anne, *A Continuation of Sir Philip Sidney's Arcadia* (1651), W1189, 199pp.

WROTH, Mary, *The Countesse of Montgomeries Urania* (1621), 26051, 558pp.

Additions to the *Arcadia:*

ALEXANDER, William, 'Supplement', 1621 edn. of *Arcadia*.

BELING, Richard, *Sixth Book to the Countesse of Pembrokes Arcadia*, 1628 edn of *Arcadia*.

JOHNSTOUN, James, 'Supplement', 1638 edn. of *Arcadia*.

2. 'Attenuated', Short Romance

BARON, Robert, *An Apologie for Paris* (1649), B888, 96pp.

BULTEEL, John, *Birinthea, a romance* (1664), B5454, 255pp.

CHAMBERLAYNE, William, *Eromena or the noble stranger* (1683), C1864, 70pp. (prose version of his *Pharonnida*, 1659).

HART, Alexander, *The tragi-comicall history of Alexto and Angelica* (1640), 12885, in Mish, *Short Fiction*, pp. 368–421.

KITTOWE, Robert, *Loves Load-starre* (1600), 15026, 70pp.

WILKINS, George, *The painfull adventures of Pericles prince of Tyre* (1608), 25638.5, ed. Kenneth Muir (Liverpool, 1953).

3. Continental Romance (including adventure romance and pastoral romance)

ASSARINO, Luca, *La Stratonica* (1651), A4016, 180pp. (*Stratonica*, 1637).

AUDIGUIER, Vital d', *Love and Valour*, trans. W. Barwick (1638), 905, 224pp. (from *Histoire tragi-comique de Lisandre et de Caliste*, 1615).

—— ——, *Lisander and Calista* (1627, 1st pub. 1621?), 905–6, 247pp. (from *Lisandre et de Caliste*).

BRUSONI, Girolamo, *Arnaldo or The injur'd lover* (1660), B5241, 190pp. (from *Novelle amorose de Signori Accademici Incogniti*, 1641).

CARMENI, Francesco, *Nissena* (1653), C599, 159pp. (from *Novelle amorose*).

CERVANTES, Miguel de, *The Travels of Persiles and Sigismunda* (1619), 4918, 399pp. (*Persiles y Sigismunda*, 1617).

CODRINGTON, Robert, *The Troublesome and Hard Adventures in Love* (1652), C1781, 283pp. (derives from Montemayor's *Diana* and Gil Polo's sequel *Diana Enamorada* (1559/1564), see Dale Randall, *BHS*, 38 (1961), 154–8).

GOMBAULD, Jean Ogier de, *Endimion* (1639), 11991, 206pp. (*L'Endymion*, 1624).

LOREDANO, Giovanni Francesco, *Dianea* (1654), L3066, 367pp. (*La Dianea*, 1627).

The Loves and Adventures of Clerio and Lozia, trans. Francis Kirkman (1652), L3260, 198pp. (French, orig. unknown).

MONTREUX, Nicolas de, *Honours Academie or the famous Pastorall of the faire sheaperdess Julietta* (1610), 18053, 323pp. (*L'Arcadie françoise*, 1585?).

QUINTANA, Francisco de, *The History of Don Fenise* (1651), Q220, 318pp. (*Experiencias de amor y fortuna*, 1626).

The True History of the Tragic Loves of Hipolito and Isabella, (1628), 13516, 153pp. (Meslier, *Les amours tragiques d'Hypolite et Isabelle*, 1610).

URFÉ, Honoré d', *The History of Astrea* (1620), 24525, Bks. I–X 373pp., Bk. XI 64pp. (*L'Astrée*, 1607).

VEGA CARPIO, Lope de, *The Pilgrim of Casteele*, trans. William Dutton? (1621), 25629, 150pp. (*El peregrino en su patria*, 1604).

4. Didactic Romance

CAMUS, Jean Pierre, *Admirable Events*, trans. S. Du Verger (1639), 4549, 357pp. (from *Les Événements singuliers ou Histoires diverses*, 1628; *Variétés historiques*, 1631; *Spectacles d'horreur*, 1630; *Relations morales*, 1631).

—— ——, *Diotrephe or an Historie of Valentines* (1641), C412, 192pp. (*Diotrèphe*, 1626).

—— ——, *Elise or Innocencie guilty*, trans. Jo: Jennings (1655), C413, 150pp. (*Élise*, 1621).

—— ——, *The Loving Enemy* (1650), C415, 112pp. (orig. unknown).

—— ——, *Natures Paradox*, trans. Major Wright (1652), C417, 372pp. (*L'Iphegène*, 1625).

—— ——, *A True and Tragical History of Two Illustrious Italian Families* (1677), C419, 281pp. (*Alcime*, 1625).

CAVENDISH, Margaret [Duchess of Newcastle], *Natures Pictures drawn by fancies pencil to the life* (1656), N855, prose pp. 396–8 [for 106–8], *—*4, II. 105–403 [pag. very irregular].

CERIZIERS, René de, *The Innocent Lord* (1655), C1681, 143pp. (*Joseph, ou la Providence divine*, 1642).

CERIZIERS, René de, *The Triumphant Lady* (1656), C1682, 142pp. (*L'Histoire D'Hirlande*, date unknown).

——— ———, *The Innocent Lady* (1654), C1679, 152pp. (*L'Innocence reconnuë*, 1634).

5. Political/Allegorical Romance

BARCLAY, John, *Barclay his Argenis*, trans. Kingesmill Long (1625), trans. Sir Robert Le Grys (1628), 1393, 483pp. (*Argenis*, Latin, 1621).

BARON, Robert, *Erotopageion, or the Cyprian Academy* (1647), B889, I. 61pp., II. 101pp., a precursor of the romances.

BRATHWAITE, Richard, *Panthalia or the Royal Romance* (1659), B4273, 303pp.

HERBERT, Sir Percy, *The Princess Cloria* (1661), P3492, 614pp.

HOWELL, James, *Dendrologia, Dodona's Grove* (1640/50), 13872/H3062, 219pp., a precursor.

——— ———, *The Parly of Beasts* (1660), H3119, 152pp., a precursor.

MACKENZIE, Sir George, *Aretina: or the serious romance* (1660), M151, 432pp.

SALES, Sir William, *Theophania, or, several modern histories presented by way of romance* (1655), S371, 206pp.

6. Religious Allegory

BERNARD, Richard, *The Isle of Man* (1627), 1946, 262pp.

BUNYAN, John, *The Holy War* (1682), B5538, ed. Roger Sharrock and James Forrest (Oxford, 1980).

——— ———, *The Life and Death of Mr. Badman* (1680), B5550, ed. John Brown (Cambridge, 1905).

——— ———, *The Pilgrim's Progress* (1678), B5557, ed. Roger Sharrock (Oxford, 1960).

CHAMBERS, Robert, *Palestina* (1600), 4954, 200pp. (facsimile, Menston, 1972: 'English Recusant Literature 1558–1640', Vol. 100).

COLERAINE, Hugh Hare, *The Situation of Paradise Found Out* (1683), C5064, 243pp.

DUNTON, John, *An Hue and Cry after Conscience: or the pilgrim's progress by candle-light* (1685), D2628, 160pp.

——— ———, *The Informer's Doom* (1683), D2629, 160pp.

——— ———, *The Pilgrim's Guide from the Cradle to his death-bed* (1684), D2632, 305pp. (plagiarizes from Bunyan, Donne, *et al.*, see A. B. Cook III, 'John Bunyan and John Dunton: A Case of Plagiarism', *PBSA*, 71 (1977), 11–28).

INGELO, Nathaniel, *Bentivolio and Urania* (1660), I175, I–IV 171pp., V–VI 219pp.

KEACH, Benjamin, *The Progress of Sin; or the travels of Ungodliness* (1684), K80, 272pp.

———— ————, *The Travels of True Godliness* (1683), K97, 168pp.

PATRICK, Simon, *The Parable of the Pilgrim* (1665), P826, 527pp.

The Progress of the Christian Pilgrim (1700), P3653, I 100pp., II 79pp. (plagiarism of Bunyan).

The Second part of the Pilgrim's Progress, by T.S. (1682), S178, 178pp.

7. *Didactic Fiction*

ABU BAKR IBN AL TUFAL, Abu Jafar, *An Account of the Oriental Philosophy . . . the profound wisdom of Hai Ebn Yokdan* (1674), A150, 117pp.

BIDPAI, *The Fables of Pilpay* (1699), B2885, 207pp. (*Les Fables de Pilpay*, 1698, from Anwār-i Suhaili, 1281).

BLONDO, Giuseppi, *The Penitent Bandito*, trans. Sir Tobie Matthew (1663, 1st edn. 1620?), P1232, 144pp. (orig. unknown).

BRATHWAITE, Richard, *The Penitent Pilgrim* (1641), B4275, 444pp.

———— ————, [supposed author], *The Arcadian Princesse*, by 'Mariano Silesio' (1635), 22553, I 254pp., II 250pp.

———— ————, *The History of Moderation* (1669), B4264, 114pp.

BURTON, John, *The History of Eriander* (1661), B6180, 208pp.

Cacoethes leaden legacy: or his school of ill manners (1634), 4326, 20pp., satirizes conduct books.

CAUSSIN, Nicholas, *The Unfortunate Politique* (1638), 4876–7, 217pp.

The Famous and Renowned History of Morindos (1609), 18108, in Mish, *Short Fiction*, pp. 4–42.

FÉNELON, François de Salignac de la Mothe, *The Adventures of Telemachus* (1699), F674, 152pp. (*Les Aventures de Télémaque*, 1699), further parts appeared later.

GRACIÁN Y MORALES, Baltasar, *The Critick*, trans. Paul Rycaut (1681), G1470, 257pp. (*El Criticón*, 1651/3/7).

The History of the Five Wise Philosophers, by H.P. [Henry Peacham?] (1672), P946, 133pp., a type of Saint's Life.

HOWARD, Thomas, *The History of the Seven Wise Mistresses of Rome* (1663), H3008, 172pp., series of exempla in romance frame.

JOHNSON, John, *The Academy of Love* (1641), J782, 102pp.

LOREDANO, Giovanni Francesco, *The Life of Adam* (1659), L3067, 86pp. (*L'Adamo*, 1640), Biblical re-telling.

PANTON, Edward, *Speculum Juventutis* (1671), P277, 403pp., semi-allegorical conduct book.

PENTON, Stephen, *The Guardian's Instruction, or the Gentleman's romance* (1688), P1439, 90pp.

———— ————, *New Instructions to the Guardian* (1694), P1440, 143pp.

PRESTON, Richard, *Angliae Speculum Morale . . . with the Life of Theodatus and three novels* (1670), P3310, 187pp.

REYNOLDS, John, *The Triumphs of Gods Revenges* (I 1621, II 1622, III 1623, IV–VI 1635), 20942–4, I–V 527pp., VI 123pp., 30 histories; 1679 edn. adds *Gods revenge against the abominable sin of adultery*, R1313, 182pp., 10 histories, probably not by Reynolds.

A Saxon History of . . . Clodoaldus (1634), 4294, 104pp., possibly a translation, original unknown.

8. *French Heroic Romance*

BOISROBERT, François le Metel de, *The Indian History of Anaxander and Orazia* (1639), B3468 (2nd edn. extant, 1657), 280pp. (*Histoire indienne d'Anexandre et d'Orazie*, 1629).

BOYLE, Roger, *Parthenissa* (I 1651, II–IV 1655, V 1656, VI 1669), O488, 740pp. (numbered to 808pp. in 1676 edn.).

DESMARETS DE ST. SORLIN, Jean, *Ariana* (1636), 6779, 328pp. (*Ariane*, 1632).

GOMBERVILLE, Marin Le Roy, *The History of Polexander*, trans. William Browne (1647), G1025, I–II. 3 240pp. II.4 35pp., II.4–IV.5 345pp. (*L'Exil de Polexandre*, 1637).

The History of Philoxypes and Polycrite (1652), H2130, 187pp. (derives from Madeleine de Scudéry, *Artamène ou le Grand Cyrus* 1649–53).

LA CALPRENÈDE, Gauthier de Coste de, *Cassandra*, trans. George Digby (1652), trans. Sir Charles Cotterell (1661, complete), L106–10, 854pp., 1661 edn. (*Cassandre*, 1642–5).

—— ——, *Cleopatra* (1652), *Hymen's Praeludia*, trans. R. Loveday, John Davies, John Coles (1652/4/5/6/8/9), L111–20, I.1–VI.4 603pp., VII–VIII 202pp., IX–X 358pp., XI–XII 254pp. (*Cléopâtre*, 1646–57).

—— ——, *Pharamond*, trans. John Phillips (1662/77), L125–6, I.1–IV.4 415pp., V.1–XII 758pp. (*Faramond*, 1661–70).

LE VAYER DE BOUTIGNY, Roland *The Famous History of Tarsis and Zelie* (1685), L1797, 330pp. (*Tarsis et Zelie*, 1659).

ORTIGUE, Pierre d' [Vaumorière], *The Grand Scipio* (1660), V162, 250pp. (*Le Grand Scipion*, 1656).

SAULNIER, Gilbert sieur de Verdier, *The Love and Arms of the Greek Princes or the romant of romants* (1640), 21775, I 177pp., II 196pp., III 225pp. (*Les amours et les armes des princes de Grèce*, 1623).

SCUDÉRY, Madeleine de, *Almahide*, trans. John Phillips (1677), S2142, I 225pp., II 267pp., III.1 107pp., III.2–3 76pp. (*Almahide*, 1660–63).

—— ——, *Artamenes or The Grand Cyrus* (1653–5), S2144–5, I 155pp., II

208pp., III–IV 359pp., V 206pp., VI 188pp., VII 195pp., VIII.1–2 166pp., VIII.3 46pp., IX 186pp., X 232pp. (*Artamène ou le Grand Cyrus*, 1649–53).

—— ——, *Clelia* (1655–61), S2151, I.1–II.3 307pp., II.4–V.3 mispag. = 519pp. (*Clélie*, 1654–60).

—— ——, *Ibrahim or the Illustrious Bassa* (1653), S2160, 398pp. (*Ibrahim*, 1641).

9. Jest-Books

ARMIN, Robert, *A Nest of Ninnies* (1608, versions in 1600, 1605), 775, ed. P. M. Zall (Lincoln, Nebraska, 1970).

BOYER, Abel, *The Wise and Ingenious Companion* (1700), B3918, 232pp., bilingual (French and English).

'CHAUCER JUNIOR', *Canterbury Tales* (1687), C3737, 24pp.

CROUCH, Humphrey, *A New and Pleasant History of Unfortunate Hodg of the South* (1655), C7286, 13pp.

Dobson's Drie Bobbes (1607), 6930, ed. E. A. Horsman (Oxford, 1955).

HEAD, Richard, *Nugae Venales* (1675), H1266, 310pp.

The Jests of George Peele (1607), 19541, 33pp.

Pasquils Jests (1604), 19451, 50pp.

PHILLIPS, William, *A New Fairing for the Merrily Disposed* (1688), P2117, 60pp.

A Pleasant History of the Life and Death of Will Summers (1637), 22917.5, 34pp.

PRICE, Laurence, *Witty William of Wiltshire* (1674), P3394, 22pp.

Robin Good Fellow (1628), 12016, 38pp.

The Sack-full of Newes, (1673), S223, 21pp.

TARLETON, Richard, *Tarltons Jests* (1613), 23684, 38pp., selection in P. M. Zall, ed., *A Nest of Ninnies* (Lincoln, Nebraska, 1970).

The Witty Jests and Mad Pranks of John Frith (1673), W3239A, 22pp.

10. Criminal Biography

DANGERFIELD, Thomas, *Dangerfield's Memoirs* (1685), D190, 37pp.

—— ——, *Don Tomazo* (1680), D185, in Peterson, pp. 185–289.

FIDGE, George, *The English Gusman* (1652), F852, 46pp.

—— ——, *Hind's Ramble* (1651), F854, 42pp.

The German Princess Revived: or the London Jilt (1684), G613, 8pp.

The Grand Pyrate: or the Life and Death of Capt. George Cusack (1676), G1505, 31pp.

HEAD, Richard, *Jackson's Recantation* (1674), H1256, in Peterson, pp. 144–75.

HIND, James, *No Jest Like a True Jest* (1674), N1174, in P.M. Zall, ed., *A Nest of Ninnies* (Lincoln, Nebraska, 1970), pp. 218–33.

KIRKMAN, Francis, *The Counterfeit Lady Unveiled* (1673), K7, in Peterson, pp. 8–102.

The Last Words of a Dying Penitent (1692), H 892, 31pp., account by Henry Harrison.

The Life and Death of Captain William Bedloe (1681), L1992, 125pp.

The Life and Death of James . . . Turner (1663), L1997, 36pp.

The Life and Death of Mrs Mary Frith (1662), British Library, not in Wing, 173pp.

The Life of Captain James Whitney (1692/3), L2025A, 32pp.

The Life of William Fuller (1692), L2039, 32pp.

The Lives of Sundry Notorious Villains (1678), B1739, 167pp., sometimes attrib. to Aphra Behn.

The London Jilt: or, the Politick Whore (1683), Harvard University Library, mistakenly attrib. to Oldys in Wing, O266, I 120pp., II 128pp.

Long Meg of Westminster (1620), 17783, in Mish, *Short Fiction*, pp. 83–113.

Malice Defeated: Or a Brief Relation of . . . Elizabeth Cellier (1680), C1661, 56pp.

ROWE, Robert, *Mr Harrison Proved the Murtherer* (1692), R2069, 28pp.

Sadler's Memoirs (1677), S282, 18pp.

SETTLE, Elkanah, *Complete Memoirs of . . . Will. Morrell* (1694), S2673, in Peterson, pp. 299–372.

—— ——, *The Life and Death of Major Clancie* (1680), S2696A, 150pp.

The Triumph of Truth (1664), T2293, in Peterson, pp. 109–36.

The Witty Rogue Arraigned (1656), S20, 47pp.

11. Imaginary Voyage/Utopia/Satire

BACON, Francis, *The New Atlantis* (1626), 1168, with *Sylva Sylvarum* (1627), *The Advancement of Learning and New Atlantis*, ed. A. Johnston (Oxford, 1974), pp. 215–47.

BARNES, Joshua, *Gerania* (1675), B870, 110pp.

CAVENDISH, Margaret [Duchess of Newcastle], *A Description of a New World Called the Blazing World* (1666), N849, 158pp.

CYRANO DE BERGERAC, *Selenarchia*, trans. Thomas St. Serif (1659), C7719, 184pp. (*Histoire comique ou Voyage dans la Lune*, 1657).

DANIEL, Gabriel, *A Voyage to the World of Cartesius* (1692), D201, 298pp. (*Voyage du monde de Descartes*, 1690).

FOIGNY, Gabriel de [Jacques Sadeur pseud.], *A New Discovery of Terra Incognita Australis* (1693), F1395, 186pp. (*Aventures dans la découverte et le voyage de la Terre Australe*, 1691).

FONTAINES, Louis, *A Relation of the Country of Jansenia* (1668), F1410, 118pp. (Père Zacharie de Lisieux, *Relation du pays de Jansénie*, 1660).

GODWIN, Francis, *The Man in the moone* (1638), 11943, ed. G. McColley (Northampton, Mass., 1937).

GUILLET DE ST. GEORGE, Georges, *An Account of a Late Voyage to Athens* (1676), G2218, 422pp. (*Athènes ancienne et nouvelle*, 1675), close to a true history/traveller's tale.

HALL, Joseph, *The Discovery of a new World*, trans. J. Healey (1609), 12686 (*Mundus Alter et Idem*, 1605), ed. Huntington Brown (Cambridge, Mass., 1937).

HARRINGTON, James, *The Commonwealth of Oceana* (1656), 11809, ed. S. B. Liljegren (Heidelberg, 1924).

HEAD, Richard, *The Floating Island* (1673), H1253, 39pp., satire on imaginary voyages.

—— ——, *The Western Wonder: or, O Brazeel* (1674), H1277, 40pp.

NEVILLE, Henry, *The Isle of Pines* (1668), N505, in *Shorter Novels: Seventeenth Century*, ed. P. Henderson (1930, rpt. 1967).

—— ——, *A New and Further Discovery of the Isle of Pines* (1668), N509, 24pp.

Pasquin Risen from the Dead (1674), P656, 245pp., satire in the manner of Quevedo.

Poor Robins Visions (1677), H1598, 133pp., satire in the manner of Quevedo.

QUEVEDO Y VILLEGAS, Francisco de, *Visions* (1640), *Hell Reformed* (1641), Q189, 344pp. in 1678 edn. (*Infierno enmendado*, 1628; *Sueños*, 1627).

SCHOOTEN, Hendrick van [pseud.?], *The Hairy Giants* (1671), S888, 16pp., satirizes travellers' tales.

VAIRASSE, Denis, *The History of the Sevarites or Sevirambi* (I 1675, II 1679), V20, I 114pp., II 140pp. (*Histoire des Séverambes*, 1677-9).

12. Picaresque Fiction

ALEMÁN Mateo, *The Rogue or the Life of Guzman de Alfarache*, trans. James Mabbe (1622), 288 (*Guzmán de Alfarache*, 1599/1600), ed. James Fitzmaurice-Kelly (1924).

BRETON, Nicholas, *The Miseries of Mavillia* (1606), 3703, in *A Mad World My Masters*, ed. U. Kentish-Wright (1929), Vol. 2, pp. 108-66.

CASTILLO SOLÓRZANO, Alonso de, *La Picara* (1655), C1232A, 304pp. (*La Garduña de Sevilla*, 1644).

CRANLEY, Thomas, *Amanda* (1635), 5988, ed. Frederic Ouvry (1869), mostly in verse.

CROKE, Charles, *Fortune's Uncertainty or Youth's unconstancy* (1667), C7008, ed. Isabel M. Westcott (Oxford, 1959), autobiography/romance/picaresque.

DAUNCEY, John, *The English Lovers or A Girle worth gold* (1662), D289A, 251pp., version of Thomas Heywood's *A Fair Maid of the West*.

DEFOE, Daniel, *The Compleat Mendicant* (1699), D830, 156pp., partly didactic.

DEKKER, Thomas, *The Wonderful Year* (1603), 6534, in *Thomas Dekker*, ed. E. D. Pendry (1967), pp. 32–64.

—— ——, *Lanthorne and Candlelight* (1608), 6485, in Pendry, pp. 173–308.

—— ——, *A Knight's Conjuring* (1607), 6508, ed. L. M. Robbins (The Hague, 1974).

The Dutch Rogue (1683), D2905, 275pp., purports to be a translation out of 'Nether-Dutch'.

The French Rogue (1672), F885, 196pp.

GARCÍA, Carlos, *The sonne of the rogue* (1638), 11550, 253pp. (*La desordenada codicia de los bienes ajenos*, 1619).

HEAD, Richard and KIRKMAN, Francis, *The English Rogue* (I 1665, II 1668, III & IV 1671), H1246–50, I 471pp., II 378pp., III 324pp., IV 304pp.

Histoire des Larrons or the History of Theeves, trans. Paul Goodwin (1638), 13523, 315pp. (*Histoire Générale des Larrons*, 1621/3/5/36).

A Historical Account of the Late Great Frost (1684), H2096, 159pp., tales/fabliaux, some Restoration novel qualities.

The Irish Rogue (1690), 11045, 181pp.

KIRKMAN, Francis, *The Unlucky Citizen* (1673), K638, 296pp., autobiography/romance interpolations.

Lazarillo de Tormes, trans. David Rowland (1576, rpt. 1624/39), trans. James Blakeston (1653), L761, 153pp. (*Lazarillo de Tormes*, 1554), see entry in Section 1.

LUNA, Juan de, *Pursuit of the Historie of Lazarillo de Tormez*, trans. T. Walkley (1622), 16927, 192pp. (*La segunda parte de la vida de Lazarillo de Tormes*, 1620).

The Pleasures of Matrimony (1688), P2565, 185pp., vivid scenes with a minimal plot.

The Practical Part of Love (1660), P3154, 84pp.

QUEVEDO Y VILLEGAS, Francisco de, *The Life and Adventures of Buscon* (1657), Q190, 287pp. (*Historia de la vida del Buscón*, 1626).

SALAS BARBADILLO, Alonso Geronimo, *The Fortunate Fool*, trans. Philip Ayres (1670), S369, 380pp. (*El necio bien afortunado*, 1621), satirical/picaresque.

13. Popular Chivalric Romance

Amadis de Gaule, see entry in Section 1, 5th part trans. 1665, 312pp.

BETTIE, William, *The History of Titania and Theseus* (1608), 3074, 44pp.

The Conquest of France (1680), C5895, 24pp.

The Delightful History of . . . St. Patrick (1685), D903, 152pp.

Don Bellianis of Greece, trans. Francis Kirkman (1671/2), F781, I 93pp.,
  II 168pp., III 78pp., 2nd and 3rd parts written by Kirkman.

The Famous and Delectable History of Cleocreton and Cloryana (1630?), 4302,
  155pp.

The Famous and Renowned History of Sir Bevis of Southampton (1689), F259,
  78pp.

The Famous History of Lord George Fauconbridge (1616), 10710, 39pp.

FLORES, Juan de, *A paire of turtle doves* (1606), 11094, 102pp. (*Los amores
  de Grisel y Mirabella*, 1495).

FORDE, Emanuel, see entry in Section 1.

Guy Earl of Warwick, by Samuel Smithson (1661), 4302, by John Shirley
  (1681), S3515, in W. J. Thoms, ed., *Early English Prose Romances* (rev.
  edn., n.d.), pp. 331–408.

HERBERAY, Nicholas de, *The Most Excellent History of . . . Don Flores of
  Greece* (1664), H1493, 62pp., an addition to the *Amadis* cycle.

The History of Fortunatus (1676), R1509, 159pp.

History of Olivaires of Castile (1695), H2919, 254pp., derives from
  Wynkyn de Worde's 1518 version.

Huon of Bourdeux (1601), 13999, 640pp.

JOHNSON, Richard, see entry in Section 1.

The Life and Death of . . . St. George (1660), L2015, 24pp.

MAINWARINGE, M., *Vienna: no art can cure this hart* (1620), 17201,
  180pp., based on *Paris and Vienne* (1540).

MALORY, Thomas, *Brittaines Glory* (1684), M339, 20pp., redaction of
  Le Mort D'Arthur.

Marianus (1641), M600, 382pp.

The Most Famous and Renowned historie of . . . Mervine (1612, 1st edn.
  1596?), 17844, 352pp.

ORTUÑEZ DE CALAHORRA, Diego, *The 9th Part of the Mirrour of
  knighthood* (1601), 18871, 346pp.

Palmerin, see entry in Section 1 under MUNDAY, Anthony.

The Renowned History of Fragosa, by W.C.? (1618), 4319–20, 134pp.

SHIRLEY, John, *The Famous History of Aurelius, the valiant London Prentice*
  (1675?), S3498, in Mish, *Restoration*, pp. 238–56.

Valentine and Orson (1637), 24573, abridged (1649), V28, 220pp.,
  abridged by Lawrence Price (1673), P3361, 18pp.

14. Popular Compilations of 'History'

CORROZET, Gilles, *Memorable Conceits* (1602), 5795, 234pp.

CROUCH, Nathaniel, *Delightful Fables in Prose and Verse* (1691), C7311,
  172pp.

CROUCH, Nathaniel, *The Extraordinary Adventures and Discoveries of several famous men* (1683), C7323, 233pp.

—— ——, *Female Excellency* (1688), C7326, 177pp.

—— ——, *The History of the Nine Worthies of the World* (1687), C7337, 190pp.

—— ——, *Unparallel'd Varieties* (1683), C7352, 231pp.

ESTIENNE, Henri, *A World of Wonders* (1606), 10553, 358pp.

GOULART, Simon, *Admirable and memorable histories containing the wonders of our time* (1606), 12135, 646pp. (*Histoires admirables et memorables de nostre temps*, 1606).

RIVERS, George, *The Heroinae* (1639), 21063, 174pp.

15. Anti-Romance

ANTON, Robert, *Moriomachia* (1613), 685, in Mish, *Short Fiction*, pp. 46–78.

CERVANTES, Miguel de, *Don Quixote*, trans. Thomas Shelton (1612/20), 4915, ed. James Fitzmaurice-Kelly (1896).

Don Samuel Crispe (1660), D1846, 21pp.

FURETIÈRE, Antoine, *Scarron's City Romance* (1671), S830, 244pp. (*Le roman bourgeois*, 1666).

The Heroicall adventures of the Knight of the Sea (1600), 18763, 239pp.

HOLLAND, Samuel, *Don Zara Del Fogo: a mock-romance* (1656), H2437, 211pp., also issued as *Wit and Fancy in a Maze* (1656), and *Romancio Mastrix* (1660).

The Knight-adventurer . . . Sir Firedrake (1663), K697, 9pp.

MONTELION [pseud.], *Don Juan Lamberto* (1661), M2492A, I 45pp., II 39pp., attrib. to Thomas Flatman or John Phillips.

OUDIN, César François sieur de Préfontaine, *The extravagant Poet* (1681), O571, 139pp. (*Le Poëte extravagant*, 1670).

SCARRON, Paul, *The Comical Romance*, trans. John Bulteel (1665), S830A, new trans. (1676), S831, 251pp. (*Le roman comique*, 1651).

Scarron Incens'd (1694), S838, 139pp. (*Scarron apparu à Mme de Maintenon*, 1694).

SOREL, Charles, *The Comical History of Francion* (1655), S4702, 300pp. (*Histoire comique de Francion*, 1623).

—— ——, *The Extravagant Shepherd* (1653), S4703, 360pp. (*Le Berger Extravagant*, 1627).

SUBLIGNY, Adrien Thomas Perdou de, *The Mock-Clelia* (1678), S6107, 396pp. (*La fausse Clélie*, 1670).

16. 'Impure' Romance

BAYLY, Thomas, *Herba Parietis* (1650), B1511, 130pp., facsimile Brummell Press (1969).

BRATHWAITE, Richard, *The Two Lancashire Lovers* (1640), 3590, 268pp.

CROWNE, John, *Pandion and Amphigenia* (1665), C7396, 307pp.

SHEPPARD, Samuel, *The Loves of Amandus and Sophronia* (1650), S3167, 140pp.

17. The Novella

AYRES, Philip, *The Revengeful Mistress* (1696), A4313, 198pp.

BOURSAULT, Edmé, *Deceptio Visus* (1671), D516, 232pp. (*Ne pas croire ce qu'on void*, 1670).

CERVANTES, Miguel de, *Exemplary Novels*, trans. James Mabbe (1640), 4914, 323pp.: 'A Storie of Two Damsells', 'The Ladie Cornelia', 'The Liberall Lover', 'The Force of Blood', 'The Spanish Ladie', 'The Jealous Husband' (from *Novelas ejemplares*, 1613).

CÉSPEDES Y MENESES, Gonzalo de, *The Famous History of Auristella* (1683), C1782, 140pp. (from *El Español Gerardo*, 1622), this edn. also contains 'the pleasant story of Paul of Segovia', a shortened version of Quevedo's *Buscón*.

—— ——, *Gerardo the Unfortunate Spaniard*. (1622), 4919, 475pp. (*Poema trágico del espagñol Gerardo*, 1615/17).

Choice Novels and Amorous Tales (1652), C3917, 247pp., trans. of twelve stories by Bianca, Loredano, Pomo, Brusoni, Pallavicino, Fusconi, and Settimo.

COX, H., *Lisarda; or the travels of love and jealousy* (1690), Newberry Library, not in Wing, 97pp.

Don Henrique de Castro (1686), D1844, 159pp.

The Fortunate, the Deceived, and the Unifortunate Lovers (1683, 1st edn. 1632?), T1088, I 175pp., II 135pp., III 104pp.

LOREDANO, Giovanni Francesco, *The Novells* (1682), L3068, 153pp. (*Novelle amorose*, 1651).

MACHIAVELLI, Niccolo, *The Divell a Married Man* (1647), M133, 8pp., redaction, full version in Quevedo, *Novels* (1671), pp. 135–99 (*Novelle di Belfagor*, date uncertain).

PÉREZ DE MONTALBÁN, Juan, *Aurora and the Prince. Oronta and The Cyprian Virgin*, trans. Thomas Stanley (1647), P1467, 87pp. (from *Sucessos y prodigios de amor*, 1624).

—— ——, *The Illustrious Shepherdess. The imperious brother* (1656), P1469, I 90pp., II 84pp. (from *Sucessos y prodigios de amor*, 1624).

The Pleasant Companion (1684), P2539, 47pp.: 'The Negro: Or, Loves Artifice', 'The despairing Prodigal: or, Lucky Surprisal', 'The Labyrinth: Or, The fortunate Thief', 'The Mistake: Or, The Intrigue at a Venture', 'Midnight Ramble'.

QUEVEDO Y VILLEGAS, Francisco de, *The Novels . . . Whereunto is added, The marriage of Belphegor . . . translated from Machiavel* (1671), Q192, 159pp. (actually a version of Salas Barbadillo, *Don Diego de Noche*, 1623).
The Spanish Decameron: or Ten novels, trans. Roger L'Estrange (1687), H2599, 587pp.: 'The Rival Ladies', 'The Mistakes', 'The Generous Lover', 'The Libertine', 'The Virgin Captive', 'The Perfidious Mistress', 'The Metamorphos'd Lover', 'The Impostour Out-Witted', 'The Amorous Miser', 'The Pretended Alchymist' (trans. from Cervantes and Castillo Salorzano).
Triana or a threefold Romanza of Mariana. Paduana. Sabina (1654), F2470, 151pp. (wrongly attrib. to Thomas Fuller).

18. Memoirs

AULNOY, Marie, *Memoirs of the Countess of Dunois* (1699), A4218, 185pp. (orig. unknown).
—— ——, *The Ingenious and Diverting Letters of the Lady ——s travels in Spain* (1691/2), B2038/40/41, I 149pp., II 162pp., III 228pp. (*Relation du voyage d'Espagne*, 1691).
BAIL, Louis Moreau du, *The Famous Chinois or the Loves of several of the French nobility* (1669), D2404, 270pp. (*Le fameux Chinois*, 1636).
BRÉMOND, Gabriel de, *Gallant Memoirs* (1681), B4347, 124pp. (*Mémoires galans*, 1680).
COURTILZ DE SANDRAS, Gatien, *The French Spy: or the Memoirs of Jean Baptiste de la Fontaine* (1700), C6597A, 371pp. (*Mémoires de Messire J. B. de la Fontaine*, 1698).
—— ——, *The Memoirs of the Count de Rochefort* (1696), C6600, 412pp. (*Mémoires de Mr. L.C.D.R.*, 1687).
—— ——, *The History of . . . Viscount de Turenne*, trans. Ferrand Spence (1686), C6598, 422pp. (*La vie du vicomte de Turenne*, 1685).
DESJARDINS, Marie-Catherine [Mlle de Villedieu], *Memoirs of the Life, and rare adventures of Henrietta Silvia Moliere* (1672), D1191, (1677), D1192, I 262pp., II 284pp. (*Les Aventures ou mémoires de la vie de Henriette Sylvie de Molière*, 1672).
Female Falsehood (1697), S303, 280pp. (Pierre de Villiers, *Les Mémoires de la vie du Comte de . . .*, 1696), wrongly attrib. to St. Évremond.
SAINT RÉAL, César Vichard, *The Memoirs of the Duchess Mazarine*, trans. P. Porter (1676), S355, 130pp. (*Mémoires de Mlle la Duchesse de Mazarin*, 1675), probably not by Saint Réal.

19. Scandal Chronicle/Secret History

The Amours of the Sultana of Barbary (1689), A3028, 176pp., Charles II and Duchess of Portsmouth etc.

BELLON, Peter, *The Court Secret* (1689), B1850/1, I 276pp., II 237pp., anti-Catholic, supporting William and Mary.

BLESSEBOIS, Pierre Corneille, *Aloisia or the amours of Octavia Englished* (1681), A2897A, 107pp. (*Aloise*, in *Les Amours des dames illustres de France*, 1680).

The Cabinet Open'd, or The secret history of the amours of Madame de Maintenon with the French King (1690), C190, 143pp.

CHAVIGNY DE LA BRETONNIÈRE, François de, *The Inconstant Lover* (1671), C3758, 214pp. (in fact a trans. of du Bail, *Le Fameux Chinois*, 1636).

CLAUDE, Issac, *The Count d'Soissons* (1688), C4586, 224pp. (*Le Comte de Soissons*, 1677).

COLONNA, Maria, *The Apology or The genuine memoirs of Madame Maria Mancini* (1679), B4344, 159pp. (*Apologie ou les véritables mémoires de Madame Maria Mancini*, 1678), possibly by Gabriel de Brémond.

COURTILZ DE SANDRAS, Gatien, *The Amorous Conquests of the Great Alcander* (1685), A3018, 178pp. (*Les conquestes amoureuses du Grand Alcandre*, 1684).

HENRIETTA, Princess, *The Amours of Madame and the Count de Guiche* (1680), A3022, 90pp., purports to be by Henrietta.

History of the Palais Royal, or The amours of Mademoiselle de la Valiere (1680), British Library, not in Wing, 78pp.

JONES, David, *The Secret History of White-Hall* (1697), D934, 494pp., almost more history than fiction.

Loves Empire; or, The amours of the French Court (1682), L3264A, 224pp. (Bussy-Rabutin, *Histoire amoureuse des Gaules*, 1665).

MAZARIN, Hortense de la Port, *Memoirs*, trans. P. Porter (1676), M1538, 130pp., orig. unknown, Mazarin purported author.

The Pastime Royal; or, the gallantries of the French court (1682), P664, I 64pp., II 122pp., not a trans.

The Secret History of the Duchess of Portsmouth (1690), S2340, 162pp.

The Secret History of the Duke of Alancon and Queen Elizabeth (1691), S2341, 233pp.

VANEL, Claude, *The Royal Mistresses of France or the Secret history of the amours of all the French Kings* (1695), V90, I 228pp., II 260pp. (*Les Galanteries des rois de France*, 1694).

20. *Nouvelle Historique*

The Amours of Edward IV. An historical novel (1700), M565, 120pp.

The Annals of Love (1672), A3215, 425pp.

ARGENCES, d', *The Countess of Salisbury*, trans. Ferrand Spence (1683), A3630, 216pp. (*La comtesse de Salisbury*, 1682).

AULNOY, Marie-Catherine, *Memoirs of the Court of Spain* (1692), A4220, 379pp. (*Mémoires de la Cour d'Espagne*, 1690).

AULNOY, Marie-Catherine, *The Novels of Elizabeth Queen of England* (1680/1), A4221, 135pp. (*Nouvelles d'Élisabeth*, 1674).

BELLON, Peter, *The Amours of Bonne Sforza Queen of Polonia* (1684), B1849, 155pp.

Beraldus, Prince of Savoy (1675), B1496, 194pp. (*Béralde, Prince de Savoye*, 1672).

BERNARD, Catherine, *The Count of Amboise*, trans. Peter Bellon (1689), B1983, 204pp. (*La Comte d'Amboise*, 1689).

—— ——, *The Female Prince or Frederick of Sicily* (1682), B1984, 230pp. (*Frédéric de Sicile*, 1680).

BOURSAULT, Edmé *The Prince of Conde* (1675), B3860, 196pp. (*Le Prince de Condé*, 1675).

BOYLE, Roger [Earl of Orrery], *English Adventures* (1676), O476, 129pp.

BRÉMOND, Gabriel de, *The Princess of Montferrat* (1680/1), B4353, I 190pp., II 190pp. (*La Princesse de Montferrat*, 1677).

The Character of Love, guided by inclination (1686), C2020, 126pp.

CROUCH, Nathaniel, *The Unfortunate Court Favourites of England* (1695), C7351, 181pp.

DELERAC, François Paulin, *Polish Manuscripts* (1700), D127, 290pp. (*Les anecdotes de Pologne*, 1699).

DESJARDINS, Marie-Catherine [Mlle de Villedieu], *The Amours of the Count de Dunois* (1675), D1187, 154pp. (*Comte de Dunois*, 1671, possibly by Mme de Murat).

—— ——, *The Disorders of Love* (1677), D1188, 148pp. (*Désordres de l'amour*, 1675).

—— ——, *Loves Journal* (1671), D1189, 126pp. (*Le Journal amoureux*, 1669).

—— ——, *The Loves of Sundry Philosophers* (1673), D1190, 230pp. (*Les Annales galantes*, 1670).

—— ——, *The Unfortunate Heroes* (1679), D1183, 281pp. (orig. unknown).

Don Sebastian King of Portugal. An Historical Novel, trans. Ferrand Spence (1683), D1487, I 143pp., II 156pp. (*Dom Sebastien*, 1679).

GIBBS, Richard, *The New Disorders of Love* (1687), G666, 167pp.

LA CHAPELLE, Jean de, *The Unequal Match; or, the life of Mary of Anjou Queen of Majorca* (1681/3), L133, I 164pp., II 174pp. (*Marie d'Anjou*, 1681).

LA FAYETTE, Marie Madeleine de, *The Princess of Montpensier* (1666), L171, in Mish, *Restoration*, pp. 4–33 (*La Princesse de Montpensier*, 1662).

LETI, Gregorio, *The Loves of Charles Duke of Mantua* (1669), L3274, 200pp. (orig. unknown).

Meroveus (1682), M1834, 115pp. (*Merovée*, 1678).

ORTIGUE, Pierre de [sieur de Vaumorière], *Agiatis, Queen of Sparta* (1686), V161, 236pp. (*Agiatis*, 1685).

PRÉCHAC, Jean de, *The Amours of Count Teckeli and the Lady Aurora Veronica de Serini* (1686), P3203, 112pp. (*La Comte de Tekeley*, 1686).

—— ——, *The English Princess* (1678), E3115, 243pp. (*La Princesse d'Angleterre*, 1677).

—— ——, *The Lovely Polander*, trans. Ferrand Spence (1681), P3207A, 88pp. (*Le beau Polonois*, 1681).

—— ——, *The Serasquier Bassa, An historical novel of the times* (1685), P3208A, 136pp. (*Le Seraskier Bacha*, 1685).

ROUSSEAU DE LA VALETTE, Michel, *Casimir, King of Poland* (1681), R2051, 204pp. (*Casimir, roi de Pologne*, 1671).

—— ——, *The Life of Count Ulfield* (1695), R2052, 139pp. (*Le Comte d'Ulfeld, nouvelle historique*, 1677).

SAINT RÉAL, César Vichard de, *Don Carlos* (1674), S353, 168pp. (*Dom Carlos, nouvelle historique*, 1672).

Secret History of the Most Renowned Q. Elizabeth and the E. of Essex (1680), S2342, 114pp.

Tachmas, Prince of Persia: an historical novel (1676), T100, 110pp. (*Tachmas, prince de Perse, nouvelle historique*, 1676).

Tudor, a prince of Wales. An historical novel (1678), T3220, 154pp.

The Unsatisfied Lovers. A New English novel (1683), U94A, 120pp. possibly by James Partridge.

21. *Nouvelle Galante*

The Adamite, or the Loves of Father Rock (1683), University of Illinois Library, not in Wing, 102pp. (*L'Adamite, ou le jesuite insensible*, 1682).

The Adventures of the Helvetian Hero with the young countess of Albania (1694), A605, 212pp.

The Amorous Abbess or Love in a Nunnery (1684), A3017/B4343, 140pp. (from François Montfort or Gabriel de Brémond, *Le cercle*, 1673).

AULNOY, Marie, *The Present Court of Spain* (1693), A4223, 379pp. (*Nouvelles espagnoles*, 1692).

BELLON, Peter, *The Reviv'd Fugitive* (1690), B1858, 144pp.

BONNECOURSE, Balthazar de, *La Montre*, trans. Aphra Behn (1686), B2595C, 243pp. (*La montre*, 1666).

BRÉMOND, Gabriel de, *The Pilgrim*, trans. Peter Bellon (1680), B4353, 2nd part by Bellon (1681), B1855, I 192pp., II 134pp. (*Le Pelerin*, 1670).

—— ——, *The Triumph of Love over Fortune* (1678), B4357, 153pp. (*Le Triomphe de l'amour sur le Destin*, 1677).

BRILLAC, J. B. de, *The Fatal Beauty of Agnes de Castro*, trans. Aphra Behn (1688), B4693A, 63pp. (*Agnès de Castro*, 1688).

CHAVIGNY DE LA BRETONNIÈRE, François de, *The Gallant Hermaphrodite. An amorous novel* (1687), C3757A, 123pp. (*L'Amante artificieuse*, 1682).

Cynthia: with the tragical account of the unfortunate loves of Almerin and Desdemona (1687), C7710A, 207pp.

GERMONT, François de, *The Neopolitan* (1683), N361, 80pp. (*La Napolitain*, 1682).

The History of Adolphus, Prince of Russia (1691), H2113, 43pp. (*conte de fée*, trans. from Marie Aulnoy, in *Histoire d'Hypolite*, 1690).

LA FAYETTE, Marie Madeleine de, *The Princess of Cleves* (1679), L169, 259pp. (*La Princesse de Clèves*, 1678).

—— ——, *Zayde. A Spanish history*, trans. P. Porter (1678), L172/3A, I 175pp., II 192pp. (*Zayde*, 1670).

LA FERTÉ SENNETERRE, *History of the Mareschalesse de la Ferté* (1690), G176A, in *Gallantry Unmasked*, pp. 81–155, separate t.p.

LA ROBERDIÈRE, Alexandre de, *Love Victorious or The Adventures of Oronces and Eugenia* (1684), L445C, 120pp. (*L'Amant cloîtré*, 1683).

Lisander or The Soldier of Fortune (1681), L2366A, 137pp.

Loves Posie: or A collection of seven and twenty love letters (1686), L3281, 153pp.

MONTFORT, François Salvat, *The Circle: or Conversations on love and gallantry* (1675), N1218, 254pp. (*Le cercle*, 1673, also attrib. to Gabriel de Brémond).

The Obliging Mistress: or The fashionable gallant (1678), O89, 104pp.

The Penitent Hermit, or The fruits of jealousie (1679), P1233, 141pp.

Peppa: or The reward of constant love (1689), P1448, 120pp. (claims to be a trans. from French, but seems to be an original work).

PIX, Mary, *The Inhumane Cardinal*, Newberry Library, not in Wing, 237pp.

POISSON, Raymond, *The Gallant Ladies, or The mutual confidence* (1685), P2745/6, I 123pp., II 131pp. (*Les galantes Dames*, 1685).

PRÉCHAC, Jean de, *The Heroine Musqueteer* (1678/9), P3206/8, 123pp. (*L'Héroïne musquetaire*, 1677).

The Religious Cavalier, trans. Gideon Pierreville (1683), 108pp. (possibly Chavigny de la Bretonnière, *La religieuse Cavalier*, although this is dated 1693 in all bibliographies).

The Rival Mother; a late true history: digested into a novel (1692), R1546, 123pp.

The Rival Princesses: or, The Colchian Court (1689), R1547, 161pp.

SCUDÉRY, Madeleine de, *Amaryllis to Tityrus* (1681), S2143, 87pp. (orig. unknown, possibly not by Scudéry).

The Siege of Mentz. Or, The German heroine (1692), S3771, 151pp., possibly by Peter Bellon.

The Spanish and French History: or Love out of season (1689), S4803, 161pp. (*Histoire espagnole et françoise*, 1671).
The Unhappy Lovers, or The timorous fair one (1694), U67, 125pp.

22. Political/Allegorical Novel

The Amours of Messaline, late Queen of Albion (1689), R2158, I 45pp., II 42pp., III 33pp., directed against James II.

AULNOY, Marie, *Memoirs of the Court of France* (1692), A4218A, 160pp. (*Mémoires et aventures singulières de la cour de France*, 1692).

CHARLETON, Rowland, *Diana Duchess of Mantua* (1679), C587, 164pp.

The Fugitive Statesman, in requital for the Perplex'd Prince (1683), F2259, 120pp., adaptation of Dryden's *Absalom and Achitophel*, see my note '*Absalom and Achitophel* and *The Fugitive Statesman*', *Restoration*, 4 (1980), 11–13.

Grimalkin, or The rebel-cat (1681), G2026, 13pp., directed at Shaftesbury.

The Pagan Prince (1690), P163, 144pp., directed against James II.

The Perplex'd Prince, by T. S. (1682), S174, 130pp., pro-Monmouth, anti-James.

The Plot in a Dream (1681), P2598, 285pp., semi-allegorical account reinforcing the 'truth' of the Popish Plot.

SERGEANT, JOHN, *An Historical Romance of the Wars between . . . Gallieno, and . . . Nasonius* (1694), S2570, 88pp., Jacobite attack on William III.

23. Oriental Tale

BONNECOURSE, Balthazar de [supposed author], *The Art of Making Love Without Speaking* (1688), A3793, 74pp. (in fact a trans. of Du Vignan's *Le Secrétaire Turc*, 1688).

BRÉMOND, Gabriel de, *The Happy Slave* (1677), B4348/9A, 191pp. (*L'hereux esclave*, 1674).

—— ——, *Hattige: or The amours of the King of Tamaran* (1676), B4350, 119pp. (*Hattigé*, 1676).

The Fair One of Tunis, trans. Charles Cotton (1674), F102, 302pp. (orig. unknown).

GRENADINE, Sebastian, *Homais Queen of Tunis* (1681), G1935, 132pp. (*Homaïs reine de Tunis*, 1680).

LA ROCHE GUILHEM, Mlle, *Almanzor and Almanzaida* (1678), L446, in Mish, *Restoration*, pp. 59–92 (*Almanzaïde*, 1674).

—— ——, *Asteria and Tamberlain* (1677), L447, 190pp. (*Thémir ou Tamerlan*, 1675).

—— ——, *The Great Scanderberg* (1690), C3801, 142pp. (*Le Grand Scanderberg*, 1688, also attrib. to Urbain Chevreau).

LA ROCHE GUILHEM, Mlle, *Zingis: A Tartarian History* (1692), L450, 176pp. (*Zingis*, 1691).

LE NOBLE, Eustache, *Abra-Mulé, or a True History of the dethronement of Mohomet IV* (1696), L1051, 132pp. (*Abra-Mulé*, 1696).

Ottoman Gallantries, trans. B. Berenclow (1687), 271pp. (French, orig. unknown).

PRÉCHAC, Jean de, *The Chaste Seraglian: or Yolanda of Sicily*, trans. Thomas Hayes (1685), P3204, 163pp. (*Yolande de Sicile*, 1678).

—— ——, *The Grand Vizier: or The history of the life of Cara Mustapha* (1685), P3205, 138pp. (*Cara Mustapha, grand-vizir*, 1684).

—— ——, *The Princess of Fess*, trans. Peter Bellon (1682), B1857/P3207B, 143pp. (*La Princesse de fez*, 1681).

DU VIGNAN, *The Turkish Secretary* (1688), D2922, 80pp. (*Le Secrétaire Turc*, 1688).

24. Restoration Novel

The Adventures of Covent Garden (1699), A604, 58pp.

Alcander and Philocrates, 'Written by a young lady' (1696), University of Illinois Library, not in Wing, 132pp.

ALCOFORADO, Marianna d', *Five Love-letters from a Nun to a Cavalier*, trans. Roger L'Estrange (1678), A889, in *The Novel in Letters*, ed. N. Wurzbach (1969), pp. 5–21 (*lettres d'amour d'une religieuse*, 1669, ascribed to Gabriel-Joseph de Lavergne Guilleragues).

The Amorous Convert (1679), A3019, 183pp.

The Art of Cuckoldom: or, The Intrigues of the city-wives (1697), A3790, 96pp., extract in Mish, *Restoration*, pp. 185–97.

BEHN, Aphra, *The Adventure of the Black Lady* (1698), B1712, 8pp.

—— ——, *The Dumb Virgin: Or, The Force of Imagination* (1700), B1711A, 34pp.

—— ——, *The Fair Jilt* (1688), B1729, 120pp.

—— ——, *The History of the Nun, or The fair Vow-Breaker* (1689), B1737, in Mish, *Restoration*, pp. 93–142.

—— ——, *Love Letters Between a nobleman and his Sister* (1683), 2nd part (1685), *The Amours of Philander and Silvia being the third and last part* . . . (1687), B1740/1, I 324pp., II 444pp. (in 1735 edn.), 1st part in *The Novel in Letters*, ed. N. Wurzbach (1969), pp. 199–282.

—— ——, *The Lucky Mistake* (1689), B1745, 40pp.

—— ——, *Memoirs of the Court of the King of Bantam* (1698), B1746, 24pp.

—— ——, *The Nun, or Perjur'd Beauty* (1698), B1712, 15pp.

—— ——, *Oroonoko: or The Royal Slave* (1688), B1749, 239pp.

—— ——, *The Unfortunate Bride: or The blind lady a beauty* (1698), B1772, 15pp.

BEHN, Aphra, *The Unfortunate Happy Lady* (1698), B1711A, 40pp.

————, *The Unhappy Mistake: Or, The Impious Vow Punish'd* (1698), B1712, 50pp.

————, *The Wandering Beauty* (1698), B1773B, 30pp.
(For all Behn's works, Montague Summers's edition, 1915, while convenient, is unreliable.)

BLACKBOURN, Richard, *Clitie* (1688), B3066, 212pp.

BLAIR, Bryce, *The Vision of Theodorus Verax* (1671), B3125, 174pp. (trans. from Erycius Puteanus, *Comus*, 1608).

BOYLE, Robert, *The Martyrdom of Theodora and of Didymus* (1687), B3986, 250pp., traces of a Saint's Life.

BRÉMOND, Gabriel de, *The Cheating Gallant or the False Count Brion* (1677), B4345, 143pp. (*Le Galant Escroc*, 1676).

CHAMILLY, Noël Bouton, *Five love-letters Written by a Cavalier in answer to the five love letters written to him by a nun* (1683), F1110, 108pp. (*Réponse aux lettres portugaises*, 1669).

CHARLETON, Walter, *The Ephesian and Cimmerian Matrons* (1651?), C3670/1, I 80pp., II 31pp., *Cimmerian Matron* in Mish, *Restoration*, pp. 147–61 (trans. from Petronius, and from Erycius Puteanus, *Comus*, 1608).

CONGREVE, William, *Incognita or Love and duty reconcil'd* (1692), C5848, ed. A. Norman Jeffares (1966).

CONSTANTINI, Angelo, *A pleasant and comical history of the life of Scaramouche* (1696), C5950, 108pp. (*La vie de Scaramouche*, 1695).

The Crafty Lady, or The rival of himself (1683), C6774, 153pp. (trans. from French, orig. unknown).

Delightful and Ingenious Novels (1685), D902, 136pp.: 'The Lucky Throw', 'The Frustrated Intentions', 'The distressed Traveller', 'The Generous Gallant', 'The Unhappy Counterfeit', 'The Champion of Honour'.

DESJARDINS, Marie-Catherine [Mlle de Villedieu], *The Husband Forc'd to be Jealous* (1668), H3805, 157pp. (*Le Jaloux par force*, 1663, ascribed to Donneau de Visé).

DUNTON, JOHN, *A Voyage Round the World* (1691), V742, I 158pp., II 115pp., III 130pp.

Erotopolis, The present State of Betty-Land (1684), E3242, 181pp., anatomical allegory, mildly pornographic.

Eve Revived, or The fair one stark naked (1684), E3475, 120pp., possibly by W. Downing.

Fatall Prudence or Democrates (1679), F544, 199pp. (trans. from French, orig. unknown).

GILDON, Charles, *The Post-Boy Rob'd of his Mail* (1692), G735A, 386pp., fictional letters.

The History of Nicerotis, a pleasant novel (1685), H2128, 95pp.

KEPPLE, Joseph, *The Maiden-Head Lost by Moonlight* (1672), K332A, in Mish, *Restoration*, pp. 166–84.

LE PAYS, René, *The Drudge* (1673), L1115, 98pp. (*Zélotyde*, 1664).

The Life of a Satyricall Puppy called Nim, by T. M. (1657), M1411, 118pp., wrongly ascribed to Thomas May.

The London Bully, or The prodigal son (1683), L2890, 131pp.

MANLEY, Mary de la Rivière, *Letters Writen [sic] by Mrs. Manley* (1696), M434, 88pp., fictional letters.

MARANA, Giovanni Paolo, *Letters Writ by a Turkish Spy* (1687/91–4), M565, selection ed. A. J. Weitzman (1970), (*L'espion turc*, 1684–6).

MONTFAUCON DE VILLARS, Nicolas, *The Count of Gabalis: or The Extravagant mysteries of the Cabalists* (1680), M2494, 183pp. (*Le Comte de Gabalis*, 1670), satire.

MOTTEUX, Peter, *The Gentleman's Journal* (1692–4), British Library, not in Wing. 1692: 'The Vain-Glorious Citt', Jan., pp. 7–13; 'The Noble Statuary', Jan., pp. 23–9; 'The Friendly Cheat', Feb., pp. 10–16; 'Loves Alchymy', Mar., pp. 11–17; 'The Adventure of the Night-Cap', Apr., pp. 9–12; 'The False Friend', May, pp. 3–7; Untitled, also in Latin, June, pp. 6–8; 'The Jealous Husband', July, pp. 2–6; 'The Reward of Indifference', Aug., pp. 3–6; '——', a fable, Sept., n.p.; 'Love sacrific'd to Honor', Oct., pp. 2–4; 'The Lady's Fortune', Nov., pp. 5–9; 'The Picture', Dec., pp. 7–12. 1693: 'The Widow by Chance', Jan., pp. 7–10; 'The Poysoned Lover', Feb., pp. 46–7; 'The Lover's Legacy', Mar., pp. 76–8; 'The Treacherous Guardian', Apr., pp. 115–20; 'The Witchcraft of Gaming', May, pp. 144–8; 'Hypocrisy Out-done', June, pp. 181–5; 'The Match-maker Match'd', July, pp. 218–21; 'The Disappointment', Aug., pp. 253–7; 'The Generous Mistress', Sept., pp. 290–5; 'A Gift and no Gift' (by Mrs Mary D.), Oct., pp. 341–2; 'The Quaker's Gambols', Nov., pp. 370–3; 'Patience Rewarded', Dec., pp. 397–400. 1694: 'The Living Ghost', Jan./Feb., pp. 15–19; 'The Rival Coachmen', Mar., pp. 49–53; 'The Cure of Jealousy', Apr., pp. 83–5; 'The Younger Brother's Fortune', May, pp. 115–18; 'The Female Husband', June, pp. 149–52; 'The Punishment of Avarice', July, pp. 187–91; 'The Female Beaux', Aug./Sept., pp. 223–6; 'The Winter Quarters', Oct./Nov., pp. 259–62.

OLDYS, Alexander, *The Fair Extravagant* (1682), Folger Library, not in Wing, 178pp.

—— ——, *The Female Gallant, Or The Wife's the Cuckold* (1692), O265, 156pp.

Olinda's Adventures (1693, 1st surviving edn. 1718), 65pp., ed. R. A. Day (Los Angeles, 1969, Augustan Reprint Society No. 138), probably by Mrs Trotter.

'OVID', *Chaucer's Ghost* (1672), O647, 121pp., 12 stories from Ovid narrated in lame Chaucerian imitation, followed by a pastiche 'medieval' tale, possibly by Charles Cotton.

The Player's Tragedy, Or, fatal love (1693), P2418, 118pp.

POPE, Walter, *The Memoirs of Monsieur du Vall* (1670), P2912, in Mish, *Restoration*, pp. 202–14, satirizes criminal biography and Francophiles.

PRÉCHAC, Jean de, *The Disorders of Basset* (1688), D1673, 108pp. (*Les Désordres de la bassette*, 1682), bassette is a card-game.

SAINT ÉVREMOND, Charles, *A Novel* [*The Irish Prophet*], in *Works* (1700), S301, Vol. 2, pp. 78–99.

SCARRON, Paul, *Scarron's Novels*, trans. John Davies (1665), S883, 336pp.: 'The Fruitless Precaution', 'The Hypocrite', 'The Innocent Adultery', 'The Judge in His Own Cause', 'The Rival-Brothers', 'The Invisible Mistress', 'The Chastisement of Avarice' (*Les nouvelles tragicomiques, traduites d'espagnol en français*, 1655).

A Sunday's Adventure, or, Walk to Hackney, by G.D. (1683), G9, 106pp.

TALLEMANT, Paul, *Lycidus: or The lover in fashion*, trans. Aphra Behn? (1688), T129, 176pp. (*Le retour de l'Isle d'amour*, 1666).

Vertue Rewarded: or, The Irish Princess (1693), V647, 184pp.

VILLIERS, Claude Deschamps, *The Gentleman Apothecary* (1670), V390, 58pp. (Donneau de Visé, *L'Apoticaire de qualité*, 1664).

VOITURE, Vincent, *Zelinda* (1671), V684, 127pp., translation but then adaptation and conclusion of this unfinished work, a faithful trans. can be found in *A Collection of Select Discourses* (1678), pp. 141–93 (*Histoire d'Alcidalis et de Zélide*, 1658).

Woman's Malice (1699), W3324, 106pp.

25. Popular Non-Chivalric Fiction

The Antient True and admirable history of Patient Grisel (1607), 12383, 31pp.

BACON, Roger, *The Famous History of Friar Bacon* (1627), 1183, 38pp.

Bateman's Tragedy (1700), Folger Library, not in Wing, in Mish, *Restoration*, pp. 276–89.

Beware the Beare (1650), B2190, 20pp.

BRATHWAIT, Richard, *Ar't Asleepe husband?* (1640), 3555, 318pp.

BRETON, Nicholas, *Grimellos Fortunes* (1603), 3657, in *Two Pamphlets of Nicholas Breton*, ed. E. G. Morice (Bristol, 1936), pp. 21–59.

BREWER, Thomas, *The Life and Death of the Merry Devil of Edmonton* (1631), 3718/9, in *The Merry Devil of Edmonton*, ed. W. A. Abrams (Durham, Nth. Carolina, 1942), pp. 225–67.

Cawwood the Rooke (1640), 4889, in Mish, *Short Fiction*, pp. 342–63.

The Cobler Turned Courtier (1680), C4782, 8pp.

The Death and Burial of Mistress Money (1664), D500, 20pp.

The Famous and Renowned History of the Memorable but Unhappy Hunting on Chevy Chase (1690), F360, 24pp.

The Famous and Renowned History of the two Unfortunate tho noble lovers, Hero and Leander (c. 1690), F361, 24pp.

GOODMAN, Nicholas, *Hollands Leaguer* (1632), 12027, ed. D. S. Barnard (The Hague, 1971).

GREEN, George A, *The Pinder of Wakefield* (1632), 12212, ed. E. A. Horsman (Liverpool, 1956).

HEAD, Richard, *The Life and Death of Mother Shipton* (1667), H1257, 50pp.

HEYWOOD, Thomas, *The Famous and Remarkable History of Sir Richard Whittington* (1656), H1780, 71pp.

The History of Friar Rush (1620), 21451, 38pp.

The History of the Blind Beggar of Bethnal-green (1676), H2146, 24pp.

The History of the Golden Eagle (1672), H2161, in Mish, *Restoration*, pp. 217–33.

The History of the Two Children in the Wood Revived (1687), H2147, 18pp.

Jack of Dover, his quest of Inquirie (1604), 14291, 35pp.

Johnny Armstrong (1700?), P2531, 24pp.

The Life and Death of Rosamund (1670), L2009, 18pp.

The Most Excellent History of Antonius and Aurelia (1682), M2882, 22pp.

The Most Pleasant History of Bovinian (1656), M2914, 12pp., continues a story of Deloney's *Gentle Craft*.

The Noble Birth and Gallant Atchievements of Robin Hood (1662), N1201, 40pp.

The Pleasant and Delightful History of Floridon and Lucina, by J. P. (1663), P64, 41pp.

The Pleasant History of Tom the Shoomaker (1674), P2552, 43pp.

PRICE, Laurence, *The Witch of the Woodlands* (1655), P3391, 22pp.

The Strange and Wonderful History of Mother Shipton (1686), S5848, 24pp. (in an early 18th-century edn.).

The Unlucky Citizen: or A pleasant history of the life of Black Tom (1686), U85, 18pp., *not* the same as Francis Kirkman's *Unlucky Citizen* (1673).

Wanton Tom: or The merry history of Tom Stitch the Taylor (1685), W716, 17pp.

Westward for Smelts (1620), 25292, 39pp.

WINSTANLEY, William, *The Honour of the Merchant-Taylors* (1668), W3064, 88pp.

Index

An asterisk preceding a page number indicates a reference to an entry in the Bibliography.